Sean Doherty did little el~~se~~ surfing. He soon realised, however, that no one was going to pay him to do so – no one apart from the Department of Social Security, anyway – so he figured that writing about it for a living was probably the next best thing.

He edited iconic surf magazine *Tracks* for the best part of a decade. His first book, a biography of surfing cult hero Michael Peterson, became a national bestseller and is presently being made into a feature film. He is a senior writer at *Surfer* magazine in the USA, contributes to several surf and sports titles around the world, and has written for the *Sydney Morning Herald*. He works regularly as a commentator at ASP world tour events and is also on the board of Surfing Australia. When not frolicking in the Southern Ocean, he plies his trade from the frigid depths of his garage. *My Brothers Keeper* is his fourth book.

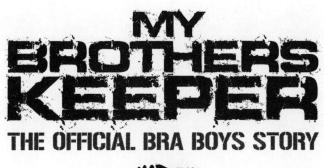

MY BROTHERS KEEPER

THE OFFICIAL BRA BOYS STORY

MY BROTHERS KEEPER

THE OFFICIAL BRA BOYS STORY

SEAN DOHERTY

HarperCollins*Publishers*

HarperCollins*Publishers*

First published in Australia in 2009
by HarperCollins*Publishers* Australia Pty Limited
ABN 36 009 913 517
harpercollins.com.au

HarperCollins*Publishers*
25 Ryde Road, Pymble, Sydney, NSW 2073, Australia
31 View Road, Glenfield, Auckland 0627, New Zealand
A 53, Sector 57, Noida, UP, India
77–85 Fulham Palace Road, London, W6 8JB, United Kingdom
2 Bloor Street East, 20th floor, Toronto, Ontario M4W 1A8, Canada
10 East 53rd Street, New York NY 10022, USA

National Library of Australia Cataloguing-in-Publication data:

Doherty, Sean.
My brothers keeper: the official bra boys story/Sean Doherty.
   ISBN: 978 0 7322 8554 8 (pbk.)
   Abberton, Jai.
   Abberton, Koby.
   Abberton, Sunny.
   Abberton, Dakota.
   Surfers – New South Wales – Maroubra – Biography.
   Suburban life – New South Wales – Maroubra.
   Suburban gangs – New South Wales – Maroubra.
   Maroubra Beach (N.S.W.)
   Maroubra (N.S.W.)
364.1066099441

Cover photos: Justin Crawford, Shorty Buckley, Nathan Smith, Glen Duffus
Pic spreads photo credits: Glen Duffus, Bill Morris, Jason Childs, Bosko, Brian Bielmann,
Jeremy Wilmotte, Shorty Buckley, Tony Nolan, Jon Frank
Chapter photo credits: Shorty Buckley, Jon Frank
Cover and internal design by Matt Stanton
Typeset in 9.5/15.5pt Palatino by Kirby Jones
Printed and bound in Australia by Griffin Press
70gsm Classic used by HarperCollins*Publishers* is a natural, recyclable product
made from wood grown in sustainable forests. The manufacturing processes conform
to the environmental regulations in the country of origin, Finland.

5 4 3 2 1   09 10 11 12

This book is dedicated to Ma and Pa Abberton for the loving oasis you gave us, and to Ma for the brotherhood you taught us.

May your legacy live on through the next generations.

Love always, your boys.

A percentage of royalties from this book will be donated to the Mavis Abberton Foundation.

Part 1
Father's Day

KOBY

THE PATERNAL LAWNMOWER OF RECONCILIATION IS PUSHED ACROSS THE TASMAN

I was sitting at Ma's place one day – I must've been about 20 at the time – when Jai's come flying into the kitchen laughing his head off. He's holding a letter.

'You gotta read this, bra! It's fucking hilarious!'

He's holding the letter away from me like a 12-year-old kid. Typical Jai – just baiting me like the stupid older brother he is. I go, 'Just give it to me, dickhead!'

> Hey, Koby,
>
> Hope you're doing good. I'm doing really good. I've got a lawnmower and a stereo. Miss you. Why don't you come over and see me some time? Castles made of sand drift away in the wind.
>
> Grant Stewart*

Me and Jai have read it and looked at each other and gone, 'What the fuck?' I knew my father's name was Stewart* and I knew my old man was a Kiwi. The letter had a New Zealand postmark on it.

Jai goes, 'Is that your dad?'

'I think so.'

'Geez, he's killing it, bra. He might send ya a lawnmower for Christmas.'

Me and Jai just started pissing ourselves. I've shown my grandma and she's started laughing as well. She was laughing harder than both of us, just hysterical.

---

* Name has been changed.

I dunno, I must've been three or four last time I seen him. I wouldn't know what he even looked like. All I remember was a tall guy with long hair who bashed my mum. Whenever my mum used to get angry at me, he'd bash her for it, 'cause I was his kid while Sunny and Jai belonged to other blokes. He'd punch the fuck out of her, turn her black and blue. I don't have photos of him … or of me when I was little either, for that matter. The earliest photo I've ever seen of myself was one someone put on Facebook, my Year 3 school photo.

But it wasn't a surprise that the letter arrived just after I'd bought two houses, had a brand-new car out the front and I'd been in the surf mags a bit. It was really strange; it almost felt like someone was setting me up – one of me mates. It had his address at the bottom and he said, 'Why don't you come over and see me some time?' I thought, you've got Buckley's, mate, after all you've done for me – fucking nothin'. Never heard from the bloke since. And Jai still gives me so much shit about it, even today; always asking how me lawnmower's going, telling me to turn me stereo down. He's teased me that badly about it, but I laugh harder than him when he does.

A couple of weeks later me and my two best mates, Jed and Ahu, are sitting out the front of Ma's place at Maroubra when this cab pulls up across the road. The cabbie – this little three-foot wog bloke, this mad little Super Mario – jumps out and starts walking towards us.

He struts across the road and starts to walk towards the front door.

'Mate, where the fuck are you going?'

He goes in the full wog accent, 'Do you know where Jai and Sunny are?'

'Who the fuck are you?

'I'm their dad.'

I just sat there stunned for a second then completely lost my shit. I was pissing myself, laughing so hard I was crying.

He looks at me and goes, 'No, I serious, I their father.'

So once I pulled myself together, I go, 'Okay, mate, I'll go in and get Sunny for ya.' This was gonna be good.

I walk inside and yell, '*Sunnyyyyy*, your dad's out the front.'

Sunny comes straight out and goes, 'Whaddaya mean, me *dad*?'

'Mate, there's some woggy little bloke out there telling me he's your dad.'

Sunny's frozen and started going all red; steam starts coming out his ears. Sunny's a mad clicker. He's real controlled, but he's also the maddest clicker out of all of us. He starts running for the door. The guy's across the street and sees Sunny charging up the path straight at him, screaming, 'Who the fuck do you think you are, turning up in my life now after you fucking left us!'

Sunny starts chasing him up the street. The guy runs for his life and jumps in his taxi. We've never seen him again.

We've all done it pretty tough for so long, we don't need a dad now. One might have been handy 20 fucking years ago when we were kids.

I went round to Jai's place later that day and said to him, 'Mate, my old man might only have a lawnmower, but your dad's a three-foot wog taxi driver.' Any time I get into taxis with Jai now I go, 'Here ya go, this bloke could be your dad, Jai,' and we both piss ourselves laughing.

We've never really talked about it. I don't want to meet someone who's never been there for me. I've had a pretty hard life at times, and for some fucker to come up and say, 'How are ya, mate? I'm your dad.' What the fuck am I going to talk to him about – lawnmowers? Not cool, buddy.

But I reckon I'd have other brothers and that out there. I've had all sorts of people come up and say they were my cousins, all sorts of people saying shit, especially after the *Bra Boys* movie came out. But it'd be cool to see my other brothers if I had any. I don't think I'd have much in common with them, but it'd be cool to find another brother.

I think Jai is still angry at Sunny about that day. Their feud started right there, I reckon. Jai really wanted to meet the guy. His last name was Stefanic, and it turns out he was Czech, I think. So Jai's real name is Daniel Stefanic. Sunny's real name is … actually, I dunno what Sunny's real name is. Mum changed their names when they moved to the hippy colony at Nimbin. They're pretty hippy names: Sunny, Jai, Koby, Dakota.

I guess being on heroin your whole life you're gonna make some crazy decisions every now and then.

JAI

My real name is Daniel Stefanic.

Serbian, my father was meant to be, but I've never met him. Other Serbs have told me Stefanic is a Serbian name. It says 'Daniel' on my birth certificate. Mum just called me Jai.

I met a bloke once who reckoned he knew my dad. But don't ya reckon you'd want to come and meet your son just once? I just want to meet him to at least find out for sure what nationality I am. I might even be Koori. Before Ma died, apparently she told someone that my father was Koori.

Ever since I was a kid, I knew I was different to Sunny and Koby. Since I was little I've liked vine leaves and short black coffee, so I reckon I might be European. I ate olives as a kid when the other two wouldn't go near 'em. Olives, salami, feta cheese, strong coffee. Sunny reckons we might have the same dad, but I know we don't. All I know is that I've got Aussie brothers and I've got Koori brothers. I can't work out where I'm from, but I know I'm more from the land than I am from money. I'm more spiritual than I am blind. I know that I'm blacker than I am a racist. But if you ever meet my father, maybe you can tell me where I'm from.

The old man pulled up in a cab at Ma's place one day out of the blue, when I wasn't there. He gets out of the cab and asked Koby and our mate Jed, 'Where's Jai?' Koby thought I'd jumped the cab without paying, and told the guy to fuck off.

'No, I'm his dad.'

This happened not long after Koby had got the letter from his old man saying he's got a new lawnmower. Fuck, I gave Koby some shit about that.

I want to meet me old man. I'll talk to him. He can't be all bad; he's part of me. If it turns out he is a fuckwit, I'll stamp the cunt for 50 and ask him where he's been. I just want to know where I'm from. I'd let him tell me where he's from, where I'm from, where he's been, and why the fuck he hasn't wanted to see me. It'd be mad to know where I'm from, see what's in the blood.

You know, I think I might go back to being Daniel Stefanic. Yeah, I'm kicking Daniel off again. Jai's been thrashed.

SUNNY

THE ELDEST OF THE SIBLINGS ON WHILE THERE'S AN 'I' IN STEFANIC, THERE'S NO 'I' IN ABBERTON

Daniel Stefanic?!

What a wanker! Daniel Stefanic. That's the funniest thing I've ever heard. Jai is the kind of guy who would think about that a lot. *'If only I was Daniel Stefanic ...'*

Our real names are Jamie and Daniel. Our mum was in a full hippy drug craze when we were born, and she wanted to call us Sunny and Jai. But Ma and Pa – her parents – wouldn't allow it; that was just too way out for them. So on our birth certificates it says Jamie Abberton and Daniel Abberton. But from the moment we were born we were called Sunny and Jai – school, passports, driver's licences for those of us who still have 'em. Koby and Dakota, well, they were always Koby and Dakota.

Mum never talked to me, Jai or Koby about our fathers at all. I've never met my father and I never want to. It's never been an issue for us because they've never been around. So it's always been just the boys; just the brothers and our mum, really. There has never been a dad around. We have never really wanted to make contact or never really given a shit about it, you know. If they're not there while you're growing up, then they're not your dad. Your parents are the ones who bring you up in a loving, nurturing environment. If your biological father fucks off and leaves you, he's never going to be your father.

The day that guy showed up in his taxi, I was so pissed off. He didn't even make it into the house. Who was that guy? We'd just been in the paper for something to do with our surfing, and Koby had just come into all this money. One of the Maroubra boys had been in a cab with this guy and our names came up in conversation. The guy just goes, 'Yeah, I'm their father.' The guy asked around and found out where we lived, then drove up. He hardly had a chance to get out of the cab; then once he jumped back in, we started booting the cab and told him to fuck off. He did a screechy, drove off up the road, and that was the last we saw of him. But I reckon he wasn't even our father. I reckon he was full of shit.

That wasn't long after Koby had got the letter from his old man in New Zealand saying how he was killing it, how he had a vacuum cleaner or something, a stereo and a train fare. We laughed our heads off. That's what I mean: why would you even want to? And for some guy to rock up while he's on duty in a taxi …? Like, fuck off, mate, we'll rip ya fucken head off. Who the fuck are ya? After all these years he decides to rock up out of the blue while he's on a shift in his taxi? You've got to be kidding me. Jai's still dirty on me, though, for chasing the guy off; still hasn't forgiven me.

If someone claiming to be my old man rocked up tomorrow I wouldn't have a second for him. I wouldn't be able to understand why he'd bother. There'd be no feeling; there'd be no nothing. To me, your father is someone who's brought you up and invested themselves in your upbringing. Maybe it might be different if you'd been adopted out, but even then I can't understand how or why people want to go back and find their biological parents, the ones who gave them away. They must really need to, but I can't understand why. People look for meaning in their parentage, and a lot of the time it's not even there.

I could not even search for a reason why I would want to go and find the guy who walked away from us before we even knew him. Why?

What would I want to say? Nothing at all. There'd be no anger, but also no curiosity. I'd probably just give him a kick in the arse for stuff I remember him doing to my mum. Obviously, it was pretty hard for us to grow up without a dad. That might create a bit of venom, but there's nothing I've been stewing over. And I certainly don't lie awake at night thinking about him. Maybe I'd just give him a whack as a square-up for some of the whacks he gave my mum, and send him on his way.

I'd be embarrassed more than anything else, to tell you the truth.

There's been a lot of 'cousins' come out of the woodwork, particularly since the court case and the movie. And I even feel a little bit weird about that stuff, let alone my dad. We're very open to new people and new cultures, but when it comes to letting people right into the inner circle, we're very cautious about that. We've worked too hard keeping it together to let it be watered down so easily.

I suppose I've always been real protective of that – making sure we don't break up what we have by bringing in strangers. I think I've always had a good understanding of how to keep everyone together.

'I'm Sunny Abberton and this is my brother, *Daniel Stefanic*'?

'So, what, youse are *half*-brothers?'

What the fuck's a *half*-brother?

Part 2
Sea Urchins

SUNNY

THE FLEDGLING ABBERTON BROTHERS MAKE THE TRANSITION FROM NIMBIN FERALS TO MAROUBRA URCHINS

I was born in Maroubra.

Our grandparents and Mum had moved from Tamarama, 10 minutes up the road, when Ma and Pa won the lottery. Most people who win the lottery would move *from* Maroubra, not *to* it. But my grandparents could at least afford a house near the beach in Maroubra, and that's what they wanted for us.

They won something like $50,000 – a lot of money in those days – and they bought a house in Fenton Avenue. It was this little red brick place, one of only two houses in a street full of unit blocks, but it was only 50 metres to the beach. I can't even imagine what our lives would be like today if they'd never bought that house.

My ma and pa – Mavis and Jim – had grown up around Zetland. Ma's side of the family were poor immigrants; we just don't know where they emigrated from. That's a bit of a family secret – as if there aren't enough of them in our family.

When my great-grandfather was dying I asked him, 'What country do we come from, Pop?'

He looked me in the eye and laughed. 'Bendigo, mate.'

'But Bendigo's not a country, Pop.'

'Let's just leave it at Bendigo, son.' And he smiled.

I suppose a lot of immigrants grew up in a very racist time, and there was a real stigma attached to coming from another country. It was bred into 'em that if you could get away with saying you were Australian or English, you would.

I've always been interested in my family's history, just not my father's. When I was 18 and on the surfing pro tour in France there was a full-on team of us driving back from the beach one afternoon, all on the drink, and we said, 'Let's all get tattoos!' So we stopped at some bar and started sketching up some drawings. The one I was going to get was the Abberton family crest. I'd seen it on the ring my great-grandfather always wore and he'd told me it was a family heirloom going back generations. He told me that when he died he was going to pass this ring down to me. Anyway, that's what I wanted to get tattooed. We drove around all night but couldn't find a tattooist, so I never got it done. When I got back I went and saw my great-grandfather.

'You would have been proud of me, Pop,' I told him. 'When we were in France I drew up a stencil of the family emblem and I was going to get a big tattoo of it on my shoulder.'

He just turned around and started pissing himself laughing.

'What?' He was still laughing. 'What?' I said. 'You gotta tell us!'

'Thank God you didn't get that tattoo, son. I found that ring on Bondi Beach in the early '20s.'

Our pa wanted us to live by the beach because he'd always been involved with the surf clubs. I traced his affinity with the ocean back to his time as a barber over the hill at Bondi. In the 1950s there was a rebel boardriders club in The Valley called the Cornell Wild Gang. *Cornell Wild* was this famous movie around at that time. It was about this bloke who wore his hair in this certain wild way and it became a really fashionable hairstyle among the guys surfing Bondi. My pa and my uncle owned Abberton's barbershop, and my pa used to specialise in the Cornell Wild. If you wanted the haircut, you had to go to Abbo's barbershop on Bondi Road. So all the surfers went to his barbershop and got to know him, and he got on with them. And despite their reputation, Pa thought surfing would be a good thing for us to get into.

Pa was a big, rangy guy, six foot at least, but the Abberton family duck arse counterbalanced his tall frame. We all got it, and if we ever put on weight that's where it goes. Pa's duck arse would be hanging out all summer because he spent the entire three months walking around in his cossies. There's a classic photo of Pa shadow-boxing, and my best mate, Ronnie Reardon, swears he's a spitting image of me. The Abberton bloodline is really strong, and no matter who the father is, it still shows through – in the eyes and the duck arse, mainly. Ronnie once said to my mum, 'Ya know, Lyn, even with all those different dads, the boys all still look the same. It must be coming from somewhere.'

Pa would become like our dad in our early years, and the only discipline we'd experience would come from him. We were really, really close. Every Saturday morning he had a ritual with us. He'd make us 'dip-ins' – that's what he called 'em – where you'd cut the top off a boiled egg and dip fingers of toast into the yolk. I remember we loved it.

Ma had a very elegant, regal look about her. She always held her head high and her chin up. She'd come from a hard upbringing – I think her father was very strict – but she was always a really strong woman.

She worked for Qantas, but spent all her spare time sunbaking on the rocks down at Tamarama. Ma walked a lot but she couldn't swim, which was bizarre considering she spent half her time either on the beach or by the pool in her backyard. She was really pedantic about her hair and she'd never go in the pool because she didn't want to ruin her hair. We'd have to full on harass Ma to get in the pool and when she did all the boys would gather round, because it was a big occasion.

I think they bought the house in Fenton Avenue knowing – because of the way my mum was going – that Jai and I would be spending a lot of time with them. They bought the place because it had two extra rooms for us, and they put in double bunks. They set this place up as a sanctuary for us.

We lived on and off with Ma and Pa from the start, and they would keep us in line. I remember Pa locking Jai in the garage, and walking back, swearing under his breath. Jai's always had a quick temper, always ready to fire up, and that's how Pa would cool him off. Ma used to take her shoe off for Jai or for Pa if she thought either of them had stepped out of line. Pa always used to lie on the floor and fall asleep in front of the telly, and Ma would take her shoe off and whack him if he started snoring. No one argued with Ma's shoe.

I don't really remember my dad. He couldn't have been playing a big part in my life at that stage, because I only have a few memories of him, and they're mostly bad. I just think my mum was easily influenced by the men in her life; that's what it was. I think she was dragged into it innocently. Experimenting with trips and amphetamines, whatever, she eventually got led down the heroin trail, you know. We couldn't get a Housing Commission place, so we were in a cycle of moving in and out of shitty ghetto houses. Sometimes Mum would be living in Redfern or out the back of Waterloo. We lived in one place near Randwick Racecourse, an old terrace house full of junk in the backyard: cars, fridges, washing machines. Jai and I slept in the same room, and we used to have a piss bucket in the corner. It was while we were living here that I started having this recurring dream. I dreamed I was lying in my bed looking up, and the ceiling would start to pulse and warp. Then there'd be a big black hockey puck and it would start bouncing around the corners of the ceiling at right angles, going faster and faster. The ceiling would start undulating like the ocean, then I'd wake up. I've had that dream forever; it wasn't until 20 years later when I was lying in intensive care after I'd been stabbed that I realised what it meant.

Later we lived in a place at Matraville where all the walls were lined with mattresses. There was a drum kit in the lounge room and motorbikes inside the house. And at every place we lived there were always strangers coming and going. So the cycle began. We'd live in these shitty houses, Mum and our dads or her boyfriends would get out of control and Ma and Pa would come and grab us. Then we'd be racing down Fenton Avenue on our Green Machine scooters until Mum had cleaned herself up and convinced Ma and Pa she was ready to have us back. This went on for years. That's why Ma and Pa's became the one place that actually felt like home.

Then we moved to Nimbin.

We lived in a hippy nudist colony just outside Nimbin, which was – and still is today I suppose – the hippy capital of Australia. I was four, Jai three, and Koby still wasn't on the scene yet. We lived there with people who'd come up from the city with us and a handful of kids. Mum's lifestyle was very communal; people would come and go and there were no defined roles like your bread-and-butter family. There was a lot of freedom, which I suppose is why they went bush.

No one worked, so there were people everywhere, all living in this one big farmhouse. It was an old Queenslander with the big, deep 15-foot-wide veranda that skirted the whole house; that's where the lounges were. People would sit there playing the guitar and smoking joints all day. It was the full hippy colony. There was an outdoor bath, which you filled with a bucket, and an outdoor pit dunny. The outhouse was really old and the wood was rotting; if you looked up while you were taking a shit there were thick spider webs everywhere in the corner of the roof. There were so many big redback spiders and snakes living in it, I was shitting myself every time I went out there. Each time you went to the toilet it was a paralysing fear. Drop a shit, one wipe, then get the hell out of there. I developed a phobia for snakes and spiders that's still with me today. One night I was asleep in my bed and this huge python crawled into bed with me. I woke up as it was crawling across me. I was so scared I couldn't even scream. I froze. Mum eventually ran in with some of her fellow colonists and I think they killed it with a shovel.

But after what we'd been through in the city, they were good times for us at Nimbin. We had chickens, we had the world's biggest backyard, and we grew our own vegies. We had horses as well, and we all learned to ride. The property we lived on had a creek running through it, and it was here during our first summer that I became conscious of the whole concept of nudity. I remember looking around and going, 'Hey, everyone's in the nude! Cool!'

The creek had a secret rockpool with a cascading waterfall. Everyone would sit by the bank all day in summer. We'd take a picnic lunch, and the adults would play guitar, swim, laugh; everyone starkers, everyone smoking joints. The kids would be in the water all day. It was so far from Maroubra it wasn't funny. I remember being there days on end, just hanging out.

We never went to school; we were left to our own devices. We were covered in mud most of the time, and Jai and I had long red hair down to our bums, dreadlocks with feathers, and pierced ears. We were like *Mad Max* kids.

The only thing I remember of my old man up there – or it might have been Koby's old man – is a dark green and purple bottle that sat on a shelf inside the house. I think it had been washed up on the beach. The colours were beautiful; it reminded me of the ocean when I looked at it because it was frosted from having floated around for so long. I remember him smashing it over Mum's head. I was holding Jai, crying, and my mum was screaming. That colour will stick with me forever.

I suppose that was the way it was with Mum's boyfriends. They played no part in our lives even when they were there, so none of us really have any memory of them apart from the violence. There was never at any time during our childhood a feeling of a family, not in the conventional sense anyway.

Not long after the bottle incident, the intervention went down. We'd been in Nimbin for about two years and during that time we'd come back to Ma and Pa's a couple of times a year. But when Ma and Pa hadn't seen us in over six months they became suspicious. Then our cousin, Kelly, who's a few years older than me and was nine or 10 at the time, came up to see us for the school holidays. Reports from Kelly eventually got back to Ma and Pa, and they finally thought they'd better get up there and see what was going on.

I remember Ma and Pa arriving in the car and us running out and cuddling them. They were really excited to see us, but at the same time shocked at the state of us. The fight with Mum started pretty much straightaway. Pa blew up, and asked if we'd been going to school. So suddenly it became fully like a snatch. Ma and Pa rushed us into the car. I remember us not really knowing what was going on, and asking about Mum. We got thrown into the back of Pa's Kingswood, and then it was straight back to Maroubra.

The next morning, back in Sydney, we were going to school, straight up.

Ma and I went and met the principal of St Mary's, and she took me to meet my teacher, Miss Back. My classroom was the last one on the corner of the block, the closest to the oval, so I thought it would be easy to make an escape and a last minute entrance straight from the beach.

She showed me the canteen, the boys' toilets and the bubblers, and then we talked about the uniform. The boys' uniform was brown and the girls' was green. The St Mary's uniform was sold at a department store so we went straight there to get our books and pencil cases and uniform, because we had nothing; we'd never set foot inside a school.

When it came down to the uniform, Ma was telling me the boys' uniform was brown, and I said, 'No, Ma, the boys' is green.' We tried asking someone and they didn't have a clue, but I was so certain that we had this big argument. I'm saying, 'Ma, I'm telling you, it's green!'

We buy the green uniform.

At this stage we hadn't had our hair cut; I still had long red hair. Ma might have combed a couple of dreads out and got rid of the feathers, but we were still pretty feral. I was hiding in the bushes, waiting for the school bell to ring. They rang the bell and all the classes lined up. I was shitting myself. It's my first day of school and I wanted to make sure there was a big huddle of kids there before I emerged from the scrub so I could blend in. Then I made my bolt straight over into the boys' line.

Suddenly everyone starts looking at me, and I'm thinking, 'Shit, they're giving the new kid a hard time.' Then the girls start looking over as well, pointing at me and laughing, and I'm wondering what's going on.

Then one of the kids shrieks as loud as he could, 'He's got the girls' uniform on!'

The whole place just breaks up. I lasted until lunchtime then I took off back to Ma's. That was the start of it. That year I got beat up several times, and it wasn't until I decked the three biggest kids that the shit about my girl's uniform stopped.

We hadn't been back in Maroubra that long when Mum returned from Nimbin and Koby was born soon after. Mum's boyfriend – Koby's dad – was a Kiwi, and we'd only been back in Maroubra long enough to start feeling settled when we were moving again – this time to New Zealand. We moved into a town called Redcliffs, just outside of Christchurch on the South Island.

It was cold there, really cold. Our house was in a pretty poor street, but it backed onto the river mouth. We had a wharf out the back that led onto this little sand island. We used to tie a rope to the wharf, and when the tide was running out we'd hold onto the rope while riding a boogieboard or a tyre tube against the current. We used to surf at this place called Taylor's Mistake Beach. I would've been seven or eight. I remember spending a lot of time sleeping in cars out the front of pubs, waiting for Mum. And there was always music in our house. Koby's old man was in a blues band, so there'd always be Janis Joplin or Hendrix or the Stones playing through the house. I also remember a lot of bikers hanging around.

There was a big open glass window overlooking the river mouth behind the house. It was beautiful spot. In the backyard there were some plants that grew along the ground that had these small, banana-looking fruits that we used to eat. Inside there was a stereo in the corner, with two lounges and a big old chair on either side. Koby's dad used to sit Koby in that chair and put these big headphones on him and blast him with Hendrix. That might explain a few things. But Koby loved it. He'd just sit there, rocking out in the chair. Koby was only just starting to walk at this stage, and in summer we'd get him out in the tyre tube. He was fearless even at that age.

It was in Redcliffs that it first clicked that there were drugs around.

I was playing armies in the backyard with my toy soldiers and I lifted up a rock and found a bag of brightly coloured pills. I'd found their stash. I took them in and showed my mum. She must have been trying to go clean at that stage, and Koby's dad had hidden them from her. There was a giant screaming match about it. That was the first time it dawned on me. Why were they fighting over these pills? What were they? I knew that whatever they were, they couldn't be good, because look what was happening. I remember my mum arguing, saying something like, 'You promised you wouldn't do them any more. What about the kids?' I knew something was going on; I'd started to put the pieces together – we were never allowed in their room; they were always sleepy. Once you get to eight, you're old enough to realise something is going on.

Koby was only one or two when I found those drugs, and I think that contributed to me feeling like I had to shelter him and Jai. Things deteriorated between Koby's dad and our mum, and it often got violent. One time all three of us kids were huddled together in a room while they were having a massive fight. Mum had made a big pot of spaghetti bolognese; that was one of the main dishes she cooked up. Koby's dad picked up the pot and threw it against the wall. The whole place was smashed up and Mum said, 'Stuff it. I'm not cleaning it up.' There was this big smear of dried spaghetti bolognese running down the wall. It stayed there for days. It looked like blood and it was really symbolic.

At that stage I didn't know if Mum was using or not, but I think our grandparents did, and they came over to visit. Soon after, Jai and I were flying back to Sydney with them. Koby was too young to be away from Mum, so he stayed in Redcliffs. Not long after we came back from New Zealand, Ma and Pa renovated the place at Fenton Avenue. I figured their plan must have been to get Mum and us home, as close to them as possible. They built an extra bedroom inside the house and made the garage worthy of habitation; they put in a ceiling, a loft, and replaced the garage door with a sliding door.

Jai and I settled straight back in. That's when we first started to get the little team together. We knew one local kid who lived around the corner from us, a kid named Bulldog. He was a wild little kid. The first time we met him he was swearing like a sailor. We're like, where's this kid come from? At school we were pretty much hippy kids. We were still quite feral because we'd been left on our own a lot, but we were more bush wild; we weren't street wild like Bulldog.

There was a school talent quest not long after we got there. We're at this full-on Catholic school and Bully has said, 'We're singing this song by the Sex Pistols.' Me and Jai were still pretty naïve. We didn't know who the hell the Sex Pistols were.

Bully's got us the outfits. He got mops and pulled the ends off them; they were our wigs and the handles became our guitars. Bully had a Sex Pistols T-shirt on, and he'd brought the tape.

'When the music starts playing, I'll sing; you and Jai just thrash around and smash your guitars.'

With all the nuns and the brothers watching, we get up in front of the whole school and Bulldog hits play on the Sex Pistols tape. We're going apeshit to the song 'Bodies'. Bully's screaming out the lyrics about animals, abortions and fucking.

The nuns grabbed the cassette, madly stripped out the tape, and immediately suspended all three of us.

JAI

A MODEST SINGLE–STOREY, RED BRICK ABODE BECOMES THE HOUSE OF DREAMS

Ma and Pa were classy. They weren't from the housos like us.

I've seen photos of Ma in the classiest restaurants in Sydney. My grandfather was captain of Woollahra Golf Club; he's got a plaque on the ninth tee. He was the trump of all trumps, my grandad. When I think about it now, we really were their world. There are things that make me sad and almost bring a tear to my eye. My first real memories of life were of living with Ma and Pa, and they were all good ones. Ma and Pa didn't even have to look after us. God bless 'em. They were like my parents, my mum and dad.

I was born not long after Ma and Pa bought the house in Fenton Avenue. We were staying with them a lot in those days. We loved that place. Koby and I want to try and scrape together the money and buy it back one day. It still looks exactly the same as it did when we were kids. I drive past it all the time, just looking at it. All my dreams as a kid were in that house. That house is in our blood.

I was banished to the garage out the back even before Pa had it set up as a room, because me and Sunny would fight so much. Some things don't change, eh? My pa would lock me out in the garage because I'd throw tantrums and smash shit; I'd be locked in there until I'd calmed down. Pa always used to say to me I was going to be a mechanic when I grew up, because I spent so much time in that bloody garage.

But we lived pretty good at Ma and Pa's. We'd go stay with our mum, you know, but just always end up back at our ma's.

I don't know what happened to my ma during her pregnancy, but it scared the shit out of her, I know that. After she had my mum she never had another kid. Mum's an only child, and she was enough for Ma and Pa to handle. Mum started writing off a bit around the time Ma and Pa bought Fenton Avenue, which is why we ended up there so often. I think a few times DOCS, or whoever it was in those days, tried to take us off Mum but she'd hide us from them. She put up a fight for us. Despite the bad situations she found herself in, deep down she always cared.

I just remember little flashes from growing up in Nimbin and New Zealand. In Nimbin a big snake crawled into Sunny's bed one day and all the older blokes in the house were into it with shovels, chopped its head off. I would've only been three. We had long hair and just ran around nude covered in mud all day.

Then my mum met Koby's dad and we moved to New Zealand for a year. The house we lived in was mad; it backed right onto the water and had its own jetty. Koby's dad had hoochie plants growing in the front yard; I remember him telling me they were tomatoes and me always wondering why no tomatoes ever grew on them. I used to go to the shop to play pinball. The Mongrel Mob would ride up the street on their bikes and the shopkeeper would bring us kids inside. I'd be sticking my head out the door and looking at these wild blokes – this big bikie gang full of huge, tattooed Maori guys – thinking it was the coolest thing I'd ever seen.

It was always cold, though. We'd walk to school, cracking the ice on the puddles; by the time we got there our shoes would be soaked and our feet freezing. It snowed one day and Mum came and got us out of school, just came hammering across the playground making a scene. 'Guys, guys … come on. We're going up to play in the snow!'

It was all right in New Zealand … except for Koby's dad.

SUNNY

MAROUBRA BEACH ASSUMES ADOPTIVE CUSTODY OF THE ABBERTON BOYS

Those first summers opened our eyes to life on the beach in Maroubra.

We already had a thing for the water. We'd been in the river behind the house in New Zealand, and in the creek in Nimbin, so it was natural that when we moved a block back from the beach at Maroubra that we were going to end up on the beach all day. We were always full-on water babies. I'd even made the cover of the *Wentworth Courier* when I was one, splashing around in the nude in the shorebreak at Bondi.

It was Pa who first got us into surfing, not long after we'd moved back from New Zealand. He brought home a board for us, a big old foamie. He stood it up against the back wall and said to us, 'Here ya go, boys. I bought you a board.'

That afternoon we did the full Bruce Lee karate kick and snapped it in half. We were destructive little bastards, full chaos kids. Pa got angry at us, but the next day he bought us another board. We snapped that one in half as well. We laid it on the grass in the backyard and started pretending to surf on it. Two boards snapped and we hadn't even hit the water yet.

He bought a third one, and said, 'Boys, if this one breaks you'll be building sandcastles all summer.' It didn't break, and we surfed the thing into the ground. I remember Pa used to take us out on that board; he'd put us on the front while he'd lie on the back.

The way my mum was, we got left with our grandparents a lot when we were young, and they had us on the beach all the time. Pa used to have this massive KB beach umbrella, and we'd all hang out under it between surfs. They both loved the beach and the sun. Ma would rub cooking oil all over her body and just bake herself brown. Those first couple of summers back in Maroubra, Ma and Pa's place just became beach central. We started surfing before and after school, as well as all weekend. You've never seen kids so happy.

The whole street was surf crazy, though. Larry Blair was the most famous surfer in Maroubra and was dating the girl who lived next door to Ma's, Nicole Selman. She was this young, beautiful surfie chick, the hottest girl in Maroubra. So we'd see Larry pretty much every day. He'd just won back-to-back Pipeline Masters, and used to surf in this white Hotline wetsuit. It was like having a rock star as a neighbour. I remember I was never star struck, though, having Larry Blair next door; he was just like any of the other guys. We'd do the knock-and-run on their door all the time; we'd even do the flaming bag of dog shit on their doorstep. I often used to hit him up for 20 cents. I think that's why he eventually ended up giving me and Jai a board, a big old McCoy. A few years later he gave Koby the board that he'd won the Pipe Masters on. It was a red board and it was so big that Koby couldn't even carry it. The older guys knew what was going on with our mum; that's why they always wanted to help us out and encourage us to get in the water and into the surf. It's always been like that here.

Glen Strange and Michael Gregory – 'Zorro' – lived on the other side of us. We were surrounded by hot surfers. Then Cheryl Moffat, one of Mum's friends, moved in next door with her son Paul. He was our age and straightaway he became one of our best mates; he would surf with me and Jai pretty well every day for the next 10 years. But it was when we joined the boardriders club that our surfing really took off. We were already on the beach all the time, and we were just absorbed into it.

The thing with Maroubra is that the boardriding clubs have always been a social barometer for what's going on in Maroubra itself. In the '70s there was the Maroubra Surfriders Association, the MSA – the one club that united the whole beach. The MSA was led by Kevin Davidson (who we called 'Woofy'). Those guys were the pros, they were respectable. A lot of them were still writing off – it was Maroubra, after all – but they wore sponsored surf clothes, their contests were run like pro tour events, and they had pro surfers like Larry Blair, Blackie Wilson and Mark Scott in their ranks. And it was huge, too. Hundreds of guys would turn up to club contests; so many they'd have to run it over two days.

But then the heroin epidemic of the late '70s came and changed everything. The surfers splintered. You were classed along two parameters: whether you were born in Maroubra or not, and whether you did drugs or you didn't. It went from one unified club to, at one stage, seven. The place fragmented. The original Maroubra club carried on, but North and South Maroubra sprung up, along with Christian, kneeboard and bodyboard clubs – seven clubs spread along a beach less than a mile long.

The first club to break away was North Maroubra Surfriders – North End – which is the one we joined when we were about 10 years old. What sparked the splintering was that a lot of the crew in Maroubra Boardriders were getting too serious about it all, and a lot of their club members were living in neighbouring suburbs like Pagewood and Hillsdale. It had become a club full of blow-in fun sheriffs. Maroubra surfers had a well-deserved, decades-long reputation as being complete surf animals. And a lot of those animals were now looking for a new home.

The North Enders were the crew who were born and bred in the heart of Maroubra and Lexington, and while the original Maroubra club was professional and slick, North End was a rough, write-off, party club. North End guys called the Maroubra guys 'Wrong Enders' because they were based on the wrong end of the beach, while the Maroubra guys called the North End guys the 'Bong Enders', for reasons that became obvious if you were ever downwind of the club's tent. The Wrong Enders and the Bong Enders, and there was real conflict between the two.

And the South Enders? Well, they had their own dialect and accent. They were another tribe altogether. But it was a write-off club as well. They were like the North Enders of the south end, and most of their guys lived in Malabar, La Perouse, and near the jail up at Long Bay.

North End Surf Riders were a write-off, the full houso boardriders club, with the old shaggy army tent and fuck-all organisation. Our logo was a guy doing a snap in a dunny bowl, holding a bong. It suited the style of the club perfectly that we were located in the north corner of the beach, because when the wind was out of the south, the shit from the

Malabar treatment works would drift straight to the north end and hole up in the corner. That's why the break there was called the Dunny Bowl. The water was black, and there was maggots and sewage on the beach. There was an old sign I remember seeing that said: 'Do not swim. Maroubra Beach 1000 times over the safe bacteria limit'.

The North End crew mostly came from the Lexo housing commission estate, and the housos at Elfinstone and South Maroubra. Jai and I fitted right in because we were starting to get a little wild by this stage. But the club was also really competitive. When you say 'surf animals', these are the guys. Search and destroy, smash every lip – the whole punk attitude. Full surf animals. And we even had chicks in our club, which was about as anti-establishment as you could get in those days. We had a lot of good hardcore surfers; not a lot of limelight pros, but good underground guys. There was Marty Lee, George Black, Geoff 'Zap' Senior, Steve 'Steamer' Lane, Tezza McKenna, Macca, Budgie, Bebbo. We just had the best time with those guys. They gave us boards, looked after us, taught us how to surf. And that's when we first felt that whole family-of-the-beach kinda thing. These guys were giving us clothes and food and taking us away, and although it was a pretty loose collective, you always knew those guys would be looking out for you.

But within that group there were the *real* surf animals, the hell crew.

Marty Lee lived in a caravan a few doors down from Ma's place, and was just about the best surfer on a whole beach full of hot surfers. It was in North Maroubra Surfriders that we first met Marty's best mates: Jason Loughnan, whose nickname was Grommet, and a guy named Tony Hines. They were like their own little team, hell-bent on destruction, and they made the rest of the guys in the club seem like altar boys. Grommet and Hinesy would often chant, 'Future, future!' That was their rally cry, and it eventually got adopted by North Maroubra Surfriders as well as the team chant.

I bought my first fibreglass surfboard off Grommet. I'd begged Ma and Pa for so long that they caved in and gave me the hundred bucks to buy it. I was so stoked. It was a Nirvana swallowtail single-fin. On one side Grommet had written 'Grommet Power!' in big letters, and on the other side he'd drawn a giant female cartoon pig with a big snout, tattoos, huge tits and fat arse. It was a female Captain Goodvibes. Underneath it he'd written in big letters 'Woofy Ted', which is what he called the board. That's the saying Grommet and those guys would use when anything was off tap – 'That's *woofy*!' Anyone from the hierarchy of Maroubra Boardriders, they were all 'woofy'. A few weeks after I got the board I was walking down the beach with it and I saw Grommet. Just as I got to him I've dropped the board on the ground. Well, he's given me the full clip around the ear and gone, 'Jesus! You gotta look after Woofy Ted!'

Our first surf trips were with the Bong Enders, and they generally ended in some form of pandemonium. Our first trip down the south coast to Bendalong ended in a famous blue. I was about 13, I reckon. It was cracker night, the June long weekend. We lit a giant bonfire in the middle of the camping ground and had a massive firecracker fight, shooting the shit out of each other. Well, the manager's come down and there was some kind of stink. One of the boys hit him and this guy has come back with 30 mates and it was on. There were fights, fires and crackers. I woke up the next morning with no shirt, no shoes, stinking of campfire and cracker smoke. They were loose weekends: surf, camp, 'cause some form of havoc, sly a few drinks off the older guys, and come home with stories amid some form of scandal.

It was an exciting time to be a grommet in Maroubra. Our pa was taking us to our first junior contests, we were surfing with Larry Blair and a dozen blokes as good as him, and Maroubra was one of the hottest surf towns in Australia. It was full Surf City.

I remember the night Ma and Pa drove us down to Cronulla to watch the night surfing contest. There were 30,000 people on the beach at Cronulla; it was the biggest thing we'd ever seen. It was like going to a rock concert. You've never seen kids more psyched about anything in their lives. There were huge grandstands, giant floodlights, rock music ... and the world's best surfers. But what we were really pumped about was that a local guy, just a few years older than us, who we surfed with all the time at Maroubra – Jay Brown – was in the contest. We knew Jay really well; he'd even occasionally sneak girls down from the Seals Club into Ma's garage where there was a little bed set up. I remember driving home that night thinking, 'Here's a guy we surf with every day at Maroubra and he's suddenly a rock star. Jay Brown just surfed in front of 30,000 people.' And I wanted to be him.

When my mum come back clean from New Zealand, the first thing she did was look for a house close to the beach and close to Ma's. When she told us she had a house next to the pub, looking out over the beach, we could hardly believe it. It was this cheap, shitty little duplex next door to the Maroubra Bay Hotel. It had a big courtyard out the front and one side of it looked down into the beer garden of the pub. It was noisy and stunk of stale beer, but you really felt the place was alive. And out the front? Well, you could throw an egg from the front yard and land it on Maroubra Beach.

Suddenly, 'cause we had the closest house to the surf, and because there was always something crazy happening at the pub, all our mates from the beach started hanging at our place. What more could a grommet want?

JAI

IN A FAMILY HARDLY OVERFLOWING WITH MALE ROLE MODELS, THE YOUNG ABBERTONS LOSE A TRUMP

We'd been going to the beach by ourselves since second class.

One day when Mum was off doing something else, she left us at the beach by ourselves, and that was it, *boom*. No looking back. But my grandfather was the guy who got us into it. He used to love the ocean. He'd take us out on the Coolite and lay on the back and catch a whitewash with either me or Sunny up on the front. He'd get you onto the wave and help you up to your feet, but then slide off the back while you weren't watching. All of a sudden you'd be up on our own. You'd look back and Pa wasn't there and you'd freak out that you were doing it all on your own.

The Coolites Pa bought us never lasted long. We broke the first two he gave us before they even got in the water. We spent half our lives at Sea Level surf shop on the corner of the beach borrowing their Coolites. They'd let you use them but you'd have to have it back before 5pm when they shut; if you didn't make it, you'd have to take the board home and they'd be a bit dark on you.

It's sad to think that all those good times we had with Pa on the beach was what killed him. He got skin cancer from all those years in the sun. We found out Pa had cancer in 1984, I think. The first thing they did was cut his boob off. Then they cut another bit off him, off his chest, and then it was just operation after operation, removing cancers that were popping up all over him. I remember the day he called us in and told us, I remember it like yesterday.

When my grandfather was in hospital dying, he was on medication and he was heaps funny. He was ringing up places randomly and ordering all this stuff. I think it was combination of his medication sending him a little crazy, and the fact he knew he was going to die. He was ordering Porsches over the phone; cars would just turn up out the front. Eventually they had to take the phone away from him. The hospital said, 'We can't do anything for him. He might have a couple of days, or if he's lucky a couple of weeks.' We said, 'We're taking him home then.' So he came back to the house and ended up lasting six months.

I remember the day he died. My aunty Jan, Pa's sister, was there, and all Ma's brothers and sisters. My mum was an only child and we didn't have fathers; we had no aunties or uncles of our own, so Mum's aunties and uncles became ours. Aunty Jan came into the lounge room at Fenton Avenue and told us Pa was gone and that he was in his room. She asked me what I wanted to do and I said I wanted to go in and cuddle him one last time before he left. I walked in there and he looked like a shadow. I grabbed him and just thanked him.

It was like we lost our dad. I was 12, and when you're 12 your dad's your whole world. When me grandfather died, Sunny kind of went into that position a bit, I reckon – the father figure. Whether he meant to or not, or whether we liked it or not, he did.

SUNNY

AT 13 AND STILL IN FLUORESCENT BOARDSHORTS,
SUNNY ASSUMES THE MANTLE OF FATHER FIGURE

We were living at Fenton Avenue when Pa got sick.

I must have been 13, and remember distinctly the day I knew something was really wrong. Pa was a real determined worker. He ran a successful business, driving around selling beach towels to chemists and tourist shops. He and Ma worked every day, because they were now supporting their grandkids as well as themselves. I can't recall either of them having a day off; it just never happened. Pa just kept on going to work, even when he knew how sick he was.

He was getting ready to go to work one day when he ran into the bathroom. I was right there, and he vomited up what looked like an egg. It was white around the outside with a big yellow yolk in the middle. I remember it scared me. It didn't look like a normal vomit; it was like nothing I'd ever seen. But then he still went to work. He went, 'Nah, I'm sweet.' He was fully stubborn and stoic like that, but by that afternoon he was in hospital, and the next day they had cut out half his chest. The cancer had spread.

The skin cancer had three goes at him. Two years before, he'd had another one, again in his side. He had a couple of operations. He had half his chest cut out at one stage, then half his stomach. It just kept eating away at him. And then he was good for another two years before it came again and got into his bones. And this time it got him.

It happened quickly.

He died in his bed. The whole scene was terrible. It was really hard on Ma. Mum was still in New Zealand trying to get clean at that stage. I think she had to go to New Zealand to get on the methadone program, whereas she had to wait for it in Australia; that's why she was in New Zealand and wasn't there when her father died. I remember that his funeral was emotional and really heavy. All our mates – all the grommets from the street – came and we were all really, really shattered.

We were pretty young, and at that age we couldn't really comprehend the loss and what it meant to the family – what it meant to Ma, and to us and our future. If Pa had lived another 10 years a lot of things would've been very different for our family. For starters, we would've had that financial support, because he was the main breadwinner in the family. He and Ma still had a mortgage on Fenton Avenue, and Pa didn't have any life insurance, so that made it really hard on Ma, who had to keep looking after us while still working enough to pay the mortgage.

But more importantly he was the father figure in our lives – the only father figure we'd ever known – and now he was gone. I remember this feeling of wanting to succeed and push on and make it for him. I still feel it today. I'm always conscious of Pa watching me today. In some situations I often think what Pa would say if he was here, or what Pa would think of decisions I've made. I still think like that because he was really similar to us in a lot of ways. It was a huge loss for us. Pa was huge for us. Pa also had a big circle of friends who we'd call uncles and aunties, who always used to visit the house, and would do Christmas with us. We lost them too.

Mum came back not long after he died. She was so upset that she was finally clean and Pa wasn't there to see her.

KOBY

INDETERMINATE BEGINNINGS INSIDE A CASTLE MADE OF SAND

Mate, I don't even know where I was born. I got no idea.

I mean, I've seen my birth certificate, and it says the Women's Hospital in Sydney, but I don't think I was actually born there. I'm pretty sure I was born at home – wherever home was at that stage. Mum was both a nurse and a heroin addict and she knew she'd get in trouble if she had me delivered in the hospital. She could lose me and lose her job.

It's just something I've never really cared that much about, not enough to find out for sure. I'm not sure if I'm New Zealander or Australian, but I know I'm me and I live in Australia and that's where I'm from. I can remember bits of living in New Zealand, but there are big parts of my life after New Zealand I can't really remember, not until I was about 12 or 13. I don't know whether I've blocked it out, or if I just got a bad memory, but there are great chunks of it missing.

I've got faint recollections of bikers coming around to our house in New Zealand, the Mongrel Mob and all that. I'm pretty sure the next-door neighbours were all bikers, and I remember guys fucking around with their bikes inside our house.

I can remember sitting on a lounge at home with my dad. He was really tall and skinny with long hair. It was a junkie house, and there were always people playing music. I mean, when he wrote me that letter, 'Castles made of sand drift away' – that's a Jimi Hendrix lyric, so he must've been into music.

But the guy was just a mad junkie who used to bash my mum. He'd hold Mum down and punch the shit out of her till there was blood everywhere. Mum slapped me once when I was playing up; he's walked in and seen it, and gone, 'You want to punch him?' And he just punched the shit out of her for it, because she'd touched me. I remember thinking at the time that it was nothing; that it was 'Okay, Mum's not going to do that sort of thing again to me.' I thought it was normal that he'd just punched her. When Sunny and Jai were there he would say things like, 'They're your kids and he's mine. Don't you touch him! You don't touch him, you touch them!' It was pretty heavy.

I remember the last time. I just watched. I sat on the couch and watched him punch the shit out of my mum. She goes, 'Yeah, you coward!' Then she left and come back with all these bikies and my dad has gone, 'I'm in trouble now, your mum's gone and done it.' Mum had gone and got her biker friends from next door and brought 'em over and they beat the shit out of my dad. She's grabbed me and we just left. As we were leaving, I remember hearing him yelling, 'It was her fault!' as the guys laid into him.

And this is the guy who sends me a letter 20 years later, with his lawnmower and stereo, saying he wants to see me?

It wasn't long after all that happened, that Pa died, and we knew it was time to go home. It must have been '83 or '84 when Pa died. I was still in New Zealand with Mum. I can totally remember the day Pa died; my mum being really upset and me just watching her and thinking that I'd never seen her ever cry like that. It must've been something bad. I was sitting on my bed and my mum told me that Pa had died. She was just sitting there on the bed, crying. I was too young to work it out; I didn't think that much of it even though I was really close to him.

As a kid you just don't take notice of death so much. I didn't really comprehend what was going on, I suppose.

SUNNY

THE WORST SCHOOL IN THE STATE, SAVING ONE
TARNISHED SOUL AT A TIME

Once Mum got home and we got the flat next to the pub on Marine Parade, we had our hang-out.

We had the pub on one side and the surf straight out in front of us. No wonder the place was soon full of kids. It was here that our first little surf gang got together.

We'd already met Bulldog. He was spending more time with us because his mum had left and his old man, who was blind, had taken to the drink. We used to be real mean to Bulldog's dad. When the wheelie bins come out, we'd hide in them out the front of his house and when he came outside we'd stick our heads up and go, 'Vince, Vince.' He'd spin around and start searching for us with his hands, but all he could feel were the bins. We must have been nine or 10 … but I'm sure we'll probably pay for that in another life.

Then came Wayno. I remember the day we met Wayne Cleveland at school, fifth class I think it was. There were two kids rumbling in the playground, with this tall, snowy-haired kid getting the upper hand.

'Who's that?' I asked.

'That's Wayno,' someone replied.

'Hmm, I've gotta meet that kid,' I thought. Wayno became one of our best mates and still is to this day. When we first met him he lived up at Kingsford, but he picked up surfing so quick. We'd moved onto fibreglass boards by this stage, so we gave Wayno one of our old Coolites to learn on, and within one summer he was charging on it. The guy picked up surfing so quick it wasn't funny. He was sharp in the water and out, cheeky like you wouldn't believe, and he was always a little trendier than the rest of us, with a better haircut and better clothes.

And then there was Ronnie. Ronnie Reardon was a small kid, but fiery as hell. He was this muscly little bloke, four foot nothing but with a heart the size of a football. 'Sport Billy' we used to call him, because he never stopped moving; he was like this little ball of muscle that just pinballed between people. He was living around the block from us, but was hanging out with some kid from Lurline Bay, a kid who got hit in the head with a hammer and ended up with brain damage. Pretty soon he was around at our place every day, and he's been a best mate to all of us ever since. Soon after we met Peter 'Jimmy' Olsen, 'Two Bob Rob' Selman and the Kingsley brothers, Jack and Luke. All these guys straightaway became part of our little surf gang.

When there were no waves we never ran out of shit to do. We used to go 'pilling' on the golf course – diving in the swamps for lost golf balls then selling 'em back to the golfers. Jimmy Olsen lived up at Lexo, and he was the master at pilling. He'd come up with five or six balls at once. He took us up to his secret golf swamp one day and we were just killing it, finding shitloads of balls, until Jimmy cut his foot really badly on a piece of glass and we had to carry him up to Prince Henry Hospital at La Perouse. Jimmy was the most energetic kid you ever met; never stopped talking, never stopped moving. We called him Ernie Devlin because the guy was the king of stunts. Whether it was jumping off cliffs into the ocean or eating a mouthful of birds eye chillies with a schooner of chilli sauce for a chaser, Jimmy would always be geeing us up to bet against him at two bucks a head.

To Mum's credit, whenever we had a house, the door was always open, so there were always kids hanging around. She's always been like that: her places were always open to all the neighbourhood kids and to our mates. I think the reason so many kids hung at our place was that most of the time no one was there to tell us what we couldn't do. I remember being in Maroubra Bay Hotel on New Year's Eve with Wayno when we were about 12, sneaking swigs of beer off tables when no one was looking. A lot of the time Mum wasn't home, and parental supervision was a pretty foreign concept to us – as it was for a lot of our mates. Most of them had come from some kind of broken family; it wasn't unusual around Maroubra.

And maybe it was because we always seemed like the odd ones out that we all banded together. We were always looking after each other because none of us were fully being looked after at home. We started to instil a lot of that stuff: don't tell on each other, always back each other up. Telling on each other was the worst thing you could do. There was a real solidarity among us already at that stage – so much so that when we finally got to high school we all got expelled on the same day.

For high school, I was enrolled at Marcellin College at Randwick, a Marist Brothers school. It was Ma's doing; she made sure we were going to get a Catholic education. It was like another world for us. We were going from zero discipline at home to full Catholic discipline at school. Most of our mates went there – me, Ronnie, Wayno, Jai the following year – and whenever it rained we'd all walk to the bus stop together crowded under Pa's big KB beach umbrella. I remember one morning while we were waiting on Maroubra Road for the school bus to pick us up, Brad Stubbs came flying down the road in a Porsche. Stubbsy was president of the Maroubra Boardriders at that stage – the Wrong Enders – and he was a bit loose. And remember, the Wrong Enders was supposed to be the professional club. Well, on this morning, Stubbsy was on fire.

He'd convinced a sports car dealer on Anzac Parade to let him take a test drive; he'd left his old Holden Kingswood at the dealership and swapped it for a bright yellow, top-of-the-line Porsche. He was flying past the bus stop with a wad of 50-dollar notes in his hand, just throwing them to the wind, and all us kids were running out on the road rumbling for them. Then he parked, walked over to the promenade on the beach, called us all over and delivered a full sermon, preaching about how we were the future of Maroubra. I've got no idea where he got the money from – and I didn't wanna know. We went from that to five minutes later being in one of the strictest Catholic schools in Sydney. When the bus pulled up outside the school, we were suddenly on another planet.

I'm surprised I lasted long enough at Marcellin for Jai to show up the following year, but together we didn't last much longer after that.

It got to the point where the principal said we were 'controlling the natural flow of the school', so they expelled our whole little gang, 10 of us from all different grades, including me and Jai together. By that stage we already had the mentality that if one of us was going to go, we all were.

So we were all banished to Maroubra Bay High, a big gang of us – me, Jai, Ronnie and Wayno among them. We all met down the beach that afternoon and said, 'Unreal, we're here. We're back where we belong.' Maroubra Bay High was about 200 metres from the surf, just up the road from our place, and right in the heart of Maroubra. We all marched up to the school together and it was like, 'look out, we're here'. It was the school's worst nightmare.

The Bay was the best school ever. Well, best for us anyway. It felt like a small-town, community school, which was great, but academically it had a reputation as just about the worst school in the state. There were classrooms where you could see the surf. I took home economics because the cooking classroom had the best views of the beach. You could look straight down McKeon Street and see the north end of the beach, and you could also see the south end from the top of the playground, so you knew what the surf was like at both ends of the beach.

By that stage we were full-on in surf-surf-surf mode, before school, lunchtime, after school. We all used to meet at the beach early each morning before school to go surfing. Then as soon as the bell rang for lunch it was *vroom*, a heap of us would bolt straight out of class and jump the fence. There used to be ways you could escape out onto Wride Street on the north side of the school oval where you wouldn't get seen by teachers. From there you'd jump the fence, run straight through the big white block of units across the road, and emerge out on Poo Hill overlooking the north end. Straight to Ma's, wetties on, boards waxed, *boom*, 30-minute surf. You'd make it back to school covered in sand, dripping wet, just as the bell rang. And then you had school surfing on Thursdays, so you'd be surfing on school time as well. Spending half of every school day in the water, the school years flew.

Maroubra Bay High was a really good school. Academically and behaviour-wise it was atrocious, but for us it had a good feel about it. Because I used to surf before school every morning I'd be late most of the time, so the girls in the office kept a signed late note there ready for me. As those years went on, I think the school realised we were young maniacs and that was unlikely to change, and they became very community oriented. They understood that most of us were doing it pretty tough, and they cut us all some slack.

However, it was still regarded as one of the worst schools in the state, so the Department of Education brought in an ex-prison warden as our principal. The big ace he was playing was this new system that was being trialled in America at the time called the SOS Program, which stood for Save Our Souls. Maroubra Bay was the only school in New South Wales where it was being trialled. That's how bad the school's reputation was.

The way the SOS Program worked was that you got three strikes and you were out. You punched a kid in the neck – one strike. Skipped class to surf – two strikes. Set fire to someone's books – three strikes. On your third strike you got sent to the SOS Room.

The SOS Room was not considered to be part of the school. You got sent to a room with one teacher who'd be rostered in there, and you couldn't leave the SOS Room until you sat there for eight periods – eight hours straight – in full silence. You'd say a word and your eight hours would start again. You had your own recess and lunch times, and you never mixed with the rest of the school. It was like being in jail. It was like they were ignoring you, and they figured without the attention you'd behave yourself. But what seemed like a good concept soon became a disaster.

Ronnie was the first kid on the first day to get thrown in there. I think he was in there for three months, maybe longer. After a week they moved the SOS Room from a single classroom to a double classroom; then it ended up going to the school hall. It didn't take long before the hundred worst kids in the school were all together in the school hall. A hundred of the naughtiest, funniest kids locked in the same room, all day, every day. It was chaos. No one was learning a thing. But the principal was this full-on warden and he stuck with it for well over a year.

The school hall had a stage, so it became like a musical. Chairs would be getting thrown around, food fights. And the beauty of it for us was that because all our little gang were in different classes, the SOS Room united us under one roof – me, Jai, Ron, Wayno, Bulldog and Jimmy. My girlfriend even ended up in there with me, and we snuck up into the loft above the stage. We weren't old enough to have sex but I was giving it my best shot. Anyway, we fell asleep making out up there one day and everyone forgot about us and went home. We got locked in there for the night.

Our early years in high school saw the beginning of the whole gang era in Maroubra. In our second year of high school, when we would have been 14, I remember we flushed this young guy's head down the toilet, just like our heads had been flushed the year before. He was a young Greek kid – we love the Greeks, we've got heaps of them in Maroubra – but we treated him no differently to any other kid, so we flushed him on his first day of high school. Tradition. Well, the next day as I'm walking home from school I see little Ronnie Reardon pinned up against the wall of the Maroubra Bay Hotel by this big Greek guy, about 20 years old. Then I see another guy jump out of a car with a baseball bat and run over. It was the Greek kid's older brother and a dozen of his mates looking for a square-up. I've just yelled out to the guy with the bat and started running at him, the guy's started running at me, and all of a sudden we're into it.

Three of my other mates – Kyle Kabbara, Jimmy Olsen and Wayno – are each into a fight across the road. Three carloads of them had come down looking for us and attacked us as we're walking home from school. Out from the pub comes Big Bitch, an ex-New Zealand heavyweight kickboxing champion. Manou, an older, full-on tough guy from the beach, was on the public phone talking to someone and he's told 'em, 'Err, sorry, I gotta go.' He and Big Bitch have joined in and next thing it's all on. One guy got thrown through the cake shop window and their cars got smashed. The guys have ended up by jumping back in their cars and taking off. We're like, 'Yeah, boys, we showed 'em!' The next day they drove back through and chased me and Ronnie into Island Aclassic surfshop down on the corner. We locked ourselves in the toilet out the back and these three big guys with baseball bats are banging on the door, trying to drag us out.

Maroubra Bay was a rough school. I used to look after this kid who worked in the canteen, who'd make these incredible chicken, lettuce and pineapple rolls for me in return. I used to love those things. We were pretty resourceful, mainly because we were often going to school hungry. When the gold dollar coins came in we mastered the counterfeit scheme. We bought a tin of gold spray paint and sprayed all our 10-cent pieces gold, and started palming them off as gold dollar coins.

The craziest guys from the beach all went to Maroubra Bay. Grommet – Jason Loughnan – especially, was jatz crackers. One day when I was in Year 8 I heard this voice outside the classroom just screaming out, 'Fuck off! Fuck off!' Into our classroom bursts Grommet. Without acknowledging anyone, without caring that the teacher was standing there, he grabs some chalk and, without saying a word, starts drawing this enormous dick on the blackboard, complete with a set of giant balls. The teacher is standing there, hands on hips, flabbergasted.

'Excuse me, who do you think you are?'

And he stares at her with psycho eyes and goes, '*I* ... am the *future*!'

His eyes bulged as he said the word. Then he turns back and starts meticulously drawing pubes on the balls with these deliberate, stabbing strokes.

The teacher has gone, 'Well, Mr Loughnan, you have no future in this school.'

He put the chalk down and just calmly marched out of the room. We could hear him chanting, 'Future, future …' as he walked down the corridor.

Grommet wasn't even enrolled at the time. He'd been kicked out of Maroubra Bay the year before, and was just dropping in during his spare time.

JAI

JAI ABBERTON GIVES A GEOGRAPHY LESSON TO MAROUBRA BAY HIGH SCHOOL'S TRUANCY OFFICER

When we were in high school they were calling Maroubra Bay the worst school in the state.

It wasn't that bad. You could see the waves from the playground, bra, and as soon as the waves were pumping everyone was just over the fence and out of there. So they brought in this new principal. He had this system where if you mucked up you got sent to the back of the class, and if you mucked up at the back of the class you got sent to this SOS Room and you had to do eight periods of silence to get out of there. It was like the full isolation room in jail; it was like solitary, in this little storeroom.

Within two weeks this bloke's SOS system had moved into the school hall, and it was full of the worst write-offs from every class just thrown in there together, not having to do a thing. You had to stay silent for eight periods to get out of there, but no one wanted to leave. You had your own lunch and recess; you didn't have to do any work. We'd have our own recess where the worst write-offs in the school would all be playing handball while the other kids were in class. We'd be throwing shit at their classrooms, throwing paper bombs of wet toilet paper. The rest of the school couldn't concentrate. Everyone wanted to get in there and check it out; it was like a nightclub.

'So, you don't have to do any work in there?'

'Nah, you just have to be quiet for eight periods to get out.'

'So, *no work*, eh?'

I think Ronnie was the first in there, but we weren't far behind. You'd get the odd strict teacher looking after you in there, and you'd behave, but then you'd have these other teachers where you'd just see how far you could push 'em.

They had to scrap it because it went so big so fast, and all the worst kids in the school were in there, including us. The principal had to bar it because there were Lexo chicks in there for months; they couldn't stay silent for eight seconds, let alone eight hours. People were in there for four months without learning a single thing. Our school was bad – one of the worst in the state – and if that was their plan to save it, it wasn't a great surprise they closed the school down not long after we left.

We surfed more than we learned. We used to go surfing heaps, fucking oath. There was one teacher, Mr Rankin, who used to do patrols along the beach looking for kids who'd skipped out and were surfing. But we had the whole area sussed out – all the units, the back lanes, fences – and we could disappear like ghosts in the click of a finger. We could travel three kays in any direction without being seen. Just in and out of flats, maybe out on the road for a second, make sure no cars are coming, then – *boom* – straight into another set of flats and over a fence. I could walk from the school to the beach without being seen.

I knew the geography of Maroubra pretty well by that stage, and geography was about the only subject I ever got into. I could draw a map of the world from a young age, and could tell you where countries are and what their capitals were. The world intrigued me. I liked to know where things were, ya know. After I went to Bali a couple of years later I started looking at maps full on. I used to love how Indonesia turns into

India which turns into the Middle East which turns into Europe which turns into Africa. It fascinated me.

SUNNY

BEWARE CROCODILES IN WHITE SUITS BEARING GIFTS

We met 'Nigel' when we were 12.

There was this kid who'd moved in up on Maroubra Road who'd started hanging with us. Whenever we had a boardriders' comp or were at the beach, we'd notice him just hanging off to the side on his own, just watching. We used to call him Nigel No Friends, but eventually he was absorbed into the group and started hanging with us. We were young maniacs; he was a little quieter, but he used to surf a bit with us. Around that time The Anchor, the big sculpture that's up at North Maroubra now, was down on the beachfront across the road from Sea Level surf shop. We all used to hang on the steps in front of it, watching the surf all day and annoying people who walked past.

We're all sitting there one day when this spiff white Jaguar pulls up. In those days we'd notice any nice car that drove through Maroubra because there were hardly any of 'em. So this Jag convertible pulls up and this old bloke in a white suit gets out. He's covered in gold. He looked like *somebody*, like that old bloke from *Fantasy Island*. He's marching straight over to us and we're looking at him going, 'Have a go at this old fag!' We're all sniggering at him.

'Whaddaya want, mate?'

He's zeroed in on Nigel, whose real name was Chris.*

'Hello, Chris. What's wrong? Don't you want to talk to your Uncle Phil?'

---

* *Name has been changed.*

We're like, 'Who the hell are you, mate?'

'My name's Phillip, I'm Chris' uncle. Boys, listen, I've got the day off, so who's up for lunch at McDonald's?' We've just gone, 'hell, yeah', and all jumped up and got straight in the car.

From that moment the bastard had him. The old bloke knew he couldn't get to any of us, we were too streetwise and we probably had parents who'd beat the shit out of him. But he planned all this to get to Chris. We piled in the car straight to Maccas, and then it was like, 'Let's go to the movies while we're here.'

We bagged Chris out the whole time, going, 'How's ya mad fag uncle! Are you a fag, too, are ya?' We had no idea what was really going on.

Anyway, this went on for a few weeks. The old reptile in the white suit would just show up randomly on weekends. We went tenpin bowling, he took us to the movies, just paying for everything. The story this guy was telling us was that he'd had a son who'd died of cancer, and Chris and his son had been best mates, so he always wanted to be close to Chris because he reminded him of his son. He was really touchy with Chris. He'd touch his leg and run his hands through his hair. We'd go, 'Look at you two, ya fags!' Chris was starting to get really upset about the whole thing, and trying to be really stand-offish with him, but Uncle Phil would go, 'Don't be stupid, Chris. I'm your uncle.'

It went on for a few weeks, him taking us out, splurging everywhere. We kept teasing Chris, but we really thought it was his uncle and we didn't really care if he was a bit of a fag if he was paying for everything.

'I should take you all to my mansion at Whale Beach one time. It's got great waves.' He kept on and on about it. We were still at that age that a trip to Whale Beach was like going to Queensland, so he finally organised to collect us one morning with our boards and take us to his place to go surfing. But he'd only invited a handful of us to go including, of course, Chris.

We get to his house at Whaley. The driveway winds all the way up the hill to this big two-storey bungalow overlooking the beach; it has the big terrace, the big barbie. We all got changed straightaway, he drove us down the beach, and we surfed for two or three hours. Then he's driven us back up to his place and put on a big barbecue for us. We're all there having a barbie, and, of course, there just happened to be two cases of beer sitting in the fridge. He'd taken off for a while, so we all started drinking. He comes back and we're all half pissed.

'Oh, you got into the beers?' he says, like he never meant it to happen. 'Okay, just don't drink too many.'

He has a few beers with us, and as the sun's going down, he suddenly says, 'Boys, we've got a bit of a problem; I'm too drunk to drive you home. You're going to have to stay here.'

He knew full well that every one of us he had there didn't have to go home because we had no parents waiting for us. That's why he'd picked us. He wasn't after us, but he'd taken us as well to make sure Chris would come. We weren't going home to any parents, and he knew that.

So when it came time to go to bed, he started handing out blankets and pillows.

'Sunny, you're on the lounge. Mate, you're over there.'

And he did that until only Chris was left, and of course there were no beds and no blankets left.

'Chris, you can come in and sleep with me.'

And we've all gone, '*Wooooooo!*' and started wolf-whistling.

Chris has gone, 'Nah, I'm sleeping out here with the boys.'

Uncle Phil carried on, going, 'Why are you making such a big deal out of this, Chris? We're family, what's wrong with you?' He almost dragged him in there.

We're like, 'Woooooo, go for it!' We were just kids who didn't faintly understand what was going on.

The next morning when we woke up, Chris came out and he was shaking. Something had happened; he was pale and he was shaken. He was telling us to fuck off and leave him alone. None of us said anything to each other; no one said anything to Chris. We were all really quiet on the drive back to Maroubra. The whole next week I don't think we talked about it once.

A week later the guy's shown up again at The Anchor and bipped the horn at us, and we all just ran at him and attacked his car. We just fly-kicked his doors, jumped on his bonnet, smashed one of his windows, and he drove off. He turned up a fortnight later and we attacked his car again, and that was the last time we saw him. We never really talked about it, and we never saw Chris again after that weekend.

Six or seven years later, I was going with a crew to the Gold Coast to a big junior surfing contest. It was late when we got there, midnight maybe. I was first heat in the morning, but I didn't have anywhere to stay. All I had was the phone number of a guy who worked at a surfing magazine up there, so I was going to call him and see if I could crash at his place for the night. I was desperate. I rung the number I'd scratched on a bit of paper. A girl answers the phone and tells me that this guy doesn't live there and she'd never heard of him.

I was desperate and, thinking I may have got the number mixed up with someone else, I fired off blindly, 'Look, I'm surfing in a junior contest in the morning. Does anyone who lives there know anything about it?'

She goes, 'Hang on, I'll ask my boyfriend.' She yells out, 'Do you know if there's a junior surfing contest on tomorrow?'

I've heard the voice in the background go, 'Who is it?'

I replied, 'My name's Sunny.'

'Sunny,' she relayed to him.

Then I heard her boyfriend go, 'Sunny who?'

'Sunny Abberton.'

'Sunny Abberton,' she relays.

The phone goes silent for a second; then the boyfriend comes and picks up the phone. It's him. It's Chris.

We rapped for a little while, both blown out by the chance phone call; then he asked if I wanted to stay. 'I've got a big place at Kirra. Come and stay up here.' It was the first time I'd seen him since it all happened. I've rocked up to his house and couldn't believe how amazing it was: big bungalow-style veranda, big backyard, artwork, huge four-wheel drive out front. He even had the beautiful model girlfriend.

I walked into the lounge room the next night and there on the wall above the TV was a photo of Chris, another kid, and his Uncle Phil in the middle. He told me it was Phillip's house, and that he was paid to be the caretaker, which meant he just went surfing most of the time. We both knew something had happened that night, and we both knew each other knew, but we never talked about it. We had no idea how to talk about it, so we swapped some small talk and I went off to bed.

I surfed in the contest the next day, and got back late in the afternoon to Chris' place. That night we're all sitting watching TV when a newsflash comes on: 'Millionaire businessman Phillip Harold Bell arrested for child sexual assault'.

By chance, I'm sitting next to Chris as this came on the TV. It was like I was supposed to be there. It turns out that the guy who had keyed Bell as the person who'd abused him was the other kid in the photo. Chris just got up and ran out the door. I was left there with no idea what to do or say. Chris' girlfriend, who knew nothing about it, was in total shock. That whole night just came flooding back as I sat there. Chris eventually came back in and denied it all. He said, 'That guy's a liar. He's trying to get Phil's money.' I left the next morning and came back to Sydney.

Once that kid came out, Chris ending up backing him, along with all these other kids. That old reptile did 10 years and died in jail. Him going down helped to expose this whole ring of paedophiles. It would eventually end up before a Royal Commission, looking into police, judges … it went all the way up. A heap of them took their own lives over it.

And you wonder why we grew up looking out for each other?

Part 3
HIM
Maroubra

KOBY

THE KID GETS THROWN IN THE DEEP END BUT FINDS
NO HOODOOS AT VOODOO

All my earliest memories of life are surf memories.

My first surf might have been with my pa, it might have been with Sunny and Jai, but it definitely wasn't with my mum. I know she had nothing to do with the ocean. I don't know whether I was too young to remember anything else, bra, or whether I surfed so much when I was young that all my surfs just blurred into each other.

I can remember walking down the beach with my Larry Blair board. It was the first board I owned, this big red thing, and it was the board he'd won the Coke Classic on at Manly. It was this really famous board, but I would drag it around by the legrope, across the rocks, across the road, just dinging the shit out of it, because I could never get my arm around it to carry it properly. One time when I got stung by a bluebottle, I was in too much pain to lug it home, so I just dumped my Larry Blair board on Maroubra Beach on a packed summer's day.

It was really Jai and Sunny who got me into surfing. When I was about 10, I remember Jai and Sunny getting free shit all the time – clothes, legropes, surfboards – and that's what really made me go, 'Fuck, that's what I wanna do: I wanna be a pro surfer.' When they started travelling, I'd watch them pack their boardbags and I'd be thinking, 'Yeah, that's me.' I hadn't surfed outside of Maroubra at all by that stage. I'd hear people talk about how good Sunny and Jai were and I'd be thinking that I wanted to be better than they were. I actually watched Sunny surfing a lot, but I didn't watch Jai much because he was a goofyfooter and I was a naturalfoot. I couldn't understand goofies. Putting their right foot forward? It just didn't add up. Why would you do it? I didn't try and copy Sunny and Jai's styles, but I did watch a lot of surf videos, those *Momentum* videos. I used to love watching Kelly Slater and Taylor Knox surf. I'd sit and watch those guys for hours – rewind, play, rewind, play. Wore the fucking tape out I did, bra.

Sunny and Jai have always supported my surfing. When I was young Jai was ripping; he was probably even better than Sunny at that stage. They didn't offer me a lot of advice, but they didn't have to. We just went surfing. We surfed a lot – all day, every day, whether it was one foot, five foot, 10 foot. Everything was about being in the water, and if there weren't any waves we'd be jumping off the rocks or playing in the stormwater drain.

And, remember, this was back in the days when you'd be surfing out at Maroubra and there'd literally be shit everywhere in the water. And not just a slick, but literally big Mars Bars out there. It was pretty filthy. But I was brought up in that shit, so to me it was just normal. I didn't travel much until I was about 12, so I never really knew what clean water was like. Then, when they extended the Malabar ocean sewer pipe miles out to sea a year or so later, you'd paddle out and wonder what was wrong with the water because it was blue. When I was a kid I just surfed Maroubra or around the corner at Voodoo, where the water was just as bad, so it never bothered me that much. When it rained it was almost worse because it'd flush out the syringes down the stormwater drain. I've spiked myself a few times with picks washed down the stormy. That was scary as shit.

I joined up with North End Boardriders when I was eight. Back then, if you weren't in the club you pretty much weren't allowed on the beach. They were good guys, all complete lunatics, but fun guys to grow up with. You had Grommet and Marty Lee; then you had guys like Brad Stubbs down the beach at Maroubra Boardriders. We did a lot of trips away with the club. My mum didn't really care; we'd go away for a week at a boardriders' trip and she wouldn't even know we were gone.

But it got to a point where I was surfing so much that it seemed easy to me, so I gave it up and took up fishing. I'd just go and sit around the rocks at North Maroubra and fish these pools, trying to catch tiny little fish. I was a bit of a loner when I was a kid. When all the boys would go up the coast together I'd just sit there with my fishing rod. I remember thinking, 'I can already surf.' It wasn't that much fun for me so I wouldn't do it. I'd mastered that. I had more fun trying to catch fish.

The only thing that was keeping me interested was riding bigger waves. Jai and Wayno set the benchmark for charging when they were young. They'd just do stupid shit, almost killing themselves trying to outdo each other: going to Hawaii, surfing big Pipeline, big Lurline Bay.

That's the mentality of everyone around here, whether it be surfing or fighting or doing stupid shit. You're always getting pushed to go harder. Jai and Wayno especially were brutal with us, bra. If the surf was big we never got a chance to say no. And if you dogged it, then you'd get ridiculed or dead-legged or torn down until the next big swell. We'd get beaten up every day by those guys, but that was a part of growing up and I actually appreciated the fact they did it.

Maroubra was so full-on like that. I think it was because there are so many Housing Commission units and so many houso kids, and every one of them is trying to climb up from nothing. When I'd walk down the beach, by the time you got there, there would be 30 kids with you. You'd just walk past their houses and whistle and they'd all come out and follow you down to the beach; then you'd all paddle out together. If there are that many kids hanging together, everything becomes a feeding frenzy, everything was a contest, especially surfing. You could never back down or show any signs of weakness, or you'd pay for it. It happened to me once, and I'm still paying for it to this day.

It was not long after I'd met Jed, my best mate. Jed was a clubbie when I met him. Quite a few of our mates used to be in the surf lifesaving club at Maroubra in the early days – Jed, Johnny and Richie Gannon, Nath Rogers, Brad Carroll. They'll all tell you it was because the clubhouse had hot showers in the winter, but the real reason was that they just used to love running around with their sluggoes pulled up their arses. We never liked the clubbies, and it wasn't long before those guys woke up to themselves, stopped mincing around in the surf club and were all out surfing with us.

We woke up that morning and the swell was pretty big. There's this rare wave that breaks along the rocks at South Coogee called The Southy.

When the swell's big, it bounces off Wedding Cake Island and re-forms into this crazy righthander. And it was firing this day.

Jed paddled out, I didn't.

I'm not even sure why I didn't go. It was massive, and I didn't really have a board big enough I suppose, so I sat there and watched it for ages while Jed paddled out with Jai and Wayno and surfed it. When I say *surfed it*, he really just sat on the shoulder watching Jai and Wayno pick them off. If I'd gone out I would've been going, so there's a big difference there, *Jed*, if you're reading this. I was probably only 12, but I got teased so bad about it. I still get teased about it today; every time I get on the piss with Jed and Wayno, it comes up, and it still burns me.

I remember vowing it was never going to happen again.

Not long after, I paddled out at Maroubra when it was about 10 foot and I had to get rescued. I jumped off from around the back of the point and got washed over the rocks; it was a miracle that I even made it out there alive. The whole time I was being dragged all over the rocks I was just thinking, 'I'm getting out here no matter what. I'll show fucking Jed!' Jed wasn't out – too scared probably – so it was my chance to redeem myself. I managed to make it out and there I was, sitting miles out to sea with a dozen of the older Maroubra boys. They were all going, 'What the fuck are you doing out here, grommet?' I didn't really know myself. They eventually had to paddle me into the beach. I was fine out there, I wasn't scared at all, but the older guys were shitting themselves that something was going to happen to me.

Then I remember my first surf at Lurline, Maroubra's big-wave spot. I jumped off the rocks no worries and was sitting wide in the channel, watching it and just shitting myself. I edged my way over and eventually a big set has come through. I'm sitting there looking at the first one, the biggest wave I'd ever seen in my life. I had no intentions of catching it, but I remember looking at it and thinking to myself, 'Why not?' I didn't have an answer, bra, so I turned around, paddled as hard as I could, and caught it. I get to my feet and halfway down I think I'm killing it. It was the greatest moment of my life – right up until the point where I nose-dived, got speared head-first into the impact zone and nearly drowned. I got washed into the inside, but I popped up and still had two arms and two legs. I was starting to realise that it was only water and I didn't have to worry about it.

By this stage I was starting to feel comfortable in big surf. Guys like Jai and Wayno would always be on your case, trying to drag you out there when it was big, but I was more the kid who wanted to do it. I was always asking 'em to take me surfing with them when it was big.

I was 12 when we surfed that big day down at Voodoo. When we left Maroubra it was six to eight foot and the swell was really south, so Vooey must have been huge. We turned up and we saw these lines running all the way down into Boat Harbour. I'm thinking, 'Y'know, it looks pretty big out there', but at the same time it also looked fun. So we walked down and waited for a break in the sets, then jumped off out in front of Suck Rock. We had to paddle our arses off to get out, and just as we got out this thing come through – 12 or 15 foot – and I thought to myself, 'Geez, that is pretty big.' I should've been more worried, but I remember I was kind of mesmerised by how perfect it looked more than anything else.

As we've paddled out wide Sunny pulled me aside and said, 'Koby, it's huge right now. I'm a bit rattled you're out here. For fuck sake, just be careful.'

That rattled me more than the waves. We finally got out there and there were only three or four guys out. We were sitting in the zone when some sets come through that we only just got over. I think Sunny then started to really worry that I was going to drown. It's still one of the biggest days I've ever surfed, even to this day. It was massive. And then I thought, 'Fuck, we're sitting so far out we're never gonna catch anything. What are we doing sitting so far out the back?' Some smaller ones have come through and I saw 'em cornering on the inside, just firing off perfectly. I've gone, 'Fuck this, I'm in there to get one of those.'

I got halfway in there when I saw it.

This huge thing just filled the horizon. I can remember all the boys just yelling, 'Koby! Paddle!'

It was fucking huge, bra. Biggest wave I've ever seen. I just scratched over it, but even as I was paddling up the face of it I looked down into the pit and I was thinking, 'You know, you could have surfed that one. They're big, but …'

Then Sunny paddled over, blowing up. 'Don't do that again! I thought you were fucking dead, little bra!'

I went, 'Sure, no worries,' and went straight back in there again and started catching waves.

When we got in later, Sunny and Jai pulled me aside and said, 'You know, if you wanna surf big waves, you can do it. We were scared for you out there, but for some reason you weren't.'

jed campbell

KOBY'S BEST MATE, THE GUY WHO PADDLED OUT WHEN KOBY DIDN'T

Koby still hates us talking about that day.

If we were on the drink right now, Wayno would bring up that day at The Southy, guaranteed.

'What happened to ya that day, Kobe? You pull a heartstring?'

I love to bag Koby about being down in Kiddies Corner that day. But to be honest, I would rather have been down with them surfing Kiddies Corner myself. But there was no way Jai and Wayno were gonna let that happen; I was going out whether I liked it or not.

The Southy is a big-wave spot where all the biggest local legends surfed, all the guys we looked up to. If you were good enough you'd get barrelled from the take-off. Then there was a big inside section – if you made it through that, you were a hero for the next 10 years. If you didn't make it, you got a two-wave hold-down.

On that day everyone was there. I paddled out with Jai and Wayno on my 6′ 3″ big-wave board. It was about a foot shorter than theirs but still too big for me, that's how small I was at the time. It was the biggest waves I'd ever surfed. I looked up and the whole cliff was lined with spectators; fair to say I was shitting myself.

You've got to understand how mad Jai and Wayno were back then. Everyone is surfing 20 metres off the cliff face, and they're about five off the cliff, bagging each other about how gay they are. They're practically sitting on the cliff, bagging the shit out of each other for sitting too wide. Meanwhile, I'm out in the channel, halfway to Bondi in about a thousand foot of water, shitting myself.

They're like, 'Get the fuck over here, ya little bastard! Have a go!' They're just into ya. I remember me first wave; me and Wayno still talk about it. I'm paddling into this one and I get to the bottom of it; I'm standing in this thing, the biggest barrel of my life. I get hammered, and go straight down.

I'm trying to get to the surface when the second wave hits me and pushes me straight down again. By this stage Wayno is racing in to try and find me. I pop up screaming, 'I got a two-wave hold-down!' I was that stoked, I was just carrying on. Jai and Wayno had seen me take off on it. Two hundred people on the cliffs had seen me take off on it. Koby saw me take off on it.

Every time Wayno brings it up I'll always laugh and gee Koby up … but today it's me surfing Kiddies Corner. Today it's Koby doing what Wayno did back then, geeing everyone up to go surf Ours or somewhere heavy like that. He's the one geeing me up to go the biggest ones. He's the most inspirational guy to speak to about surfing heavy waves … and every time he does I wonder how much that day he didn't paddle out at The Southy contributed to that.

I remember the day I met Koby. I watched him go running across the beach with his big red board. The surf was huge, and I said to the guys I was with, 'If that kid goes surfing, I'm going surfing.' No one else wanted to go 'cause it was pretty big and wild. Koby was paddling out on his own, so I just grabbed a board from the surf club and paddled out with him. And that was it, instant best mates. That was the first day I ever met him and next weekend I was staying at his house.

The guys we hung with on the beach at Maroubra were spilt into two gangs. The older guys – which included Sunny, Jai, Wayno, Moff, Ronnie and Jimmy – called themselves Ma's Hell Team after the Abbertons' grandma. The younger guys – which included me, Koby and our mate Ahu – called ourselves Ma's Madness soon after.

To be in Ma's Madness, you had to surf Maroubra whenever it got big. It didn't happen real often, but when it did you had to go out. You didn't have a choice if you were in our crew.

Ma's Hell Team were the biggest legends in the whole world to us. They were the hottest surfers on the beach and they all knew how to have a good time. They also knew that though we were all from different walks of life, we'd all had the same kind of upbringing as they had, with busted families or whatever, and they just took us all in. They'd say, 'You're the future.' And because they were the hottest surfers on the beach, you felt like you were part of a select crew. I'd go to school and no one would ever muck around with me because I was mates with Ma's Hell Team. The other kids at school were always worried about Jai. I could be the biggest smartarse in the world and they wouldn't touch me in case I told Jai. But the reality was that Jai would rather let you get beaten up to teach you a lesson. They loved us, but when the waves were flat and those guys had nothing to do, you had to look over your shoulder. When they were bored shitless you'd just end up running all day, and you'd cop all sorts of crazy grommet abuse. It was fun, but you were always nervous whenever the surf was flat and you saw Wayno and Jai coming down the street. They were your best mates and your biggest nightmares, all rolled into one.

Those guys taught us so much. I remember Sunny put a lot of time in with Koby's surfing. A few years later when Sunny was on the pro tour, Koby and I would turn up first thing in the morning and we'd see his boardbag there and we'd just go, 'You beauty, Sunny's back!' and it'd be a race to see who'd go surfing with him first. Koby and I would sit there and ask him everything about the tour. We'd pester him with questions but he'd throw it back at us. He'd throw a surfing mag at us and go, 'Which photo is the best and why?' He was really good like that. Jai was just mad. He'd go, 'I don't wanna sit here and talk about it. Let's go.'

Jai will surf and charge anything, whereas Sunny is a little more calculated. Koby was the perfect mix of both of them. Koby's always had it. He's always been nuts. When we were young, it would be six foot out the back of the Maroubra Dunny Bowl and we'd be happy to surf the reformers on the inside. But Koby would go straight out the back on his own then get paddled back in by some older guy going, 'You're not allowed out here, grommet!'

JAI

SELF–PRESERVATION TAKES A BACKSEAT AS THE BOYS TAKE A HARDLINE AT LURLINE

If you didn't charge, you deserved the backseat.

We just pushed each other. I remember me, Wayno and Sunny surfing the first day of a big Clovelly Bommie swell. After we got out and put the boards on the roof Sunny jumps in the front seat, and Wayno just goes, 'Where are you going, mate? Get in the back. You got nothing out there. Were you even out there, Sunny? We didn't even see you out there, mate.'

Whoever charged the big days got the front seat. They were the trump that day. I got a couple of biggies that first day, and I remember Wayno got a biggie that ended up on the cover of *Tracks*.

It's always been that way here, bra, and it starts when you're a kid. We always used to take Koby to Voodoo. We had to push him, because when he was young Koby was more into fishing. I'd tell him to come surfing and he'd just go, 'Nah, I'm going fishing; I don't really like surfing.' And he'd sit on the rocks at North Maroubra all day and just fish. The kid needed to be pushed.

Me, Sunny and Wayno would always take Koby and his mates and push them. We'd try and scare them, get them to catch something big, get them stoked, harden the little cunts up. We were making those kids go whether they liked it or not, 'cause that's what Blackie Wilson and those guys had done with us. Blackie was always out there when it was big, and he used to say to us, 'It doesn't matter if you catch waves or not, as long as you're in the ocean. I don't care if you guys just come out and sit in the channel; you've just got to feel the ocean.' He always knew that if he managed to get us out there, we'd go, 'This isn't that bad,' and just pluck a couple off.

Blackie's real name was Steve Wilson. He was my biggest hero in the world. He used to charge so hard. He surfed in pro contests and was rated in the top 16 in the world at one stage. He owned Impact surfboards and ran Sea Level surf shop on the corner of Marine Parade. He was a really important figure for us when we were kids. Blackie shaped me my first new custom board. It had the big Tommy Carroll stripe across the deck of it. I'd never had a new board. I'd only just got it when one day me and Ronnie were in the garage at Ma's; we were so psyched to get out there that we ran into each other, and the nose of Ronnie's board went straight into my brand new board and put a massive ding in it. I hadn't even had a surf on the thing. Fuck, I nearly had tears in me eyes, I've never been that shattered in my life.

At this stage we had signed up for North End Boardriders, who were mainly just mullers and ratbags. They were the guys at the pub, the guys on the street; guys like Hinesy and Marty Lee. Blackie was in Maroubra Boardriders down the beach – Maroubra had all the pro surfers. But that didn't matter – he took us under his wing more than anyone. Blackie played a big part in our surfing. He was the guy who showed us what to do out there. He shaped our boards. He was a legend, the biggest legend. Maybe he could see our situation a bit and wanted to help us out.

Voodoo was our wave, bra, our proving ground. That's where we did all our surfing in bigger waves. There's other big spots around here like Lurline, The Southy, Cloey Bommie, but they don't break real often, whereas Vooey is pretty consistent. It was isolated and powerful, and 'cause the water there was dirty because of the outfall it even felt like Maroubra. All our reef surfing was done at Vooey, and that's why we all like surfing heavy reef waves today. I remember surfing it for two weeks straight once with Blackie; we were onto it every day.

My best surfing mate was Wayno. I've had all my best surfs over the years with him and to this day it's often just us, going wave for wave. Except Koby's in a league of his own these days. I'm lucky to make a takeoff – I need the ski.

One day me and Wayno surfed big Lurline Bay on our own and had to get rescued by the chopper. It was massive. Wayno's jumped out there and been sucked straight out to sea over at Larry's Left. It's about 12, 15 foot; it was nearly closing out the bay across to Lurline which you never see happen – that's how big it was. He's there and – *boom* – lost his board. I look around and all of a sudden I'm the only cunt standing there on the cliffs with a board; all the boys had come in and gone home 'cause it was getting dark. So I've pulled on me wettie and jumped straight off the rocks to go out and get him. As I'm paddling out, I hear the helicopter above; the cliffs were packed with people watching and someone had phoned it in. Wayno's copping a fair few sets on the head and I'm right there beside him. I give Wayno my board to sit on, but forget I've still got the legrope on my ankle. The chopper has come over and they've dropped the rescue harness. I've just grabbed it 'cause I was right near it; then the chopper's gone to take off. I'm getting winched up and then next thing the legrope pulls tight. I slingshot straight back down into the water, just as this set's about to come and hammer us. Wayno's there blowing up: 'You stole me helicopter, ya fuckwit!' Then – *boom* – we were there fighting in the water. When we finally got into the chopper the bloke looks at us and goes, 'What the fuck were you blokes doing down there?'

The whole lot of us were never worried about drowning in big waves. We were too busy trying to trump each other. It was always a competition when we paddled out together.

In those days Maroubra was all about surfing. We all used to hang out in the surf shops – Blackie's Sea Level, Doigy's Island Aclassic; then later David Gyngell had his shop, Maroubra Underground. Those guys would always be helping us out with boards and clothes and wax. Walking back through the streets from the beach to Fenton Avenue, Maroubra was always packed. The pub was packed, the beer garden was packed, the beach and the car parks were packed. Surfing was huge then.

Maroubra was where it was happening, and the place was alive, brother.

SUNNY

IT'S ALL FUN AND GAMES UNTIL SOMEONE CALLS THE CHOPPER

It was a huge day at Lurline, and Blackie turned around and said he'd give a free board to whoever paddled out.

There was me, Jai, Wayno, Ronnie, Jimmy and Moff. We're all about 12 or 13 at the time. We've all just looked at each other and gone, 'We're fucking out there!' Blackie was already paddling out with a few of the other older guys when I climbed down the cliff and jumped off the rocks. As I started paddling out I looked back, expecting the boys to be there, but there was nobody. The swell was huge and still building, and the other boys couldn't get out off the rocks.

By the time I got out the back it began to dawn on me how fucking big it was. It was 12 foot, probably bigger, but it was getting bigger with every set. I snuck over a couple of smaller ones and I was in the channel sussing it out when I saw this enormous set rolling in. The horizon just went black. I was just scratching out to sea, yelling at the older boys to get the hell out of there. It was a 15-footer; I remember almost coughing my heart out as I scratched up the face of it. Blackie and the boys hadn't seen it, and were right underneath it, diving off their boards. I just scratched for my life over the first two, and suddenly the third one was there in front of me. I was in the perfect spot, and with all those guys there I had to go. As I was riding it I saw two of their boards float over me in the lip and get washed in. I kicked out in the channel and there was Blackie, Rissole, Red Johnson and Brad Coulis, all floating there without their boards.

I yelled out to Blackie, 'One of your boards almost hit me!'

'Well, paddle in and get it for us, grommet!'

The board had been washed way over towards Larry's Lefts, where all the water from Lurline Bay flushes back out to sea. I paddled over, grabbed the board and brought it out to him, but it turned out to be Rissole's board. I gave Blackie my board, Rissole jumped on his board and I jumped on Rissole's back. By this stage we were all out of there. The ocean was boiling and it was getting too wild, even for those guys.

The rocks are the only way out, and Blackie scampered up the cliff like a crab. But suddenly there's this massive set and Rissole and I are caught in the rip; we're duck-diving eight-footers. We were caught right in front of the cliff. If a big set had hit us, we were gone.

Even though it was a really dangerous situation, I was confident because those guys were there. In the end we had to get choppered out, because there was no way we could get up the rocks. There were ambulances and crowds, the full scene, and I remember being winched up the rope and claiming it to the crowd.

The rescue guy blew up at me. 'You think this is funny, mate?'

I was in Year 7 at school and all the chicks were digging the fact I'd surfed this huge day and been rescued and made the newspapers. I lapped it up. I was pretty quick to tell Jai to get in the backseat every day we went surfing after that. The newspaper clipping of me being rescued was still up on the wall at Sea Level surf shop years later.

Jai and me would bag the shit out of each other, but out in the water it was a healthy rivalry. You always want to see your brother getting amazing waves and surf them well. There was always hooting when we surfed together. Out at Voodoo, Jai was pretty hard to beat. But even though Jai would charge big surf, I'd still be outsurfing him and charging just as hard; it's just that you'll never hear Jai say it. Like Jai, Koby was instinctively fearless. The pair of them never worried about a thing out there, but I had this parental vibe where I couldn't help but be worried about my brothers when they paddled out in heavy surf. I was always holding my breath when they took off on a heavy wave, which Jai and Koby were doing all the time. It was just a natural reaction, a blood thing. That's why I freaked out the day Koby paddled out at big Voodoo.

The kid just got off on danger. When Koby was five, I remember we pushed him down this giant hill on a little plastic three-wheeler. He got all the way to the bottom and got the death wobbles, crashed into a parked car and got six stitches in his head. The next day he was straight back up there again, ready to go, stitches and all.

Koby was always a hyperactive kid, but he'd also have these quiet moments. When you'd take him to the beach sometimes he'd just disappear off around the rocks on his own. He wasn't clinging to you; he'd always be off exploring. He went through a full fishing stage, which turned into a boogieboarding stage, which turned into a snake-catching stage, which then turned into a big-wave surfing stage. Each one he'd just lose himself in totally.

Jai was like Koby – fully hyperactive. Like any brothers a year apart, we were competitive, but as we hung with the same friends we were always on the same team. Jai was just the master of pushing everything that little bit too far. Jai and I shared a room and we would punch the shit out of each other. Often. We didn't have boxing gloves – Mum wouldn't buy them for us – so we'd hold a rolled-up pair of socks in each fist then put a footy sock over our hand to make our own boxing gloves. When Jai and I would fight you'd know he'd wanna knock your head off. One time we'd had this big blow-up and he'd rung me and said, 'Brother when I get home, it's *on*!'

So I've run around the house and hidden all the bats and all the sharp objects. Thinking I was safe, I was sitting on the lounge when I heard the key crunch in the front door. It was at that instant that it hit me – *the golf club behind the door*! It was the big wood that we used to hit golf balls at the streetlights over in Coral Sea Park. The second I flashed on it I grabbed a pillow off the lounge and rolled over and *whump*, the head of the golf club went straight into it.

SUNNY

HOW A KINDLY 50–YEAR–OLD GRANDMOTHER UNWITTINGLY AIDS IN THE FORMATION OF THE WORLD'S MOST NOTORIOUS SURFING TRIBE

That's how the cycle worked: Mum would come back and say, 'I'm clean, everything's good. I'm going to take the kids back.'

To prove it, she'd rent a house, we'd move back in with her, and then within six months the wheels would fall off. She'd be a mess, we'd be on the streets, the rent wouldn't be paid and we'd be back living at Ma's again. That's what happened with our place next to the Maroubra Bay pub.

Living right on the beach and next to the pub was paradise for us at first, but the novelty of living with Mum again soon wore off. Mum just wasn't there. Just *wasn't* there. We wouldn't see her for a couple of days, and when we did see her she wasn't any good to us anyway 'cause she was fried. Back then, if Mum was around, a good meal was sausages, eggs and chips. If she wasn't, it was cereal and toast for dinner. We were lucky that Ma's was just around the corner; if we got really hungry we'd either go to her place or snowdrop from the early-morning bread and milk runs.

It was just pretty much do what we wanted. If your mum's either not there or she's shuffling around the house with a bunch of strangers all on the nod, you're out of there, doing whatever you liked, whenever you liked. We were the kids who were on the beach all day and on the streets all night. Around that time, when we were living next to the pub, I remember it got really bad. We were on the streets non-stop. We never had a time when we had to be home; we had no real rules to follow. That's why we began building a new family.

When we eventually got evicted from the place next to the pub we moved up the road to Bona Vista Avenue, just one street back from the beach at North Maroubra. The place was an old abandoned house, half of which had been burned out and just left there, charred. We used to all leave our boards in the burned half, and it also kinda became our hangout. I remember hardly seeing Mum when we lived there. We had a Salvation Army Christmas in that house; you know, when the Salvos come around and give you Chrissie presents and Christmas lunch. Go the Salvos. We had Spam and canned pudding for Christmas lunch that year, some bonbons and a few presents.

Sure enough, we were soon moving again. I hated moving between these shitty houses. Hated it. The only saving grace was that we weren't moving out of the area; we were in Maroubra the whole time so it meant we could keep surfing and building our group of mates. Luckily, this time we were moving back to the only place that had ever felt like home – Ma's place.

The detached garage out the back of Ma's was where Koby and Mum lived when we moved back in, while Jai and I shared a room inside the house. When we were kids, one Christmas Ma and Pa had given us the option of going on a holiday to Hawaii or a pool. We chose the pool, and it took up most of the small backyard. For us it was heaven – all the houso kids now had a pool. When there were no waves we had somewhere to hang, and Ma's quickly became a second home for all our mates. Ma's was so close to the beach they could leave their boards there, hang out between surfs, sneak a cheeky feed off her.

We'd hang in the backyard or, when Mum moved out, in the garage. It had originally started out years before as, 'Okay, boys, you can leave your boards in the corner of the garage; just keep away from Pa's towels,' to the full-on storage shed for all the boys' boards and wetsuits. It was like a second-hand surf shop in there.

We'd jump up on the roof of the garage, shimmy up to where the pool fence met the wall, and check out the surf; we could get a glimpse of it from up there. If we wanted a better look, we'd just jump our back fence, jump the fence across the lane, and scramble up onto the roofs of the shops across the road from the beach and have an uninterrupted view. The bloke across the lane eventually put barbed wire on his fence to stop us getting up. A few years later, when the scene in Maroubra had deteriorated, we strung barbed wire across the back fence of Ma's as well to stop crew getting in.

The other great thing about living at Ma's was that you had an open ticket to hear Australia's best rock bands. The Seals Club, which towered over Ma's place from across the back lane, would have AC/DC playing, Midnight Oil, Cold Chisel, you name it. And when someone opened the toilet door, AC/DC would come blaring through your bedroom window. They were literally playing 50 feet away from you. It drove Ma crazy, but we loved it.

But living under Ma's roof, you were also living by Ma's rules. Ma used to sit there on the veranda on a long wooden bench drinking her coffee in the afternoon sun, listening to her AM radio and monitoring our comings and goings. She was bloody cunning, too. When the lawns needed mowing she'd leave the lawnmower across the path so you couldn't get through to check the surf; the only way she'd let you through was if you mowed the lawns for her. She kept us honest.

The one thing you knew – that any of the boys knew – with Ma, was that the door was always open. She understood that a lot of our mates were from busted families and were often in trouble at home, and she always made them feel welcome. My mum inherited that trait from her. That's where Ma's Orphan Christmas came from. We'd bring in our friends who had nowhere to go for Christmas, Mum would invite her friends who had nowhere to go, and we'd all have Christmas at Ma's.

Ma's place was crucial in us forging such a tight group of friends. It's because she gave us that base that all of those guys from that group are still our best mates today. That's why we named our little gang after her.

There was a cabinet in the lounge room where Ma would proudly keep all our surfing trophies. After a few years there were hundreds of 'em. But the first trophy that went in there was the Ma's Hell Team trophy that we won at Maroubra Boardriders in 1988. It's the only trophy I've kept.

The boardriders club held an annual teams pointscore. All our mates banded together and entered a team to surf against the older blokes. When they asked us what we were gonna be called, we came up with Ma's Hell Team in honour of Ma. We just thought it was classic having a 'hell team' named after our grandmother. It was a strong club at that stage, and we won that year's overall team pointscore. At the presentation we made an impromptu performance of the Ma's Hell Team song, which was sung to the tune of George Thorogood's 'Bad to the Bone'.

Ma's Hell Team lived on and became the name of our little gang. There was me, Jai, Ronnie, Wayno, Moff, Jimmy, Jack and Luke Kingsley, Darren Bailes, the Nass brothers – all the crew who hung at Ma's place. Koby and his two best mates, Jed and Ahu, were too young. We said, 'You kids can't be in Ma's Hell Team,' so they went and formed their own little gang called Ma's Madness. Ma's Hell Team would form the nucleus of what would eventually become the Bra Boys.

There was even a girl in Ma's Hell Team. When we lived next to the pub our neighbours were a guy named Bullet McKenzie and his little sister, Lynette. Bullet was a great guy and a natural waterman. When he was young he'd carve these miniature surfboards out of esky foam and shape little plasticine surfers to ride them in the Maroubra shorebreak. He went on to become one of the world's best boogieboarders. Lynette was the best chick surfer on the beach, hands down, and we signed her up for Ma's Hell Team straightaway. She surfed like one of the guys, charged big Lurline Bay, did whatever we did, and within a couple of years she was surfing on the women's world tour. She was a gnarly competitor – which was the Maroubra coming out in her I suppose – and I reckon she would have won a world title if she hadn't moved out of Maroubra and lost a bit of that mongrel.

There were plenty of girls in Maroubra at the time, but they weren't like the girls you found at Bondi and Bronte. You're talking about a beach that was full of sewage most of the time, and a beach where at any given moment there'd be nudity, drugs, burn-outs and fights, so it wasn't like chicks were busting down the door to come and sunbake here, you know. The Maroubra girls were a little more rough and ready, a lot like us. Rachel Nass lived next to Ma's; she was one of our good mates. Nassy and her group of friends all surfed, hung out with us, gave us shit, and would start random egg wars with us when they got bored. There's a bit of graffiti on the wall of the Sun Club that's still there today. It says, 'Nassy's got balls' because she and her crew were full chargers. That's why we loved having 'em around. They were fun chicks.

Ma's place got robbed three times over the years, and we're pretty sure it was Mum's boyfriends every time. They did it two Christmases in a row. One of the times me and Jai unwittingly helped 'em do it. It was when were living next to the pub, and we were really young, eight or nine. One day me and Jai are walking up Fenton Avenue towards Ma's place when we spotted Mum's boyfriend at the time and his mate sitting out the front in their car. As me and Jai went past they've gone, 'Geez, boys, we're starving, we're so hungry. I wish we could get a feed. What are the chances of getting something from your grandma's place?' There's no one home at Ma's, and the place is locked up. We've gone to the front door and they've started trying to jimmy the lock. They made out to me and Jai like it was all a big game. We were like, 'Yeah, let's get in and get something!' They had it all planned. They got a jack from the car and wedged it between the bars on the bedroom window and the brick wall, bent the bars open wide enough for us to squeeze through, and sent us in to open the door. We came out and it was like, 'Yeah, we got in! What are we gonna eat?' Me and Jai sat in the kitchen and ate cereal and then we all left, with them closing the door on our way out.

We came home later that day from a surf and everything was gone. They'd stolen the TV, our Christmas presents and all my ma's jewellery, including her wedding ring. We realised straightaway that we'd helped them do it. We had broken in and helped them rob our own grandparents' place. I really remember just the *hatred* I felt for my mum at that stage. She may not have been there, but she had brought those guys there. As a kid, that was really hard to come to terms with.

Ma never got her wedding ring back.

While Ma loved having us under her roof, she was never comfortable with Mum's friends being around. That's why Mum stayed out in the garage. Ma just couldn't trust Mum's friends. I remember the vibe between my ma and my mum, you know. She wasn't allowed to have a key to the house. We were allowed a key each, but it wasn't to be given to Mum under any circumstances, and the door was always to be locked and the place secure.

Ma was feeling really pressured. Pa hadn't long died, but the stress wasn't only from the loss of Pa himself. He died with no life insurance and Ma was left to pay the mortgage as well as support us kids. Ma was under a lot of emotional and financial pressure, as well as worrying about her daughter.

One day Ma didn't get out of bed. I remember she was just lying there, and she seemed really sick. For Ma to stay in bed, no matter how sick she was, was so rare. I don't think we'd ever seen it before. She asked for some Bex, and in typical Ma fashion she said she'd be okay. The following morning she was still in bed and still sick. There was a doctor across the road – we used to call him Doctor Death because he looked like an extra out of a horror movie – so I ran and got him. He said Ma was stressed and gave her more Panadol and told her to rest. The third day she was still in bed, just as sick, so we went and got him again. And again he said she was okay and only needed aspirin. He'd hardly walked out the door when I called my aunty; she came over and we called an ambulance straightaway.

Ma had had a stroke, and her brain had been bleeding for three days. Initially, she was totally incapable of doing anything. She couldn't walk, couldn't talk, couldn't lift her arms. Nothing. I remember us all going in to see her up at St Vincent's. It was so sad. Such a proud woman, robbed of everything. When she finally got out of the ward she stayed in the hospital to begin rehab – physio on her hands and legs, speech therapy. And we're all thinking that if only she'd been taken to hospital on that first day then maybe none of this would have ever happened.

With Ma in hospital, we thought we'd have to sell the house. We had no money and the mortgage had to be paid. Mum was in a bad way – she wasn't an option – so Jai and me ended up moving in with my aunty Jan, Pa's sister, who lived down the coast at Gerringong. Koby was still pretty young, so he stayed with Mum.

It was a heavy time, because we were getting really settled with life in Maroubra. We had this hell group of mates, we had the beach, and we didn't know if we'd ever be going back to it. We couldn't really look after

Ma the way she was, and we knew Mum couldn't look after her, so the plan was that our aunty was going to look after us all – me, Jai and Ma. We were going to sell Fenton Avenue, buy a place down in Kiama, and live with Ma and look after her with our aunty's help. We had a huge going-away party with all our mates before we left, and it was a really sad time for us.

Me and Jai ended up moving down to Gerringong and waiting for the house to sell and Ma to move down. We enrolled in Kiama High School – I was in Year 10 and Jai was in Year 9 – but we didn't last long. We were Sydney street kids, and we got to this school and it was, like, so sleepy, so country. On our first day of school we met the principal, went to our first classes, and by lunchtime Jai and me just looked at each other and said, 'Let's get the fuck out of here.'

From Kiama High School to Gerringong it's about 10 kays, along a real windy highway. So me and Jai are hitchhiking along the side of the road in our school uniform on our first day, going back to our aunty's place. The principal stops, picks us up and goes, 'You guys aren't going to last long here, are ya?' He dropped us back to our aunty Jan's. Our aunty was really great with us and we loved her to death. We liked Gerringong, we liked the surf and we liked the kids there, but it just wasn't Maroubra. It was never going to work.

We started coming back to Maroubra for weekends. Eventually our grandmother recovered enough so she could cook for herself and bath herself. The decision was made that we were going to move back in with her at Fenton Avenue, which hadn't sold. It was the best move for her – the only other option was a nursing home, and Ma was never going to go for that.

And it was the best move for us. We were back in Maroubra.

Ma made progress. After a while she taught herself to say a handful of words, one at a time. She could communicate a bit. But it wasn't until she got out of hospital and moved back home with us that she really improved. She just wanted to be home. When we moved back in we had to go back to square one with her. Ma's very independent, she really liked to cook for herself, but at the start she wasn't up to it so we had to do it. It was a really hard time, because every sentence was a full-on charade. Her hand movements weren't steady enough for sign language, but we eventually got a system going where she could communicate with us. She'd point towards Mum's house, and that meant Mum. Another direction for the supermarket; the bank was to the west.

We roped in a few of our mates to help too; they were mowing the lawns and cleaning the pool, because they knew she was obsessive with this stuff. If we didn't clean the pool within half an hour of her asking, you'd walk back in later that afternoon and here'd be Ma trying to clean the pool herself with an arm and a leg that didn't work.

The worst job Ma would give you, though, was to go under the house and get Zac out. Mum had saved Zac from the dog pound a few years before; he was a racing greyhound who hadn't cut it and had been turned out onto the streets. We had him for years. You couldn't lock Zac up, 'cause he'd hurdle Ma's back fence in one leap. I remember being in Ma's little Datsun 200B before her stroke; we'd be driving past the University of New South Wales, four or five miles away, and I'd look out the window and Zac was still beside the car, keeping up. He couldn't chase a rabbit but he was okay with 200Bs. Anyway, when Zac got old we called him Zac The Leatherback, because he got all arthritic and mangy. When he was crook he'd go and hide underneath the house. He'd stay in there for days, until Ma sent you in to get him. Even on his deathbed he'd fight you all the way. His little cave was full of fleas, spiders and dirt, and all the hair he'd scratched off himself. It was horrible.

Ma was so strong that after the stroke she didn't want people to see her the way she was. She withdrew a bit – not from us, but from her old life, from her old friends. It'd be a really hard struggle to get her to come out to dinner with us because she couldn't use a knife and fork properly. She was a really proud woman, and having to rely on other people really got under her skin.

They were hard times, because we had to look after our ma, you know, with just a bit of help from our aunties. Years later Koby took on the responsibility of looking after Ma, and he'd do that for almost a decade. We all lived with Ma for quite a while, and that was really hard. We loved her to death, but it was a tough thing for young kids to be dealing with.

JAI

THE MAGNANIMOUS AND MARVELLOUS MAVIS ABBERTON

Why wouldn't we like it? We went to school when we wanted, we could surf whenever we wanted, and we could stay out as late as we wanted. We could have as many mates as we wanted to sleep over. Bra, living with Mum was great, because she didn't care what we did. We were free to do whatever we wanted. I didn't mind it, living with Mum. I liked it.

I remember not eating much, though. Seeing them all on the nod and that, I remember always thinking, 'Fuck, there's something in the food. Have a go at what it's doing to 'em! There's something in the food for sure. There's no way I'm eating that shit.' And I'd watch my little brother; I'd always take Koby aside and say, 'Come and eat here with me, little bra. Don't eat with Mum and her crew. Who knows what's in their food.'

When you're young you kind of don't really know what's going on. It just seemed like we got it really good. It wasn't until we were a bit older and we added it all up that we realised why it was like that, and then we got a bit angry.

But Mum fought hard to hang on to us. Through four different blokes she never wanted us split up, but at times it all just got too much for her … and that's when we realised how lucky we were to have our grandma. Ma's place was our rock, Ma was our rock. Living with Mum gave us all this freedom, but it was just chaos. Ma's place was stability, it gave us a bit of discipline, and it was right near the beach. Everybody listened to Ma – not just us boys, but our mates as well. If she said you're going to school, you went to school. Ma had this way about her; you just respected what she said. And that went for all the boys. I think back now about my grandmother taking us all on. She was a bit of a legend. Fucking oath. We really were her world.

When we first moved into Fenton Avenue, Ma was working two jobs: she worked for Qantas and she had a cleaning job. She'd work a morning job at Qantas, come home for an hour, then go work until 10 o'clock at night. Me and Sunny had a room inside, sharing bunk beds, and Koby lived in the garage with Mum.

It was when we moved into Ma's place that our group of mates got really tight. Ma's place just became home for all those guys. There was me, Ronnie, Moff, Wayno, Jimmy, Bailsey, Kinga ... we were hanging real tight. The boys would leave their boards at my grandmother's house and there were always guys coming and going all day. Ma's place was alive, and I reckon she liked it that way. Ma used to give us a dollar each for lunch and we'd get a pie and a drink. She used to give us all a buck; not just me, Sunny and Koby – she used to look after all her boys.

A lot of the older Maroubra guys – guys like Hinesy, Grommet, Blackie, Red – knew me mum and what was going on with her, and I think they all really respected how my grandmother was looking after us all. A lot of them would drop by as well. I suppose they dropped in to check how things were going, maybe borrow a board, because the place was like a board factory there were so many of them there. But I think Ma looking after us rubbed off on some of the older guys and they started hanging with us; you know, keeping an eye on us as well. Ma really liked that too; she loved that whole idea of a big family of friends.

We were still out on the streets pretty late and that, even at Ma's, but the older boys were always looking after us. And then when Christmas time come round, Ronnie and Wayno would always spend it together with us at Ma's, like we were kind of each other's family. I still look at Ahu and Jeddy as my little brothers as well.

Then my grandmother lost her voice. She had a hectic stroke and didn't speak for the last 15 years of her life. Shortly before it happened, my mum got pinched; she was gonna get locked up so she said to Ma, 'You're going to have to look after the boys.' Well, my grandmother went to bed and didn't get out until the ambulance came three days later, and in that time she had three strokes.

So first we lost Pa ... and then Ma. It was like we'd lost Ma without actually losing her. My grandmother was the world to us. When she got out of hospital she was all there in the head; she just couldn't talk to us.

She had the sign language going, and she didn't need to speak out loud for me to know what she was talking about. We just had a sixth sense; you'd just feel what she was trying to say without her even having said it. One action was enough. It was a huge battle for Ma to recover. She fought so hard and it frustrated the fuck out of her, bra, it really did. It was sad to watch. She was so staunch. I just think of the happy times with Ma.

While Ma was in hospital we moved down to me aunty's place at Gerringong. Our aunty Jan was such a special lady. She was real spiritual and she was the first one to plant a seed in my head and make me think that there's more to this world than meets the eye.

Me and Sunny enrolled at Kiama High, which was all right, 'cause we had the chicks on tap. It was this little country town and we were the full city boys. But it wasn't like going to Maroubra Bay; we'd be lucky to last half a day at the Bay before we took off to go surfing. Kiama High was a *real* school. We took off from school to go surfing a couple of days after we got there and – *boom* – we had truancy officers at the door dragging us back to school. I think down in the country they had more time on their hands, those blokes. They actually do their jobs. The truancy officer at Maroubra … we're not sure what that guy did.

KOBY

MAROUBRA, LAND OF CHOCOLATE MILK AND HEROIN

Though we lived in these shitty houses, we had the best TVs.

We'd have massive TVs, stereos and videos, but no food. Then the next week the TVs would be gone. But I was still too young to notice things and put it all together what was going on with my mum and her friends.

Before we moved back in with Ma we lived in these shitty rentals all over Maroubra. The one up in Bona Vista Avenue was so fucked up; it was haunted. I was only a kid at the time, maybe eight, and I remember we'd hear banging on the doors. We'd hide and Mum would say it was ghosts. It wasn't ghosts; it was guys looking for their money – money Mum owed 'em. There were always people knocking on the doors. Mum would say the house was haunted. She wouldn't answer the doors. She'd tell me to be quiet or the ghosts would get us.

My morning ritual when we lived in those houses was I'd wake up, go for an early surf, then we'd steal all the bread and chocolate milk we could find because we had no cash and we were starving. That was in the old days when bread and milk got delivered to your door. I usually just picked it off the doorsteps of the Chinese takeaway shop in Maroubra. I did it for years and was pretty good at it. Eventually they wouldn't leave the yoghurts and chocolate milk any more because we'd clean 'em all out; they just stopped delivering them.

Then after about three years I got done. All the bread and milk truck drivers hid up the end of the street and waited for me. I came flying up the street with a loaf of bread in my hand and the fat bread-truck driver just hammered me, just crash-tackled me to the ground; I got held there until the coppers come along. There was a boardriders' trip leaving that morning and everyone was getting on the bus to go away surfing for the weekend. I remember watching it drive away just going, 'No! This is fucked!'

We'd get the bread and milk and have breakfast down the hill at Ma's. Ma would ask us what's been going on up the hill, what Mum's been up to. She was worried and kept pretty close tabs on Mum. Living up the hill with Mum was pretty loose. We never knew if there was going to be any money or food, but we always knew the beach and Ma's house would be there. They were the only stable things we had. When we were living in those rentals we'd leave all our surfing stuff in Ma's garage. Pretty soon I was living in there.

Jai and Sunny had a little bunk room inside, while me and Mum slept outside in the garage. When we lived there it had grease-stained concrete floors, bars on the windows and Pa's old tools everywhere. We had to move out all the boys' surfboards and wetties to fit in our stuff. It was one big room with a chipboard wall for privacy. The wall had got wet 'cause the roof leaked and it was all swollen and crumbling. The little chips of wood would get in your bed and itch the shit out of ya. I slept with my mum on a double mattress on the floor.

I recently spoke to the guy who owns the Fenton Avenue house now, and he said we can go there whenever we want, which is cool. I was going to take Jai around there and sit by the pool and have a beer. The best times of my life were in that house, I reckon.

Ma knew that if all those kids were in her backyard, under her roof, they were doing better than out on the streets. But she was pretty strict, bra, so you didn't like to ask her for too much. If she ever gave you anything she made sure you earned it: you mow the lawn, you clean the pool, you get up on the roof and pull the leaves out of the gutter. But at that time she was by herself too, so it must've been hard for her. Even though it seemed fucked for us at the time and we used to whinge about doing it, when you think about it, she was letting 20 kids hang in her backyard all day and making them all lunch.

If we weren't at our grandma's house, we'd be surfing. And if we weren't surfing we'd be running around in the laneway behind Ma's place. We'd get up on the roofs and awnings of the shops and check the surf. When we were young we knew that whole block like the back of our hands. That back laneway was our own domain: busted fences, barbed wire, corrugated iron, burned-out cars.

That's where the boys formed Ma's Hell Team. They wouldn't let us be full Ma's Hell Team members because they reckoned we were too young, so we became Ma's Madness – me, Jed and Ahu. We always used to have these challenges against Bazza's Scum Team. They were all mates of ours who'd formed their own little gang and hung across the road from us. We used to have our crew of 20 and they'd have their crew of 20 and we'd either surf against each other or just beat the shit out of each other.

I always wondered why it was me and Mum who had to live in the garage. Why couldn't Sunny and Jai sleep out there? I was at the age where I was starting to piece shit together, and the first thing I worked out was that my mum was a junkie. She wouldn't come home some nights; it was like she was nocturnal. Then she'd get home and sleep, so even when she was home there wasn't much happening. We didn't even want to think about what she was up to when she walked out that door every night.

At that stage a lot of the older guys on the beach would egg junkies whenever one wandered down onto Marine Parade. If they came in a car they'd have rocks thrown at them and told to fuck off and not come back. The older guys hated smackies because they'd seen what that shit had done to the place.

I was about eight or nine when I followed the older kids one day and we come across a carload of smackies. We were going down this laneway and I could see the old brown Holden sitting there and my mum in the front seat. I said, 'Stay here, boys,' and I walked over to see what was going on. As I got closer to the car, they just took off. I watched the car drive off and then I looked down and saw that I had a dirty pick sticking out of my foot. It went straight through my shoe and into my big toe. When I got home, Mum was already there. I told her I had to go to hospital, and she asked why. I told her how I'd kicked the needle down in the laneway and she asked me where.

'Right next to the car where you were shooting up!'

I can remember the look on her face. It was one of her needles, 100 per cent, and I knew it. Here I was, throwing rocks at junkies and my mum's one of them. Ma knew, of course, and that's why we lived out in the garage – Ma didn't want any of Mum's friends in the house. She didn't even really trust Mum in the house, for that matter. I was Mummy's boy, and wherever Mum went, I had to go too.

But despite everything that was going down, she was still my mum and I was still close to her. She was a good mum, bra; she was just in the grip of some bad shit. When she was there, she was great. She'd take all the boys up the coast in the car and go surfing. She took us all up to Norah Head one time to go surfing and fishing. Other kids we knew went on family holidays to Bali or some other cool place every year; we went to Norah Head. She was a loving mum when she was there, but, bra, she just wasn't there enough.

I grew up pretty fast in that garage. When you're young and your mum goes missing, you're having a ball, you're doing anything you want, so it was good in that respect. It wasn't until I got a bit older that I realised, you know, she hasn't been here for a week. Where the fuck is she? Ma would have to work and we'd be on our own. That's when I started to cultivate a real disrespect for my mum.

But Ma and Mum were so close it wasn't funny. Ma was just a good mother and I think she acknowledged the state my mum was in – that Mum had this disease and that it's her daughter and that's just how it was. That's the thing – when Mum was well, she'd be round checking on Ma all the time, right up until the time years later when Ma died.

Pa had only died a few years before. Ma still had the mortgage, she was working two jobs, and looking after us kids and dealing with all Mum's shit. It all got to her. Ma got real stressed with everything that was happening. That's when she got sick; she had the stroke. She survived, but she was never the same. She couldn't talk, and she lost movement down her left side. It was so sad. She was a proud woman, and watching her having to deal with suddenly being like that was fucking heartbreaking.

SUNNY

THE BALLAD OF GROMMET AND HINESY

The laneway behind Ma's place in Fenton Avenue was our playground. It ran between the backyard of Ma's place and the Seals Club, along the back of the shops on Marine Parade all the way up to the shops on McKeon Street. It was the full ghetto. We were like alley cats in there. We used to bounce across the roofs to get around; we spent so much time up there we even formed a little gang called The Rooftops. We built a bridge across the laneway with a plank of wood so we could get from one side to the other to check the surf. If a yard was fenced off we'd cut a rabbit hole in the corrugated iron with tin snips. We'd jump along the shop awnings and get all the way to The Cue, the old pinball parlour owned by Lenny Holt the wrestler, the son of Harold Holt the prime minister.

The Stackhouse was the famous little restaurant next door to the Seals Club that Marty Lee's parents owned. Red Johnson's girlfriend Melissa was working there as a waitress and she got me a job one summer as a dishpig, washing dishes. It was the coolest little restaurant. All the surfers used to eat there; Larry Blair might pop in, or Stubbsy or Blackie or Red. Melissa would deliver the food and she'd tell me if any of them were out front and I'd make some excuse to bring out a plate or stick me head around from the back and start talking to those guys.

Marty used to live out the back of the restaurant in a caravan, so he, Hinesy and Grommet would be out the backyard all the time plotting various acts of anarchy. The back fence of The Stackhouse, which backed onto the same laneway that ran behind Ma's, was eight feet high and topped with barbed wire. Those guys had turned it into the full compound. We were never silly enough to try and get in there.

The Stackhouse used to have a resident budgie that lived in a cage by the door.

Well, one night there was a talent quest upstairs in the Seals Club, run by Maroubra Boardriders. Predictably, it got out of control. When his turn came around, Lee Stubbs ran down to the restaurant, grabbed the budgie out of the cage and ran back upstairs. He got up on stage and, in front of the whole room, shoved the thing in his mouth and bit the head off it. The place erupted. The audience turned on him; there were girls throwing up, people screaming. He had to fight his way out of there. It caused headlines, and the RSPCA was called in.

Marty Lee moved out of the caravan and into a block of units with Hinesy and Grommet. I remember one time the SWAT team surrounded the place to raid it. Who knows what those guys had been up to. Us grommets had run across from the vacant block next door to watch, hiding in the long grass. There's cops at the back door and front door, waiting to kick the doors in. All of a sudden we've seen Marty jump off the second-storey roof, a 20-foot drop. He's landed in the long grass not far from us, and rolled into a crawl, full commando style. We couldn't believe it. He's sprung straight up like nothing has happened ... and he's dressed as an old lady. He's got on a wig and old dress, he's got a cane, and he's just waddled off. The cops had no idea. The cops got the rest of them and dragged them all out. Marty was right next to us and he whispers, 'C'mon, fellas, walk with me, walk with me,' motioning for us to follow and give him a bit of cover. We were flabbergasted. I think he may have rolled his ankle, he was limping a bit, but because he was dressed as an old woman it suited the act perfectly. It was, at the time, the best thing we had ever seen.

Marty, Hinesy and Grommet were good mates. They were four or five years older than us, and they were just extreme Maroubra. They were born out of a chaotic time. It was a full-on time to live through, and it spawned guys like these three. A whole new generation of housos got built in the '70s. Then the heroin epidemic hit and these guys were the crew who grew up amid all that.

Ma told me about meeting Jason Loughnan – Grommet – for the first time. Behind the old Maroubra Pavilion down on the beach there was a kids' playground. She was reading a book on a park bench, and here's Grommet with a heavy cast-iron sprinkler on the end of a hose. He was swinging it like a lasso, six inches from the heads of all these kids who were totally shitting themselves.

Grommet was one of those kids you heard a lot about before you ever saw him. He had a big reputation. He was The Grommet, the grommet of all grommets. He was known up and down the coast, from Newcastle to Narrabeen to Nowra; wherever the boardriders club had gone he'd left an impression. He was the gnarliest ADD kid, chaos on legs, and the funniest, best write-off we'd ever seen.

Beyond hyperactive, super confident, good looking, hysterical, and the hottest surfer on the beach, Grommet was into everything. His biggest hero was Bruce Lee: he moved like Bruce Lee, he talked like Bruce Lee, and he even surfed like Bruce Lee. He really thought he was Bruce Lee back then. But more than anything, he exuded this confidence and charisma. He had the stare and the belief ...

But Grommet was one of those kids who was addicted to trouble, and went searching for it. That could mean anything from taking off on a 10-foot wave in front of dry rocks, to throwing an egg at a copper, to stealing a car.

We'd be down the beach at Maroubra and we'd see this sports car just flying down the road with three cop cars in pursuit. Grommet. He'd get up the south end and escape, then double-back past the boys at the beach and claim it. Everyone would be out on the street cheering him on. He'd always get away. Then he'd go and do giant burn-outs out the front of the Maroubra Police Station, beeping the horn, goading them into another chase.

Tony Hines and Grommet always hung together, but we got along better with Grommet. He was always a lot more light-hearted with us than Tony. Hinesy was always a bit darker. I remember the first time we met Tony. All us kids used to share this bike that we'd ride around the streets on, this old flower power dragster with no tyres on it. We'd fly down Fenton Avenue and McKeon Street on it and sparks would shoot out the back. It was the legendary bike this one summer. One day we came around the front of the beach on it and Hinesy was there.

'Give us a go on ya bike, boys.'

We didn't want to give it to him, but he pressured us, and we weren't going to say no to him, ever. There's a stop sign on the corner where someone had ripped the no parking sign off it, so it was just a big metal pole. He's picked the bike up above his head, spiked it straight down over the pole, and then he jumped on it about 20 times.

'There's ya bike, grommets.'

We were gutted. None of us was tall enough to get it off. We walked up to the corner surf shop, to Blackie and Doigy's, and we told 'em Hinesy had smashed up our bike. They've gone, 'That's fucked. We'll deal with him for ya.' But the square-up never happened, 'cause Tony was too big and gnarly by this stage, even for those guys.

Marty Lee eventually moved into a block of units on Poo Hill, overlooking Maroubra Beach, on the corner of Marine Parade and Severn Street, just up from the pub. They called it Poo Hill because it faced southeast, the direction of the predominate wind that blew across from the old sewerage works on the headland at Malabar. Marty, Hinesy and Grommet – that was the Poo Hill Gang. They all hung on that hill and checked the surf from up there. They had written on the road in giant letters, eight foot high, 'Poo Hill'.

Marty actually lived in an indoor swimming pool. They'd drained it for some reason, so Marty put a tarp over one end and just moved into the pool. He had his bed down the deep end and all his boards and other stuff was in the shallow end. You used to walk down the pool stairs at the shallow end to get into his place.

The Poo Hill block was built by an old Maroubra guy named Athol. The place was pretty dodgy. It took him 12 years to build; when he had some money he'd do some more on it until it was finally done. He'd also built all these secret passageways in the back. One of them looked like it finished in a dead end, but you could squeeze through and it opened up into a secret basement that was their full underground hideout. They got up to some really, really loose shit down there, and we avoided the place like the plague.

Our mate Ronnie actually ended up living in the Poo Hill units, above Marty. Ronnie's mum had gone to jail, and Ronnie's stepdad, Mick, had moved into the unit on Poo Hill with him. All our guys used to hang at Ronnie's a lot, so all of a sudden we're basically living in the same unit block as Marty, Hinesy and Grommet.

Those three and their mates had all grown up playing these war games around Maroubra. We used to hear them when we were really young; running through the laneway behind Ma's playing these urban skirmish games. Once we got to 10 or 11, and without really choosing to do so, we started playing them as well.

I remember Hinesy ambushing us, just grabbing us by the scruff of the neck, and going, 'You weren't ready! Always be ready. Just remember … *I could get you at any time.*' These games started to become more frequent as time went on, and they got way more brutal. It was partly for their own entertainment, but I think they were also trying to train us up to be ready for life in Maroubra. At that stage Maroubra was pure anarchy. There were these big fights out the front of the pub between gangs of Asians and bikies, and the Seals Club became Friday night fight night out on the street at closing time. It was always going on at the beach. That's why these guys were always saying, 'You've gotta be ready.' We were their young urban soldiers.

If Grommet or Hinesy showed up, we'd just scatter like cockroaches when the light turned on. We'd disappear down the laneway behind Ma's, into little tunnels, onto roofs. We knew every nook and cranny and every escape route, because we had to.

Those guys were our mates, but at the same time they'd push it. If they did get you, you were in for an ordeal. There was no crying and putting on the tears and being let go home. The older guys, the boardriders guys, would dish out grommet abuse to us, the kind of stuff you see on every beach. Encouraging us to egg crew, making us do the runner from Maccas, nude runs … just harmless stuff. But these war games were something else.

There'd be five or six of them, and they'd give you 10 minutes to get away. Then they'd come and hunt you down. Hinesy would wave you away by saying, 'Let the games begin.' Most of the time we'd bolt down to South Maroubra; there were plenty of places to hide there. Down near the rifle range it was all still wild and full of snakes, but there were tunnels and gullies everywhere, so it gave you a bit of a chance to get away. There were old World War II tunnels that linked Maroubra to La Perouse, the full underground labyrinth. They'd chase us through these, through the sewer pipes, the scrub. They'd chase you through the back of the rifle range and, deadset, there'd be bullets flying just over your heads. They'd chase us up to the hill on the rifle range, and we'd crawl over the hill to escape. Facing live rifle fire was way safer than getting caught by those blokes.

Whatever happened, you didn't want to get caught. They had to draw blood for you to be out of the game, so when they caught you they'd have these wooden daggers they'd made and they'd slit your throat with them. You were desperate not to get caught. Once when they were hot on my heels, I happily dived into an open sewer pipe to hide from them. You'd get in these big bitou bushes down near the rifle range and you could hide under them they were so thick. I remember being in them one day just frozen as Grommet and Hinesy have stopped a couple of feet away, discussing where they thought I'd gone. I wasn't even breathing. It was like they fair dinkum thought they were in Vietnam, and they were discussing ways of flushing out the Vietcong, that's how serious they were.

It was house-to-house, corner-to-corner, urban warfare. When they got you they'd beat the shit out of you, tie you up, lock you up. There was grommet *abuse*, but this was grommet *torture*. They'd tie us up in bins and fill 'em full of water and push the bins down the hill. They'd fight us, and because I was the biggest I had to fight Grommet every day. I remember turning up to school with black eyes all the time. They used to tie us up in boardbags and bury us alive in the sand. One time Grommet locked me, Jai, Ronnie and a kid called Robbie, in a cupboard at his place for 16 hours. He'd pushed the bed up against the cupboard to lock us in. We only got out when the police turned up. When we didn't come home, our folks called the police, who found out we were last seen with Grommet. They went around to his place and I remember hearing them at the door asking if we were there, and Grommet saying, 'Nah, mate, haven't seen 'em.' We're just screaming these muffled screams. Then the cops came in and opened the door and we just fell out. We were blinded by the light, and so stiff we couldn't even move. This was, like, 10.30 at night.

We tried to all turn on him once, but we never did it again.

We were outside his garage up in Torrington Road. He'd get us all up there and he'd stand in the middle; then, one by one, we'd have to go in there and take him on. One by one, he'd beat the shit out of us. When I was fighting him, after he'd beaten everyone else up, I fired up. We all just looked at each other and went, 'fuck this', and we 10-outed him. We all jumped on him, held him down and bashed him. All of a sudden he's screaming.

'Fuck! I've broken me arm! I've broken me arm!'

He's howling in pain, almost crying. We get off him, thinking we'd really hurt him. In a heartbeat his expression has changed.

'Big mistake, boys.'

And with his broken arm, he's beaten the shit out of all of us.

Grommet had grown up in a house in Torrington Road, a few doors down from Tilly Devine's house. Tilly Devine was an English immigrant who'd controlled organised crime in Sydney in the 1920s and '30s. The house she lived in had been the scene of two fatal shootouts, and five men had died in there. Tilly's place was on the corner of Malabar and Torrington, and for as long as anyone can remember no one had lived in there. The house had been abandoned for 30 years or more. We all thought it was haunted by the ghosts of the guys who'd been shot there … and the ghost of Tilly herself. We wouldn't go anywhere near it.

Well, this one time Grommet made us go in. We had no choice; he stood outside. We walked in and there were axes and a pitchfork in the wall, so straightaway we're shitting ourselves. Then we've heard this noise coming from upstairs. We eventually worked up the courage to climb the stairs and found the only thing in the room was an old cupboard. We've crept over and slowly opened the door. As it creaked open, we've all screamed. No word of a lie, there was a mannequin in the cupboard dressed up as Tilly Devine, in this furry overcoat with a 1930s hat and shawl. It was the scariest thing I'd ever seen. We bolted down the stairs, out the door, and we didn't stop until we got to South Maroubra.

In retrospect, just remembering how hard Grommet had cajoled us to go up there, he'd probably planted the dummy and the axes to scare the shit out of us. It didn't matter, 'cause we never went back there. Even today, every time I drive past it I make a sign of the cross.

But sending us into Tilly's house wasn't nearly as scary as what Grommet did to us next. Me and Jai were walking to the beach and he's pulled up in this full-on hotted-up Monaro. We knew enough by this stage to know the car wasn't his.

'C'mon, grommets, get in. Do you like me new car?'

'Nah, we're going for a surf.'

He's really adamant. 'Jump in! It's me new car. I wanna take yas for a spin up the street. We'll be two minutes, I promise.'

So me and Jai have got in and the second the door has closed behind us he's done the biggest burn-out you ever seen and has just taken off up the street with this full evil laugh.

'Got ya now, grommets.'

He did burn-outs all the way up the street, did a U-turn at North Maroubra, and came all the way back down to Fitzgerald, left onto Beauchamp, then straight out to the Botany quarter-mile. The car had 240 on the clock as its top speed, and once the needle hit 240 the whole car has started shaking violently. Grommet's reaction was to punch it even harder, and I swear we went even quicker. He reckons we were going 270. There were these pillows in the back and me and Jai had 'em wrapped around us, screaming. Grommet was pissing himself laughing.

But this was vintage Grommet; totally addicted to trouble, and completely unafraid of the consequences. It wasn't a great surprise when he ended up in a boys' home at 16. He was in and out of those for a couple of years, and we'd see bits and pieces of him. He'd get out and come and surf with us for two weeks, then there'd be another famous car chase and he'd be gone again.

As soon as Grommet turned 18 he was tried as an adult and was sent to jail. We heard about a month or two later that someone had tried to rape him in there, and he'd turned around and killed the guy.

Grommet got 15 years for it.

JAI

THE EXEMPLARY ACTS OF THE OLDER GENERATION LEAD TO AN ADMIRABLE SOLIDARITY AND THE DEGUSTATION OF A BRIGHT BLUE AND HIGHLY TOXIC MARINE INVERTEBRATE

Hinesy and Grommet ... they were hectic. When we were young, the older boys we mostly hung around were Tony Hines and Jason Loughnan – 'Grommet'. At that time those guys were running amok.

By this stage it was me, Sunny, Jimmy, Wayno, Ronnie and Moff in our gang. We were family, you know. We were the young guys, surfing together every day, surfing in North End Boardriders, hanging sick together every day. Then you'd have the older boys – you know, Grommet, Hinesy, Marty Lee – who were all about four or five years older than us.

There was a lot of shit happening in the street around that time. We'd be surfing all the time, always trying to stay in the water and avoid trouble. That was the best way to do it. But it was Grommet, Hinesy and Marty who taught us about life on the streets and how to deal with it. Stick together, be strong, don't run. Just be there for each other. They were the ones who said, 'Ya never tell on anyone.' That's what we had bred into us, and that's what we believe to this day. We're not sure where they got it from; I suppose they had it preached to them as well. But they were way looser than anyone who had come before them, and way looser than anyone who's come after.

We were young, and my grandad was dead. We'd listen to Ma but she was just too kind. Who else were we going to look up to around here? They were funny. They were mad fighters. They had money. That's who we were looking up to. Besides Ma.

We were on the streets all the time, and Hinesy and Grommet used to look after us a lot back then. They were good. They'd take us to Bondi for a cruise, buy us lunch, make sure we were all right … look after us if we ever got into any trouble. They used to buy us eggs so we could egg the smackies. Back then, if ever we found a couple of people going on the blink in the street, there was Hinesy with, 'Here's a dozen eggs, boys.' Hinesy and Grommet just kept telling us, 'Don't touch that shit.' We were partying pretty hard, but we knew not to touch smack because those guys had told us not to.

Grommet and Marty were both incredible surfers. Grommet was sponsored, but he was mad, ya know. He'd be surfing 15-foot Lurline out there on his own. When we were young he'd come flying past us all down on the beach in Porsches and all sorts of fancy cars he'd stolen. Remember the 'Porsche Kids' back in the '80s who'd rip off sports cars?

He was one of the original Porsche Kids. Back then every third day he'd be flying past in some hotted-up car with half-a-dozen cop cars chasing after him.

Hinesy and Grommet were training the whole time. It was them against the coppers, them against everyone else; them against us, even. They used to take us down to South Maroubra and to play war games with us. If they caught you, you'd have to fight them or they'd pretend to cut your throat. They were doing this shit non-stop.

We didn't have much money or boards and stuff back then, and Jason – Grommet – had plenty 'cause he was sponsored, so we'd be like, 'Jas, lend us a board?' But fuck, what we had to go through to borrow a board off him. We had to fight him, we had to fight each other; we were tied up, whipped. He made us earn it. One time he locked me and Bulldog in the boot of his car for, fuck, I dunno how long, but the car didn't get home to me mum's until 11 o'clock that night. We'd been in there since that arvo. My mum came out schizing, going, 'Where the hell are they?' Me mum made him open the boot and there we were. It was only that me mum went looking for us that we got let out. Me mum gets written off, but it was 11 o'clock and she was out looking for us.

To borrow a board meant two hours of getting fucking tortured. I mean, he'd put us in an Otto bin, shut the lid and sit on it. He'd let it fill right to the top with a hose, nearly drowning us, then kick the bin over at the last minute.

'See, I love youse!'

And then there was Tony.

I remember one time I was walking back from the beach round to my grandmother's. Me and my grandmother were sitting in the backyard having a cup of tea when all of a sudden Tony's come running down the lane then – *bang* – he's jumped our back fence. He's jumped it in one bound and it was pretty clear something had happened. He's just gone, 'Fuck, Jai, can you fucking go around to the post office and check if the bloke's dead?'

'Fucking check if *what bloke's* dead?'

I had just been sitting there with my grandma having a cup of tea! But it was Tony, so I said, 'Sweet, no worries. Just stay here and I'll go check.' So I walked around to the post office and there he was – the postman – in a pool of blood. When the bloke was doing his run, Hinesy had stolen his postie bike and rode it around for a while. When the postie pulled him up, Hinesy chucked him through the window.

I walked back to Ma's place and Tony was still in the backyard, sitting with my grandma.

'Yeah, he's pretty fucked up, Tony, but he looks alive.'

'Oh, sweet, sweet. So he's all right?'

'He's all right. I'm pretty sure he's not dead, anyway.'

Ma was worried, because she knew what Tony was capable of. She was into me, trying to say, 'What did Tony do?' pointing at Tony. Tony was more worried about being in trouble off Ma than he was of getting in trouble off the cops. He was always heaps respectful to my grandmother, always had been. My grandmother was like everyone's grandmother, even the older boys.

I was never going to the police. We just didn't really go to the cops ever, you know. It wasn't in our nature to go to the police; they were kind of hated by all the boys. Hinesy had drummed that into us: don't trust 'em, never talk to 'em. You just didn't ever go to the police. It's the way Hinesy taught us.

The postie didn't die, by the way.

Those guys had a huge influence on us. We were tougher and tighter for hanging around them. I remember one day walking down the beach with the boys for a swim and being dared to put a bluebottle in my mouth. It was a full Grommet move, that one.

'No worries.'

I lowered it all into my mouth and had started chewing when I felt the first wave of pain. I stung the fuck out of myself. My whole tongue got stung and started swelling up, and I nearly ended up in hospital. Good joke, that one.

Once, when I was about 15, I went into the pub to play pool with Ronnie. Ronnie's a really good pool player, so we'd set up on the table and hustle for money. We played a couple of bikies for 20 bucks. Sure enough we won the game, but the bloke wouldn't pay. Ronnie, who was boxing by this stage, has just left-hooked this bikie, the biggest one, straight to the chin and put him out, snoring. That's the first time any of us had fought an adult, and I remember standing there, going, 'Yeah! That's my mate Ronnie. Don't take the knock on our 20!' Ronnie started training full on not long after and eventually fought for the Aussie title. Ronnie's worth his weight in gold, bra.

Wayno was beyond his years as well. He was always setting the pace from a young age, pushing the limits hard, in and out of the water.

KOBY

THE ABBERTONS MOVE ON UP TO THE PALATIAL SURROUNDS OF THE LEXINGTON PLACE HOUSING COMMISSION ESTATE

We'd waited five years for a houso flat when one finally came up.

It was just up the road from Maroubra Beach in Astoria Circuit, up in the Housing Commission capital of Sydney, Lexington Place. It was a big unit with a backyard, and we only paid 60 bucks a week rent. It was in a block of four and we were upstairs, but we claimed the backyard as our own. Me, Jai, Mum and her new boyfriend Paul moved in.

There were a lot of kids up there which was great for us. We'd walk down the hill and whistle out as we went. All our mates would just appear at their front doors with their boards under their arms, and we'd head off down the beach as a group of 20. There was never any shortage of kids up there.

We still never saw a lot of our mum in Astoria Circuit. I remember her saying to me, 'I've got this new system, and if I go away anywhere you're going to have food to eat.' Using a whole loaf of bread, she'd make half-a-dozen Vegemite sandwiches and half-a-dozen devon and tomato sauce sandwiches, then put 'em all in the freezer. I asked her what she was doing, and she goes, 'You'll need to eat.' Frozen sandwiches, bra. And when she wouldn't come home for a few days, that's what we'd live on – frozen Vegemite sandwiches.

Life in Lexo would be hot and cold. When Mum and Paul were home we'd be eating steak Diane, lasagne, and these mussels Paul would cook up in this secret sauce. But when they weren't around it was mostly Rice Bubbles and Corn Flakes.

Jai and I relished the freedom. What kid wouldn't? We'd try and hide it from Ma that Mum hadn't been home for two weeks. We wouldn't go to school. Me and Jai would just look at each other in the morning and go, 'Well, there's no one here to tell us to go to school. Let's go surfing.' We'd just walk down and hang out at the beach all day. If Mum come home later on she'd go, 'How was school?' and I'd go, 'All right I suppose,' and I'm sunburned and my face is still covered in zinc.

But when all you're eating is frozen Vegemite sandwiches, bra, you're not doing it that good. The thing was that when Mum would come home she'd stack the fridge up, you'd get money; it'd be mad. But then she'd leave and all of a sudden you were struggling again. Every Christmas, we always scored. Every Christmas, bra, I'd get a motorbike or a surfboard. The stuff would always be hot, but when you get a motorbike or a surfboard you don't care if it's got someone else's name on it. She was always good to us at Christmas and birthdays. But the thing was that a month later it'd get hocked; anything you owned that was worth anything would slowly disappear. Like, Mum, where's my motorbike gone?

It didn't affect us too much until I got to a stage where you start to piece together what's going on around you. There's all these people in your house and you're not allowed in the lounge room for an hour while they're there. It was just off to your room or go to the beach. It'd be eight o'clock at night and Mum'd be like, 'Koby, how about you go to the beach for a while.' As a kid you'll go, 'Fuck yeah, I'll go to the beach. It's eight o'clock!' But I didn't really start realising what a bad scene it was until my friends started coming around and I'd see the way they looked at my mum and her friends. They saw it more than me.

I'd be sitting in the toilet and I'd look around and there were all these red dots all over the wall. I couldn't work out what they were at first. It was blood spatter. When they got the belt around their arm and hit the vein with the needle, the blood just squirts out.

Then it started to get really bad. I remember one guy; his name was George. I was sitting there one night and there was Mum, Paul, George, and this guy Nick. This night, this George guy OD'ed. I remember walking into the bathroom and seeing him out cold. They're pouring water over him, slapping him. They're all yelling, 'He's dead! He's dead!' They had to get the needle out of his arm; he had froth coming out of his mouth. It was like a full-on *Pulp Fiction* scene, bra. I remember them dragging him out of the bathroom and into the lounge room before Mum yelled at me to get into my room. I heard the car start up and they took him away. I never ever saw the guy again.

That sort of shit didn't really scar me that much, though. I was a weird kid, and I never really thought that much about it. The only impression it really left me with was that I didn't ever want to be like that; I knew I never wanted to touch that shit. I never seen 'em doing it, because they'd never let me see it; they'd never do it in front of us. But what did rattle me was when my friends would come around and Mum and Paul and their friends would all be on the nod. You've got all your friends in the house and your mum is sitting there asleep in her Rice Bubbles. It was embarrassing, bra. I hated it. I really hated it. Everyone knew what junkies were like. Eventually I started telling Mum and Paul to go into their room. I was sick of it.

Jai was real rough with them when they had the sleepy arm. He was a fair bit bigger than me, and he'd slap 'em in the face real hard. Jai was really affected by it, and started getting aggro. He started rebelling pretty bad. When these people would come to the house Jai would want to fight them, and when they were on the nod he'd slap them in the head. One time Paul fell asleep at the sink while he was doing the dishes, and me and Jai were just sitting there laughing. Then Jai went over and held his head down in the dishwater until he woke up. Jai was pretty ruthless. That's when they moved him out. They said, 'You're not good for the house,' and they moved him into a caravan in the backyard that they rented for $20 a week.

Paul had a streak in him, but he'd been with my mum since I could remember and I knew he'd never do anything to hurt us kids or her. We just didn't have that much to do with him to be honest. He was the best boyfriend Mum had ever had, but he didn't have much competition.

Paul was covered in these tattoos he'd done himself. He'd get a pen, a needle, some elastic bands and a little portable CD player and rig up a tattoo machine and just start on himself. He was also a boxer, and he loved his training. He had a couple of pro fights; he fought pro because he was only really interested in the money. He got bashed up a bit, but didn't give a fuck. He made his $500 a fight.

Me and Jed used to go through Paul and Mum's room, and one time we came across this secret compartment in the cupboard. Inside was this big bag with two sawn-off shotguns, two handguns and a balaclava. We just looked at each other and went, 'What the fuck!' The bed they had was high off the floor, and Jed and I would be on opposite sides of the bed with shotguns, pretending to shoot each other. We never checked if they were loaded.

Paul went to jail soon after for two years. This guy from down the road, Carl, had stolen my motorbike. We'd bought it off him not long before and he stole it straight back off us. We knew it was him, because the idiot was burning around Lexo on it. So I said to Paul, 'That cunt stole my motorbike!'

We drive down there and I'm going, 'Fuck, Paul, you've gotta get him. I want me bike back.'

Paul goes, 'No worries.' He never said much, Paul, but you knew he had something planned.

And then I've seen Carl across the street.

Paul said, 'How badly do you wanna get the guy?'

'The bastard stole me bike. He needs to learn a lesson.'

As we drive in, sure enough there he is on the bike. He hasn't seen us, but then he's disappeared and come back a minute later without it. Paul's stopped the car and yelled out to him, 'Carl, how are you, mate? Come over here for a minute.'

Carl was onto us that we were onto him. He knew what was happening and wouldn't come over. Paul's just gone *whoosh* and pulled out a big handgun and put it on his lap and gone, 'Don't worry, little bra, we're gonna get him.' I've just gone, 'What the fuck!' I remember Paul looking at me, a real weird look. He's gone again, 'How badly do you wanna get him?'

Anyway, finally the guy comes over. He didn't know we'd seen him riding the bike. Paul goes, 'Where's that bike, mate?'

'What bike?'

'Where's that bike, mate?'

Carl's starting to shit himself by this stage.

'No, Paul, I didn't take it, mate. I didn't take it, honest.'

He knew Paul, and he knew you didn't fuck with Paul.

'I swear, Paul, I didn't take it. I wouldn't take Koby's bike.'

And Paul, all mellow, goes, 'All right, Carl, you just find out who took it for me then.'

Paul's put his hand out to shake Carl's, and I'm just seeing what's gonna happen. This guy was fucked. Paul grabbed the guy's hand and just ripped him in through the window and done the full movie trick – wound the window up on Carl's neck, then stuck the barrel of the gun straight in his mouth.

'Where's the fucking bike?'

I was sitting there, hearing people yelling out, 'He's got a gun! He's got a gun!' Paul's just smashed him round the head with the gun then wound down the window. I'm just yelling like a kid, 'Yeah, Paul, we got him!' And I'm screaming out at Carl, 'I want that bike back!'

So Carl brings the bike back up to our place five minutes later, 'cause he's thinking, 'Well, I'm gonna get shot here if I don't.' He walks up the stairs to knock on the door. I see him coming and go, 'Paul! Paul, c'mere. He's here with the bike.' Carl knocks on the door, Paul opens it, and Carl goes, 'I've got your bike here, Paul.' Paul just goes *whack* and knocks him clean down the stairs.

We were lying in bed that night when we hear cop cars and choppers. The cops raided the house and took Paul away. I got woken up and opened the door of my bedroom; everyone was on the floor. They raided the house, dragged us all out and laid us on the floor as they've ripped the house apart. They were searching for the gun, and stupid Paul had thrown it in our own garbage bin downstairs. The cops found that gun, and they found another gun.

And this is one reason why I've always hated police. For some reason, as this copper has walked past as I'm sitting on the couch he goes, 'I feel sorry for you, mate.'

'Why?'

'Because your mum and dad are junkies.'

I was 12. I thought, 'You scumbag, what do you have to say that shit for?' Now I look back, that was a big moment for me. I started to question whether I actually *was* a scumbag. It was such a shitty moment, and I'm gonna remember it till the day I die.

There's a photo of me in the family album that I reckon was taken just after Paul got carted away. I'm on my bed, and I'm drawing up this poster in thick black crayons. In giant letters it says, 'Fuck the police!'

SUNNY

SAWING THROUGH A THREADBARE PARENTAL ANCHOR ROPE AND FLOATING AWAY ON THE SEA OF TEENAGE INDEPENDENCE

Mum was a little more together when we first got the place at Lexo.

She'd been on the Housing Commission waiting list for years, and finally she managed to get a flat. It was an upstairs flat in Astoria Circuit in the Lexington Place estate. Lexo had a huge Housing Commission population, eight families per block, and some bigger four-storey places. Some of the houso estates, like the one at Elfinstone at the south end of Maroubra, were these dark, communist-looking things, but the Lexo estate wasn't quite as depressing, and it had cool street names like Minneapolis, Portland and New Orleans, named after ships in the Battle of the Coral Sea.

The best thing for us was that it was only two minutes up the hill from the beach. We'd either ride or skate down to the beach from Lexington every morning to surf, picking up our mates who lived in the other houso flats on the way.

We used to play 'Thursday night under lights' in the park across the road. We'd play touch football and the lights would stay on in Coral Sea Park until 10 o'clock at night. All the street kids – our beach mates, the local Koori kids, the girls even – we'd play this rough and ready game of tackle footy. Mum was always screaming at the top of her voice out the back window, which faced over to the park, 'Suuunnnyyy! Jaiiiiiiii! Koooobyyyy! Get home *now*!' Who knows what she was screaming for, but she'd stick her head out that bloody window and her voice would echo down the road and across the park and out through the whole estate.

Koby was starting to go a bit feral by this stage. He used to make slingshots, and the little bastard could – and would – hit you from 50 yards. And then there was the snake. He'd caught this poisonous snake and kept it in a fish tank inside the house. He'd sit there and feed live lizards to it. Every time he fed it a lizard, he'd put his hand closer and closer and closer. It'd strike at him, and he'd pull his hand back. It wasn't even funny, but he was just seeing how quick he was. He loved his snakes, whereas I was petrified of the fucking things after Nimbin.

Ma was living by herself down in Fenton Avenue at that stage. My mum, our aunties and us boys would be down there all the time helping her out. We'd still hang out down there with our mates all the time anyway, so she was never short of company. After the stroke and her rehab she'd actually gone and stayed with her sisters for a while in the country. She'd lost most of the movement on her left side, and she'd lost her speech, but she pretty much could walk, cook, clean and shower by herself. And she needed the space. Having us boys living there 24 hours a day wasn't helping her get better.

So up at Lexo it was me, Mum, Jai, Koby and her new boyfriend, Paul, living in a three-bedroom unit. Paul was from a Maltese family, and had grown up in the housos a little further out from Maroubra. He'd been quite a good surfer when he was young, but he was hanging around the beach when the heroin epidemic swept through in the '70s and he got caught up in it, along with my mum. That's how they first met.

From day one there was a whole lot of wild stuff going on. Mum and Paul were using pretty heavily at certain times, and they had these extreme mates who used to hang around. We used to tell Mum that we didn't like those guys being around. You could tell they were up to no good. We had the police raid the place a couple of times. The cops were saying they'd robbed a post office, a chemist, but they never found anything, which was a surprise.

There were times up at Lexo when there was just no food in the place. There were other times when there was tons of food. Whenever she had money, Mum would go and do this massive shop of groceries. She was a good mum, she was a loving mum, but she was just a heroin addict. When her habit was good, she was good. Things were normal. She'd cook a spaghetti bolognese or a bacon and egg pie. It'd almost be like a normal family. But when she was bad, they wouldn't be home for three day or four days.

Often we'd wake up and there'd be no food. No milk or bread, no cereal or fruit. So we learned all the routes of all the milk and bread deliveries in the neighbourhood. It was like, you'd wake up and look in the fridge and go, 'Okay, no food. All right, what day is it today? Wednesday. What time is it? Eight. Okay, the milk truck should be at number 27 Astoria so I gotta be quick, I can still make it.' The suburban hunter-gatherer. Throw on a hoodie and run down the street, jump the fence. We were pretty smart about it, because we'd just take one carton of milk. Then we'd know that number 49 New Orleans had the milk and bread as well, so we'd bolt down and pinch the bread from them. We knew all the days, and we knew never to do the one place five days in a row. Maybe once a month for each, that was enough. Then there were the shops at Lexington. In the morning they'd deliver the bread in these big baskets, and the milk and chocolate Mooves in milk crates. If you got in early enough, you could take what you needed, but you'd have to resist your natural urge to take 10 loaves and a crate of chocolate Mooves. You'd have to be smart about it. Two loaves of bread, two litres of milk, then the shopkeeper thinks the delivery guy has miscounted and he doesn't wait in the bushes the next morning to find out where his crates of chocolate milk are going.

Koby wasn't real clued up on the subtleties of it. We eventually got Koby onto the milk squad as well, but he was snowdropping a little too much, getting a little bit too greedy and doing the same shops in the street a little too often. There was one morning when Koby has swooped in to snowdrop a loaf of bread and all the shopkeepers in the street had been lying in ambush, waiting for the phantom bread thief to show. So Koby's grabbed the bread and all of a sudden this big circle of shopkeepers and delivery guys are surrounding him. They finally had their man.

You know, I suppose because Jai and Koby were a bit younger, I felt a little more responsible for making sure there was food. I was always a real protective older brother to those guys, and as I got a bit older and started to understand fully what was going on in the house I tried to shelter them from it. The easiest way to do it was to just go surfing. I reckon we spent more time on the beach than we ever did at home.

It was a heavy time for us. We'd already lost Pa, our grandmother was half lost to us, and our mum was a raging junkie. What happens if Mum dies? What happens if we come home and Mum's overdosed or in jail? I remember being in the car with Mum when she fell asleep at the wheel, rolled through a red light, and a bus hit us. We could look after ourselves, we were already doing it, but we'd never be allowed to live on our own if anything happened to Mum. Would we get split up? We lived with that fear of what would happen if I came home and she was dead. We were hearing of heroin overdoses all the time; we knew so many friends and surfers who had died from overdoses. It was a pretty realistic fear.

It was becoming more and more obvious to me and Jai that things were getting pretty bad. The unit got broken into a couple of times, and a lot of Mum and Paul's smackie friends seemed to have moved in on a semi-permanent basis. Then they'd all move out for four or five days and we wouldn't see them at all. We didn't want to come home; we were all basically living down on the beach or at Ma's. It was like our world didn't connect with theirs any more. They did their thing, we did ours. We'd come home and find the place empty but could tell they'd been there. You'd find the odd needle, a burnt spoon, a drop of blood in the basin, blood spatter on the walls. It was obvious they were creeping around trying to hide the signs from us, but they were so fucked up at the time it only made it more obvious to us.

We all started rebelling. By this stage Jai and I were 14 and 15; we were big enough and knew how to handle ourselves. You'd come home and all of a sudden there's 10 strange junkies in your house? Like, fuck off! At the time all our friends and all the older guys from the beach knew what was going on up there, but no one ever really said anything. It was a strange standoff, because here we were, bashing junkies and egging them and running them out of town, and, you know, my mum was one of them. I suppose that was pretty big for them, a mark of respect for our friendship that Mum's habit never became an issue with them. Back then in Maroubra the community was very protective of the beach kids. Thieves, junkies or people looking for trouble, you know, they'd pretty much be dealt with.

At home it was just getting heavier and heavier. The cops spent more time there than we did. And with all the shifty guys who were hanging around, it was obvious that shit was going down. They were just off their heads. We were just at that stage where we were so embarrassed we just didn't want anything to do with it.

As soon as we were old enough, we were out of there. I couldn't wait to get out of Lexo.

Me and Jai both moved back down to Ma's. Part of my motive in moving was also to try and get in my girlfriend Melanie's pants. Up at Astoria she used to sleep in Koby's room if she stayed over. I was a million to one of getting any action up there, but my odds weren't that much better at Ma's place, because Ma was strict with girlfriends. 'Not under my roof' was her saying, which she'd charade by pointing to the ceiling and shaking her head vigorously whenever the subject came up. I got around this, however, on a technicality, by sleeping out in the garage.

Once I moved back to Ma's, it was all about becoming a pro surfer. I had to forget about Mum and Paul if that was ever going to happen. When I made the pro tour a year or so later, I hardly saw Mum at all. I'd just come home long enough to be reminded why I didn't want to live there and that nothing had changed.

Koby was 10 when I left. I felt like shit that he was going to have to fend for himself up there. But if surfing was going to be the way out for all of us then I had no choice, I had to go.

SUNNY

THE MOST POWERFUL MAN IN AUSTRALIA INVITES THE DIRTY SOUTHSIDE BUNCH OF CUNTS AROUND FOR A BEER

That's how we first met Dave Gyngell.

Jai and I were surfing a lot of amateur and junior events, and we were making finals and doing okay. Dave Gyngell owned Bondi Surf Co, his surf shop in Campbell Parade, and he also ran Bondi's boardriding club, which at that stage went under the name ITN – In The Nude. He'd often surf Maroubra. We surfed a lot of Bondi versus Maroubra club contests, so we got to know him pretty well. One day he's approached us and said he wanted to sponsor us, which meant we could get free legropes, wax and ding repairs. From there, Gynge always tried to help us out with sponsors and a bit of career advice, because he had strong links to the guys who ran pro surfing, and he had a pretty good gauge on how the whole thing worked.

We were actually really close with the Bondi and Bronte guys. That was back in the days when Bondi was still known as Scum Valley. Bondi was still far trendier than Maroubra, but it was a long, long way from what it is today. The same shit that washed into Maroubra also generally washed into Bondi, and in those days it was populated with a menagerie of surfing animals who all became our good mates; guys like Ben and Will Webber, Dave Davidson, Jason Kitzler and the Cookie brothers. We saw these guys all the time in the surf, so we were pretty close. There was still that real competitiveness between beaches, but there was still that south of the bridge solidarity. When we surfed in the NSW titles we'd compete on the same team. We called ourselves the Dirty Southside Bunch of Cunts, which just about said it all.

Anyway, one time we had a junior contest over the bridge at Avalon, on Sydney's northern beaches, and Gynge drove Jai and me over there from Maroubra. We surfed on the Saturday and made the finals, which were gonna be held the following day. We were in the first heat of the morning, so Gynge has gone, 'I'll call my godfather and see if we can stay at his place up at Palm Beach.'

We didn't know who the hell his godfather was.

Gynge has picked up the phone and gone, 'Is Kerry there? Hey, Kerry, can I crash for the night? Oh, and I've got two mates with me, is that okay? Sweet, we'll see you soon.'

'Who's Kerry?' Jai asked.

Gynge told us, and me and Jai just shit ourselves. It was Australia's richest man – Kerry Packer.

So we drive up to Kerry Packer's place at Palm Beach. We rock up to the biggest house either of us had ever seen. The place was the size of our entire Housing Commission block back in Maroubra, with concrete angels and water features. We walk in with Gynge and straight into some big formal dinner that's going on up there. We met Neville Wran, the premier of New South Wales who was in a black tuxedo. James Packer was going out with Jennifer Flavin at that stage, Sylvester Stallone's ex, and they were both there, along with an assortment of politicians and businessmen all wearing their bags of fruit. It was the full movers and shakers black tie dinner, most of them there, no doubt, trying to curry favour from the Big Guy.

Gynge is just the king there at Kerry's place, and his persona doesn't change at all from how he is down on the beach. He's just cruising around the place in his boardies, leaving sandy footprints, grabbing food out of the fridge.

Then Kerry comes out wearing a dressing gown, just strutting about, filling the room. I was that stoked to meet him. We were blown away enough by the fact that he had an entire fridge stocked exclusively with soft drink, let alone to be sitting there chatting to the richest, most powerful man in Australia. The guy had such an aura. So we meet Kerry and he's hanging out with us in his dressing gown. He had a beer with us, and then he heads back in to the party.

It turns out we were going to have dinner with them all. We're sitting there chatting, and everyone disperses to get changed. Then Ros, Kerry's wife, comes out and says, 'David, can I have a word with you?'

It turns out the problem was they were having a black tie event and we're all dressed in boardies. We just went, 'Sweet, no worries.' We were blown away to even be there. There was a little separate outdoor area and we said, 'We'll just hang out here.' The chef was gonna cook us whatever we wanted. We were stoked.

Well, one of the politicians walked into Kerry's room, and seconds later we hear this huge, booming, '*Get out!*' The guy scurries out with his tail between his legs, grovelling. Then another one goes in and he gets marched.

'*Out! Out!*'

Then Ros went in and her and Kerry had a bit of a blow-up. Then Gynge goes in and soon comes back out.

'Kerry said that if we're not dressed enough to eat with them, then neither is he.'

Kerry, still in his dressing gown, has come out, sat down, and had dinner with us! What a legend! He left all of them in there by themselves, some of the most powerful politicians in the country. The chef cooked us up a chicken pasta, and Kerry's had pasta with us. We're all just sitting there joking and laughing. Gynge has got his feet up on the table, just being himself, and Kerry Packer's hanging out with us. We were just talking about surfing with him. Kerry loved big waves, and he respected surfers and surfing. Gynge was his godson; he'd dropped out of school to be a surfer, but they all still loved him. He was still a fair way off Channel Nine at this stage. But for Kerry to say, 'If they're not dressed enough then neither am I', for two houso kids from Maroubra like me and Jai – mate, we thought the bloke was God.

The next day both me and Jai made the final together, and I don't reckon either of us have had a better weekend in our lives together.

SUNNY

MAROUBRA'S PRIMORDIAL SOUP OF SEWAGE AND SYRINGES SPAWNS AN AS YET UNCLASSIFIED ANTI–AUTHORITARIAN LIFE FORM

When we were growing up, the water at Maroubra was so bad that when you paddled in it you couldn't see your arms. Although it would occasionally go a black-brown colour, the water was usually bright green and had a soupy consistency to it, and there was a mist that rose up off the water surface like you see in horror movies. It was a rank steam, like the water was farting.

Malabar was the biggest sewerage outfall in the Southern Hemisphere at the time, and there'd be days after heavy rain when it'd overflow and pump out raw sewage across the beach. And then, while they built the new plant and extended the pipeline 10 kilometres out to sea, it pumped out basically raw sewage for four years. The full dunny bowl churn. It was full raw – tampons, syringes, turds. I trod on two syringes in my time, and we were always really careful walking down to the waterline to paddle out. You'd walk in any set of fresh footprints you could find.

I remember as a kid standing under the street run-off flowing out of the stormwater outlet and getting fully barrelled under it, thinking I was killing it. I suppose we were so used to it that it didn't even faze us; it's all we'd ever known. Our immune systems were working pretty well. Country guys who surfed in pristine water at home would come up to surf Maroubra for contests and they'd get sick after one surf. Some of them used to gargle with Listerine and disinfect themselves like a toxic response unit after they got out of the surf. They used to be horrified. But that's how we grew up, on a beach infested by rats, maggots and sewage. There were times when it became so bad the beach literally became alive with maggots, the whole shoreline teeming with them.

Shitty water became so much a part of the Maroubra psyche that it was incorporated into the local ceremonial greeting. Spitting the Winkle became the Maroubra equivalent of the *haka*, a party trick without peer to be performed at only the most distinguished occasions. It involved the spittee sticking a hose up his arse, filling his bowel full of water, then bending over and unleashing a geyser of rusty colonic in the general direction of whoever was unlucky enough to be there at the time.

Gooba's real name was Mark, and he was one of the top surfers in Maroubra. He was so good that in 1980 he won the world amateur title in France, beating guys like Tom Carroll and Tom Curren. It was a huge coup for Maroubra. The story that has become Maroubra surf folklore goes that prior to the presentation, Gooba had a fair idea that he'd won, and he prepared accordingly. He's waddled out to receive the winner's trophy from the French cultural ambassador, has said thanks very much, turned around, dropped his dacks, and let fly all over the crowd. Apparently he was banned from France outright as a result. Then there were stories of Brad Stubbs going to America and coming back bragging, 'When I was there, son, I spat the winkle from the west coast to the east.' Apparently he almost got killed after spitting the winkle all over the wrong crowd, the Americans unable to appreciate the cultural significance of the act.

There were periods when the water at Maroubra would be bearable. There were blue-ish days. Any time the wind blew northeast, which is most of summer, you were fine because it would blow all the shit down to Malabar and Cronulla, but any time in winter when the wind blew from the south it was disgusting.

The water at Bondi at the time wasn't much better, and when we heard there was a pollution march at Bondi we started screenprinting T-shirts up in Darren Bailes' garage. He played in a band called The Dead Shits at the time and used to make the band's T-shirts. We called ourselves the Anti Shit Squad – ASS. We led the march down Campbell Parade, and at the rally we got on the ground and started doing the worm, like maggots on the beach.

And then Ian Cohen, the Green senator, contacted us. I think the NSW premier was visiting the Malabar headland to inspect the new ocean outfall plant they were building. Cohen was trying to push them to make the outfall secondary treatment, not primary, because they weren't really fixing the problem; they were just pumping the shit offshore and out of sight. It wasn't that long after Ian had paddled out on a surfboard and clung to the bow of a US nuclear warship in Sydney Harbour. The guy was a champion, and the full master of the environmental stunt. He wanted to prove that a turd as big as a human being could fit through the screening process. So what he wanted was for us to jump the fence and create a diversion, while he, dressed as a giant turd, slipped through the security system and dived into the shit tank. We immediately said, no worries, if you're keen to dive into a swimming pool of raw shit, the least we can do is create a diversion for you.

So we went in, jumped the fences and stormed the sewerage plant. We knew that whole area from playing war games as kids, and we'd been chased out of there by security on numerous occasions. We got inside the perimeter and into one of the tunnels leading down into the facility. A whole lot of us stormed it and we got chased by all the security. We didn't get arrested; we got thrown out. But Ian got in. He got in and jumped into the tank but got arrested before he could submerge himself. What a legend.

But when they switched the new plant on in 1990, mate, it was like night and day. It took a few days to clear completely, but I remember the shock of sitting on my board and being able to see my hand in the water. It was like we were surfing a new beach. Fuck, where are we? Within weeks it was crystal blue and you could see the bottom. Within a year they were doing tests and claiming it was the cleanest the water had been in 70 years. There's an old shipwreck out beyond the stormwater drain at the north end, and that summer on a really low tide we saw it for the first time. Everyone had a real spark of enthusiasm for surfing. For us, it was like we were surfing in the tropics, it was like we were surfing in Indonesia. The place just came back to life.

But that also signalled the start of the end for Maroubra.

By that stage the council had finally put the plans together for a huge refurbishment of the beach. We had our beach back, but the developers had dollar signs in their eyes, and having people like us around wasn't going to be good for business.

SUNNY

A STOLEN SUMMER ON A COAST WITHOUT CONCRETE, BLACKIE AND RED ADD SOME COLOUR TO THE DRAB GREY OF CITY LIFE

As a kid, surfing ate up everything else in my life.

I would have been about 12 when I first knew I wanted to be a pro surfer. I gave up junk food, started doing sit-ups, push-ups, stretching, running, surfing every day. At Ma's house there was a gate with a welded doorframe above it, and I couldn't walk past it without doing 10 chin-ups on it. If I forgot something, it was 10 on the way back in, and another 10 on the way back out. I was already anti-drugs because of my mum, and I didn't want anything impure in my body. I was so obsessed with surfing it was ridiculous. I'd be riding down the street and I'd be surfing my bike in between the cars, mindsurfing between traffic like I was on a wave. I'd lie in bed at night and do re-entries off the walls. I'd devour anything surfing – movies, magazines – just pull them apart for hours, looking where Tom Carroll's feet were on his board, where his eyes were looking when he was on a wave. I had to work a lot harder at my surfing than Jai, who was a more natural surfer than either Koby or I. We had to work a lot harder at it, whereas Jai could not surf for three months and then go out there and rip.

I was a pretty obsessed kid, full stop. When I was younger some of my upbringing channelled itself into weird obsessions. I couldn't finish my food unless the last pea, the last carrot and the last bit of steak were all in the one mouthful. If that didn't happen, if I screwed it up and there was something left over, I had to make more of everything and go again. I also used to blank out a lot when I was young and lose great chunks of time. I'd close the front door and then suddenly I'd be on the water's edge with my board, not able to remember how I got there ... not remembering which street I walked down, who I spoke to, how I got changed. I don't know whether it was me focusing too heavily, some reflex I'd developed to block out some of the shit we were going through, or a combination of both.

We grew up in a family where there were no real rules and the only real disciplinary figure in our lives was our grandfather, and he passed away when we were right at that crucial age, 12, 13. We didn't have much discipline at all, but what we had, surfing gave to us. Surfing was our life, but we also saw it as our escape. We wanted to make a living out of surfing.

But the two guys who really shaped our surfing were Blackie Wilson and Red Johnson. Blackie and Red were both board shapers and both great surfers. Blackie was Aboriginal, while I think Red always liked me and Jai because he had red hair and freckles like us. Me and Jai both got sponsored by Blackie, and rode his boards with the big black fist logo on them. Blackie and Red would take us surfing all the time, and it was them that first got us surfing the heavy reefs around Maroubra and Cronulla. Those guys were unreal to us, but Maroubra had a real nurturing culture like that.

I eventually got a job in Blackie's board shaping bay, sweeping up all the foam dust. He gave me a shovel then pointed me towards a bay that was waist-deep in foam dust. By the second day I'd turned bright red and I was itching like a dog. I was allergic to surfboard foam. The dust got into my pores, and I was rashed up, sweating, and my eyes puffed up. I was never going to be a shaper, that was for sure.

While I loved surfing in North End Boardriders, I realised that if I was going to be serious about my surfing I couldn't stay there, so I defected down the beach to Maroubra Boardriders. From the Bong End to the Wrong End. I left mainly because Blackie was in Maroubra. Me joining the other club was a big drama … half the older guys wouldn't talk to me for a year, and even me mates were giving me the cold shoulder. The older North End guys were saying, 'Stubbsy's brainwashing ya', 'cause Brad Stubbs was the president of Maroubra, and he was making this big professional push. They even had a team tracksuit, which was unheard of for the Bong Enders. Maroubra were all, like, *pro*, and I wanted to be a part of it. I'd be their gun junior surfer, and we'd be surfing against all the big clubs like Merewether and Newport and Snapper. What fuelled Stubbsy's whole push for professionalism was a feeling of resentment that Maroubra were the poor cousins of the surf industry. We'd grown up on a beach covered in shit and syringes, and we thought there was a real conspiracy to keep Maroubra in the shadows.

On one Maroubra Boardriders trip to Queensland for a national teams contest, Stubbsy wanted to make a statement that we were the 'New Maroubra', that we'd lifted our game. He'd gone out and bought a circus tent. It was big enough to fit a circus under it anyway, and if you listened to some comments around the beach from the other teams, that's exactly what they believed was going on. We had matching white team tracksuits, we had matching sunglasses. He'd bought a big barbecue, and he even brought an actual kitchen sink down onto the beach just so that he could say he'd brought the kitchen sink. He was feeding us this great food, he was feeding the judges; it was incredible. Stubbsy was on fire.

Eventually North End imploded and everyone joined Maroubra. Those six years North End was in existence were just hilarious, but something that fun and that chaotic couldn't last forever. But it was also a sign that Maroubra was changing.

There was a huge exodus of the older guys. Maroubra was becoming just too intense, too violent, too riddled with drugs. Guys like Marty Lee, the best surfers on the beach, were being harassed by the cops and driven out. Others couldn't afford to live and surf on the dole any more now the developers had moved into Maroubra and started pushing up the rents. Some escaped to the Gold Coast, some to the south coast; others moved overseas to remote Indonesia and Reunion Island to get as far away from Maroubra as possible. We couldn't understand why they all suddenly left, and we wouldn't find out until we were their age.

Red and Blackie moved up the north coast. Jai and I would go up there in school holidays and stay with them. Jai used to stay with Blackie in Ballina, and I'd stay with Red at Lennox Head. We'd both get the McCafferty's bus up there together but we'd stay at separate places, I think because Red and Blackie knew we fought like cats and dogs and the two of us under the one roof was always trouble.

The first time I went to Lennox I was 12 years old. Red had just bought one of the first houses up there on Sunrise Crescent overlooking the point, this beautiful old pole house. There were only four or five houses there at that stage. My bedroom was upstairs, and Red goes, 'When you look out that window in the morning, you're not going to believe what you see.' I was that excited I couldn't sleep.

I woke up at dawn the next morning, rolled over in my bed and opened the curtains and there it was – Lennox Head, eight foot, offshore and perfect. It was like a dream, just lines of swell to the horizon. We had nothing like it anywhere near Maroubra; I'd never seen anything like it in my life. It was paradise.

We got down there on the rocks with our boards. I'd left Red behind and sprinted straight down to the water and I can hear him back up the track going, 'Be careful, those rocks are bloody slippery!'

'Yeah, yeah, grandpa, whatever,' I muttered.

I ran straight down the rocks and have seen a wave coming. I went to run and jump off this one rock and have slipped straight off it, gone arse over, and been pinballed between these gnarly black boulders. Washed up with what was left of both my dignity and my surfboard, I discovered I'd snapped two fins out. I had to walk back up the hill past Red – the walk of shame – with a useless board. Luckily for me, Red owned San Juan surfboards in Byron Bay at that stage, so he had plenty of boards back at his place, and we just surfed all day. It just felt good to be out of the city, away from the concrete. It allowed us to concentrate fully on our surfing, which was what we were all about at that stage.

Blackie, meanwhile, had taken a job as the caretaker of the Ballina Surf Club. Red and I would drive down and surf with Blackie and Jai, so we kinda hung between Red and Blackie's places. We spent heaps of time down at North Wall there, at Ballina, and it was there we met Simon Baker, the actor. He was a couple of years older than us, about 14, and he lived next to the surf club at Ballina in a caravan. We did a heap of surfing together, and he was a cool kid. I saw him years later one day in Bondi, after he'd made a name in Hollywood, and had a coffee with him and caught up. We had a rap about those days surfing North Wall, and he asked all about Jai and how he was going, 'cause he and Jai had been really good mates.

That summer was unreal, and we stayed up there for the whole school holidays. Then we did it for the next two or three years, every holiday until we were about 16. Red and Blackie would pay for our bus fares, they'd pay for our food. They'd ring Ma and organise it all with her. I think they enjoyed having the grommets up there with them.

They were the best summers. David Parkes and Albert Whiteman, two classic old kneeboarders from Maroubra, lived up at Byron and they hung with Red and Blackie a bit. We never ran out of stuff to do with those guys. I'd fix dings at the San Juan shop with Red. We'd take Albert's four-wheel drive on the beach with a towrope and surf behind it in the shallows. We surfed huge Ballina river mouth. Their mates were all fishermen and big-wave riders, and Albert played in a blues band so we'd sneak into the Great Northern at Byron and watch him play. It was unreal. Red was still working on his house, so he'd put us to work helping him build the patio. We had to earn our keep, full grommet labour. They'd also take us on these mad adventures. I remember being dressed all in cammo gear, our faces smeared with Vegemite, running around playing commandos with them up in the rainforest on Mount Warning. They didn't tell us, but I was sure they were on mushies, because they didn't stop laughing for eight hours.

We used to lie to Ma when she'd call. We'd tell her there'd been a flood up there and the highway was cut and we couldn't get back. Then she'd watch the news and it'd say: 'north coast, sunny and 30 degrees'. Or we'd get Blackie to ring up and make up some bullshit excuse. That was the thing – Ma couldn't argue with you on the phone. You'd hear her grunting and you could tell she was trying to say the word 'Bullshit!'

There was another enclave of Maroubra refugees down at Urunga, outside of Coffs Harbour, and Jai, Wayno and me did a few weeks with them as well. It was that North End crew: Rod Saunders, Scotty Scar Back, Rod Duncan, Bebbo. They were a crazy bunch of guys who fully looked after us, cruising round with us all day chasing waves in their old Valiant.

That was the trip where we met Billy Barnes. We'd gone surfing one morning on this long, empty stretch of beach, and we noticed a guy surfing on his own about a mile down the beach. The guy was ripping, so we've ended up walking down there and surfing the same bank. Turns out it was a Koori kid about our age who introduced himself as Billy. We surfed with him all that day and he hung with us for the rest of the time we were up there. He became a good mate to us in no time, helped no end by the fact he saved my life a few days later.

The Maroubra boys had moved up there and were caretaking a local tourist park that had this huge waterslide. At the end of the day when the waterslide closed, we'd jump the fence and have it to ourselves. They'd turned the water off, so we'd each carry up two buckets of water from the pool down below, then throw them down the slide and jump in. Because the film of water was so thin, it was like sliding on oil, and you'd end up going twice as fast as normal.

So me and Billy are up the top of this slide, which was an enclosed tube and was pretty high. I've thrown my buckets down, jumped on my boogieboard, and off I go. I was flying. The end of the slide had this big kicker that launched you out into the pool, but as I get to it I start to realise, 'Fuck, I'm going way too fast for this thing.' The last thing I remember was flying into the final drop-off and smashing my head against the roof. I've knocked myself out, flown out the end, and sunk like a stone. There's no one around, only Billy. He's come flying down, has landed in the pool then wondered where the fuck I'd gone. He found me, dragged me out, then started pumping my chest 'cause I wasn't breathing. I started vomiting up water and have come back to life.

'You bloody lucky there, cuz. I thought you were ratshit.'

It was a pretty eventful trip, that one, because it was also the first time I'd ever taken drugs. Me and Wayno had come back to the boys' house after a surf and found a mushroom omelette sitting on the stove. We were starving, so we've heated it up and scoffed it. All of a sudden we're pissing ourselves laughing, tripping out, with no idea what was happening. We went straight over to the waterslide, where, after my first run down the slide, I convinced myself I'd travelled into the future. Then I lost Wayno, so I went over to the paddocks nearby and lay on my back for four hours and played with the sky. Wayno, meanwhile, had gone walkabout. The Maroubra guys had come home, found the omelette gone, and come looking for what was left of us. They found Wayno walking along the highway, heading south, talking in some strange dialect. Wayno didn't come down for a day; I figure he must've got the gnarliest part of the omelette. I was pure as the driven snow up to then, not a toke on a joint, nothing, so my system didn't know what to do with some of the north coast's finest fungus and I was all pins and needles for three days.

Billy Barnes came back to Sydney with us. Billy was adopted, and his mum had died not long before he met us. He really had no one. So we said, 'Why don't you come down and live with us?' We turned up at Astoria Circuit with Billy in tow.

'Mum, we've got a mate here. He's coming to live with us.'

She looked at Billy, standing there with his bags and his surfboard.

'No worries. Just make sure he does the dishes.'

Within a couple of weeks he had a job up at the fruit and veg shop, was boxing with Ronnie, and had hooked up with a girl from across the road. You could say he fitted right in.

JAI

WHY A RAINY MONDAY MORNING BEATS THE HOLLOW GLORY OF A SURF MAGAZINE COVER EVERY TIME

'Okay, boys, we're gonna stay up at Palm Beach. I've got a mate who lives up the road.'

We were surfing in a junior contest over on the northern beaches, and Dave Gyngell said to me and Sunny that if we got through our heats he had a surprise for us. So we've rocked up to this place and there's all these Rolls and pimping cars parked out the front. We just go to Gynge, 'Where the fuck are we?'

'We're at my godfather's place.'

We walk up this big flight of stairs and there's Kerry. He's in this big dining room and it's full of politicians and big wigs. He goes, 'G'day there, boys. Hang on, I'll be out with you in a minute.' He had a big function on. All his guests are dressed up in penguin suits, and Kerry's sitting at the head of the table in his dressing gown. Just pimping like Hugh Hefner. Just like, 'I don't get dressed up for no one, mate.'

We sat out the back and had a feed. Then Kerry Packer come out with us and sat down. He goes, 'Shit, boys, I'd rather be hanging out here with you blokes than with those jokers in there.' He was a full-on lad. They were all still talking shit in there, and he just coated them for half an hour to come and hang with us. He was just one of the boys. He was fully quizzing us about what the surf had been like.

The chef brought out the full menu for us to choose from and there were all these ice creams. I used to love Weis Bars and there was a whole fridge full of 'em. Bra, I'd died and gone to Heaven. I reckon I ate about nine. But it was good to meet an Aussie legend, and that was mad of Gynge to take us up there and meet him.

I was actually doing all right in contests at this stage. I won the NSW junior title, which meant I got a start at the Australian Titles, which were held down in Victor Harbor, South Australia that year. I lasted about five minutes.

We were staying at the local caravan park and we'd been out on the piss and these chicks came back to our room. One thing led to another and I ended up taking their car and driving it straight through the boom gate of the caravan park. I thought that'd go down sweet. Fuck! The next day it was like the team manager, the caravan park owner, the mayor, the prime minister, they were all over me.

'Jai, there's been a breach of conduct ...'

'Yeah, yeah, sorry, boys. I smashed the boom gate, it was me, sorry. I'll pay for it.'

'Sorry, Jai, you're out of here, mate. You're on the next plane home.'

I was still going all right in contests, but all the signs were telling me it wasn't my game. And it was around then that I got sponsored by Rip Curl. I never got any money in my contract; they used to just take me on the odd surf trip and give me free boardies. They'd just started on their whole 'Search' campaign, and that's what they signed me for. The whole idea was to travel around, find some perfect waves, and come back with a bunch of photos for magazines and ads. It was what I wanted to do, so I was stoked.

I was still surfing contests and doing okay, and the following year I made the Aussie Titles again, this time down at Bells. I got through two heats no worries, and then it was a day off. They had a skateboard ramp out the front of the Rip Curl shop, and someone's gone to me, 'Jai, I bet you can't drop in on that ramp.'

The fucking idiot I was, I just shoulda said, 'No, I can't,' but seeing as though I'd been challenged that was it – 'I can fucking do this.' I've survived the drop-in, but then gone and done a turn and just fell on my ankle. I remember thinking, 'Ahh, my ankle's sweet, I haven't broken it.' My mates are going, 'Is your foot right?' and I was going, 'Yeah, it's all right.' I was in full denial.

I was staying with Michael Anthony, the board shaper, and at two in the morning I woke him up. 'I think it's broken, bra.' It was just throbbing. Michael drove me up to the hozzy, and sure enough it was broken, and I got plastered up straightaway. He's a legend guy, Michael. I haven't seen him in years and often wonder how he's doing.

The next day the contest was on down at Johanna, two hours down the coast. This left bank down the beach was six to eight foot and firing. Chad Edser and Joel Fitzgerald were the only two out. It was like G-Land – the best beachbreak I've ever seen. I didn't give a fuck about missing the contest, but missing those perfect waves down the beach was what really hurt. The best beachbreak I'd ever seen and I was stuck on the hill watching it.

It was the start of a real chalky run for me. I got back to Maroubra, and was out of the water for a month, which was doing my head in. I waited four weeks to take the plaster off – the doctor told me six – but I was walking on it the whole time, just being stupid. It never really healed properly, and I just ripped the plaster off myself and went surfing.

A week later I broke it again, worse than the first time.

I was surfing this mad left bank out in the middle of the beach at Maroubra. It was only my second surf back, and this wave's just closed out on me and straightaway I've felt it go again. It broke worse than the first time. I was laid up for months. I couldn't surf, I couldn't work. It felt like I was in plaster for three years, and I lost all interest in doing comps.

I don't really have a competitive streak in me. Never have. I'm the keenest cunt in the world when the early surf is on, when the waves are good, but surfing to compete always used to shit me a bit. I wasn't really that patient, and I didn't have the head for it.

So I stopped surfing contests. I couldn't handle getting beaten in shitty waves by some bloke you know you'd smash if the surf was big. I just didn't really have the patience for it. I reckon I should have just believed in myself more. When you look back on what you were doing, you realise you were blowing cunts out of the water. If I'd believed that at the time I could have gone 10 times further, made a career out of it. A lot of people have the talent to do it – the skill is avoiding the partying. I was too much into partying and trying to make money. But I got no regrets about it. I don't regret a lot of partying, a lot of girls and a lot of cash.

Me and Wayno would just surf hard. We didn't give a fuck about going in contests. That was us from a young age. Sunny might be on the tour, but when The Southy's on or Voodoo's on, he knows who's trumps, bra. Me and Wayno were inside him every wave, so we really didn't give a fuck about the mags and the contests. We used to have a saying: 'Rainy Monday mornings'. That's when ya go and charge your hardest – no one around watching, no photographers, just you and your mate.

People had stopped paying me to go on surf trips 'cause of the stupid stuff I'd done, so now if I wanted to travel and surf I had to find a way to fund it myself. I started to lay carpet. Work enough to save up enough money to travel, that was the plan. I used to lay carpet with my mates Jimmy Olsen and Wazza Fox. They were just legends, but fuck, I used to hate it, though. I've done carpet laying and roof tiling, the two hardest trades. I used to work with an old Maroubra guy called Digger Wilson on the roofs. He was an old staunch bloke. He'd say, 'Okay, we're not setting up the conveyer belt today,' and I'd have to carry the tiles four at a time on my shoulder up the ladder. After three days of that I was getting to the top of the ladder nearly delirious a couple of times, I nearly fell. I just hated working there. I done that for a few years, off and on, working between surf trips.

I remember how I paid for my first Indo trip, bra. They used to have these big dance parties up at the Hordern Pavilion. I was only young, like 15, and I used to buy these packs of No-Doz and sell 'em to the kids up there as eccies. One night I made, like, 1800 bucks. I was getting these cunts coming back to me after dancing, going, 'Those pingers were mad! Give us another one.'

'Fair dinkum, mate?'

They're going, 'Give me five!' I go, '250,' *boom boom boom*. I made 1800 bucks one night and bought a ticket to Indo the next day.

SUNNY

A JAILHOUSE VISIT TO A FALLEN IDOL SETS THE BOYS ON THE PATH TO SURFING RIGHTEOUSNESS

The first Australian Titles I went to were held at Bells Beach.

It was going to be almost a thousand bucks for the whole trip, and I was 15 and didn't have a cent to my name. Maroubra Boardriders chipped in a hundred bucks, and some friends threw in another hundred, but I was still 800 bucks shy. So ensued my first real entrepreneurial adventure.

At the same time, the girl who lived across the street from me in Astoria Circuit, Billy Barnes' girlfriend Lisette, had made the Australian athletics championships in Brisbane. Her parents were German immigrants, and her dad had had a stroke, so she was struggling for money as well. So Lisette and I teamed up.

It was the middle of summer, so we went to Franklins supermarket and bought these cheap cans of cola and lemonade, then we went to the fruit shop and bought big watermelons, and we organised some ice and two Eskies to lug it all around in. We'd get dropped at beaches around the area: La Perouse, Gordon's Bay – beaches where there were no shops. We'd have a big Esky with watermelons and ice, and then another Esky with cold drinks and we were going around the beaches selling them. We made a killing on it, so we both saved the money to go.

I got on the bus to Bells carrying a plastic bag, and wearing just a pair of boardies and a T-shirt. My entrepreneurial venture had covered my costs, but I was still light on for spending money. I've walked onto the NSW team bus, didn't know anyone, and I was totally in awe. The bus was full of Australia's best surfers; it was like one of my surfing magazines had just come to life and these guys had climbed out of its pages. Guns N' Roses' 'Sweet Child O' Mine' was playing on the bus stereo as I walked down the aisle, past all my surfing heroes, trying to find a seat.

I ended up sitting next to a guy named Saul Baker from Wollongong. He was surfing in the juniors as well, and we talked surfing for the next 12 hours as the bus headed south. Saul was a straight-up bloke and we became good friends in the years to come. Even though he was from Wollongong there was a lot of Maroubra in him; the guy had no reverse gear.

When we started surfing, I get to the third round and I've won all my heats so far. I'm psyched to win the Australian junior title. I'm gonna win this fucking thing; I've worked so hard to get here. But then I've had a hassle out in the water with one of the Western Australian surfers. We've both gone over the falls on this wave, and my board has speared back at me and I cut my heel on the fin. I didn't even look at it because I knew it was probably bad, so I've stayed out there, kept surfing the heat, and have made it through. I get to shore and find I've knocked the fin out of my board, and sure enough there's a big gash in my foot. They've taken me straight into Geelong Hospital where I got six stitches. I hardly ever wore shoes at home, so my feet were like leather, and the doctor snapped two needles trying to shoot a local anaesthetic into my heel.

I got back to Bells two hours later and my quarterfinal is in the water. It'd been going for five minutes, and I still had a board that was missing a fin. I was on crutches and had my foot all bandaged up. The guys have had one look at me and shook their heads.

'Sorry, mate, even if you could surf, it's too late.'

'Fuck that, I'm out there!'

I whacked on my wettie, grabbed Saul Baker's board, hobbled down the steps still with my foot full of painkillers, and won my quarter. I made the final the following day, but the cut had turned nasty, the painkillers had worn off, and I ended up getting a third, which was a huge result for me.

It was soon after I got back that we got news that Grommet wanted to see us. We hadn't heard anything from him since he'd gone to jail, but he was writing letters to our surfie chick mates, Rachel Nass and Karen Jepson. In one of his letters he asked the girls to ask us to walk up the hill and visit him, because he was up the road in Long Bay at this stage. We'd known all our lives that the jail was just up the hill – you can see the guard tower from down the beach – and we'd heard all the stories from the guys who'd done time up there. The police had cracked down hard, and a lot of Maroubra guys had been sent up to Long Bay – Marty, Grommet and Bebbo among them. We'd been close to Bebbo – Mark Bebbington. The guy had nothing himself, but he used to bring a big box of hand-me-down boardies and shirts around to Ma's place for us. He was one of those guys who really connected with us and tried to look after us. Bebbo never made it out … he hung himself in jail. Marty was released and was pretty much told by the cops to get out of town. And then Grommet, well, he'd called us in and wanted to see us.

There was me, Ronnie, Jai, Jimmy and Wayno who walked up there. He wanted to see all of us. We were about 15, and walking through the gates we were shit-scared. I think that's part of what Grommet wanted to happen. The place was freaky enough, and we had no idea what shape Grommet would be in. He was only 19, but he'd been crazy when he'd gone in, and now he'd just killed a guy. Was he twice as gnarly and twice as crazy? What'd he grown into up there?

Well, it was the complete opposite.

He sat us down and said, 'Boys, I've fucked up. Have a look around and see where I live now. Youse have got your whole lives in front of you. I thought I was this tough kid. I thought I was invincible. But look what I've done.' He was still upbeat and charismatic, his usual self, but he was now looking at what he could do to stop us going down the path he'd chosen. Here was the baddest guy in town, the anti-hero cult figure who we respected and feared, saying, 'Don't go down the road I went down. Do you know how hard it is for me to smell the ocean up here? How hard it is to be stuck here thinking about you guys surfing out in the Dunny Bowl?' He singled us all out and asked us what our plans were and gave us words of encouragement like only he could. 'Sunny, chase the world tour, mate; you could be top 10, easy. Ronnie, I hear you're boxing. I reckon you could take it all the way. You've got a good style and you're tough.'

We walked out of there inspired, but sad and hollow at the same time. Here was a guy with so much talent and charisma and so much energy, a guy who could have done anything in the world, and here he was trapped in a concrete cell for the next 15 years. He wanted to teach us kids not to make the same mistake he'd made, to not have a big chip on your shoulder. If you had a chip on your shoulder in the street then you'd end up in jail. If you had a big chip on your shoulder in jail, then this is where you could end up – doing 15 years. What a fucking sad story.

Jay Brown was another of our heroes. He surfed for Mango clothing, surfed in the big pro contests, and was right in there with the next generation of hot surfers, but he'd been swept up in the Maroubra party scene, and it was affecting his surfing career. Around the same time that we'd gone up to see Grommet, I remember Browny pulling me aside as well. We used to sneak in the pub a bit, and it's there he worded me up. He pointed around the room and said, 'Don't get caught up in this, Sunny. Follow your surfing. Don't get caught in the Bermuda Triangle here.'

It was a really crucial time for us. Maroubra was exploding, and there was trouble all over the place. We'd been tuned from an early age by guys like Blackie and Red on how to avoid it, but now they'd moved away we'd been left to our own devices. We could have gone either way. If we hadn't had those serious word-ups from Grommet and Jay Brown, I don't know where we'd be now. And the thing was, they were guys on both sides of the Maroubra coin – Grommet from the North End write-off crew, and Jay from the slick Wrong Enders – and we were getting the same advice off both of them. We listened.

Me and Jai started winning a lot of local contests. I'd win my heats by surfing smart; Jai would win his on natural talent. I was consistent. Jai was hot and cold. Jai was less competitive than me; he just wanted to go surfing. Jai was a really, really natural surfer; he could not surf for six months and then go out there and totally blaze it like he hadn't missed a day. He'd go out in 10-foot waves and surf them like they were three foot … totally fearless.

Right about that time, Jai told me he wanted to go to Bali with a friend of ours, Scotty Linford. Jai had lost interest in the contests by this stage, and just wanted to surf the best waves he could find. He didn't have a passport, so I forged Mum's signature on his passport application. I think some of the older guys on the beach helped him with some money for the airfare to Bali.

Jai asked if I wanted to go. I didn't. I wanted to concentrate on the State Titles, and if I went to Bali I was going to miss them. That one decision, right there, was where our lives split apart. Jai went to Bali and ended up sailing over to Grajagan. Scotty cut his leg and came home but Jai stayed on his own, a 15-year-old kid, and just blazed. He just blew everyone away. He came back after two months, penniless and about a stone lighter. But what he did have were all these photos of him surfing big G-Land. And that was the start of Jai's new life. He'd travel for the next 10 years, to Indonesia mainly, chasing surf, while I travelled the world chasing the pro tour. We didn't realise it at the time, but me not going on that trip was a huge point in my life.

I surfed for Maroubra Boardriders for a while, but then made the decision to also surf for Avoca Boardriders up on the Central Coast. I was an ambitious little fucker at that stage, really hungry, so I joined Avoca just for the competition. They had pretty much the best junior team in Australia with guys like Shane Powell and Sam Chell. They also had older guys like Mark Sainsbury and Ross Clarke-Jones who were travelling the world on the pro tour, so I joined them as my second club.

Turns out it was a good move, because that's how my sponsorship came about. Bruce Turner, who worked for Rusty, was a member of Avoca Boardriders, and Rusty was in the process of sponsoring Shane

Powell when I joined. Bruce – and I'm forever in his debt for doing this – convinced them to sponsor me as well to do the world tour. Me and Powelly would be their main two Aussie juniors. The first deal was $25,000 a year with 25 free surfboards. It doesn't sound like much now, but when someone comes up to a houso kid in Year 11 who's got nothing and says, 'Do you want to be paid 25 grand to travel the world?' you're hardly going to knock it back.

I went back to Maroubra, walked up to Maroubra Bay High and told them I was out of there. I went home and packed my bags.

MY BROTHERS KEEPER

Part 4
Sun club

SUNNY

A COMICALLY OVERLOADED CITROEN FULL OF IRATE
FRENCHMEN WELCOMES SUNNY ABBERTON TO THE
WORLD SURFING TOUR

Flying out for France, I had no idea what I was doing. It was 1988, my first year on the pro tour. I'd be spending three months in France, three months in America, then a month in Hawaii. I'd never set foot outside of Australia before.

I got off the plane at Biarritz airport on my own, and I was stuck in the airport for hours. No one was there to pick me up, I couldn't speak a word of French, and I didn't even have anyone's phone number. I eventually got on to Pierre Agnes from Quiksilver, who got Steven Bell, an Aussie guy who lived in France, to come out and pick me up. Belly took me to some house and said I could sleep on the lounge. I've looked down and the lounge was made of driftwood – it was the most uncomfortable thing I've ever fucking slept on.

A big junior contest had been scheduled, and there was a bit of an Aussie contingent with me – Jake Spooner, Jake Paterson, the Bannister brothers, Shane Herring, Todd Prestage – and we were all pretty much roughing it. There were no team managers, no minders; we were living by our own devices. We all chipped in and bought a shitty old Citroen wagon, the full comical French car that we made even more comical by spray-painting it with flames.

We head down to Capbreton. There's no one around, but there's beautiful waves and beautiful weather. We went straight to the Rockfood nightclub that night, the craziest club anywhere on the pro tour. The owner, Roland, was the DJ there, and here we were, 16 years old, and he was introducing us one by one as we walked in on the red carpet with a spotlight on us like we were rock stars. There are hot French chicks *everywhere*. It's safe to say we were just in heaven.

We had nowhere to stay, though, so we asked if we could sleep in the contest scaffolding on the beach. They had built this big four-storey tower on the sand for the contest, and that became our home for two weeks. It sounds shithouse, but it was so much fun. We'd get blind every night, take chicks back to the tower and try and get a root, then wake up in the morning to perfect, empty waves. We'd eat our cereal then go surfing in the nude. All the chicks were nude on the beach so we thought, why not?

We were living off baguettes and Laughing Cow cheese. Some rorter told us that you couldn't get arrested in France for shoplifting as long as every item you stole cost less than 50 francs. So we'd get dressed in the afternoon in our nightclub gear and go to the supermarket and just literally have a picnic in there. We'd get stuck into the 49-franc beers, the 49-franc bread and the 49-franc cheese. People would be looking at us and we'd be fully unfazed, not even trying to hide it, just having the best time. Then we'd go down to the Rockfood and party there all night.

If we didn't make it back to the tower, we'd often sleep in the car at the beach car parks. We'd pull the car up, lay out our boardbags, and just crash right there on the asphalt. You'd wake up at 10 in the morning in the blazing sun, fully hung over. It's the middle of summer, and you know how crowded those French beaches get. All these people are walking past with strange looks on their faces. Here's a dozen Aussies, all passed out, with baguettes and cheese and wine bottles scattered everywhere. But we were having that much fun. We were getting perfect waves, living on the beach, rooting all the local chicks, surfing in the nude. How good was life? It got even better for me when I made the final of the world's first international pro junior. The field included guys like Rob Machado and Shane Dorian – guys who'd go on to be superstars – as well as all the best young Aussie guys. I made the final against Jake Spooner from Wollongong, and only lost it because I got done on an interference.

It couldn't last, though. The local French guys had been watching all this and had started to really get the shits with us. We'd parked the car one morning and walked down the beach to have a surf out the front of our makeshift apartment block at Capbreton. There was this one aggro French guy out in the water who kept hassling us. He was a big bloke too; not tall, but really stocky. I caught a wave and this guy blatantly dropped in on me. I've come up behind him and overtaken him. He's tried to tackle me off the board and he's missed. Well, he's got to the surface and he's gone, 'You *farkeeng* drop in on me!'

'Fuck off, mate,' I replied, '*you* tried to drop in on *me*.'

'*You* tell *me* to fuck off? I *keeeeeeeel* you!'

And he's just come at me, swinging punches. I'm still sitting on my board, and I managed to kind of lodge my foot up into his neck and kick him off his board. Then he tried to stab me in the eye with the nose of his board. It came right at my eye; I just tilted my head back and it's missed my eye by an inch. So I've just gone, 'Fuck you, mate,' and came back with a full king hit that got him flush under the eye; his whole head just split open. That was it.

'I *keeeeeeeeeeellllllll* you!!'

Then our mate Bunter from Narrabeen paddled over. He was a bit bigger and a bit more solid than me, and they had a windmilling fight in the water without many connecting. The French guy eventually paddled in, screaming, 'I'm going to *keel* you! You wait here, you dead! Aussies ... dead!'

We were looking at each other going, 'Shit, that was a bit heavy.' We thought there might be a bit of trouble up on the beach later, but we weren't really freaking out about it. We just kept surfing.

We get back to our car and it's smashed to pieces. Trashed. Some locals came over and gave us the number plate of the guy who'd done it – our mate from the surf. He knew it was our car – I can't imagine how he guessed with the racing flames on it – and apparently he'd pulled up in front of it with a full screechy, jumped out with a tyre jack and smashed the front windscreen, the back windscreen and the two side windows. He'd jumped on the roof and the bonnet, both of which were caved in. There were two boards in the car, one of which was Brett Warner's, and both of those were trashed. We've just gone, 'Fuck, this is bullshit.' He did it in front of 50 people and didn't care. Someone had called the cops while he was trashing the car, so five minutes after we got there the cops showed up and took photos and our names. Then Tom Carroll, who'd been surfing down the beach, walked past and we explained to him what'd happened. We chatted to Tom, cleaned up the glass and kicked the roof back into shape. It was already a piece of shit, now it was a battered piece of shit. We're thinking, okay, he's got us, all square, end of story.

There was me, Jake Paterson, Brett Bannister and Brett's mate Bunter in the car. Our boards were tied to the roof and we'd just pulled out of the car park when someone's gone, 'Geez, imagine if they came back.' And I swear that within five seconds we heard this car fanging towards us. But it wasn't one car, it was three, and there must've been 15 guys with baseball bats and chains, all hanging out the windows yelling out in French, '*Allez!* We fucking *keeeeeeel* you!'

The first car rammed us from behind. We all knew it was on; these cunts were serious. *Boom boom* – they fully rammed us again. And they had a nice car too, and they were willing to trash it. That worried us. This wasn't a bluff. These cunts were mad. Looking back at it, I suppose they wanted to send a message: 'You Aussies, you come over here and think you're ruling the place, rooting our chicks and stealing our waves?'

It turned into the full car chase. Bunter was driving, and doing a good job too, as the chase went from Capbreton back to Seignosse. It's not far as the crow flies, but it's all back streets, so it takes you 20 minutes to get there. What we wanted to do was get back to the contest site where we could jump out and there'd be another 10 or 20 crew there to help us. We were totally outnumbered, and they were fully armed.

Those little laneways and streets are all cobblestone, and every building has a lane or a street running off it, so it's like a maze. We started on the highway, got to a traffic jam at a roundabout and have flown through it on the wrong side of the road. We must've done that two or three times – straight through red lights and roundabouts. We lost one car at a roundabout, but still had two chasing us. We got onto this major road and we're gunning it, but their cars are too fast for the shitbox Citreon and they come up straight beside us and rammed us twice again at 80 kays, swinging the bats out the car window. If we stopped long enough at any lights or roundabouts, they weren't going to give a fuck who was there – the cops, people in the street, whoever – they were gonna beat the shit out of us.

As we're flying down the highway, them swerving next to us, one guy has leaned out the front window of their car. Me and Jake Paterson were in the backseat and this bat come straight through our car's remaining window and glass exploded all over us. Realising we weren't going to outrun them, Bunters hit the handbrake and locked it up on the highway, U-turned, and took off back the way we came. Driving back on the gravel verge on the wrong side of the road, we just turned right at the first street we could find, straight into the full alley maze. It was like something out of a Bond movie. There were people diving out the way, we were running red lights, cars were locking up. Bunter had one hand on the wheel and the other fully on the horn.

I had a frypan to defend myself with. I was getting pissed off by this stage, and I was shaking the frypan going, 'Fuck you, ya cunts!' There were two cars still hot on our heels. I looked back and saw the second car make a sharp right. He was trying to take a shortcut and block us off. I was screaming, 'Left! Left!' 'cause I knew they were trying to block us from the right. We're all screaming, 'Turn left!' For reasons known only to himself, Bunter turns right. We flew down these other streets and the road has bent around to the right and, sure enough, here's their car coming straight at us. Bunter skidded and we crashed through a fence and into the front yard of someone's house.

Bunter and Brett took off out the driver's side door; I bailed out the window with Jake not far behind. Me and Jake are suddenly standing on the driveway of this French chateau. We could see that the back door was open, and the guys with bats are right behind us, so we run for the door. We've burst into this house and run straight into the living room. Here's this French family peacefully having their afternoon meal, 10 of them, and me and Jake are just yelling, 'Help us! Help us!' The family thought they were being robbed by these psycho foreigners and just freaked. They didn't have a clue what we were saying; they were just trying to kick us out of the house.

I looked out the door and saw these three cunts on the bonnet of our car, just baseball-batting our boards to pieces. I just clicked. I had my only board on the roof, my tradesman's tools, and I needed that thing to survive. I ran back into the house, pushed the old man out of the way, grabbed this huge antique chair and just went charging out into the driveway. I think they must've seen the look in my eye, because they've jumped into their car. I'm running screaming at them, and I've thrown this big heavy antique chair straight at the driver's window … and it's just bounced off it. I swear, it was all quiet for that little split second where it dawned on them that there was three of them and one of me. They were now trying to get back out of the car, and I was using the chair to keep 'em in there like a lion tamer.

It was right about then that the cops turned up. Three cop cars. The family had rung the police. These guys didn't give a fuck; they even wanted to fight the cops. They had their bats out and there was a full standoff. We still didn't know what had happened to Bunter and Banno. Turns out they'd been chased the other way by three of them. Bunter reckons he could hear the air swooshing as they swung the bats behind his head. Then he run out of puff, just turned around and has thrown a big haymaker; one guy's run straight into it and been knocked out. Then they ran into a restaurant and the two guys run after them and turned the restaurant upside down. Bunter had a bit of a cut because he'd fought one of them, but somehow they were the only wounds we had. It was a miracle.

It's got a postscript to it, this story, though. About 10 years later I'm at home, coming out of the surf at Maroubra, and I see this guy on the beach with all his bags and his boards. It's about 8pm, it was almost dark, it was raining and the guy's sitting there. I've gone up to him and asked him what he was doing. His name was Estuban and he was a Basque guy. He's said he was supposed to stay at his friend's house, but his friend hadn't showed. I've gone, 'Mate, you better come and stay at my place.' He was a good bloke, and he ended up staying three or four days. He gave me his phone number back in Spain and gone, 'Sunny, if you ever come to Basque country, call me and we have big barbecue.'

Well, a couple of years later I had a Spanish girlfriend named Irace from Bakio, right next to Mundaka in the Basque country. While I'm there we've broken up, and I'm stuck at Mundaka with a hire car and my trip all paid in advance. What the fuck am I going to do? Then it hit me – call me old mate Estuban. Biggest karma ... Estuban's got a mansion right on the beach back up the coast in Anglet, France, with a boxing gym, a swimming pool, the works. First night at dinner he's got the whole family there, as they do. They ask how we met, and I tell the story of how I met Estuban on the beach at Maroubra, so I was suddenly a saint.

Estuban tells me there's going to be waves in a few days, and there's a secret spot he's gonna take me to. As it's March, there's no other foreigners there, just French surfers. His secret spot is a little peak, and there's a really competitive French crew out. No one says hello, and there's a very aggro vibe in the water. After about half an hour this nuggetty guy comes down the hill. He looks familiar, but I can't place him. He comes running down the beach, screaming in French at someone out in the water. I'm looking around at the guys out there, thinking, 'Shit, one of you blokes is in trouble here.' We're all staring at him when the French guy sitting next to me, who hasn't spoken a word since I paddled out, looks over at me and says, 'It's your old friend.'

JAI

FROM A CARAVAN IN ASTORIA CIRCUIT TO A FISHING CANOE IN THE TIMOR SEA, JAI GOES A WANDERIN'

I never really got kicked out of the house in Astoria Circuit, bra, I kinda just *evolved* out of there.

I didn't want to be up there, so I moved into a caravan downstairs. I could play Body Count as loud as I liked down there, and me and the girl could do whatever we liked. I had to get out of Lexo eventually, though; it was a bad scene. It wasn't much longer before I moved back down to Ma's place.

Paul, he was all right, he was pretty mellow, you know. Never touched any of us, never touched me mum; that's why he's all right. Probably spoke five words to me in 10 years, though. He just didn't talk.

The first time I ever went to Indo was 1988, the bicentenary year. I was 15. I had a good mate, Scotty Linford, who's dead now – he got knocked in Bali they say. I told Mum I was going to Bali with Scotty and his parents.

'Nah, Mum, it's all sweet, me, Scotty and his folks.'

Mum was freaking a little and Ma was freaking a lot. Mum's taken me to the airport, and there's Scotty on his own.

'Where's his mum?'

I told her she was already over in Bali and we were meeting her there. Mum knew straightaway that was bullshit.

'Scotty's folks aren't coming, Mum, but it's too late. I've already got the tickets.'

'Well, look after yourself then.' And she drove off.

It was fucking mad, bra. I'd just turned 15 and was going to Indo by myself. The first day I got there, I was shitting myself. I remember thinking, 'Why the fuck would anyone come here?' I was that culture shocked. It was just the traffic and all the hagglers – and why wasn't anyone speaking English? I'd hardly been out of Maroubra in me life, and I wanted to go home after one day. This was the dirtiest, most hectic place I'd ever seen in my life. On that first day I was so ready to go home. Then we got out to Uluwatu the next day and I've thought, 'Hang on, this is the best place in the world!'

Scotty was a few years older than us, and he was always in the middle of everything, a little hustler. When we were young he was always pulling out the wads of cash. But he was always looking after us; there was nothing that guy wouldn't do to help any one of us.

Scotty had been to Bali a few times and knew what he was doing. We met up with a big group of Maroubra guys – Wazza Fox, Marco Signetti, Bindi, Chewy. They were all staying at the same place as me and Scotty, so they looked after me. After a couple of weeks on Bali me and Scotty headed over to G-Land. Within the first two days Scotty sliced himself up, the biggest reef cut; he had to skol a bottle of tequila while they stitched him back together. He just skolled it while this bloke named Kev put 15 stitches in him. I don't think Kev had held a needle before, and it looked like it was him who needed the tequila, but he got the job done. Scotty had to get out of there straightaway; the thing was bound to get infected and that could be a death sentence in Indo.

'If your leg's fucked, boot it,' I told him. His leg was pretty bad.

But I wanted to stay. I was a 15-year-old goofyfoot and it was four-foot perfect G-Land. That was the dream, you know, so there was no way I was going home. So Scotty took off and I was there on me own. When Scotty come back to Maroubra by himself and me mum found out, that's when she really started tripping.

'What do you mean *he's over there on his own!*'

But the older Maroubra boys were still there to keep an eye on me, so I stayed. Glad I did, because the surf pumped. I got three barrels on one wave, and Bobby Radiasa, the guy who owned the camp, saw it. He couldn't believe I was only 15, so he let me stay an extra three days for free. I loved it, living in the jungle at G-Land. The surf got up to eight foot, but I'd just turned 15, so to me it was like 15 foot. I was getting full stand-up barrels. I just surfed myself to a standstill, 10 hours in the water a day. I stayed in Bali for another three weeks until me money run out; I didn't have a cent left when I got back. But that was it for me. I'd just had the most insane time, and I was counting down the days until I went again.

I'd already left school by this stage. I'd worked around a bit carpet laying, doing a lot of surfing, but then I had the idea of going back to school. I went back and did Year 11 and 12 as a mature age student up at Maroubra Junction High. I would've done it at Maroubra Bay, but they'd shut the school down soon after I'd left. I'd never finished Year 9, never done Year 10, but I rocked up and told the teachers at Maroubra Junction, 'Yeah, I've got my School Certificate.' They didn't believe me, but I think so many kids up there had left at Year 10 that they were willing to take pretty well anyone into Year 11, so they said no worries.

So I got my HSC, bra – the only Abberton brother to finish school. I didn't really apply myself, though. It was pretty much like before, and I just went surfing most of the time. But I did finish school and I lodged my Austudy form before the due date. If you got your school record stamped by a certain date you got back paid from Austudy. I got eight grand back pay as a lump sum, so I took a month off school and went to Hawaii with Wayno.

When I got to Hawaii, Wayno had already been there for two weeks. The first day I ever surfed Pipe it was eight to 10 foot and just perfect, bra. By this stage Wayno had snapped all his boards, so he went under the house where we were staying and pulled out this old 7' 6" single-fin with dirt an inch thick on it. You had to thread the legrope through the fin, that's how old the board was. I remember paddling out through the channel next to Pipe. Wayno had paddled out before me and I watched him go the biggest, ugliest one straight off the bat. His second one was even crazier – this big, double-sucking ugly cunt that no one wanted – and he just pig-dogged it and got the biggest barrel. That was my first surf at Pipe. Wayno surfed so hard on that single fin that this big Hawaiian guy came up to him on the beach.

'Bra, do you smoke pot?'

Wayno's gone, 'Fucking oath!'

'You wanna smoke a joint, bra? You just ripped on that board.'

Wayno was the best bloke to be with over in Hawaii. He charged like no one you'd ever seen. Back home we'd be lucky to have one big Lurline or Southy day every year, but every day was like that over on the North Shore.

That first trip to Hawaii was mad. We stayed at Johnny Theodore's place at Sunset. He was a funny character, bra. One day we were surfing Pipe in the morning. It was big and getting bigger – too big – and the wind went onshore around lunchtime, just howling. We went back to the house. About an hour before dark the wind's swung back offshore. Johnny's come in the room and said, 'We're going down to watch Pipe. It's as big as it gets.' I was only young and still didn't know what the fuck I was doing over there.

'Should I bring me board, Johnny?'

Johnny's laughed and gone, 'Yeah, bra, bring your board.'

So I've put my board in the car and we've driven down to Pipe: me, Wayno and Johnny. We've pulled up at Pipe.

'Johnny, we're just checking it, right?'

'Nah,' said Johnny, 'get your board out, Jai. I wanna lock the car up.'

So I got me board and started walking down the track at Pipe. I run into Shaun Munro, an Aussie pro surfer who I only knew from being in surf mag ads. He's looking at me like I've got two heads.

'What have you got your board for? Have you seen it? You're out of your mind.'

I remember coming to the end of the track. I just froze. It was Third Reef, massive, but soooo perfect. Pipe was as big and clean as it gets, 15, 18 foot. If I hadn't seen Shaun Munro on the track I might not have gone out, but after him asking me why I had my board I was always gonna go. The beach was packed. Everyone was watching, 300 people, but there was only Johnny Boy Gomes and one lifeguard in the line-up. I'd never seen anything like it in my life.

I started paddling out.

Johnny Theodore is going, 'Fuck, bra, *are you going out*! You're out of your fucking mind!'

I'm shitting myself. But I've paddled straight out there in the rip. Then I've looked around and gone, 'Okay, now what the fuck do I do?' It was 20 minutes before dark, the sun's gone down, and I'm sitting out there between Second and Third reefs on my own. Then Johnny Boy came up to me and said, 'Hey, bra.' He didn't say that shit to any *haole*, ever. Meanwhile, Wayno and Johnny Theodore are on the beach; Johnny's freaking out, thinking, 'I've geed this kid up. I didn't think he was going to go out … *I've just killed this kid!*'

I'm out there on me own, but Wayno's there on the beach going, 'Nah, he'll be all right.'

Then this massive one stands up on Second Reef. I just went, 'Fuck, if I don't go this, I'm going to die out here.' So I've paddled into this big one – the only one I could get – and I've just completely airdropped into it, just falling blind, fully shitting myself.

But I've landed the cunt.

It wasn't a real deep tube, but I got barrelled and it basically just spat me up onto the beach. I'd just got the wave of my life and hardly even got me hair wet! This was the best day of me life, right there, bra.

By the time I'd got to Wayno and Johnny, 10 guys had high-fived me, going, 'You're a sick little cunt.' I was puffing bungers all the way up the beach. When I went back to the house, I got upgraded to the big room, the trump room, all 'cause I went out. It was my day – probably the proudest day of my life. Any other day and I could still be floating around out there now, face down, bra. But it was meant to be.

The boys in the house reckoned I wouldn't have gone out if I hadn't seen Shaun Munro that day.

'What have you got your board for?'

I started thinking, 'Fuck this bloke, who is he talking to? He hasn't got a fucking board!' Bang – I'm out there without even thinking about it.

Later in that trip I paddled out at Sunset and it was huge again, 15 foot, but onshore and windy and messy as hell. I was way out to sea, and there was one other guy out there. It was just the two of us in the middle of the ocean. He was a big guy, a big Hawaiian guy. Considering how Johnny Boy had paddled up to me and said 'Hey, bra' at Pipe, I figured that if I could get a 'Hey, bra' out of him, I could get one out of this guy if we're the only two out and it's 15 foot. So I paddled up to him, thinking I'm on a roll here.

'How's it going, bra?'

'Who the fuck are you, haole boy! You don't say hello to me, haole boy!'

There's just two of us in the middle of the ocean and I thought I might be able to keep an eye on him and he could keep an eye on me. Only fucking two of us out there and 'Who the fuck are you, haole boy!' I had to laugh.

I travelled to Indo a lot in those next years; I reckon I did six trips in two years. I've been to Indo, like, 30 times all up. Usually it's Bali, but I remember the only time I sailed up through Timor. That was with Scotty

Linford again, and my mate Brook Silvester, who was making surf movies. I flew up to Darwin and then went to the Merpati Airlines counter. I needed to be in Timor the next day 'cause the boat we were sailing on left from Kupang that afternoon.

I walked up and said to the Indo bloke at the counter, 'I need to get on the next flight up to Kupang in Timor.'

'Sorry, sir, tomorrow's flight's booked.'

I pulled out 200 bucks cash and waved it around.

'Okay, get here early. I'll get you on the flight.'

I got there early the next day and saw this little school kid walking up and down near the check-in; I knew straightaway I had his seat on the plane. The kid's finally worked up the courage to come over and ask me whether I had his seat number.

'Sorry there, little mate. Nah, it's not me; it must be someone else.'

I felt like a cunt, but in the end he sat on his mum's lap the whole flight.

From Kupang, we first sailed to Roti Island where we hired these two sketchy little fishing boats from a guy called Pork Chop and sailed all the way up to Sumbawa through some pretty rough ocean. The boats were taking water the whole way, and there were a couple of times when we thought the things were going to the bottom with us in them. Even the Indos were shitting themselves, and they'll go to sea on a floating palm tree.

We pulled into this bay that had this sick lefthander. Never in my life have I seen sharks like I did that day. We pulled up next to these Indo fishermen and within two minutes they'd each hauled in a big shark. I saw another two sharks in the water, then another boat sails in and it's full of sharks. It was this full shark bay, halfway between Roti and Lakey Peak. It was late in the day so we threw out the anchors and decided to sleep there for the night. I was on one of the boats with Scotty Linford, but the chronic weed was on the other boat. I'd seen all these sharks just on dark, swimming between the boats, fully patrolling, but I was hanging for a smoke. I'm thinking, 'Fuck, there's no way I'm paddling across there for a smoke.' The boats were about 50 metres apart, but I was hanging for a smoke by this stage so I figured I'd take Scotty with me to cut my chances of getting eaten by half.

'Fuck this, Scotty, I need a smoke. *You* need a smoke. We're going.'

'No way, mate. How many fucking sharks have we seen, Jai? No way I'm going.'

So I've just grabbed Scotty's board and thrown it in the water.

'You're coming, bra. If I'm going, you're going.'

'Fuck that, Jai. We're gonna get eaten for sure!'

Well, while we're arguing his board has floated off into the dark.

'That's a shit game, Scotty, leaving me to go on me own.'

'Fuck that, mate. You owe me a board!'

So I've dived in and swum after his board. I've found it, paddled me arse off and got onto the other boat, then punched two cones straightaway to settle me nerves. I stayed and had a couple more, but then had to make the fucking paddle back to our boat again. Bra, by the time I got back I was straighter than I was when I left! I'd never been so scared in my life. That whole way back I just had this feeling that something was underneath me just raring to take a chunk out of me. I nearly fucking walked on water to get back.

And when I climbed back on board Scotty was sitting there going, 'See – as if that was worth it!'

SUNNY

FROM *FAVELA*-CRAWLING IN BRAZIL TO A NUDE JAPANESE DISCO TO AN INADVERTENT SLICE OF DURBAN POISON CHOCOLATE CAKE, SUNNY EXPERIENCES THE UNITED COLOURS OF THE WORLD SURFING TOUR

My surfing was an escape from where I came from, but it was also a full attack – an attack on the waves. You paddled out and you were challenging the ocean, not the other way around.

That was a common theme with all Maroubra surfers, but for me it was totally about that. Athletes reflect the places they come from, and I liked chaos. I felt my best out in the water when there was no one out and it was stormy and rainy with lightning flashing all over the place. That's where I felt the most relaxed, most at ease. We lived on the most urbanised beach in Australia and I was raised in chaos, so when it came time to do the tour I was ready for it.

What I wasn't ready for, and what I really struggled with on tour, was the fact that it was largely every man for himself. The hardest thing was dealing with the lack of a brotherhood. It was the complete opposite of Maroubra. On my first few years on tour the older guys were arseholes. Straight up, they were. There were only a handful of them – Rob Bain, Gary Green, Mark Sainsbury, Matt Hoy and Rod Kerr – who gave the grommets any respect and any type of a go. Most of the guys treated us arrogantly. They saw us as threats and treated us accordingly.

During my first year on tour we were in Spain, down in a place called Zauratz. The contest was right in the middle of a local festival, and we rocked into a town full of 50,000 mad locals all dressed in the traditional Basque outfit with white shirts, big red berets and scarves. We surfed the contest and on the last night we all went out. The boys had all said, 'You won't pull a girl here,' but I think Spanish women are beautiful, so I went out, picked up a chick and went back to her place.

I rocked up to the hotel the next morning all stoked 'cause I'd scored a hot chick, but nobody's there and my stuff's down in the lobby. Everyone had left me. The guys had packed the car and just brushed me. I grab my gear and head down to the contest site to see people are packing away the scaffolding. The next contest starts the next day in Portugal, so I'm thinking, 'Fucking hell, what do I do?'

I see this car with all the windows up, and in it I can see two guys and this little orange glow among all this smoke. I go up and knock on the window; it's wound down and all this smoke has just poured out like something from a Cheech 'n' Chong movie. It was Mark Sainsbury and Gary Green. I didn't know either of them at this stage, or, more to the point, they didn't know me. I'd surfed with Sanga at Avoca Boardriders, but he was one of the world's best surfers at this stage and I was just a kid, so I don't think he even recognised me.

'What are ya doing, grommet?'

'Look, I don't really know you guys, but I went out last night and pulled a chick and everyone's left me and I've got to get down to Portugal.'

Sanga's gone, 'Fair dinkum. Don't worry, we'll look after you, grommet. Jump in.'

So they let me throw my board in and they just looked after me the whole way down to Portugal. They were good mates with Robbie Bain, and that's when I first met Bainy. There were only a few of 'em at the time – guys who actually acknowledged the existence of the younger guys.

The other adjustment I had to make was to some extremely underwhelming surf. All my surfing up to that point had been about attacking the waves; burying your rail, putting yourself in the heaviest part of the wave. When the waves pushes, you push back. That's what Maroubra surfing had been known for, the full animal style. We mightn't have had too much else here, but we had good, powerful waves. We had reefs. We had waves with grunt.

I turn up at Huntington Beach, California, for my first contest in America, and the surf is literally half a foot, knee-high at best. And to add to the irony of the situation, I've got Brock Little in my heat. The Hawaiian was the best big-wave rider in the world, he was one of my all-time heroes, and here I am drawn against him in waves neither of us would even dream about getting out of bed for back at home. There were thousands of people on the beach. I remember sitting out there thinking, 'First up, how the fuck can I surf half-foot waves? And, second, how can I hassle the world's best big-wave surfer to surf half-foot waves?' While I was sitting there trying to find answers to these questions, Brock was busy catching enough waves to beat me. I lost the heat and I was really bummed. On my first full year on tour, 11 times I got to 49th place – which was one spot off the main event and one spot off the prize money. Frustrated? You bet I was.

I had a really good time in the States, because we hung out with the Wetherly brothers. Rusty, my sponsor, was based in San Diego so we stayed with them and they hooked us up with Benji and Jason Wetherley, who also rode for Rusty. It was really cool for us, because apart from becoming really good friends with them, their parents owned a house at Pipeline in Hawaii, right next to Jack Johnson's house. It was where all those American and Hawaiian guys hung out – Todd Chesser, Taylor Knox, Rob Machado, Kelly Slater, Jack Johnson, Taylor Steele and the Wetherleys, the whole *Momentum* crew. That was the first year I went to Hawaii, and for me, a young Aussie, that was *the* house to hang at. They had a big trampoline out the front, and everyone hung there just watching and surfing Pipe all day. This was before any of those guys had made surf movies or won world titles or sold millions of records.

It was good to have a little crew over there, because I was only 16, and a place like Hawaii is intimidating enough as it is. One time me and another young Aussie surfer, Marcus Brabant, were hitchhiking on the Kam Highway at Pipe, and when this car's gone past without picking us up, Marcus has stuck his finger up. The brakelights went on and one of the heaviest Hawaiian guys you've ever seen has got out and slapped him around the head. There was just a vibe to the place; you fuck up and it's on.

We got on really well with the American guys after that year in Hawaii. Benji and Taylor Steele came out and stayed at Ma's place the next year; that was before Taylor made his first *Momentum* movie. Koby was like a 10-year-old grommet and he was just driving these guys mad asking questions. That's what Koby used to do: ask surf questions non-stop. 'Who'd win a heat out of Kelly Slater and Rob Machado at eight-foot Pipe?' All night, all day. We'd be watching a movie and Koby's still going at it.

'Barton Lynch and Tom Carroll at six-foot Bells?'

'Occy and Tom Curren, three-foot Huntington?'

We're just going, 'Fuck, I dunno. Can you shut the fuck up for a while?' But I was already warning those guys to look out for Koby in a couple of years, because even at that age it was pretty clear he was gonna rip when he got older.

The tour was a wild ride in those days. If you wanted, it could be this never-ending party with the same people that just changed venues every few weeks and was often only interrupted by an occasional surfing contest. You'd be partying with Sepultura in Brazil one week, then dancing nude at a disco in Japan the next.

That disco dancing happened a week after I'd beaten Kelly Slater in Miyazaki, so I was in celebration mode. He was seen as pretty well untouchable on tour at that stage; he had this new bag of tricks – airs, reverses – and he was just making everyone else look silly. He was revolutionising surfing in front of everyone's disbelieving eyes, and for me to beat him was huge. I think I was the only Aussie junior that beat him all year.

Sonny Miller, the American filmmaker, had somehow acquired 20 full disco outfits – flared pants, platform shoes, vests, wigs, you name it – along with a huge old-school '70s ghetto blaster. We were all pissed, 20 of us, and we've put on our disco suits and jumped on the train into Tokyo. We took over the whole city; we danced single file down the street singing, goofing off. Matt Hoy was there, along with Rod Kerr, John Shimooka, Brad Gerlach, Sonny Miller, Marcus Brabant ... the usual suspects.

We just went wild. The mild-mannered Japanese didn't know what the fuck was going on as 20 semi-nude, fully pissed disco clowns started dancing down their main drag. We'd partied at four or five nightclubs, and by this stage we had a full entourage of people following us down the street. It was like a music video.

It was during a moment of nudity – these guys would drop their pants at the drop of a hat – that we met these Aussie chicks. One of the chicks has gone, 'Look, if you guys wanna party properly, I own a club in the city. Let's go to my bar.'

Once we get there, the first thing she's said is: 'Let's have a nude dance-off; the winner gets a thousand bucks on the bar.' It was this huge Japanese club, totally surreal; 500 people were in there, and suddenly we're up on the bar in a line with a microphone and a spotlight. The DJ goes, 'This is John Shimooka from Hawaii!' and Shmoo struts out onto the bar nude and starts dancing round. The place went nuts. The bar was packed, and there were Japanese girls' hands reaching up trying to tickle your ballbag. All the chicks are screaming, trying to grab your cock. There were flashes going off everywhere. I went last. I had a bit of a pull back stage to rub some blood into my dick. Then it's, 'Sunny Abberton from Australia!' With a full mongrel I've just stomped onto the bar, pulling out all my best disco moves – because if it's one thing all the Maroubra guys can do, it's dance. There were chicks screaming, hands all over me. It turns out I won. The thousand bucks didn't last long between us.

I can't remember much about the rest of the night, but I do know it went for two days. We were like a fucking rock band.

The tour had a pretty healthy drug scene at this stage. Party drugs like coke thrived in that kind of environment, and there were also quite a few guys smoking weed. I never did any drugs, not consciously anyway. I was staunch against it. I'd get on the piss pretty readily, but because of my mum and my upbringing, I was pretty obsessed with avoiding drugs. They did, however, catch up with me in South Africa.

I was staying in a house full of Aussie surfers in Durban. Shane Powell and me had just come back from a surf and there was a chocolate cake on the counter, which was convenient because we were starving. We made a cup of tea and ate a slice of what looked and tasted like perfectly normal chocolate cake. Within half an hour I was on the bed; I felt like I'd been hit by a bus. I then locked myself in the toilet and just started laughing and laughing. The boys came and knocked on the door, but I couldn't tell 'em what was happening because I was laughing so much. I was so paranoid; I didn't want them to see me. But I knew I needed to find Powelly – who'd apparently taken off down the street – because he'd eaten some as well. So I ran down the beach at Durban. There's this big round restaurant on the beachfront down there with huge windows facing the ocean. I'm walking along the windows with my face pressed against them, moving along like Marcel Marceau. I'm walking like I'm on the moon, on one side of the window looking in. Suddenly I freeze. On the inside, looking out, doing exactly the same thing as me, was Powelly. We've both looked at each other for a second then just broken up laughing. Powelly suddenly bolted and ran into the restaurant kitchen. I've chased him through there, and then the chase has gone on for the next two hours, all through the streets of Durban. It was just the funniest, funniest time.

Apparently we weren't the only ones to fall foul of the same hash cake. A South African guy who, like me, hadn't ever touched drugs before, also innocently scoffed a piece of the cake. He didn't fare quite so well, and had to be rushed to hospital. He was a Christian, and the cake freaked him out so much that he called for a priest to come to the hospital and deliver him his last rites.

But the beauty of the tour for a kid from Maroubra was the diversity of places it took you. You had Japan, which was like being in a cartoon; America, which was like being in a circus. Europe was like a history book and Hawaii was like being in a wrestling ring. Then you had places like South Africa and Brazil that really made you ask some big questions of yourself and where you were from.

The first time we went to South Africa, apartheid was still in place. It was freaky and it was fucked. It was such a depressing vibe. Walking from the hotel to the beach, you could feel the hatred between the whites and the blacks. I remember a lot of the surfers boycotted that leg of the tour – Tom Carroll, most famously – but as a young surfer your sponsors want you to go.

The next year when I came back, apartheid had ended, apartheid was gone, and black and white people were on the beach together. But no one was acknowledging each other. Even the kids who were playing right next to each other were just invisible to one another. We met a lot of the South African surfers and I started asking them about the whole thing, and whether they had any black friends. They were like, 'Yeah, we're sweet with it, we're not racist.'

One night I wanted to check out Durban, so I went to the local nightclub. The first thing I noticed was that there were no black people in the line. I went inside and didn't see one black face. A bit later I look around and there's two black guys sitting at a table, so I thought I'd cruise over and buy 'em a beer and have a chat.

'G'day, boys, I'm from Australia. Do youse want a beer?'

They were that shocked they couldn't talk. I ended up sitting down and getting on the piss with them all night. We ended up pretty well blind, dancing around the place; I had the best night with them. They said they'd been going to that nightclub for three months and I was the first white person to speak to 'em. It was a bit of a shock for me to see that places like that existed, because Maroubra was a full mongrel mix of races, and no one ever really even thought about it.

Brazil was much tougher. Right from the very start, Brazil is hard 'cause in some places you're seeing real poverty. I've seen it in Indonesia and I've seen it in a few other places, but in Brazil there's just this desperation. You see the look of hunger in their eyes; they're willing to do anything. We were there when there was a crash in the currency, so the cost of bread and the basics just skyrocketed overnight. There was panic in the streets.

One time while we were heading from Sao Paulo to Guaruja we were in this traffic jam, and suddenly these people have come out from under this freeway overpass; these people were living under there. They've rushed our car, begging for money. They were banging on the windows and pressing their faces against the glass. It was pretty tense, and even the Brazilian guys we were with freaked out.

I remember being down on the beach and this kid has cruised along on his skateboard, covered in grazes. I got speaking to him in what little Portuguese I knew and he told me he'd just come off his skatey. The Brazilian guy I was with kind of ushered me out of the way and told me I shouldn't be talking to that kid. He was worried I would get mugged – which over there was a valid possibility – but you sensed it was more than that. It was a class thing.

Then one of the maids in the hotel we were all staying at was raped. No one was charged, but it was assumed it was someone involved in the contest, a surfer. That rocked me. Here we were staying in a hundred dollar a night hotel, and this Brazilian girl working on a dollar a day gets raped by one of the guests. It disgusted me. The lower class just seemed disposable, just there to be used by the rich.

I saw the jobs the street kids were doing, which was just shitty labouring, pretty much, and I thought, 'Ya know, that's what most of the guys in Maroubra do.' And these Brazilian guys were just shunned. It gave me some real perspective on our situation back at home.

This was like Maroubra, just on a giant scale, and I realised the kid on the skateboard could have been a kid like me.

KOBY

KOBY ABBERTON'S SCHOOL DAY

I've never been diagnosed, but I'm sure I've got ADD.

That was my big problem at school. If I wasn't enjoying what we were doing – which was pretty well anything to do with schoolwork – I'd just drift off somewhere else. I just can't sit there, bra. If I wasn't into it I'd sit there and, no shit, I'd be watching the teacher's lips move but I wouldn't hear a sound. Then I'd start imagining they're telling me the surf's pumping. My maths teacher would be explaining an equation on the board and all I'd hear coming from his lips would be, 'Koby, that sick little bank out the front of the surf club would be fucking pumping right now. Get out there, grom.'

I was never a school person. I never enjoyed it, never liked being told what to do. Coming from my background, it was hard for me to listen to anyone really. I still don't listen to people today. No one in my life had ever really told me what I should and shouldn't be doing – Sunny has tried unsuccessfully for years – so a teacher telling me to stop firing paperclips at the other kids had no chance.

My earliest memory of Maroubra Bay Public School was almost choking to death on a 50-cent piece. It was cake day at school, and I had 50 cents to buy some cakes. I was holding the coin between my front teeth and flicking it to spin it around. The teacher told me about 10 times to stop doing it; then sure enough I've flicked it straight down my throat. Someone had to stick their hand down my throat and pull the thing out. I spewed up all the cakes I'd already eaten, and the 50-cent piece was there right in the middle of this stinking puddle of half-chewed lamingtons.

I was definitely hyperactive, but I wasn't the worst kid in the school by a long shot. The houso estates fed straight down into the school, so there were some pretty rough kids in there. Out of the kids I went to primary school with, there's 20 of them who are either dead or have done jail time. I can get a class photo from Year 6 and point 'em out: 'Bank robbery, 10 years. Drug overdose, dead. Manslaughter, six years.'

My two best mates, Jed Campbell and Ahu Taylor, didn't go to primary school with me, but we spent more time on the beach than we ever did at school, so it never really mattered. Jed used to hang out with the clubbies until I rescued him from 'em, and we started hanging out and surfing together in Year 4. Then me and Jed started playing footy with this Maori kid named Ahu who lived up the road. We all started surfing together and pretty much became best mates straight up.

We're still best mates today, 20 years later.

The year before I started high school they closed down Maroubra Bay High, they gave up trying to make it work, so I had to enrol up the road at Maroubra Junction High. They were pretty chaotic years. I never learned much, not at school anyway, and I'm pretty sure I stopped a lot of other kids learning too much as well.

Jed was at the centre of most of my trouble in high school, although he'll probably tell you exactly the same thing about me. One time he come up to me and said, 'I've got this chick who's hot for me. I'm meeting her around the back of the classroom.' This was where the guys would take their chicks to fool around, so I figured I was gonna watch and see how Jed went.

While Jed walks around with his chick, I climb onto the roof and shimmy over to the edge. I stick my head over, look down and go, whoa! Jed's getting a blowjob off her. As I'm trying to edge over so I could get a better view I've stuck my hand straight in a wasp's nest and the things have started to buzz me. I wigged out. While I'm trying to swat them away, I've rolled straight off the roof, landed on my arm and broken my wrist. All I remember is Jed looking across at me grovelling on the ground and pissing himself laughing while saying, 'Keep going, keep going!' to the girl. Still to this day that's the only broken bone I've ever had in my life.

My other good mate in high school was a kid named Theo. He was Greek, and because his English wasn't real good he and I were all in the same classes. We were just ratbags together. He was one of my best mates in Years 7 and 8. He always wanted to come to the beach and I tried to talk him out of it every time. I said, 'Bra, you can't come down to Maroubra on ya boogieboard!' The boogieboard thing just wasn't cool. But the way things turned out I guess I should've made more of an effort to get him to surf. A few years later Theo ended up stabbing Sunny on New Year's Eve, before Jai hit him with a schooner glass as payback. Theo went to jail for six years before he died of a heroin overdose.

By the time I was in Year 8, Jai had come back to school. He'd been travelling and surfing for a couple of years, and they let him come back and enrol in Year 11 at Maroubra Junction, even though he'd never even finished Year 9. He did good being the only Abberton brother to finish Year 12. But if they'd let me skip two years I would've done it as well, no worries. I don't know how much schoolwork Jai did, though. I remember walking past his caravan up home at Lexo one day; the door's swung open and all this smoke poured out. Jai walks out of the cloud, followed by one of his teachers from Maroubra Junction, both of them clubbed. I looked at the teacher, he looked at me.

'Whoa,' I said, 'what are *you* doing here?'

I was just down at the beach most of the time and rarely went to school. I'd just surf and hang out and have a fucking good time. At that stage – Year 8 – anything was better than school, you know what I mean. It's not the time to learn. Year 8 is the time when you start seeing chicks. You just want to be out and about, doing your thing, hanging out, surfing, chasing chicks. No one was at home making me go to school, so most days I'd just wake up, go surfing, have another surf before lunch, wait for the boys to get home from school, then surf again. Three surfs a day for 10 years … perfect life. The school would have cracked down on me, but they just couldn't find me. This is how seldom I went to school: a couple of times I turned up for school in school holidays and wondered why no one was there. I hadn't been there in weeks and didn't even know.

I was a nightmare at school anyway and I was never destined to last. I remember the day I was expelled. We had a maths class in the music room – nothing made much sense at this school – and this substitute teacher is trying to make some stupid joke. I'm just being the full smartarse, really giving it to this guy. I'm pissing myself laughing at my own jokes, but the teacher is fully clicking out, telling me to shut up. Everyone's freaking out and I'm still pissing myself at the back of the room.

All of a sudden the teacher pulls a saxophone off the rack and throws it at me. I was about four kids away from him, and he's got me fair in the head and knocked me out. There's a big scar there on my hairline, 12 stitches. Now everyone thinks I'm going bald, which I'm pretty furious about. I woke up and everyone was standing over me; I was covered in blood. I got up, threw my chair at the guy, and marched out of school forever. That was my last day, a few weeks into Year 9.

I couldn't get back into school, they wouldn't let me, but a few months later I thought I should try and do Year 10, so I enrolled in TAFE up at Randwick. On my first day at TAFE I turned up there with all my books. I'm sitting there at the desk, and the teacher walks past and goes, 'Have you got your books there?'

I thought I'd welcome myself to this school on day one and let 'em know I was there.

'Sure have!'

I reach into my bag, pull out my pet python and throw it on top of the chick sitting next to me.

On my way home on the bus, half an hour later, one of my good mates, Greg Winter, has seen me.

'Weren't you starting TAFE today?'

'Yeah, and I think I just finished.'

SUNNY

A FREE WEEKEND BEHIND BARS IN THE COMPANY OF
CRIPS AND BLOODS, ALL FOR THE HEINOUS CRIME OF
ILLICIT SKATEBOARDING

This happened during my last year on tour.

Coming into the Hawaiian leg I was rated number 44 in the world, and needed to make a couple of heats to qualify for the next year's world tour. I'd just lost to Vetea David in Brazil, had flown back into LA, and was due to leave the next afternoon to fly straight on to Hawaii.

A guy named Darren Brillhart, who was the Rusty rep, had picked me up from the airport at one in the morning. He'd only just started with Rusty and I'd never met him before, so we introduced ourselves, loaded my stuff in the car, and drove off to his place. I'm so tired I fall asleep on the way there. He takes me to my room, I drop my stuff on the floor, say goodnight and fall asleep.

He stuck his head in early the next morning and said, 'Look, I've got to go to work. Make yourself at home.' So I go back to sleep and wake up around lunchtime.

There's nothing to eat, so I grab a skateboard that was lying around and skate down the street to get something to eat. I'm just inland a bit from Newport Beach, so I skate out to the main road and down towards the beach, not really taking particular notice of where I've gone. After about 10 minutes I get to Newport Boulevard and started skating along the beach, smiling at hot chicks on rollerblades, watching the waves, having a top old day.

Then all of a sudden – *boom* – I've been crash-tackled from the side, straight off the path and head first into the sand. I lifted my head up, spat out a mouthful of sand, and look up and see I've been tackled by this giant cop. He's dragged me to my feet and screamed, 'You've been arrested for skateboarding in a *non* skateboarding zone!' I'm still spitting sand as he's dragged me away; then he's asked me to show some ID.

'Mate, I haven't got any ID. I'm Australian, and I only flew in last night.'

'Where's your passport then?'

'Mate, I was just skating down to get lunch. I kinda didn't think I'd need it.'

'Where do you live?'

'I've just skated the road. I don't know the address.'

'Who are you staying with?

'Err … Dazza?'

I haven't got a name, a street number, a phone number or ID. I suggest to him we jump in the car and drive back to the house so I can get my ID, but he doesn't want a bar of it. Then he gets another call on his radio, something urgent. He handcuffs me to a pole then drives off. I'm on Newport Boulevard handcuffed to a pole, there's hundreds of people walking past, and he leaves me there for three hours. *Three fucking hours!*

Eventually he's pulled up and he's got two of the biggest Mexicans you've ever seen handcuffed in the back of the car. I've gone, 'Mate, there's no way I'm getting in the back of that car. I've got to catch a plane in a few hours! I gotta be in Hawaii! I'm not getting in this car!' Once I get in the car who knows what's gonna happen. No one even knows where I am.

The cop and I have a full-on wrestling match, which I lose. They take me to the Newport Police Station, fingerprint me, and take my mug shot. They dead-set don't believe me that I'm Australian, and I start to get really scared. I suppose I'd been doing so much travelling over the past four years that my accent had mellowed; they expected an Australian to look and sound like Crocodile Dundee. This one big black sergeant says, 'You're staying here until you can prove who you are. You're allowed one phone call.' I tried to ring Rusty in Australia but the operator barred the call; I tried to ring my mum and the operator barred that call too. I was fucked.

To my absolute horror, I was then fully processed and sent to the LA County Jail. I was chained together with this assortment of heavy-looking crims and marched onto the prison bus like in the movies. Everyone was chained into their seats, and I'm off to the LA County Jail.

I just went skateboarding, for fuck's sake!

We arrive and there's one big cell with two small cells inside it. There's showers, a shitter, a table. There's a bunch of guys in the big cell: a big bikie guy, a guy looking up at the roof just chanting 'the colours, the colours', and a pair of meth heads who looked like they were ready to chew through the steel bars. I'm looking around going, 'Where the fuck am I?' I thought, 'If I don't say anything, they won't see any strengths and weaknesses in me.' I was just sticking to myself, staying invisible.

It was a Friday – shower day. After a few hours later they've come down with towels and asked who wants to shower. I said to myself, 'Fuck that, I'm not dropping the soap with these blokes lurking around.' Then one of the guys tells me they only let you shower every three days, so I'm like, okay, I better have one. I shower – and hang on so tight to the soap I leave fingerprints in it. That night I'm lying on a rubber mattress, covered by an itchy woollen blanket, my head resting on a rock hard pillow. I stayed awake all night.

Day two: I spend the whole day and another night in the cells. More psychos added to cell.

Day three: court.

Off on the bus with the prison gang all chained together. We arrive at a big courtroom; the judge and the prosecutors are in the middle, while all the other inmates are around the outside of the room, looking on from behind toughened glass.

Maybe I was wrong, but it seemed like the prisoners had been grouped together. This is 1992, when the LA gang problem was full-on. It looked like the Bloods were in one section, the Crips were in one section, the Hispanics were in another and I was in a mixed population with about 50 other guys.

We waited there the whole day. They processed you group by group. When it was the Crips' turn, they'd read out, 'Pablo Ramirez'. He'd step forward, the door would buzz open and he'd step out; they'd chain him to another prisoner and he'd walk off. I looked over at the Hispanic crew. There was this one huge guy. He's got his blue shirt buttoned to the top button, white shirt underneath, just slicking his hair back and death-staring everyone. It looked like he was ready to kill there and then on the spot.

I'm in there the whole day. Late in the arvo they're still calling guys out and marching them upstairs to the court. I'm starting to think I'm going to be in here overnight. They're calling out names randomly; then they call our old mate, the heavy-looking Mexican guy.

The guy next to me goes, 'I'd hate to be chained next to that guy.'

'Sunny Abberton,' the voice boomed. 'Step forward!'

They chain me behind this freak, and the guy is just shooting lightning bolts at me. We all walk along the circle and up this dark, vertical staircase to the courtroom, where we sit behind a table, chained together. This Mexican guy is just dragging me along, fully ragdolling me. On the stairwell I'm thinking that maybe he's just gonna shank me in the throat with a sharpened toothbrush. We get upstairs and there's a judge, a DA and a Spanish interpreter. They'd call your name and read your charge. There's murderers, armed robbers and rapists in my line. I'm the last guy and they call my name – and I know what's coming.

'Sunny Abberton. The charge is illegal skateboarding.'

Everyone just looks up and goes, 'What!' The judge is stunned.

'No other priors? Illegal skateboarding?! You've got to be joking.'

Then the guy next to me, the armed robber, fully elbows me and he's cracking up. I explained to the judge what happened and she's said, 'Well, Sunny Abberton, how do you plead to the charge?'

'Guilty.'

'Time served!'

The whole place erupts. Suddenly I was the hero, and everyone was clapping and cheering. But I was still going to have to spend another night in there, because it was too late to process me. I stood up and said, 'Excuse me, your honour, I was supposed to be on a flight to Hawaii two days ago. Is there any way I can get out now?' She's gone, No worries.

I was processed and they dumped me out on the street with my skateboard, and that was it. I was in the middle of LA. But by this stage my crew had discovered what was happening. One black sergeant in Newport had believed me and had spent two days on the phone, calling people and asking whether there was a kid called Sunny Abberton staying at their address. On the second day he found Darren's house. They thought I was missing and had filed a missing persons report.

I got on the plane to Hawaii swearing I was never going back to California again.

ahu taylor

KOBY'S OTHER BEST MATE

I arrived in Maroubra from New Zealand when I was about six and I didn't know anyone.

I was living on Malabar Road, just across from the primary school, which is where I met Koby. I still had a pretty heavy Kiwi accent and the teacher would make me stand up in front of the class and say 'fish and chips' and the number 'six' over and over. I never got what the joke was, but the whole class would be pissing themselves.

Koby took me down the beach one day, I think I might have been eight, and he introduced me to Sunny and Jai and the rest of the boys. I used to just follow Jai around like he was an absolute legend. Jai was the man. He was sponsored by Rip Curl and was doing the Search trips at the time so he was the king around here. Then Sunny took us down the beach one day with a board and showed me the fundamentals. I never looked back.

We'd leave our stuff at Ma's place, but when I got a brand new surfboard I never left that down there. If you left your shit at Ma's it was open slather. But we'd be hanging there all the time, and if there was no surf we'd all be out by the pool. The backyard was pretty funny. We'd have contests trying to do the most laps underwater, and when we got old enough we'd put beers on the bottom of the pool – this is when we were about 14 – and you had to dive down, open it, and drink the beer underwater without taking a mouthful of chlorine pool water. Hanging in the backyard was pretty cool except for when Jai and Sunny and the other boys would rock back … we'd just bail over the fence and run from 'em.

The grommet abuse we would cop was ridiculous. Jai, Sunny, Wayno, Frog and Johnny all used to hammer us. You'd be tied up inside a wheelie bin. You'd be stripped naked to a telegraph pole on Marine Parade on a hot Sunday. There used to be this prickly thorn bush out the front of Maroubra Underground, the old surf shop. We'd get stripped naked and one guy would grab your arms, another would grab your legs, and they'd just drag you backwards and forwards across it; you'd have these grazes and cuts all over you. You never went to the surf shop while those guys were loitering out the front. Apart from Ma's, that was their other big hangout.

Koby has always been the smallest out of all of us. He had this squeaky, cheeky voice, which got squeakier and cheekier when he was talking to someone he didn't like. Koby used to go all right with the chicks for a guy with a pretty boy haircut. It was shoulder length, brown and blond, and he'd fully brush his fringe over to one side. We always used to think he was in the bathroom jerking off, but he was probably just doing his hair.

It was ridiculous how much surfing we used to do. We were surfing early, sneaking for lunchtime surfs, then in the arvo – three times a day. Then on the weekends we'd be surfing five times a day. Most of it was down the front at Maroubra, but then Scotty Linford started taking us up the coast for weekend trips. Basically it'd be me, Jed, Koby, Jack Kingsley and occasionally Ben Johnson. On the way back Scotty would double-park in the middle of the Sydney Harbour Bridge and make Koby jump out of the car, grab some mud from under the wheel arches and rub it across the car's number plates, 'cause by that stage we'd be completely out of money and wouldn't have a cent for the toll. Koby would jump back in and Scotty would drive straight through the tollgates.

We used to do a lot of road trips; we'd go to team events and weekends up at Seal Rocks. There was one trip when me, Koby, Jed and our mate Kev went to Port Macquarie to see Scotty Linford, who was living up there at the time. We drove up with Kev, who'd just got his licence and a car, and between me, Jed and Koby we probably had 50 bucks if we were lucky. We're leaving Port to come home, we've got no money and the tank is empty. Kev was driving. Koby's looked at Kev and gone, 'Pull into the petrol station ... we're gonna do the runner!' Kev's absolutely shitting himself.

'Nah, I'm not doing it. It's my car! I'll get done.'

Koby's eventually convinced him to do it. So Kev fills the car, jumps in and turns the key in the ignition, but when we've driven out of the driveway the car's pumping a cloud of black smoke. We're wondering what the fuck's going on. Kev was shitting himself so much that he'd gone and filled the tank with diesel! The car's stopped about 50 metres down the road.

Me, Jed and Koby have just jumped out of the car and done the bolt, leaving Kev to deal with it. Good mates. We look beside us and there's Kev running along. Suddenly he's stopped and gone, 'Me car ... I've gotta go back for it.'

Koby, meanwhile, is already hitchhiking to the next train station and is halfway home. Me and Jed have gone back to Scotty's. We're shitting ourselves, thinking Scotty is gonna bash us, so we've broken into his car out the front and slept in it for the night. Scotty's come out in the morning with Kev, who's been upstairs all night in a warm bed, and he's gone, 'Where the fuck is Koby?' Scotty was blowing up at us only because we'd split up and left each other. Kev's eventually got the car fixed, we drove home and it was all sweet. We got home and go around to Ma's and Koby was sitting there like nothing had happened. He'd shined us. He was always the first one to start the trouble and the first to disappear ... and it's me and Jed who usually have to come in and sort out his mess.

This other time we'd all been surfing and had gotten out of the water before Koby. On his way back up the beach Koby found this pair of Webs, the paddling gloves, sitting there on the beach. No towel, no one there … Well, this is Koby's version of the story, so it might be bullshit. He said, 'I just saw 'em sitting there and picked 'em up. No one owns 'em.' Next thing he comes running into Ma's going, 'I've just been chased by these guys trying to beat me up!' There's half-a-dozen of us at Ma's at the time, so we've just bolted out, put T-shirts over our faces and ran straight for the Paki's general store next to the Seals Club. Although we used to do it every second day, for some stupid reason they always used to keep the eggs right near the door. So we've run in there all balaclavaed up, grabbed all the eggs they had, and run over and started egging the car Koby had told us belonged to the guys who'd chased him. All of a sudden that car became six cars. We thought, 'Fuck, we're in trouble here.' Suddenly the tables have turned and they're all out of their cars chasing us. We're running down the street and I'm going to Koby, 'What the fuck have you done!' Koby's split and left me.

I've run into the middle of 'The Stadium' – the park where we'd play footy – thinking I'm sweet. There were a heap of older Maroubra guys there having beers and a barbie, so I'm thinking they'll back me up here. The guys chasing us were huge, way bigger than us. We were 14, they would have been 30. This one guy has walked straight into the middle of all the boys, just took it on, and said, 'I want no dramas with any of you blokes, but this young guy and his mates has stolen our shit and egged our car.'

'No we didn't!' I protested. They've looked over – his car is covered in eggs; they've looked at me – I'm covered in eggs.

'But they were gonna bash Koby!' I offered in my defence. The boys have tapped me on the shoulder.

'Time for you to step up and be a man. You're on your own here, buddy.'

I looked at Koby, who was standing across the field watching, thinking, 'What have you done to me here!'

Koby's the biggest agitator you've ever met in your whole life and always the first to bolt. Trouble was always attracted to him, without fail.

I went to Maroubra Bay in Year 7 but it closed the next year, so I went to Maroubra Junction, where I got expelled. I ended up at Marcellin where I finished Year 10 mainly because they found out I could play footy pretty well. I could've gone places with it but I liked smoking pot a bit much. Koby, meanwhile, was fully focused on his surfing. We'd start drinking before blue light discos but Koby wouldn't have anything to do with it. All that mattered was his surfing. We'd be drinking and he'd be saying, 'Fuck that, I'm gonna be one of the best. You watch.' And look where he is. It's exactly what he said he was gonna do.

But you can't fault Koby as a mate, and it'd be hard to find a better bunch of mates than the crew we grew up with. Even to this day, 20 years on, we're all still in Maroubra and all still tight as. We might argue but we'll drink and laugh about it a day later. If you blow up at your mate he'll sit there and write you off, and next thing you're laughing back. And Koby's the best at that. He'll know something's wrong with you and he'll go, 'Bra, are you all right?' I'll start spewing out this sob story and then he'll start laughing at me and walk away.

He's one of a kind, thankfully. Another one of him running around and the world would be chaos.

SUNNY

A CURSORY STUDY OF THE SUBURB'S HISTORY OF UNSCRIPTED GUARDIANSHIP REVEALS ONE OF MAROUBRA'S FINEST WASN'T EVEN MAROUBRAN

Scotty Linford lived next door to Lucy's lolly shop on Malabar Road.

He'd grown up a couple of suburbs away in Mascot, and didn't know one end of a surfboard from the other when he moved here. Localism was really strong back then, and it wasn't easy for Scotty to get a toehold in Maroubra. The North End guys were the born and bred

Maroubra crew, and they made life tough for anyone who moved into the area. They'd call 'em 'flash-ins' and tell 'em to 'get back to Mascot'. It was really localised. So when guys like Scotty, and our mate Shane Chaplain, moved in, it was tough at first for 'em to fit in, especially seeing they didn't surf when they got here.

We met Scotty when we lived in the burnt-out ghost house up in Bona Vista. We didn't take him in at first, but we didn't shut him out either. Our generation was a little more open than the older guys to crew coming in and making a new start in Maroubra. Scotty first gravitated towards us 'cause we weren't telling him to fuck off when other people were; then his personality did the rest.

He was this rough and tough little AC/DC-looking guy. He was short, hyperactive and polite, with a laugh like Muttley the cartoon dog. He'd readily admit he was only just starting to surf, but he'd also tell you how psyched he was on living in Maroubra. He was a guy who really bought into the whole idea of the Maroubra brotherhood. If he felt someone was questioning his loyalty to Maroubra and the guys who lived here, he'd arc up. That's what we loved about him.

Because he was three or four years older than us, he became the guy who took us surfing after Blackie and Red moved up the coast. Scotty drove this strange-looking ute with a bubble hatch on the back; we'd all pile into it and drive down to Voodoo. He was an easy gee-up, as well. We could call him at work and tell him we were going down the coast, and if he had something else on we'd just go, 'Geez, mate, you're soft,' and he'd be in. We even convinced him once to drop his girlfriend to come down the coast for a weekend because she was being a handbrake. He'd drop tools in a heartbeat to come surfing with ya; you only had to call him chicken.

'Scotty, Voodoo's 12 foot. You're in, aren't you?'

'Naturally, bra.'

It didn't matter that he wasn't the world's best surfer; he'd paddle out into anything.

When we started competing, Scotty would be the one driving us – me, Jai, Wayno and Jimmy – to the events up and down the coast. We were like his kids; he'd be the one to stand up for us, even though he was only about four foot tall. One time he took us to this pro junior over at Narrabeen and we stopped in at Kentucky Fried Chicken on the way home. We were in line when these big footy players came in and pushed straight in front of us. Scotty's reached up and tapped the guy on the shoulder.

'Mate, we were waiting.'

'Beat it, shorty.'

Scotty has fired straight up.

'Outside! Now!'

Scotty has marched outside, just screaming at the guy. The footy player was about three times his size, but I think he saw the look in Scotty's eye and thought better of it.

When I was a little older, me and Wayno used to stay at Scotty's place and he'd get us into our first nightclubs. He'd lend you his going-out clothes – his shitty white shoes and bad Hawaiian shirts – and then sweet-talk the bouncers into letting you in the door even though you were 15. And if they didn't let you in he'd want to fight 'em for ya. He was right into the dance party scene. Scotty was out every night, outside the pub dancing, inside the pub dancing; he was just this ball of perpetual energy. The thing was, we could never take chicks back to either Astoria Circuit or to Ma's place. Never. You could never bring a chick back under Ma's roof – she was fully staunch no sex before marriage – so Scotty would always let us crash at his place when we had a girl with us.

But to us he was so much more than a lift to the surf or a ticket into a nightclub. He'd do anything to help us: drive you to a contest, write you a resumé, lend you $50, offer you some career advice. He was always there. He knew what we were going through at home, and that we could do with some support. And he fully believed in us.

When I left for the pro tour, Scotty pulled me aside and told me that he'd look after Koby for me, and you knew his word was gospel. I knew Koby was going to be looked after and I knew Scotty would be true to his word.

He always said to us that he was going to marry a girl one day and move away from Maroubra. And when he and Jai did that boat trip up from Timor, Scotty did it. He met a local girl while they were in port on Roti, then went back and ended up marrying her and having a baby girl. When they moved to Bali we'd hang with him every time we went over.

We did G-Land, Uluwatu, and me, Jai and Koby even went down to Sumbawa with Scotty. Scotty had a fight with a French guy down there. That's the way it'd always happen on our trips with him. We were all pretty good surfers and bigger guys than him. So as Scotty was the smallest and the guy not surfing as well as the others, he was the target. But it was the worst thing they could do. The French guy dropped in on him at Lakey Peak. Scotty had been waiting for ages for this wave, and the French guy just swung around and burned him cold. Scotty has just come up swinging and took the poor guy out.

Later, I think he just got caught up in the Bali party program; he just pushed it too far. He was always having a good time – and that's what killed him eventually.

I wrote the eulogy for Scotty's funeral. Here was the guy who'd taught us more about the Maroubra brotherhood than anyone ... and the guy wasn't even from Maroubra.

JAI

THE TRAGIC AND CAUTIONARY TALE OF SCOTTY

I didn't know it at the time, but Scotty Linford had met a local girl on Roti Island before we'd sailed up from Timor to Sumbawa.

After we'd left Scotty in Sumbawa and had flown back to Australia, Scotty travelled back to Roti to see his new girl again. He stayed down there for a month or two and fell for her. Next thing they were married, living in Bali, and they had a kid together. He was happy most of the time anyway, but he really seemed like he'd found where he wanted to be over there.

MY BROTHERS KEEPER

I hadn't seen him for a while, and when I next caught up with him in Bali, something was different. He was saying some really weird things.

'Listen, Jai, you're going to have to look after me kid, I'm not going to be here much longer. Bra, I think my run is coming to an end.'

I've spoken to a few people now in the weeks before they've died, and that's the way they talk. God gives them insights into what's going to happen.

I said to him, 'Fuck, bra, it's dangerous. What you say, someone hears. God hears what you say.' But he kept saying it; he said it four or five times.

'Scotty, you better pull up saying that shit. You're married, you've got a kid.'

The following week he was dead.

A few years later, I met a guy from Kauai who'd been there that night.

'Jai, let me tell ya what happened. We were partying and, bra, I just turned around and Scotty was blue. If I was in another country or something I might've hung around and rung the coppers, but we were in Bali and we all just got out of there. I've felt bad about it every day since, but we could have got 20 years just for being there. It was just a bad scene.'

Scotty was the coolest, funniest, loyalest mate a bloke could ever have. I loved him with all my heart – all the boys did. Scotty took me to my first nightclub, my first trip away was with Scotty, the first time I surfed big waves was with Scotty. I loved him dearly as he loved all of us dearly.

It was a huge funeral. He was one of the first of the boys to die. All the boys thought they were invincible at that time, just partying hard, going mental. When Scotty died we suddenly started thinking we weren't so invincible. It was a massive reality check. That could have been any one of us. From then on I always wanted to live for Scotty. From that time, every minute we lived was a bonus, ya know.

Maroubra was starting to change. Scotty and a handful of others were dead, Grommet and Hinesy were both in jail, and a lot of the other older guys had moved away. It quietened down heaps, bra. Our generation, we wanted to stay out of jail, stay out of trouble, because so many of the older guys went to jail and so many of them got killed. There's a photo I seen somewhere with 15 of the older core Maroubra crew in it, bra. I counted two of them still alive.

KOBY

KOBY LOSES A FATHER, BEST MATE, MENTOR, MANAGER, TAXI DRIVER, CASH MACHINE AND HORTICULTURAL ADVISER ALL IN ONE. RIP THE MAGNIFICENT SCOTTY LINFORD

Scotty Linford was like my dad and my best mate rolled into one.

Whenever he saw me he'd slip me 10 bucks; if I had nowhere to stay I'd stay at his place. He'd take us all surfing up and down the coast. He also got me my first surf sponsor, Mango clothing. They'd pay for my surfboards, which was huge for me, 'cause I had nothing. It was the best thing that could have happened to me at the time.

We had some good times together, me, him, Jed and my mate Beastie; some mad trips up and down the coast. He'd do anything for ya. To me he was everything – everything you want ya dad to be. If you got stuck somewhere you could call him and he'd come and pick you up, wouldn't think anything of it.

No matter where he was he'd come up to the school and vouch for me, tell the teachers to cut me a break, explain to them what was going on at home. Sunny was travelling on tour so he wasn't there and Jai was doing a lot of travelling, so I was kind of alone a lot at that time. In return,

Scotty never fucking asked anything of me. He helped me out with my surfing, told me I could be anything I wanted, you know. I reckon he would have thought of me as his kid. And it was strange, 'cause he would've only been 22 and I might have been 12 at the time he was helping me out.

We all heard different stories … weird circumstances. We heard he died of a heroin overdose, but we didn't know what really happened. I think he'd been partying and tried to come down with a shot of heroin. They found him in a hotel room in Bali, and he'd been there so long he'd turned black. It wasn't how a guy like Scotty should have gone out; there was no dignity in it.

I wish he was here, mate. I think about him every day. I've got him here tattooed on my arm with me, and a couple of times a day I'll stop and look at it and think about him … wonder what he'd be like if he was still here with us today, what he'd be doing.

KOBY

WHILE A NEW ABBERTON MAKES HIS DEBUT
ON THE SHAGPILE OF ASTORIA CIRCUIT,
ANOTHER IS SHOWN THE DOOR

Not many people can say they watched their little brother being born on the bedroom floor, bra.

I watched Dakota being born on my mum's bedroom floor. I was 13. Mum and Paul had been together a long time by this stage, and she'd fallen pregnant. It was near the end of her term, and I remember her telling me to make sure I'd be home that morning. She had a feeling she was going to have the baby, and she wanted us to be there.

I think Mum had the baby in the house at Astoria because she was an addict, and didn't want to have the baby in a hospital and risk having the kid taken off her. Or she might have just wanted a natural birth at home.

I just remember Mum screaming.

'Koby! Koby, get in here!'

I walk into Sunny and Jai's room and Mum's on the bed with the midwife. Sunny's there too, and Paul's holding the door. I sat there and watched Dakota's head pop out and the rest of him follow. It was pretty amazing, but freaky as shit for a 13-year-old.

'Koby,' Mum said, 'if you're not careful, this is what's going to happen.'

Mum made me watch Dakota pop out for a reason. I'd lost my virginity a few months before. This semi hottie, who was a few years older than me, had put it on me. I was like, all right, I'm on.

For the next week I thought I was killing it, until Jason Hunt, my lunatic mate, has pulled me aside.

'Koby, you know that girl from the other night? Well, she's pregnant ... and you're the father.' I was freaking! I was freaking so much that I told my mate Benny Burndred's mum Deb about it.

'Deb, I'm in trouble. I had sex with this girl and I think she's pregnant. What should I do?'

Deb was like my second mum at this stage because I stayed at their house quite a bit. I don't know if she set out to teach me a lesson or not, but she said, 'Listen, you're going to have to tell your mum.'

'I'm not telling my mum, I can't.' I was more embarrassed than anything.

Debbie gets on the phone and rings me mum and tells her. Deb was pretty fired up.

'Lyn, Koby and Benny have been out having sex. They're 13 years old!'

So I walk into Astoria Circuit and get the biggest backhander off Mum.

Three months later – three months of me thinking this chick was pregnant and I'm going to be a father at 13, three months of getting worked over by Mum and Paul – Jason Hunt calls me.

'Nah, it's all bullshit. I was only joking. Suck cocks, dickhead!'

I'm like, well, thank fuck for that. And after all that Mum went, 'Well if you're going to be out there doing that stuff, you better know what the consequences are. This is what you'll get.' She was trying to scare me off sex for life.

With Dakota on the scene now, Jai and I were on our own a lot more; we saw even less of Mum and Paul. But it was fine, 'cause by this stage, Jai and me could fend for ourselves pretty well.

Sunny had started travelling on the pro tour from a very young age. He started when he was 16. He wasn't there so much, so it was me and Jai in the house a lot. That's why we're really close now, because we were there through all of that shit. When he was there, Sunny was really supportive, but when he travelled for all those years it was at the time that most of this shit was going on with my mum and Paul, and Jai and I went through the hardest times.

We were pretty bad thieves as kids. We had nothing coming from my mum, so we got pretty good at shoplifting. I still remember a rort I used to do. I'd walk into the supermarket and wait for someone to buy their groceries then as they were walking out the front I'd ask them for their receipt. You walk back in with a plastic bag from that supermarket in your pocket and fill it full of the items on the receipt. Then you walk up to the checkout and pay for an apple, tell them you've already paid for the rest and flash them the receipt. I never got pinged for it. I also used to get the older blokes to put bets on the horses for me at the TAB, and even at that age I had a pretty good eye for a winner.

The whole situation couldn't last forever, though.

This one day I'd wagged school at about one o'clock in the afternoon because I thought Mum and Paul would be out. The door at Astoria Circuit was locked, so I climbed up the drainpipe into the house. As I got to the top of the drain I thought I saw someone walking into the bathroom, which was strange seeing as the place was locked up and quiet. I've climbed over onto the veranda and ran in and chased 'em, because I thought someone was burgling the house.

As I've got into the lounge room I remember looking down and Mum had a belt around her arm with a needle hanging out. She just screams, 'Get out! Get out!'

And I just scream back, '*You cunts get out!*'

There were six or seven of them there. Paul jumped up and grabbed a baseball bat and hit me across the back with it. It was one of those hollow silver ones, so it didn't hurt that much, but he's hit me with it. I grabbed a big knife and I'm just yelling, 'I'm gonna stab him!'

Then I put the knife down and just said, 'I'm outta here.'

I never went back. I was 13 years old then and I've never been home since.

SUNNY

THE SAVIOUR IS BORN, ALTHOUGH HIS DIVINE HOME BIRTH CANNOT PREVENT THE IMMEDIATE DISINTEGRATION OF WHAT WAS ADMITTEDLY A REASONABLY FRAGILE FAMILY UNIT

We looked at Dakota as a glimmer of hope for the family. Maybe he might be the one to bring it all back together.

We were stoked that Dakota was a boy. At that stage all we wanted was another brother who could surf with us. I also thought having Dakota would be really good for Mum because it would straighten her out, which it did for a while. She'd quite often pull herself out of it and straighten up, but she always fell off the wagon. That's what made it even harder for us, because you'd get hope and then you'd just have your heart broken again. There were always all the promises: 'This time it's for real.' And I think that's why Ma became really cynical, because she'd seen it all before even more than we had.

But we always thought that Dakota would be all right. He'd be one of us, and we'd look after him. We were really positive about it. And Paul really loved Dakota too, really loved him. We all went out to Paul's family's Christmas a few times, and we took Dakota to the beach with us whenever we could. They were really good signs for us as a family. That's why what happened next changed things forever.

I was surfing out at Stormy at Maroubra late one afternoon when I looked towards the shore and seen Koby running down the beach. I could hear him whistling at me. Even from out there, I could tell from his body language that something was wrong.

I came straight in on a wave and found him fully hysterical.

He hadn't said a word at this stage and I was really scared. I had no idea what had happened, but I knew it wasn't going to be good news. He told me what had happened – how he'd been locked out and had climbed up the drainpipe out the back and found my mum and her friends shooting up, and that Paul had hit him with the baseball bat. He was crying, but he was angry more than upset. I just grabbed him and gave him a big hug and said to him, 'Don't worry, Kobe. You'll show 'em, mate, you'll show 'em.'

I understood what he was upset about – the betrayal – and how he felt like he didn't have anyone. I just said to him, 'We've got our own family, Kobe. You've got us. We're never gonna leave you, mate. And you'll show 'em – put it all into your surfing.'

And I knew he would. That was our only way out … the only way. I knew what he was going through too. It was a huge moment, for sure. So after he's calmed down a bit I said, 'Okay, we'll fix it. C'mon, let's go.'

So we walked back to Ma's, got changed, and we got the details out of him as to what had gone down. Then we called Jai; he came over and we met in Ma's garage.

'Righto,' I said, 'we're gonna go in there and grab all your stuff and bring it down here. Koby, we'll start looking for a unit tomorrow where you can move in with me and Rowena. We'll be sweet.'

We were angry, mate. We wanted to bash Paul. Me, Koby and Jai went and got baseball bats with the full intention to beat up our mum's boyfriend and anyone else who was there. We drove up there and kicked the door in. They'd cleared out, knowing they'd stepped over the line. They knew they could never touch Koby. We were aggressive and wild enough that we weren't going to take it. It was 10 years of shit exploding in two minutes. Luckily for them they weren't there. We turned over the kitchen table and smashed up the house. If Dakota wasn't living there we would've smashed the whole place to pieces, that's how angry we were. Dakota would've only been two at this stage. But we left them a message that if you ever fucking touch us again, you know we are going to kick your arse. We took Koby's bed and his TV, we just took everything we needed for Koby, and that was it. We never went back.

We barely saw Mum and Paul after that. For two years we didn't see Mum at all, and I didn't speak to her for six. We heard Paul had left her, and that she'd moved out of the Lexo house. She'd got a new houso in New Orleans Crescent, and when her friend Annie's house burned down and they lost everything, Annie and her two girls, Holly and Sam, moved in with Mum. They still live with Mum today.

Mum would drop Dakota down at Ma's place and we'd play with him there, but we never went back to Astoria Circuit. We'd spend time with Dakota and take him to the beach, but we didn't see him much because we didn't want anything to do with Mum. Especially me and Koby; we were pissed off. Jai was always less angry; he was still angry, but mine and Koby's resentment lasted a lot longer. Koby's only slowly coming around now, 15 years later. Every year, though, regardless of what was happening with Mum, I'd make sure I was there for Dakota's birthday.

That day changed us. We used it. It galvanised us, made us wanna be something better. And our motivation was to show our mum that we didn't need her. I remember being out in the surf when mad crazy shit had been happening at home and everything was falling apart. I'm in the ocean, it's rainy and stormy and no one is there and I'm thinking, 'We are going to be the best, you know. We'll show them. They'll fucking see, they'll all fucking see!'

That was the day when, for us, the Bra Boys were really born. That was the day we realised the brotherhood was our family; the brotherhood was the only thing that counted.

KOBY

A NINE–MONTH TOUR OF THE BEST SECOND–HAND COUCHES THE 2035 POSTCODE CAN PROFFER

I went straight down and found Sunny.

He was out in the surf at Maroubra – he happened to be home from the pro tour at that stage. I've called him in and told him what had happened. I was really upset. Sunny started crying too.

He said, 'Don't worry. This day was always going to come. We all knew this day was going to come. We'll start looking for a joint. Don't worry. Just try and forget about it and put everything you've got into your surfing. That's our way out of this life.'

I never went back to Lexo, but I did break back in soon after it all happened to steal the video recorder and get my snake back. I had this massive diamond python, the biggest snake I've ever seen. Me and Scotty Linford had caught it up at his family's house at Port Macquarie one time; we'd put it in a backpack and brought it back to Maroubra. Minding his own business in the bush one day, eating rats in a glass tank at Lexo the next. You'd feel sorry for it if it wasn't so evil. It didn't have a name; it was just a big, nasty snake. It was 10 foot long, as thick as my upper arm. It lived in a tank at my house, and we used to go to Paddy's Markets to buy mice and rats to feed it. I went in and took my snake back, and gave it to my mate Shane Chappo to look after until I found somewhere to live.

Sunny was living with his new girlfriend, Rowena, at this stage, and he'd just paid a heap of money to renovate Ma's garage. I couldn't really move back in with Ma because she was still recovering from her stroke and I just would've been too much for her. I was still only 14, and I was a naughty kid. So for almost a year I just stayed on my friends' lounges; Benny Burndred's house at Hillsdale, Jed's house. I was sleeping on lounges at night, and in between that I was more or less on the streets. Benny's mum and dad became pretty much like my family at that stage. They let me stay there for months on end without asking a question. They knew I was going through a hard time, they knew my mum.

Mum didn't try and contact me at all. That's why I still don't really talk to her now. She should have kicked Paul out, not me. I was really close to Dakota when I was up at Lexo, but when I got kicked out I didn't see him for about three years. It was hard, but while I wanted to spend time with Dakota, I didn't want a bar of Mum or Paul.

I didn't see Mum for about eight years. It was a long, long time. It was hard not seeing Dakota. Looking back on it now, Dakota knows the situation we were in and understands what happened. He knows I had no respect for our mum and didn't want anything to do with her. He knows it had nothing to do with him.

I was on the young homeless allowance, which was $184 every fortnight. Because I was staying at my friends' places I was saving $100 a fortnight; I just kept saving and saving. I stayed at the boys' houses for about eight months I reckon, just dragging around my clothes and my surfboard.

I started channelling all my energy and anger – and I had plenty of both – into surfing and getting strong. I used to watch Jai and Sunny and all the boys train in the backyard when I was a kid. I'd sneak out there when they'd finished and just copy their routine, do what they'd done, and I started getting better at it, stronger. Hinesy was out of jail by this stage, and I used to go to his place a fair bit. He had a boxing ring in his backyard and I'd spar with him. When we were kids, Hinesy was the toughest guy on the beach; I thought that by jumping in a boxing ring with him some of it would rub off on me.

Considering I wasn't going to school, my surfing started to get really good. In the South Side regionals I won the under-14s and under-16s all on the same day. That was the first day I really got noticed by guys outside of Maroubra. I'd won both divisions, so they thought, 'Fuck if this kid can do that, he must be pretty good.' Soon after, Scotty Linford got me my first sponsorship. It was with Mango clothing; they'd pay for half my boards and gave me free clothes. New boards were about $200 back then, so Mango would chip in $100, and Gunther Rohn at Local Motion would shape them for me and cover the other hundred bucks. That was pretty big time for me.

By this stage I was searching for bigger challenges, and starting to look outside Maroubra. It was made pretty clear to me the day I surfed against Sunny in the final of a Maroubra Boardriders club contest. Those contests had a lot of good surfers, and everyone wanted to win the fucker. I was 15 and my surfing had come along to a stage where I was getting close to Sunny and Jai. Every time we paddled out I was surfing my arse off to try and beat those guys.

So there it was, man-on-man, me and Sunny in the final. All the boys were there on the beach, because it was the first time we'd surfed a final together, and they all knew it was going to be on.

I smashed him. I did a big reverse and got a perfect 10. I took the Abberton Cup that day. Hammered him. That was the end of Sunny Abberton's surfing career, right there, bra ...

SUNNY

THE SOBERING RESPONSIBILITY OF AN EXPECTANT
GIRLFRIEND, A 14–YEAR–OLD COLA–FUELLED SIBLING,
AND A RECALCITRANT 10–FOOT DIAMOND PYTHON

She was sitting on the rocks at the Maroubra Dunny Bowl when I first saw her. She just blew me away; she was beautiful, a Koori princess.

I had some front on me, so I ran down and introduced myself, and we started chatting. Her name was Rowena, and she'd just moved down from the Central Coast to study at the University of NSW.

About a week later I was coming back from Manly. I'd caught the ferry across the harbour and had climbed on a bus at Circular Quay. And there she was. We got the bus all the way from Circular Quay down to Maroubra together, just rapping about life. I think we both knew. That night she and a group of her friends were down the Maroubra pub, and we hit it off. That was it. I was 21, she was 19, and before I knew it we were in Europe together.

I didn't know it at the time, but this was going to be my last year on the pro tour. After I surfed the French contests, me and Row drove down to Portugal, even though neither of us could actually drive. I had no licence at the time and had only driven a car a handful of times.

So I get to the counter, and hand over my Australian learners' permit to the guy behind the counter. I'm waiting for the guy to say, '*Impossible!*' but he's gone, 'Okay, this is fine. How do you want to pay for the car?' So my mate at Rusty hands over the credit card, pays for the thing, and the bloke hands me the keys. Then to my horror the guy goes, 'Your car is waiting right out the front.' The car rental guys are all right there watching, the Rusty guy is there next to the car he's just paid for, and they're all waiting for me to get in and drive off.

Rowena's in the car, and I'm shitting myself. I've gone, 'Okay, I can do this.' I jumped in, turned the key in the ignition and slowly started lifting my foot off the clutch. The car has just started violently kangaroo hopping for about 20 metres then stalled, dead. I've looked back at them and put my hands up, laughing, as if to say, 'Geez, the cars in Australia aren't like this!' The exit road hooked back around and ran past the hire car place again before it led out to the main roundabout for the airport. So I've bunny hopped the whole way round and stalled a dozen times; it must have been pretty obvious by this stage that I couldn't drive. By the time I got to the second lap, all the hire car place staff were sitting there watching me trying to get out, no doubt thinking that was going to be the last time they ever saw that car again.

I've eventually got to the roundabout, turned down the wrong road, and a cop has come running over, blowing his whistle. I've just yelled, 'If I stop now, brother, I'm not going anywhere!' I sped around him and took off out of there.

On the way to Portugal we had three crashes, and lost both the mirrors on the car. On the freeway, three or four cars were overtaking us at a time. We were lucky to be doing 30 miles an hour and we were sitting in the fast lane thinking we were in the slow lane. Cars were beeping us and abusing us the whole way.

Once the Portuguese contest finished we stayed on at Ericeira for a couple of weeks, just hanging out, me and Row. We'd picked up a local chick who was hitchhiking, and asked her if she knew of anywhere we could stay. She told us her mum owned holiday houses in the area. It was the biggest karma score. The house we rented had three bedrooms and looked out over the ocean at Coxos – one of Portugal's best waves.

It was October, heading out of the European summer, and the mornings were crisp. Row and I would grill some toast on the old wood-burning skillet and sit in the backyard overlooking the ocean and have a cup of tea. Then we'd head down to the beach. I surfed the righthander at Coxos by myself, just pumping, and I felt it was the best I'd ever surfed. We had a great two weeks together. I completely forgot about the stress of competing in shitty waves, performing for the cameras, and the endless chase for ratings points. After travelling for so many years on tour, it was the first time I'd really got away from the contests and travelled for myself, and it made me wonder why I hadn't done it earlier.

It was the first time that I actually felt settled, and I was thinking about it a lot. Rowena was my first serious girlfriend and I'd really fallen for her. Touring the world for four years had changed me. Back home at Maroubra, everyone came from fractured families. But travelling on tour, I was staying with families all around the world, and I saw them at their best. The second year in Hossegor we stayed with a local French family who would all sit down every day and have a full three-course lunch around the table with a bottle of wine, everyone talking and laughing. I loved the European sense of family, and I started craving it in my life. I'd stay with Rusty Preisendorfer, my sponsor in California, and I remember being so stoked about simply stacking his dishwasher. I'd never done it before. I stayed with families in Portugal, Brazil, Hawaii and Japan, and they were nothing like the families I knew at home. They worked normal jobs, they sat down to meals, they celebrated birthdays, and chaos was restricted to kids under five. It opened my eyes to the rest of the world and to the fact that what was going on in Maroubra, and what was going on with our family, wasn't normal. Suddenly, that's what I wanted – a normal family life of my own. Those two weeks in Portugal with Rowena were the first little window I got into what my life could be. And I liked it.

When it came time to drop the car back, we just dumped it at the airport and run. The guy from Rusty eventually called me and told me they'd been billed five grand for the damage.

My surfing year to that point had been hot and cold. Whenever the waves had some size I'd beaten a lot of the big guys, but as soon as a contest was held in shitty waves, that would be the end of me. In Portugal my surfing felt so good, and with only three events left I needed just one decent result to make sure I'd have enough points to qualify for the tour the next year. We were going to Brazil next, and the waves for that contest had traditionally been pretty well flat every year, so before I left Europe for Brazil, I traded all my bigger surfboards for snowboards to take back home. In Brazil, I surfed through and made the second round. When I go to bed the night before the third round, the surf is half-a-foot. I'm drawn against Tahitian Vetea 'Poto' David the next morning. Poto is the biggest guy on tour, and needs a three-foot wave to get to his feet basically, so I'm drifting off to sleep that night feeling pretty confident.

I wake up the next morning and the surf is a solid eight feet. It's double overhead and has come up from nowhere. I haven't got a board over 5' 10". And guess who's the only surfer on tour who takes a 7' board to Brazil? Poto. I get down the bottom of an eight-foot wave and just slide straight out 'cause my board's way too short; Poto just kills me. When I get to Hawaii I have to do all right at Haleiwa and Sunset; I go out early in both – and that was it. I'd missed out on the elite tour by four places, and was relegated to the qualifying tour the next year. I was 21.

That result spoke to me. It was a sign. I was basically living a double life. They were fully two worlds, and I didn't know who I was in either. On the road I was this super-obsessed professional surfer, a bit unsure of myself, and struggling for a bit of guidance and responsibility. Then I'd come back to Maroubra and there'd be fights every day, my 13-year-old brother had just been kicked out of home, and I was the one being looked up to for a bit of guidance and responsibility. Maroubra was all about a brotherhood, while the tour felt like every man for himself. Where was Koby going to live? How was he going to survive? It began to dawn on me that I couldn't be both a father figure for the family *and* a travelling pro surfer. I was going to have to pick one.

Mark Sainsbury had died earlier that year. One of the few guys I actually felt any real connection to on tour was gone. He'd travelled home from overseas just to surf in an Avoca Boardriders contest; he'd suffered a brain aneurysm while surfing Avoca Point and drowned. What brotherhood there was on tour was scattering. I was just burned out at 21.

A month after Portugal, me and Row have gone to Hawaii, where we've hung out most of the time at the Weatherleys' place at Pipeline. Kelly had already won the world title by the time the tour got to Hawaii, so he was hanging out at the Weatherleys' a lot with his girlfriend at the time, Bree, so the four of us were together quite a bit.

We got back to Maroubra just before Christmas. Rowena and I were still living in the garage at Ma's place. Because I was away so much, it was stupid to pay rent on my own place, so we'd fixed up the garage with running water and a little bathroom to make it more comfortable.

Rowena, meanwhile, had developed this little potbelly. She was on the pill, was still getting her periods; she had two pregnancy tests that both came up negative. We went to the doctors because we didn't know what was going on. She was bloating up, getting cramps and morning sickness, but everything was telling us she couldn't be pregnant.

'Congratulations, Rowena,' said the doctor. 'You're four-and-a-half months pregnant.'

We went and had an ultrasound straightaway. As soon as we saw our baby kicking around in there, that's when it became real. I wanted a family, and here it was. I vividly remember walking around the front of the house to talk to Ma that afternoon. She was at the front door, as if she was waiting for me. I don't know if it was the look on my face that gave it away, but she's said straightaway, 'What's up?' with a kind of half grunt, half shrug of her hands.

'Nothing, Ma.'

Straightaway she's pointed at me, then pointed out the backyard to Rowena, and then started rubbing her belly. She knew. Ma had sensed it.

'No, Ma, she's not.'

Ma's just looking at me, smiling and nodding. I just started cracking up. I said, 'Yeah, okay, Ma, she's pregnant.'

And that pretty well sealed it. With Koby being kicked out and Rowena now pregnant, I knew my days on tour were over. I had a kid on the way. I was looking after Koby and, to a lesser extent, Jai, who was still living with Ma. I surfed the first contest of the new season up at Kirra, telling myself that if I did no good, I was done with it. I bombed out in the early rounds. A few days later when Rusty rang to see what my plan was for the year and to book my tickets, I said, 'Boys, I don't want to go. I don't want to do it any more.' Even though everything had been telling me to quit, and I was sure in my own head I wanted to quit, it still wasn't an easy call to make.

We weren't going to have the baby in a garage – Maroubra wasn't Bethlehem – and with Koby sleeping on lounges, we needed to find somewhere for us all to live. Luckily for us, a unit in the block next door to Ma's was up for rent and it was cheap. It was nothing special, but I think the fact that it was ours, we were paying for it, and we were this little family – me, Rowena, our unborn child and Koby – made it feel like home. And it was in the perfect position – right next to Ma's and a stone's throw from the beach.

Koby was a pain in the arse to live with, though. He was the hypo-est little kid you've ever met. He never stopped talking, never stopped fidgeting or moving around, never stopped tapping stuff, which in a small unit really got on our nerves. He used to drink heaps of Coke, four two-litre bottles of the shit a day. He'd just walk around the house carrying a two-litre bottle of it, swigging out of it from breakfast to bedtime. It's a wonder he's got any teeth left. And he's the last guy who needs to be drinking Coke. I'd go home and try and relax, watch TV, and he'd be sucking on a bottle of Coke, feet on the table, chewing gum at 100 miles an hour while bashing out this drum solo with a chopstick on the coffee table. The full ADD pest.

It took a little while for Koby and I to rebuild that same kind of relationship we'd had when I left for the tour four years earlier. In that time he and Jai had got really close. Even though there's only a year between me and Jai, and six years between Jai and Koby, those two have kind of always teamed up against their older brother. They'll say it was my travelling that did it, but it's always been that way. I think it was to do with the fact that I took on the role of the father figure, and I was the one who'd be telling them what to do. I was the authority figure and they didn't like authority figures. That brought 'em together. We all had close relationships, but it was different with me; I was like the old man. I think Koby resented the fact I'd left him, because he's blocked out a lot of those good times we had before I went. But by the time I'd quit the tour and was back on the scene, Jai had started travelling a lot, so I kind of filled that void a bit.

Rowena was still in the early stages of her pregnancy when her brother Ben came down from the Central Coast and stayed with us. Ben had only been surfing for a couple of years but had got right into it. He and Koby used to hang out and became good little mates. Ben was the full bush kid, which is part of why Koby liked being with him. Anyway, Koby had this huge fucking diamond python that must've been at least eight foot long. I'd already told him he wasn't allowed to keep the snake in the house because both Row and I had real snake phobias.

So we're all sitting in the unit one night, Koby and Ben included. We've just had dinner and Row says she's tired and she's gonna go off to bed. Row has turned off the light, pulled the sheet back and jumped into bed. Next thing there's this full horror movie scream. I've jumped up and ran in. Row is in the corner of the room, white as a ghost.

'There's a fucking snake in the bed!'

I turned around just in time to see Koby and Ben bolting out the front door. Row was so scared, she was bawling for hours. They didn't come back that night. I caught 'em outside the flat the next day; I've grabbed 'em and kicked both their arses.

Not long before that, I'd gotten suss on Koby. He was up to something. I'd smelled pot on him. I pulled him up and asked him whether he was smoking and he made some excuse about someone smoking in the car he was in. I was staunch anti-drugs, hated the shit, even pot. I've gone into his room and I'm looking at his cupboard, thinking I'm hearing things, because his cupboard is humming. I didn't gerry at first. Then a few days later I looked in his room and pretty well every stitch of clothing he owned was in a pile on the floor. It struck me then that I'd never seen the cupboard opened. And that's when it hit me. I've just gone, 'That little fucker's growing pot in there!' I've stormed in and busted the cupboard open and there they were. He had the full hydro set-up. There were only four plants, but they were pretty big. I've grabbed 'em and ripped 'em out; I was clicking. When he got home I marched him into his room and gave him a bit of a lashing, told him his plants were gone and if he ever did it again I'd bury *him* in a pot plant.

I didn't care that it was only pot. I just didn't want him going down that road at all, especially not at the stage of his life he was at. He had all this talent and I just didn't want to see him waste it. Turns out he wasn't smoking the shit, but he wasn't going to tell me what he was really growing it for.

KOBY

A BEDROOM CUPBOARD WITH HYDROPONIC TENDENCIES
BECOMES KOBY'S SURF TRAVEL TARDIS

Yeah, I was growing a lot of hydro in my room. I'd lie in bed with the lights off and my cupboard would be like a spaceship, just lit up and humming.

I started selling weed because I didn't have a cent. I was getting a homeless allowance, but now that I'd moved in with Sunny and Rowena it was costing me $100 a week in rent. Scotty Linford taught me how to grow the shit in my bedroom. I'd seen other guys selling it and straightaway I saw it was a chance to make my own money. I learned how to grow the chronicest hydro, and I was selling it for about $600 an ounce, which was just ridiculous. I wasn't that big a fan of drugs myself, after seeing my mum and what they were doing to her and all, but I was smoking a little bit, sure. I was about 15 when I started smoking it, but I didn't like it that much, bra, and I'd stopped smoking it altogether six months later.

But Sunny was starting to get suspicious. I'd stashed a lot of my money away, which I was going to use to travel, but I was also flashing a fair bit of it around. And he also wondered why my clothes had never ever found their way into my cupboard. Sunny is so anti-drugs, hates 'em. While me and Jai have both taken drugs, Sunny is straight-up staunch. If he walked in and you were halfway through a rail of coke he'd grab the bag and flush the lot down the toilet, then stick your head in there and flush that too. When you backchatted him he'd punch you. Well, I came in one day and my plants were gone and Sunny was just standing there, fuming. It kind of put an end to my dope days, but I was off and running by then.

I still had the snake at this stage. Sunny's chick was pregnant and me and her little brother Benny came home one day and put the snake in her bed. They've come home and I've heard Rowena scream, then heard Sunny yell, 'You fucking little cunt!' We just bolted.

Now, me and Jai have had a lot of fistfights, but me and Sunny never have. When Sunny caught me the next day he just punched the shit out of me. It's the only time he ever beat me up, but I deserved that one, Rowena being pregnant and all. I ended up selling the snake for $500 to my mate Chappo, but he cranked up the heater in its tank and burned its head off. I moved out of Sunny's place soon after and went back next door to Ma's. I was pretty loose at that stage and, with a kid on the way, I think Sunny was pretty relieved when I told him I was moving out. Anyway, I was cashed up and planning to travel, like Jai, so it made more sense to move back in with Ma where I wasn't paying rent.

My weed money I had stashed away got me travelling. I went to Bali first with my mates Jack Kingsley and Jamie Gore – Frog. Bali is the first place we all went to overseas; it's got perfect waves, chicks, clubs, and you can basically do whatever you like. It's still our favourite spot today. I must've been 15 on that trip, I reckon. We went down to Sumbawa. We were pretty clueless at the time, and we went in March, so the waves were pretty shitty. We stayed a month, but for about four of those days we just had it firing. As soon as I got back I was thinking to myself, 'I've got to go away again.' I pulled out another wad of weed money and a month later went back to Bali.

Later that year I went to Hawaii for the first time. I went by myself and stayed at Mark Foo's backpacker hostel. It was so good over there, bra. The best waves I'd ever seen, all my surfing heroes, surf photographers – the whole deal. I surfed myself stupid. I didn't surf Pipeline much because it was too crowded, but I surfed heaps at Sunset and Backyards.

And then I surfed Waimea Bay for the first time. It was 20 foot, and I should have been shitting myself, but for some reason I wasn't at all. It was just like surfing big Lurline back at home, just in boardies and with a hundred Hawaiians out there. I paddled out on a 7' 6", the longest board I had, which was like a toothpick compared to the boards the Hawaiian guys were riding. I caught the biggest wave of my life that day, and annoyed the shit out of those guys, paddling inside 'em all. I got some good ones, I got flogged on a couple, and got caught inside by a 20-footer, but it was no worse a flogging than I'd already had a heap of times surfing big Lurline. There was no tow surfing back in those days, so Waimea was about it as far as big-wave surfing got. I was stoked I did all right that day. At least I could go back to Maroubra and tell the boys I'd surfed Waimea, which is the reason 90 per cent of guys paddle out there.

That trip really got me noticed, though. I got back and Billabong wanted to sponsor me. They had so many good guys on their team, though, that I was way down the list. I hated that. I wanted to be the top guy. So I went over to Rip Curl, but they wanted to get me on to this freesurfing, travel program. At this stage I wanted to surf contests as well and win prize money and world titles and shit, so I didn't last long there either. I eventually signed with MCD, which was cool because I was being paid in American dollars, so I was getting two Aussie dollars for every US dollar in my contract.

I really had a taste for the travel now. Jai had made a surf movie up in the islands of Indo the year before, and he asked me if I wanted to go on the same boat the following year. You can guess my answer – 'Fucking oath, bra. When do we leave?'

The islands we were going to, Asu and Bawa, were way up off north Sumatra. On the way there, me and Jai decided to take a quick detour. We took a boat out and surfed this big, perfect righthander called Apocalypse, which breaks off these perfect, uninhabited jungle islands full of tigers and monkeys and shit. To get there, you've got to sail out from Jakarta for a day across open ocean; and that was the first time I discovered I get chronically seasick.

When we get out to Apocalypse, it's 10 foot and the most perfect wave we've ever seen. By this stage, though, I was so sick I was paralysed. I was just lying there on deck. I could hear everyone whistling when the sets came through and I could only just muster the energy to lift my head off the pillow to see Jai inside another giant barrel. It was bad enough I was crook as a dog, but to be missing perfect waves made it a thousand times worse.

They thought I was going to die. I was throwing up for days on end. I was completely fucked, the sickest I've ever been in my whole life. I must've been close to being dead, 'cause I had nothing to eat or drink for a week. I remember Jai trying to give me water and me just telling him to fuck off. The only thing that was going to help me was to get back onto land again. I thought if I didn't get to land soon I was gonna die. I couldn't be out there any more. So one morning I jumped overboard, swam in, and just crawled up the beach and fell asleep. I was hoping a tiger was gonna jump out of the jungle and chew my throat out, 'cause I just felt like shit. I was a fucking corpse.

By the time we got on another boat to head out to Asu and Bawa I'd finally got my sea legs, although I'd dropped almost a stone in weight. That was a huge trip for me; it really opened me up to travelling and surfing. They called it 'Davo's contest' – Dave Davidson from Bondi had organised it – but it was just a heap of Jai's mates, all top Aussie pro surfers, hanging out and having fun in perfect tropical surf. At the end of the trip they nominated a winner.

The waves got really big, and we were all charging hard. Jai was winning the contest when he got head-slammed and busted his eardrum, so they subbed me in his place. It was a wild trip. I was the grommet of the trip, and they cut my hair and tortured me – the usual stuff – but when you're out on those boats you all become pretty good friends. It was one of the first times I actually got treated like one of the boys by the older guys. I was still pretty young then, only 16, but I could see I was surfing as good as those guys; they were just smarter and more experienced.

I realised this was what I wanted to do with my life.

The boat sailed back to the famous island of Nias for the annual world tour contest there. I got a start in the contest – the biggest contest I'd been in up to that point.

We got there and just went, 'Holy shit.' The wave wraps into this perfect bay lined by palm trees; it's one of the most beautiful places in the world. We stayed there for a month in the best *losmen* overlooking the point. It cost us about three bucks a night, and you'd just wake up in the morning and look out over this perfect wave. Still to this day it's probably the best place you can go in the world for surf.

The contest started and the surf was eight foot and as perfect as it gets. It was my first big contest, I was the youngest guy in the field, and I made the fucking semis, bra, straight up. If I'd given myself more of a chance I reckon I could've won it, but I was so surprised I'd even made the semis that I was almost happy enough with that. The waves were eight foot, square as anything, and just running. I just got paid four grand to surf perfect waves. Like, where do I sign up for this?

That four grand didn't last me real long, and if I wanted to go away again on another trip I was going to have to work for it. Bra, I went home and worked as a fucking garbage man for a while. Three days. I'd had enough by then. I was on the trucks but I hated it. I did it over Christmas, and the whole place stunk of prawns and seafood that had been sitting out in the sun all week. Then I worked with my mates Jimmy Olsen and Gary Fox as a carpet layer for six months. In a way, I wished I kept it up, just as something to fall back on one day. Jimmy and Gazza have helped a lot of the boys out with work over the years. Everyone looks up to those guys. If you're not a carpet layer here, there's not much else to do. You're either a carpet layer or a pro surfer or a bit of both.

I went back to Hawaii later that year, staying with my little mate Lee Winkler who I'd met when we done a few junior contests together. Wink's so funny, the full country boy from Coffs Harbour, drinking his beers and JDs every afternoon, smoking his cigarettes, but such a good bloke. When I started doing the tour in the years to come he was one of my main travel buddies. But we almost lost him in Hawaii that year.

Backdoor was about six to eight foot late one afternoon, and Wink and I thought we'd go for a quick surf right on dark. The crowd had settled down, everyone was getting out, but it was warpy Pipe, it wasn't perfect. So we went flying out and got a couple. Me and Wink were always really competitive, ya know. I snaked him for the first wave of the last set of the day, and I rode it all the way to shore. I walked up the beach and was watching him. It was getting real dark by this stage and Wink was the last guy out there. He missed the second one, missed the third one, and then I seen him take off on the fourth. I'm going, 'Don't get a better one than me, ya little cunt.'

Wink took off and went to bottom turn, his board has skipped out and he's landed face first at the bottom of the wave. I was laughing hysterically at this stage. Sometimes when ya fall in the flats the wave will push you out in front of it and wash you in. Well, this wave has dragged him back up into it instead. All I see is this dark, hairy little shape going up and over in the lip. I'm still laughing.

I never used to wear a legrope over in Hawaii. I reckon that's always how you break your board. But Wink *always* used to wear one; he'd say to me, 'If anything happens, how are they gonna find ya if they can't see ya board on the surface? You're just gonna be under the water, dead.'

Well, I seen him go over in the lip face-first like a dumb bodysurfer, and I was still laughing. Then I saw the next wave come through, and he was still right in the impact zone. The wave had just held him there. The next one has just *whoomped*, fully detonated, and has picked him up and just destroyed him. It was then that I noticed he looked weird. He looked limp. I stopped laughing. It was like he wasn't fighting it. I kept watching as the last one picked him up and slammed him. I've gone, 'Fuck, he's in trouble.'

I grabbed my board and paddled out. Luckily, the last wave had pushed him out of the death zone and washed him in a bit. Backdoor's only a 50 metre paddle, but by this stage I thought he was dead. I found his board and followed his leggie down to him. I pulled him up by his leggie and managed to lay him on my board; I lay down on top of him and started paddling.

I knew he was fucked. There was no use me going, 'How you looking, mate?' There was no time. As I've swung him on the board I saw he had a big hole in one side of his head and the other side was all sliced up. And I could see the colour of him: he was white as a ghost. He's always been pretty white, but this was something else. He was purple-white. He was out cold.

Then I tried to catch a wave in, forgetting that his board was dragging behind us, still attached to him by his leggie. I've gone to catch this wave and we're off. Then all of a sudden his board has grabbed in the water and stopped us dead. I'm holding my board's rails with Wink underneath me, and suddenly we've just stopped dead. Wink's head has snapped back, I've snapped forward, and I've fully headbutted him. It was a gnarly headbutt, but it brung him back to life.

Suddenly Wink's gurgling and whinging, but we've lost the wave. Then he's back under water and we're separated. When I pulled him up again his eyes were moving, there were signs of life. I got him to the beach and Kelly Slater, Chris and Dan Malloy and Brock Little were all there. It was late, and there were no lifeguards. Wink was fucked. He had a pulse but he was out. So we've started pumping his guts to get the water out of him.

He got airlifted to Honolulu. I was filthy because I didn't get a ride in the chopper. We drove to the hospital, but they wouldn't let us in because he was still in intensive care. We rang his mum and she came straight out from Australia. Three days later we're finally allowed to see him. He's lying on the bed, out cold. He'd busted his eardrum, had a hole in the head, broke his collarbone, stitches in his head, fractured jaw. He'd fucked himself up.

We're there with his mum and the doctor goes, 'Who pulled him out?' Wink's looked up at me – and this is when I knew he was all right. He's smiled his dumb Wink smile, pointed at me, and gone, 'Fucking him!' He was filthy it was me who'd rescued him, 'cause he knew I'd give him shit about it for the next 70 years.

I'm going, 'Yeeeeeeeah, Wink. I'm the man.'

Then his mum goes to me, 'What do you want?'

'What do ya mean?'

'I'll buy you whatever you want.'

'I want one of those new Club Sport Commodores, thanks.'

I remember Wink's head going all red; he's trying to jump out of bed with all these wires hanging out of him, and the machines are all beeping, going crazy. He tries to attack me. 'You're fucking kidding me, aren't ya! Asking my mum for a new car!'

'I shoulda left ya, Wink.'

We all just started pissing ourselves laughing.

About a year later Wink pulled me aside after a few beers and he's gone, 'Fuck, mate, you saved my life. The doctor had said one more wave and I was dead. One hundred per cent. They couldn't even believe I survived.'

JAI

EQUATORIAL PISSINGS AND THE EMERGENCE OF MAROUBRA'S NEW SURFING *WUNDERKIND*

The ocean was our escape, you know, fucking oath. All our lives it's been an escape.

When Koby come running down the beach that day, that's what Sunny said to him. And it's true. When Koby jumped through the window and found Mum and Paul on the nod, then had a fight with 'em, pulled a knife on 'em, got hit with the bat and then ran out, that day changed a lot of things, bra. I remember Koby was heaps upset.

I know Koby didn't talk to Mum for 10 years after that – Sunny also. I never turned my back on her. Never, no matter what. She was my mum. I felt bad for Koby sometimes, like maybe I should be with him and Sunny and bar her. Koby knew how much I loved him. He knows if it came down to it, I'm with him, before anyone else in the world. I just felt if I barred her, maybe she'd just give up or something.

That day, Sunny was going, 'Don't worry about it. There's none of those problems in the ocean.' That's why we'd always just surf, why we'd always be in the water. No worries in the ocean. Life for us always seems to be better when we're in the ocean.

Koby was obviously listening, 'cause surfing's pretty well all he did for the next few years. He overtook me, for sure. But he never used to surf any comps; he'd just surf Red Sands and Voodoo with us, the heaviest waves he could find. He was a little madman. So we made a plan to go to Indo together, get out on the boats off Sumatra and just surf the heaviest, most perfect waves we could find.

The first place we went to was a place called Apocalypse. We hooked up with a boat in Jakarta called *Just Dreaming*, and we told the skipper to take us to the heaviest wave he can find. The skipper's gone, 'I've got this wave I know, but you blokes might be shitting yourself. I've taken heaps of guys to this place and everyone's shat 'emselves.'

He took us there, and we just had it perfect for two days, bra. To this day they're still the two best backhand sessions I've ever had. And I could surf all right then too. I surfed that right eight to 10 foot by myself for two days on my backhand.

Our mate Brook Silvester was up there with us filming for a surf movie called *Idyllic Indo*, and a heap of my waves from Apocalypse didn't make it on there. Koby, though, the poor little cunt never even got wet. He was that seasick he couldn't lift his head off the pillow, couldn't even come out on deck to watch. Meanwhile, I was just getting stand-up barrel after stand-up barrel. He was shattered. He got so seasick, I felt sorry for him. He lost a heap of weight. I was worried about him, but he bounced back.

Then we went to the islands up north and caught up with our mate Dave Davidson. He'd invited a heap of his mates up there and we were going to surf a contest. It wasn't a real contest, more just eight guys going surfing.

We had the maddest waves at Asu and Bawa. Tommy Carroll was there on another surf trip and he surfed with us. The set of the day came through and he was paddling for it, fully going to drop in on me. I've just yelled, '*Oooss*, Tommy! What are ya doing, brother? I'm taking off 15 foot deeper than ya! What's up, Tommy?'

I've come out of the barrel and just stood tall and claimed it. It was a mad wave. That was me first wave in that comp at Asu. Then I popped me eardrum. I got a sick one in the end bowl; I've gone to pull off the back of it and the lip's hit me in the chest and taken me over with it. I landed on the side of my head and popped me eardrum. I was fucked, bra. It hurt like hell, and all my balance was gone. That was the end of my trip. The boys let Koby take my place, and he ripped. He was only 16, he was the grommet on that boat, but he really stood up, drawing these sick lines in pretty powerful surf. That's when he came of age, I reckon, that trip. I was so proud of him.

Then we sailed in from Asu to Nias. It's on the equator there, so it's hotter and steamier than anywhere you've ever been. It's a beautiful place, but I hated the village. The villagers there at Lagundri on Nias were ripping each other off, robbing the tourists. Two of our old Maroubra mates, Sean and Matty, had gone up there to run boats and surf charters out of the village, and a few of the locals set 'em up with mull plants in their backyards. They ended up doing a fair bit of jail time for something they didn't do. When we got there, they were under house arrest in the village. They were allowed out of jail but they weren't allowed to leave Lagundri, so they couldn't come home to Australia. 'Prisoners of the barrel' we called 'em, because even though they were technically in jail they could surf as much as they wanted. They were in jail, getting barrelled in perfect waves. I'd say to the boys, 'I could think of a lot worse places to be jailed than here.' I wouldn't have minded doing my time there.

Soon after we got there, I had to fly home. I had to get out of there; I couldn't sit there and watch perfect waves. They said I couldn't fly with my ear, because of the pressure. But I just couldn't sit there and watch pumping waves and not be able to surf 'em. That would've hurt 10 times more.

After I went home all the boys, including Koby, surfed in the world tour contest that was on there at Lagundri. Bra, I knew Koby would do well there, God bless. I seen the footage later and he blew the house down. It was a world-class field, some of the best surfers in the world, and Koby made the semis. He just drew different lines to the other guys. All the overseas guys were just tripping on him, wondering where the fuck this kid had come from. No one had heard of him outside Australia. No one had really heard of him outside Maroubra. He shined on that trip.

I was doing a shitload of travelling at that stage. I did a Mentawais trip with Gary Green. He'd dropped off the tour and was really the first guy who got paid to go freesurfing for a living, which, looking back, is what I probably shoulda been doing. The Mentawais were called The Sinking Islands back then, and it was before they got popular. There wasn't a soul up there and there's these perfect little waves wrapping around these perfect, empty islands. It was paradise up there.

But Bali was always my favourite. One year I did four Indo trips in the season, three of them to Bali. It's a bit of a ritual with the Maroubra boys, ya know, has been for years. Whenever you went over, you'd run into more Maroubra guys there than ya do walking down McKeon Street. Wherever you go you team up, but I've flown over to Bali one-out a few times. You start one-out, then within three days there's 20 of you drinking and going mad at Double Six. The Maroubra guys just like getting the fuck out of Maroubra I think, and Bali's their favourite.

One of my early trips to Bali, I started realising there's higher powers out there. It's a powerful place, bra. We were somewhere up in the mountains, and I saw this guy in this Balinese Hindu ceremony with a full-on metal sword, ramming it in his guts and bending the sword. I was thinking, 'How the fuck is that guy doing this? What kind of spirit has he got flowing through him?' One time this bloke was telling me about how he was in Bali and had been fucking up on drugs and was in a really bad place in his life. Then one day he was walking down this street and he suddenly felt a presence. He kept walking along then *boom*, his dead father's spirit stopped him like he was hitting a brick wall. All of a sudden his dad was standing there in front of him, wearing this mad Balinese mask, saying, 'You better pull up, son.' His dad had been dead for years. And I believe stories like that because I've experienced things too, you know what I mean. The spirits channel through Bali; you can feel it.

In the mid-'90s we went through a big dance party phase over there. Once me and Nath Rogers were at this sickest dance party, this Nyang Nyang party, which turned into this huge day party out past Uluwatu. Those Nyang Nyang parties were massive. We just walked out in the bush and I'm going, 'There's no party out here, these cunts are tripping!' We went down this little dirt track and we just hear the music – *boom boom boom*. The strobe lights were going off and the jungle was going mad with thousands of people. The forest was full of Euros, full of Indos, all hacking it up, all pinging, even though it's a year in jail if you're caught.

And then there's the motorbikes. The boys always get on the bikes over there and rip it up. Me mate Johnny, the sickest cunt, he always gets this souped up 250 bike when everyone else is on Tigers over there. We're going out to Ulu one day and this copper is standing on the side of the road, and he's going to Johnny, 'Pull over, pull over.' Johnny's just hit it and burned off around him, weaving in and out of traffic. Johnny always said, 'Fuck 'em. Just take off when the Indo cops try and pull ya over on the bikes.' Johnny went so sick in that chase – blew 'em.

The next day I was hammering out to Ulu for a surf. I was one-out because I'd got up late. I was punching it out there, and here's the same copper standing on the side of the road. After seeing Johnny's effort I've just lined this guy up and gone for it, straight around him. Bra, he's just dived out of the way; I just missed him. He's got up and jumped on his big *CHiPs* bike. I look behind and here he is, pegging after me. I raced him all the way to Uluwatu trying to outrun him on the windy little road, dodging trucks full of chickens and whole families on motorbikes.

I got to Ulu, quickly hid the bike, got me board and bolted down the cliff, got out there and went surfing. For two hours the boys reckon he was doing laps of the car park waiting for me to show up. He asked the boys where the guy on the bike was, reckoned he was going to shoot him.

I'm smart about riding bikes there. I drive hard when I'm straight, and slow when I'm not. It's a sweet tactic, bra. When I'm pissed I take it easy, drive like a grandma. I'm here to survive, mate. You gotta have survival tactics over there. In the early days I wouldn't eat meat over there, outside of Bali. Who knows what you were eating, bra? Dog satay for sure. It's the easiest way to get sick, so I'd always eat vego or pick the meat out of my rice. That's changed today. Once you've eaten jail food, everything you eat starts to look pretty good.

I'll always come home from Indonesia with nothing. I've had the best fake Rolexes, I've had the best fake Omegas, and I just give 'em away. I can't help it; it's something in my nature. I don't need material things, especially over in Indo when I see how the Indonesians live. I give away my boards, my T-shirts, and I do the same every time I go over there. That's what I want to do, that's my dream: I want to make millions then give it all away. I never go without anything, I eat every day, I've got a roof over my head, so what more do I need?

I always felt at home when I was in Indo. The poorer the village, the more I liked being there. I just like living with the people. I like to stay in villages on bamboo floors, living how other people live. I've only ever stayed in a motel in Indonesia a handful of times. It's bullshit. To me, staying in a Hilton is just a waste of money. People come back and say, 'Gee, the food was nice in Bali,' and they didn't set foot outside their resort. I'd rather stay in the cheapest, shittiest joint with the locals; I'd rather stay in the ghetto with the people. At least I know it's all real.

SUNNY

SUNNY ABBERTON BURIES HIS PRO SURFING AMBITIONS
MAROUBRA UNDERGROUND

I was fighting it.

For two years after I quit, if I heard anything about a surf contest I felt sick in the stomach. I felt ill, they disgusted me. I couldn't watch a surf video or read a surf magazine; they made me nauseous. Maybe I had that athlete's crash. I started at 15 and retired at 21, when I should have just been starting. In my last year, I'd beaten all those guys; I was in my prime when I quit. I regretted it in some ways, but I knew the decisions I made were for the right reasons, and they all led me to where I am today. I dropped off the tour to try and have a normal life, to raise a family, to surf and throw myself into the culture of the beach. My life had all been about contests and getting my photo in the mags and all that bullshit. This was just about living.

My normal life started when I began managing Dave Gyngell's Maroubra Underground surf shop. It was my first full-time job. I was working mainly at his Maroubra store in McKeon Street, but I'd also do some days over at his Bondi store. Working in the surf shop, I was amazed by the number of people who would come in and ask, 'Where do I go if I want to learn how to surf?'

'Err, you know what, I don't think there is anywhere.'

Then the light bulb appeared above my head. My surf school idea seemed like a winner. Gynge set me up with George Quigley, who was the head beach inspector at Bondi. We went to No Names and had lunch and a beer, and it was all sweet. I sent my letter in to the council and I was off and running – the only surf school in Sydney's eastern suburbs. Before long I started a school at Maroubra as well, and I was making shitloads of money. I couldn't believe I was the only guy in Sydney doing it.

The surf school money was so good I could use it to pay our rent and buy our food, and sit on my surf shop wage for months without touching it. But more than that, I was happy to be at home and have a girlfriend and a normal life. I'd fully moved on.

Most of the shops on the beach at Maroubra have a bit of history, a lot of it shady. There were rumours that the pizza guy melted down gold in the pizza ovens, and rumours that the Seals Club was a meeting place for some colourful underground identities. The fish and chip guy was shot up in Kings Cross. No wonder Gynge called his surf shop Maroubra Underground.

The shop also doubled as a surf check for the Maroubra guys who were in jail at the time. We were a hotline to the outside world for several correctional facilities, providing surf checks and daily updates on the vagaries of the Maroubra social scene. No surprise we were under surveillance from the very start with phone taps. One day this detective dropped in to the shop to ask me about some drama that had happened in the area. I could hear the shop phone ringing while the cop was talking to me, but I let the answering machine pick it up. I'm sitting there talking to the detective when a mate of ours who was in Long Bay starts leaving a message, just asking what the surf had been like, who'd been fighting at the pub, whether any of the boys had been getting roots. Then, without a word of a lie, while this same detective is in the shop, another two guys have rung up; one from Silverwater, one from Goulburn. The cop looked at me after the last call and goes, 'Mate, maybe I should interview your answering machine.'

Then Gynge got out of the surf shop game and decided to sell up. We bought Maroubra Underground off him – me, Jai and Koby, along with the Rogers brothers, Nath and Bunch. The surf shop was more for the lifestyle than a serious money-making concern. It was just natural for us to take it over when Gynge left. Koby was too young to work in the shop, but Jai worked with us for a while. He'd sell boards and the hardware – leggies, deck grip, boardcovers – and he'd bring a lot of people into the shop.

It was good, and it gave us our first taste of playing around doing our own clothing line. We started printing Maroubra Underground shirts, and that little enterprise started us doing our own label, PSA – Pure Surf Addiction. It was stuff reflecting what was happening at Maroubra. We'd use rap lyrics and street design, so it was a bit more urban than other surf labels, but it sold really well. I remember one of the T-shirts we printed said, 'Never did a crime I didn't have to do'. We must have known something.

We were still running the surf lessons out of the shop, and everything was going well for a while, but retail's tough. A year after we took over, the council closed the beach for redevelopment. One summer they closed the northern end of the beach, then the next summer they closed the southern end. It was like a ghost town for two years and that cruelled us. But we ended up doing all right and eventually sold the business and made a bit of a profit.

It was good, but I still wasn't happy. I'm the kind of guy who always thinks there's something better for me lying around the corner. I'm open for it. The surf schools were a great way to make money, but dealing with backpackers and fat Pommies was doing my head in. Then George Quigley rang me one day and told me that this girl named Brenda kept ringing him, wanting to put in an application for a surf school on Bondi. I told George that if she wanted the licence that badly, then let her have it.

I gave away the licence for the surf school on the world's most famous beach. Brenda Miley-Dyer still runs the surf school at Bondi. I don't even want to think about what that thing turns over today.

Not long after that we got the news about Saul.

I'd met Saul Baker at the Aussie Titles five years before and the two of us became good mates. He'd come up and stay at Ma's, he got to know all the Maroubra boys really well, and he'd hang out and surf and party with us quite a lot. At the time he and I had the same dream of making it to the pro tour. We were both battlers in that way; we never got it easy, we didn't have much sponsorship, and we both had to work for it. Saul finally picked up a sponsorship off O'Neill and Byrne Surfboards, just a few months before he and I were going to go off and surf on the world tour.

One night he'd driven up from Wollongong and we'd gone out to a party. He was acting a little strange, and he said he wanted to go home early and sleep it off at Ma's place. I asked if he was all right; he said he was okay and took a cab home.

I was worried about him. I left the place soon after to go back and check on him. When I got to Ma's I jumped out of the taxi and looked across the street; the blinker on his van was going and he was just pulling away from the kerb. I yelled out to him but he was off.

They reckon you can see his house from where he crashed. He'd already pulled over at Cronulla and slept, but then drove on. He nearly got all the way to his place at Bulli. He was probably thinking about crawling into his own bed and under the covers when he's fallen asleep at the wheel. It was a horrific accident. He nearly lost his leg and he fractured his skull. They said he'd be lucky to walk again, let alone surf.

I went and stayed at his place soon after he got out of hospital. He was shattered. He fully fought with his rehab and he fully believed he was going to make it. In the end he was a champion to even be surfing again at all, but he was never going to be pro and he just couldn't deal with his dream being shattered.

I kept in contact with him in the months after, ringing him to see how he was going, but pretty soon I took off on the world tour and was in Europe and Hawaii. Meanwhile, Saul had a breakdown and ended up in an institution. Me and a girl from Maroubra, Lisa Keen, who was also a good friend of his, went and seen him. The institution was out west in Sydney, and it was heavy. He was so heavily medicated that he was like a little kid. They were putting on *Home Alone* for him to watch, and he wouldn't talk to me. He told me to be quiet because he wanted to watch it.

He eventually got out and battled his depression for another year and a half. He never used to do a lot of drugs, but suddenly he was taking a lot of acid.

He was living up on the north coast when he walked down the beach one night with his board and his guitar and hung himself off a pandanus tree.

The police found my phone number in his wallet and called me. It was devastating, it really was. I carried his coffin at the funeral. I remember looking through his diary at his sketches and paintings. He was a great writer and a great artist, and if he'd made it out of his depression he could have been anything.

Some time after that, Rowena and I moved out of our unit in Fenton Avenue, because we needed somewhere bigger for the baby. I don't know if that got Ma thinking or not, but it was right after then that Ma told us she wanted to sell her house. Ma's place had started falling down. It had been 10 years since anyone had spent any money to maintain it. The guttering had rusted, the pool was like a swamp; it needed a new roof. It needed 75 grands' worth of work. We tried to refinance her mortgage and get a loan on the house, but Ma had no real income so no one would lend us the money. She was struggling to keep up with the mortgage payments as it was. We didn't want her to sell the house – that was the only real home we'd ever known – but Ma's mind was made up. I think it was the quiet that did it. She was so used to the place being full of life that now we were all off travelling and doing our own thing, it seemed empty to her. It was just her and the memories of Pa and all the good times that had happened under that roof. She regretted it once she'd done it. She didn't know how much it meant to her until she moved out.

We were going to put Ma in a nursing home, because she needed proper care and we didn't think we could give it to her. But she didn't want to go, and we didn't want to send her. Then we all went in together and bought a cheap block of units in Maroubra, and Ma moved into one of them with Koby. There was no way Koby could live in the same house as our kid, and Ma still needed help with a few things after the stroke, so it worked out well. We initially looked at renting. Ma inspected a few places with us but she was really down and upset, because most of the units were too hard for her to get around in.

I remember the day we bought the units. We walked Ma through one, showing her the unit, pretending we were looking at renting it.

'What do you think of this one, Ma?'

She loved it.

Koby said, 'Well it's yours. We just bought it.'

Ma was just so bloody happy, you know, the happiest we'd seen her in a long, long time.

And amidst all this I became a father.

Kiyahna was born in Sydney Women's Hospital; this tiny, beautiful little girl. Row's family are from Mornington Island in the Gulf of Carpentaria, and up there *kiyahna* means 'sea breeze from the north'. Rowena wanted a natural birth; she didn't want drugs or an epidural. And it was hard work. To see your first child being born is an incredible experience. When you look at something you've created, something that comes from someone who you love, it's overwhelming.

Rowena was a deep sleeper and I was a light sleeper, so I was straightaway on night duty with Kiyahna. I think that's why Rowena and I are still really close today, even though we're apart, because of that time when Kiyahna was a baby and how well we worked together.

Rocking her to sleep, changing shitty nappies at night – that was all me for the first couple of years.

They were happy times at first, but they got tougher. I think we were just too young and there was too much going on. Rowena was still at uni when she'd fallen pregnant, but to her credit she finished her degree. I was trying to run a business, look after Kiyahna, Koby and Ma, and deal with what was happening on the streets of Maroubra at the time, the random violence. It was a really heavy combination of things. I'd tried really hard to make things happen, but there was just too much going on for it all to survive.

In terms of our relationship it was pretty hard making that adjustment – from carefree teenager to the job, the long-term girlfriend, the child, the family. It was a huge transition, a really heavy adjustment, and I just wasn't mature enough to deal with it. Something had to give and, over the next couple of years, it was my relationship with Rowena.

Rowena's mum eventually came down and moved her and Kiyahna out. I remember how I felt that day – cold. I slept on the floor with a curtain for a bedsheet because there was nothing left in the house. She took everything except one pillow and the curtains. There were eight little curtain panels, so I took one down and it just covered me. I lay there on the floor looking up at the ceiling, wondering how the fuck it had come to this. I was about as depressed as I've ever been.

I blew it, and I regret it even today. Rowena was a princess, my Aboriginal princess. But at least out of it all we have Kiyahna, and I have the best relationship with her to this day. She's a full daddy's girl, the biggest angel ever. I still get on well with Rowena, even though we're not together; we do our best to make sure Kiyahna gets the best from both of us.

And maybe, subliminally, there was another reason that it happened. I was scared. I didn't want my family to be anywhere near Maroubra. The place was changing, it was descending into chaos. It was getting violent; it was being overrun by idiots. It was no place to raise a family.

SUNNY

STRAIGHT OUTTA COMPTON AND STRAIGHT TO MAROUBRA

It was a Bondi Boardriders presentation night, some time in the early '90s.

We had the best time; a dozen of the Maroubra boys, a dozen of the Bronte boys, and all the Bondi guys. We have a sick night at the North Bondi RSL, the presso's finished and we're walking back to the Icebergs to have a beer and kick on. We're only about 200 metres down on the promenade on Campbell Parade when one of the Cookie brothers, who'd just been crowned the club champion and is walking alongside his girlfriend, is hit in the head by a flying longneck bottle. This thing comes flying past everyone and smacks him straight in the side of the face. It didn't explode, but it scalloped him, cut him above the eye. We've looked around and there's a big pack of two or three carloads of, well, let's call 'em unproud Australians, shouting, 'C'mon, c'mon!' down in the car park.

A few of us Maroubra boys looked at each other, and we've gone to the Bondi guys, 'C'mon, let's go get these fuckwits.'

They've gone, 'No, no, don't do anything.'

Well, next thing that's happened is another bottle has come flying through the air and has hit the guy's girlfriend in the face and explodes into a million pieces. We've said, 'That's it, let's go!'

The Bondi guys have full on grabbed us and said, 'Don't do anything, boys.'

We're like, 'Fuck that! These guys just smashed bottles in ya girl's face!'

'We've got to live here; we've got to deal with it tomorrow.'

And we're like, 'Whatever. It's not our fight.'

But the Maroubra guys just looked at each other and shook our heads. We knew they'd let it go too far. They hadn't done anything about it when they could have, and it had got to the stage where it was too late to rectify the situation. We all swore – just in the way we looked at each other that night – that we'd never let it get to that stage at Maroubra. We had the advantage of getting to see that first. It was working its way south from Bondi down. Bondi was the main place where a lot of the crew from the suburbs would hang out late at night, but all the eastern suburbs beaches were starting to get pretty wild.

It didn't take long for it to find its way down to Maroubra, though. Even while I was on tour I remember I'd come home from trips and there'd be three big skirmishes happen in the space of a weekend in Maroubra. It was happening all the time. People were getting robbed in the park and rolled for their shoes. They'd opened up new houso estates out the back of Maroubra, and moved people in from other areas and it unsettled the flow of things. The Seals Club had also been having these nights for crew coming in from the western suburbs, from Cabramatta and Bankstown, where two to three thousand people would turn up. It was like a deadset cyclone coming through the town. It was chaos. The beaches on the south side were like a full-on battlefield with different groups of kids from all around the place, all congregating on the beach.

It was also the height of American gang culture, and all these fuckwits were coming into Maroubra 20-strong – 20 fat and skinny white kids thinking they were in a NWA film clip, just trying to act like gangsters. There was a stage where that was happening every week, a new gang coming to attack. It was so normal. In the early '90s it got to the stage where we decided we were going to war with those fucking idiots. It was the time when 10 guys ambushed Jai with baseball bats and broke his arm just two doors up from Ma's. It was the time Koby got cornered with guns held to his head. It was the time they were moving in and trying to say they were taking over this beach. But on top of these wannabe LA gangsters, there were carloads of ethnic and unproud Australians, bikers, you name it, all coming through and causing trouble.

It led me to being stabbed.

It was New Year's Eve, and I went out to dinner with Rowena, who was six months' pregnant at the time. We'd been to dinner down on the beach at Coogee – I hadn't even been drinking – and we were walking back to the car when I've heard this bloke screaming for help. This was a scream of desperation. We looked around and these five or six guys were stomping this bloke who was curled up on the ground. I couldn't walk away from it. Maybe I was a little stupid for getting involved with my pregnant girlfriend there, but I said, 'Get off him. C'mon, mate, he's had enough.'

There were a lot of people around; it was only about seven o'clock and still broad daylight. Next thing they just turned on us. I got Row out of there, told her to run over the road and lock herself in the car. There were about three of us there who'd tried to help, and this whole gang of homeboys suddenly began attacking us. We started fighting them off and were doing pretty good; we gave a couple of those blokes a solid hiding.

It wasn't until after the fight had finished that I realised I'd been stabbed, twice – once above the heart and once in the back. Someone asked me what the blood was on me, and I said, 'What blood?' The stab wound in my chest had been made with a knife, while I'd been stabbed in the back with a broken bottle. I hadn't felt it when it happened; it just felt like being punched. I've been stabbed four times over the years, and it always just feels like a punch.

I went straight to the hospital in an ambulance. I couldn't breathe; my lung was filling up with blood. That's when I looked down and saw this big blood bubble coming out of my chest. I felt all right but I just couldn't breathe. I was starting to gargle on my own blood. Another inch down with the knife and I was dead; it would have gone through my heart. The doctors straightaway knew I had a punctured lung and they had to get a tube in there and drain it.

But then it got heavier. The same homeboys came up to the hospital looking for me, the same half-dozen guys. While I was getting operated on they attacked the emergency department, trying to get in and have another go at me. I was lying there and I heard it all happening outside. I was just angry more than anything that they had the hide to do that.

They didn't know who I was; they'd just come at me again 'cause we'd given them a bit of a flogging when it all first started. It was just the beginning of these gangs that moved in to try and take over and forge a reputation. These guys wanted to make their mark, and what better way to show you were serious than to attack the hospital, to say we haven't finished with ya.

I got out of hospital the next day. By this stage word had got out I'd been stabbed, and these guys had tracked down where I lived. They attacked the house the next night; lucky we had bars on the windows. I'd asked Ron to stay over with us so it wasn't just me, Rowena and Koby. They attacked the house with bricks and baseball bats and tried to smash their way in. They hadn't been able to get in and have eventually driven off, but that night was a signal to us that things had escalated. This problem wasn't going away. This is our place, we live here, we've grown up here – and you expect us to hide in our houses and be scared to walk along the beach?

When they attacked our house that night, that's when we really went, 'Well, this is war.' That one got personal. One of the guys who'd attacked me and attacked the house that night was a kid called Theo, who'd been one of Koby's good mates at school years before. Before too long both our families would be dragged into it, and it became this gnarly family feud. It would end up with Jai going to jail a year later.

Things snowballed from there; it went from random attacks on individuals to full-scale 20-on-20s. There was one time up on Poo Hill – The Battle of Poo Hill it became known as – when Jimmy and Ronnie were walking up the hill and some car has swerved at them. They've missed them, but they've stopped the car up ahead. One of our boys has run up and punched one of the guys through the car window. The guy has said, 'You wait. You're gonna die, motherfucker!'

They must have driven up the street and done a U-ey and watched which unit Jimmy and Ronnie had gone into. The boys were holding a party that night in Ronnie's unit on the corner of Poo Hill; there must've been 20 or 30 of us there, guys and girls. Next thing the place was under attack. Ten bricks hit the place simultaneously – *bang bang bang* through the windows. We looked out and there was maybe 40 guys fully attacking the house. They had baseball bats, bricks, rocks, bottles. I come out onto the balcony and saw three of them trying to get over the fence. I reached into the tub of empty beer bottles and just pegged the bottles at 'em, trying to stop them getting over. Half the boys charged out into the street in the first wave of defence, and a full-on battle has erupted. I remember seeing this one small kid run up to one of the guys attacking us and smashing a walking crutch into his face. I ran straight out at 'em and got hit by a tomahawk. This guy threw it at me and it's hit me in the shin and opened me up.

What do you do if this shit is happening every day? Call the police every time it does? No, you shouldn't. To a point, communities should look after themselves. And we didn't trust the cops. Maroubra was like a black hole for the police and the media back then. It was like the poor, forgotten cousin. A lot of stuff that would make a headline today and draw the SWAT team onto the streets never rated a mention back then. And when anything did happen, we'd still get the blame for most of it. You'd get a group of guys coming in from 50 kilometres away with baseball bats and we'd get charged. I was charged with an assault once. A guy lifted up a baseball bat to hit me and I've gone in with a short right cross and dropped him just before it hit me. I got charged for assault and he got off. I got charged with it when there was a guy trying to knock my head off with a baseball bat?! There was still that feeling that regardless of what happened and who was provoking it, we were the ones getting charged for it.

We'd grown up being harassed by police. When we were eight years old we'd cut across the school to check the waves at Clovelly Bommie and we got charged with trespassing. From the very start it just felt like any little crime or any little thing they could pin on us, they would. The way crime is enforced in a Housing Commission neighbourhood compared to a well-off neighbourhood is totally different. By the time you're 15 or 16 you have a rap sheet and you owe a lot of money in fines. That's what had happened to us. We owed money in fines for loitering and affray and not wearing a helmet while riding our pushbikes. Just shit, nothing. But you've already got this 'us against them' mentality, and if anything happens from now on you're running, not waiting around, because you know you're gonna get charged and you know you can't trust them.

Hinesy was the one who told us from a very young age that if guys come here looking for trouble, you give 'em trouble and they won't come back. And it was the best way to keep the area calm. If people came looking for trouble, you let them know they'd find it very quickly and it'd keep things peaceful. Win, lose or draw, you don't wanna come back if someone's gonna really give you a fight. Human nature tells you that if someone's going to make it tough for you then you choose an easier target. 'Well, let's not go to Maroubra today. How about we try and take the Bronte boys? What about Cronulla?'

Before all this there was still a lot of division on the beach. There were still a lot of different boardriding clubs. The Maroubra guys hated the La Per guys who hated the South End guys. The footy players didn't like the surfers who didn't like the clubbies. The fact that the beach was being targeted by outsiders and was being made a dangerous place brought us all back together. We knew we'd be stronger as one, rather than a heap of splinter groups. There were so many people in the community who were being affected by this trouble coming into Maroubra that the whole place began to unite and galvanise. Petty disputes were consigned to history. The shopkeepers, the residents, the clubbies, the surfers, we were all committed to fighting this and making Maroubra a safe and fun place to live again. Unless the whole community was committed to fighting it, we'd never stop it.

KOBY

A LATE NIGHT TRIP UP TO SLEEVEMASTERS AND THE BRA BOYS ARE FORGED IN INK

The car drove down McKeon Street and swerved at us, trying to run us down on the footpath. I woulda been 15, I reckon.

My mate Ben Johnson has grabbed an empty bottle out of the bin, run after them, and thrown it through their window. They've jumped out of the car and me, Ben, Jed and Jason Hunt have just run at them and started fighting outside Maroubra Underground. They were a fair bit older than us, but ever since I was a kid we were taught that you don't run from a fight. A dog instinct is that if you run, the dog will chase you. So we've always been taught to run *at* them, not *from* them.

So we ran at 'em and started fighting. I was smashing the car, kicking the doors so the other guys couldn't get out. Ben and Jason Hunt were fighting the other two. They've jumped back in the car and kept driving down McKeon Street, stopping out the front of the laundromat. We see 'em running in, running out, running in, running out, and we're wondering what the fuck they were doing. By this stage we were all on the street, a heap of us, standing there waiting to see what they were up to. Suddenly these guys start running at us, so we start running back at 'em. There's about 10 of us and five of them, but they were big guys and we were kids. As we've got close to them, 20 metres away, we saw they were holding these long shiny things; then all of a sudden we hear, *boom*! We've just gone, 'What the fuck!' They were firing shotguns. One had a baseball bat; another one's got an axe.

We all U-turned on a 20-cent piece and bolted straight back up McKeon Street, down the promenade onto the beach. They're right on our arse and they were still firing shots. I didn't turn around to see whether they were shooting at us or firing warning shots; we all ran into the bushes at the south end of the beach and hid. I'm in there next to Ben. Somehow they knew Jason Hunt's name, and they're doing the old, 'Jason, we can see you, mate! You might as well come out!' I'm just thinking there's not a chance I'm falling for that one … but Jed does.

'All right, I'm sorry, I'm sorry!'

They've come straight over and just smashed him in the face with the butt of the shotgun, then turned it around and put the barrel in his mouth.

'Where's Jason Hunt?!'

They wanted him bad, 'cause they thought it was Jason who'd thrown the bottle. I'm just going, fuck, Jed's about to get his head blown off.

Jed's going, 'Fuck, I dunno what was happening. I just turned up and then we were running.'

Then all of a sudden Jed's called their bluff. He knew by this stage that we had 20 blokes who could be there in 30 minutes, and they'd all be ready to go. He's stood up and gone, 'Listen, you blokes wanna fight? We've got 50 guys who'll be here in five minutes, and we know you live in the laundromat!'

And they've backed off and bailed! Still not sure why, bra, but we were fucking happy they did. We've all jumped out of the bush and Jed's turned around.

'Thanks for the back-up, ya cunts!'

The next day we were sitting down the beach. This car drives past us slowly; we've seen the big ding in the door and knew it was the same guys. They've driven past with the shotgun hanging out the window, and the guy pointing it at us has gone, 'Someone's gonna die!'

As they've driven off one of us has thrown another bottle and smashed it on the car and we've all bolted again.

Maroubra was starting to get pretty heavy. We didn't even know they were gangs, you know; they were just packs of guys who used to hang around. It was the start of the Marrickville Legends and the Parkside Killers, the start of all those gangs. But to us they were just groups of guys coming to the beach causing trouble. We didn't know 'em, we didn't have history with them; they just turned up. Maroubra was a magnet for it. We all grew up around that shit; there've been so many fights here. But around then it was escalating. There were so many gang fights and wars in the streets. There'd be mad stinks in the streets, fighting in the pub with the bikers; there was all sorts of shit going on. The only way we were going to stop these guys was to form our own crew.

One day not long after, my friend Jack Kingsley and I were talking about getting tattoos, something like 'Maroubra Boys'. Jack's a good artist, and he's sketched one up and gone, 'Look at this.' We're all going,

'Yeah, "Maroubra Boys".' Then someone, I think it was Sunny, goes, 'What about "Bra Boys"?'

Jack's drawn it up and we've all gone into SleeveMasters up at the Cross to get it done. There were half-a-dozen of us who went up that first time: me, Headley, Goldy, Sunny, Ronnie and Mumbles I think. I went third. I saw the first two and I went, 'They're shit, they're tiny.' I got mine three times the size of the first two guys; my tattoo was the biggest. But within a week, once all the boys started going up there, it was about the smallest.

Now that I think about it, I reckon we should've stuck with Maroubra Boys, but I guess the Bra Boys will have to stay. And we weren't a gang; we weren't a fucking brotherhood. It was just me and my friends with the same tattoo. You know, we all stuck together, and that's it. Do anything for each other. It was just me and my friends, and if you call it anything else you're reading too much into it … just me and my mates.

We didn't sit down and say, 'Let's form a gang.' It started as a tattoo, but the tatt reflected what we were all about. Around here, especially back then, if you didn't have someone looking out for you, you were pretty well going to go to jail, bra. We were talking about it the other day. The fighting, the surfing, the partying – it's such a fine line between having a good time and going to jail. To be going the hardest at it, you're sometimes going to end up on the wrong end of the law. The older guys had formed the MRA – the Maroubra Republican Army – but this was the young crew coming through, and we were taking the Bra Boys to a whole new level. We had to.

Everyone around here was always training up, always boxing. The house up in Bond Street was the full training gym; we had a garage set up with boxing bags. Everyone would do the focus pads, everyone would spar, everyone was fighting. You'd be trying to take your mate's head off, it'd be always out of control, but you'd have gloves on so no one ever got hurt too much. A few loose teeth and bleeding lips, that's just about it. This guy named Big Bitch took the training. He was New Zealand heavyweight kickboxing champ. He was a nice guy, but a gnarly fucker. He'd take all the boxing classes, and Johnny Gannon would do most of the training.

The Parkside Killers, PSK, we hated their guts. I wouldn't say I respected them – they were all maggots – but, y'know, I respected them for the fact they'd have the balls to come and try and get us. Their place was up at Lexo, up at Duffys Corner. Matraville was UTB, United Tongan Brothers. Bra Boys was just Maroubra.

Most of our fights were with PSK. We went through years of wars with those guys, probably 100 fights. They'd come in a couple of carloads and try and get you one- or two-out; then we'd try and get them back. Jai got beaten up by five of them with baseball bats and broke his arm. They stabbed Sunny. We'd get them and they'd get us, and it just went on and on. When you're 16 years old, fighting's pretty well what ya do.

I remember one time walking across the pedestrian crossing on Marine Parade, and this car with six PSK guys in it has pulled up. They've jumped straight out of the car. Before I even knew what a club lock was, some bloke has jumped out of the car with one and started running at me. I had nothing, but I told him I was ready to go. Then they all jump out of the car and I'm there by myself. Anyway, I've gone to hit the guy holding the club lock. Turns out it wasn't a club lock; it was one of those retractable batons the cops use. He's stepped back and flung this little thing at me and it's just gone *whzzz* and hit me straight in the forehead and split me open. I've still got the scar from it. I dropped. He smashed me in the mouth with it on the way down and then they just kicked the fuck out of me. We went back up to their house and threw a petrol bomb at it and attacked them later that night.

People started to get singled out. Matt King was the number one PSK guy we wanted to get, then this Dion guy and this guy called Boof. Funnily enough, most of them live in Maroubra now. The other day I gave this young grommet five My Brothers Keeper T-shirts and he goes, 'You know my dad!'

'What's his name?'

'Boofa.'

What the fuck! I realised I've been saying hello to the guy I fought for 10 years without even realising it. He's working on the council and I'd been talking to him for the last year without recognising him. Next time I seen him, I go, 'I can't believe I fought you for 10 years!'

We sat there and laughed.

The violence that was going on got pretty bad, though. People were getting stabbed down here regularly. It was happening once every couple of weeks. We'd just say to the other gangs, 'We'll meet you at Byrne Reserve at eight tonight,' and we'd do it. Gang wars. It was usually in McKeon Street because it was hard for 'em to get out. We could smash up cars at each end and keep 'em blocked in. There was always massive fights out the front of the pub; bikies, guns, baseball bats, fence palings. You'd pull the rubbish bins out of their cover, stash all your bats and weapons inside and put the bin back. You'd stash stuff so if anything happened you'd be armed in a few seconds. You'd put rocks on the roof. That was the kids' job.

One time there were about 30 of us hanging around the bus stop on Marine Parade for some reason. These three guys and this one chick walked past, just looking at us. One of them has gone to my mate Nudge, 'What the fuck are you looking at?'

'Mate,' I said, 'there's 30 of us. Just keep walking. Don't be stupid.' I knew what would happen. 'Just get away from here. We don't come to your place and do that. Now fuck off.'

The guy kept walking, but he was still eyeballing my mate.

He goes, 'But ya know I woulda smashed your head in!'

Well, Nudge has gone off after him as the guy has kept walking backwards, mouthing off. All of a sudden Nudge went *whack* and has started into the guy against this garage door of a unit block, which has swung open. The pair of them have spilled inside the garage, fighting. Then the other two guys have run in and they were all into Nudge. I've said, 'Boys, only two of ya run up.' 'Cause you wanted even numbers; you didn't want 20 guys beating up three. That was bad form.

All of a sudden I heard a scream, and one of the Baldwins has come out of the garage and he had a huge hole in his stomach. He's just yelling out, 'I've been stabbed!' He moved his hand and there was this little ball of intestines hanging out. He was just trying to push them back in, freaking out. So then Dumpster, another one of our friends, ran in, and he got slashed across the neck and had his lung punctured. Then Shane Seccy ran in and got stabbed in the back. These three guys are all in serious trouble.

Fuck the numbers, bra. We've all run up and looked in and the cunt had knuckle-dusters on and a knife about a foot long. The other cunt had a massive knife. Next thing I look around and the chick's out cold somehow; someone hammered her. Then everyone's got milk crates and as these two guys have come out they've just been set upon and taken apart. These cunts have ended up in worse shape than our guys.

The Bra Boys got me into a lot of trouble but they kept me out of a lot more. I was a pretty bad kid, I did what I wanted, but I had them there to pull me out. I had them to watch over me. And they were good days. They made everyone what they are, and it taught us all to fight and stick up for ourselves. With all that shit happening on the streets, our crew got solid. We started with a core crew of about 20 or 30 of us; then it gradually turned into 50, then 100. Today it's about 300.

Around here, you're going to be the best footballer, the best chick puller or the best surfer. It's just a massive race to be the best. And it's not just my brothers or the Bra Boys; it's the whole area. The fact that most of us have come from fuck-all means we fight that much harder to climb out of it. If you're going to do something, you go the hardest at it. It's all about being number one. If you're not number one and not going the hardest, you shouldn't be living here.

SUNNY

THE WAGONS ARE CIRCLED AS A TRACKSUITED ARMY OF QUASI-AMERICANS DESCEND ON THE BEACHSIDE SUBURB

I just remember watching *The Warriors* on TV as a kid, over and over.

It was in the house that had all the mattresses on the walls and the motorbikes in the lounge room. I must've watched it a hundred times. I think I would've been eight or nine at the time. All those freaky gangs, the guys dressed as baseball players with their faces painted, the guys on rollerskates, the guy with bottles on his fingers clinking them together, going, 'Warriors, come out to play-yay!' The Warriors had to stick together and fight their way across the city before dawn. I remember that movie really resonated with me.

And the thing was, because we'd grown up with chaos, we felt comfortable around it. Whenever there was a big storm at night we'd go down and sit under the pavilion or in one of the rock caves and watch the storm and the ocean. The back alley at Ma's with the noise of the pinball parlour and panel beater … the cars, the people, the pub. We felt comfortable in chaos, so when it descended on Maroubra we were ready for it.

By this stage the gangs were getting audacious. There was one time when three guys were in the pub, walking around, shoving people, agitating, looking for trouble. One of the boys said something to 'em and they've pulled out knuckledusters and bowie knives and started punching and stabbing people. They stabbed three or four of the boys.

What were we supposed to do? We weren't going to let 'em get away with it. And that was the whole thing. We were all fit and healthy; we were charging waves and charging life. We don't care if you've got a gun or a knife; we're not going to give you respect just for that. We're not going to drop everything we believe in because some skinny piece of unhealthy drugged-up shit in a tracksuit pulls a knife on us. *You think we're gonna give you respect for that?* You might pull a knife and stab someone, but you're not getting away. None of us are running. We're standing up for what we believe in. Sooner or later they stopped coming back … it just took a lot of stab wounds for that to happen.

We just said to ourselves we wouldn't accept anyone coming in here wearing gang colours – hats, whatever. We wouldn't accept any of it. It was full control. We weren't accepting any shit. No gangs, no bombers; anyone who came in was asked to remove their hats.

But what do ya do? What do ya do when gangs come into your street and start beating up innocent guys? Coming to the beach to try and fuck someone up? When the Bra Boys started, we wanted to take back the beach and make it safe again. We weren't accepting this shit happening in our town.

One of the boys had a connection up at SleeveMasters in the Cross, Greg his name was. There were about six of us: a couple from my generation and a few from the generation above us. There was Scotty Gunzer who's about 12 years older than us, Goldy and Mumbles who are like six years older, then there was me, Ronnie, Head and Koby. We'd always been known as the Bra Boys, especially among the surfing fraternity. For 40 years Maroubra surfers had been known as Bra Boys, so it was pretty natural that's what we'd get tattooed.

It was really taking that step of uniting the beach under a single banner. We weren't a gang. The whole thing with the gangs at that time was graffiti – putting your gang colours up, trying to spread your gang's name. But we were the opposite. You weren't allowed to show anyone your tatt; you weren't allowed to get it photographed. We didn't want to be known as a homeboy gang, didn't want that whole LA gangster thing attached to us. We were against that. That's who we were fighting with. We weren't trying to be these homeboy gangsters. All these guys were trying to be these big thugs. They'd look at a blond guy with a suntan and go, 'Look at this fag.' We're like, 'No, mate, have a go at yourself.'

None of this is new; it's been happening for decades. It's part of the Maroubra folklore to not let outsiders come in and run riot in the town. You've been brought up with all those stories of the surfers fighting the rockers in the '60s. Whenever it would happen, everyone would be real proud that you repelled them and haven't let a gang come in and do whatever they wanted in the town. We don't drive out to Bankstown train station trying to start something.

And it wasn't just outsiders coming in; there was a lot of shit going on in Maroubra itself that needed to be sorted out. I remember this young kid, Harley, who'd been coming to Ma's orphan Christmases with us for years. He was down at the beach one day and we saw this older guy screaming at him, threatening him. The guy bolted and I've asked Harley who it was. He said, 'It's me mum's boyfriend.' Turns out the guy had been bashing him and his mum, and both were scared shitless. I asked

Harley where the guy lived, rounded up a few guys and we went and paid him a visit.

The Bra Boys were a necessity, because we were on our own and we had a lot of these situations to deal with, both on the street and at home. It was all the kids who'd been left to fend for themselves. We really wanted to create a family for those kids. We'd grown up in the ocean, so it was natural to create a family around it.

We had this house up on the corner of Bond Street and Marine Parade. It was an old, run-down house, but we all moved in and fixed it up, and it became the full-on Bra Boys house. Jed and his girl were sleeping in the kitchen on a double bed. There was a campfire in the middle of the lounge room floor.

One night this bikie gang turned up down the beach and one of the boys has had a fight with one of their guys over a parking spot. That night 30 guys from their bikie gang turned up in McKeon Street. They'd run into one of our boys who was sitting down at the beach and beat the shit out of him. We're all up in the backyard having a barbecue, the full fire is going, when next thing this car pulls up. One of our boys yells out from the window, 'There's a bikie gang at the beach attacking! Let's go!'

So we've all pulled flaming logs and sticks out of the fire, grabbed whatever we could. A lot of the boys were tradesmen, so there were three or four utes at the place. Twenty of us have come flying out of this house with flaming sticks and down Marine Parade in the back of the utes. About halfway down McKeon Street we see two of our guys lying face down on the ground surrounded by about 20 bikers with chains and baseball bats with nails in 'em. So we flew down the street, jumped out of the utes and charged.

I'm running straight at this big guy when I see him pull out two pistols, point them at me and just blaze away. He's let four rounds go. I've jumped over a car for cover and come back around behind him. By this stage the guy has the gun pointed at our mate Frog. The biker's mate is screaming, 'Shoot him! Shoot him!' When he didn't fire, the guy has gone, 'Fuck ya, I'll shoot him,' and grabbed the gun. Just as he's reached to grab it, one of our guys has come in from the side with a flaming log and smashed him in the head and this giant explosion of embers has lit up the street.

jed campbell

HAM AND EGGS AT THE BRA

Marty Lee used to come up to us and go, 'You know, you blokes are the future.' Then a minute later it would be 'fuck this', 'fuck the police', 'fuck the world'. We'd just walk away at 12 years old going, 'I hate everyone!'

I miss all them guys around here now, though – the hardcore surfers who lived out the back of their cars and in garages. That's all long gone. You had the Bob Hawke Surf Team – Mumbles, Headley Walsh, Marty Lee, Bebbo – guys who lived to surf and guys who ripped. They would pay 100 bucks rent between three of them to live right on the beach. That's the difference now; if you wanna live around here you have to have money. The boys who never had money, or just laboured and were happy to drink a litre of milk for breakfast and a banana roll for dinner, they're all gone. They're in the mines in WA. They're the guys who made the place good. It was always so loose and fun and cheap. Those blokes would have a heart attack here today. The hamburger they used to buy down here for two bucks would cost 'em seven bucks, and it'd be half the size!

I used to love the way when we were kids the police car would drive past three times, and one of the older guys would go, 'Here's five bucks. Go and buy some eggs and egg the coppers next time they drive past.' And there was no way we'd say no to that. 'And when you're finished with the cops hit the parking officers.' One time we sat up on top of the Bay pub – me, Koby, Ahu, Jack – and we egged the coppers; got 'em good too. The only reason they caught us was that we had all these eggs left, so later, when we got bored, we started egging each other. The cops grabbed us and we're covered in eggs going, 'We got no idea who threw those eggs at ya earlier.' It got written up in a story in *Tracks* titled, 'Ham and Eggs at The Bra'. I'll never forget that article because it said, 'It's always a hop, skip and a jump from Long Bay' – 'cause you can see Long Bay jail from here, that tower on the top of the hill.

In those days, wherever I was, Koby was. The older guys were always geeing us up, going, 'Who's toughest out of you two?' and we'd just start beating the shit out of each other. As far as madness, well, Koby's a year or so younger than me, so he was always madder. But whenever us grommets would get picked on we were smart enough to bond together and start picking back. We had a pretty cool crew: me, Koby, Ahu, Jason Hunt, Jack Kinga, the Burndreds.

Boardriders trips were always fun. You'd come down to the beach in the morning and the president would be billeting you out into the older guys' cars and they'd say, 'You know what's gonna be funny? Getting you drunk!' You'd just go, 'Fucking oath!' The maddest ones were the surf trips down to Cronulla. The local guys down there would just throw mud all over the boys' cars, 'cause there'd always be some kind of chaos that we'd started. Those guys weren't that different to us. You know how now we're made out to be this tough gang; we were copping it back then too. Everyone was surf rats – Maroubra, Cronulla, Bronte, Bondi – and we were all mad. The Cronulla guys were just the same as us – surf nazis – just that the guys here in Maroubra would be in and out of jail. You'd hear a lot of jail stories. The Maroubra guys would always just take it a little further, a lot further.

Then a few years later all that stuff started happening. It was when all those gangs were forming, the Lebanese and the Islanders; it was that whole rap homeboy era. We were like 15, 16, and we loved it too, but we were too busy surfing to be interested in trying to beat up other crew. It was crazy times. It became like a warzone. I shouldn't say that, because compared to some places out west it was probably not as full on. I lived down here on the beach and we forever had a team always ready to roll and those guys were always coming down to get us. We couldn't understand why. We're like, 'What's at Maroubra Beach? There's a pub here with 10 people in it. You don't need to come to our beach and fight us; there's nothing here.' Maybe they came because they knew they had someone to fight.

We just started getting madder, our crew kept growing and we wouldn't cop anything that was going on. But the older guys were blowing up at us, because they felt they couldn't walk up the street without some drama happening, and they were blaming us for it. The younger guys blamed the older guys for not doing anything, and the older guys blamed the younger guys for inciting it. That changed the place as much as anything. When I was a kid there were the Sunnys, Jais, Waynos, Ronnies and Moffs who you'd idolise, but above them were another generation – Mumbles, Marty, the older Chappo, Headley Walsh – a whole older crew who you also idolised. That all got broke apart when that shit started happening.

I got into a lot of trouble as a kid and spent two-and-a-half years away from here. When I come back I noticed the place had changed.

But I think the bigger the Bra Boys got, the more the fun kind of toned down. It took some of the fun out of it, just because we got this heavy reputation. The guys from Cronulla would go, 'Okay, I'm gonna throw a mud bomb in the window of that Maroubra bloke's car.' Now all of a sudden they worry about the repercussions. 'Hang on a second, there's a hundred of them; they might come and get us.' All of a sudden we're a gang, but we're just going, 'C'mon, you blokes, have a joke with us.' What everyone thought we were wasn't us at all. But then when you read the papers it makes you think twice. We all paint ourselves as choirboys … maybe we're not, 'cause we've all been in a lot of trouble in our time.

There's the crazy gang side, and the things you do to survive and help your crew. But then there's the other 99 per cent of the time when you surf in the morning and have a barbecue on the hill in the arvo and there's a guy running past you with a roll of dunny paper on fire hanging out his arse. That's what the real Maroubra is to me.

KOBY

A hundred people fighting in the streets is not something the police could ignore, but they did.

They did nothing about all these gangs coming into Maroubra and randomly taking people out. The whole reason the Bra Boys formed was because the cops weren't doing anything. Instead, the police added it up and come to the conclusion we're drug gangs fighting over territory. There were people selling drugs in Maroubra, sure, but it wasn't organised crime gangs and it's not why we were fighting. The cops never wanted to help us, because we were from Maroubra, and Maroubra has just been known as scum forever. We'd never see the cops down here day to day trying to smooth things out. But then when anything happened that involved us, the SWAT team would be down here in 30 seconds.

I remember one time, a funny one. A few of the boys are driving past the beach in their van when they see a fight in the park. They've pulled up to watch it and one of the guy's mates has gone, 'What the fuck are you looking at!'

My mate's gone, 'Fuck you, mate, I'm watching the fight.'

'Get out of the fucking car, smartarse.'

So my mate got out of the car and has just knocked him out, and his mates have all turned around and chased after him. My mate got in his van and bolted; soon these other guys are chasing him in their car. My mates look in the rear-vision mirror and they see the guys leaning out of the window shooting at the van; they can hear bullets hitting it. The chase has gone on through the back streets of Maroubra, and finally the boys have driven up to Maroubra Police Station. They run into the police station and the guys chasing them are still shooting out the front of the cop station. When the boys run in, the cops are hiding under the front desk going, like, 'Get the fuck out of here! What are you guys doing?'

Mate, they should be thankful we were there, because we were doing their job for 'em. I never seen 'em arrest one person for smack in Maroubra, ever, and the shit was everywhere. Once we started the Bra Boys, that's when we said there's not going to be any heroin in Maroubra, we don't want drugs in the place. We just wanted to stamp it out. We'd hear of a house that was selling it and we'd go and kick the door in and sort it out. It was the evolution of us egging them when we were kids. We'd just confront 'em and tell 'em to leave. We'd fight 'em if we had to, even though it's not much of a fight against a junkie. Living with them my whole life I know it's not an easy thing to kick, but it was their choice to do it, and if they're around the kids here all the time it's not a good scene. What comes with junkies is thieving and crime and you don't need that anywhere.

We were doing our own policing down there, bra. This one day, Ma was crossing the road on the pedestrian crossing on Marine Parade. Jai was out the front of the surf shop, and Ma was walking across in my direction. Ma's hobbling across the road, 'cause walking wasn't that easy for her after the stroke, and it was taking her a while to shuffle across. Well, this guy in a hotted-up, pissy little Gemini has pulled up at the crossing and has just started beeping his horn at her because she's taking so long. I see the guy beeping then I look straight over at Jai. He's watching like a hawk. I'm just thinking, 'Mate, you'd want to stop beeping in the next two seconds or something bad's gonna happen to ya.' Ma's still hobbling, and the fuckwit isn't just beeping any more, he's holding the horn down without taking his hand off it. Ma's starting to freak out. Well, I see Jai just take off. Next thing he's on the guy's bonnet, jumping up and down like it's a trampoline. He gets up onto the guy's roof and he's jumping so high and hard that the car's windows are popping out and the whole roof starts to collapse down onto the guy. By this stage Ma has made it across to the other side. Jai's jumped off the car and the guy has driven off down the road with his head hanging out the driver's window because the whole roof of his car had been squashed down a whole foot. Jai had flattened it. I remember Jai walking over to Ma, and Ma just shaking her head, going, '*Raaaaggghhhh,*' in disapproval. Fuck, bra, it was the funniest thing I'd ever seen. Priceless. The whole beach was laughing, just watching this fuckwit beeping an old lady and having his car compacted by Jai.

When I was 17 I wasn't allowed on the beachfront at Maroubra. I'd been charged with an assault, and while I was waiting for my day in court, they put this stupid fucking ban on me – banned me from Maroubra. I wasn't allowed between Curtin Crescent, all the way down Broom Street, up Fitzgerald then out to Anzac Parade and all the way north to Coogee. They gave me a street directory with a big cross through the area on the beach, and it highlighted the roads I was allowed to travel on. I wasn't allowed within a kilometre of the beach. I wasn't even allowed to surf my own beach. They were saying I was one of the instigators of the violence. And this is how stupid it was: the guy who I had a fight with lived at fucking Marrickville, which is 20 minutes from here, and we'd had the fight half an hour away from Maroubra, and yet here I am banned from fucking Maroubra Beach? How the fuck did the beach come into it? It was a joke. I kept surfing, but I had to be careful I wasn't spotted, 'cause I'd end up in juvenile detention. I didn't really care, 'cause I soon found a way around it.

'See ya later, boys, I'm off to Bali.'

I come back after a month, went to court and got let off, like I knew I would.

I've been charged and in front of the courts that many times, 13 I think, and been found not guilty every time … well, until the Tony thing, anyway. The cops just loved getting me in there. One time I got charged with punching this boogieboarder out here at Maroubra. I was in the water with one of my friends and I had an argument with the boogieboarder. We had a wrestle, which was nothing. Then my mate saw him on the beach, gave him a smashing, and the guy blamed it all on me. I got charged with assault.

When it came to court, the boogieboarder said he knew it was me because I had a big tattoo on my back.. My lawyer asked the guy to describe the tattoo and he said it was a big 2035 running vertically down the length of my spine. The police were that certain they had me. My lawyer has said, 'Are you sure it was my client?'

'One hundred per cent.'

So my lawyer, Jason Dimmock, said, 'Koby, can you stand up, take your shirt off and turn around.' No tattoo. The judge throws it out straightaway.

I knew why they kept doing it. They thought that by taking me out of the picture – getting me in jail or banning me from Maroubra or whatever – the Bra Boys would splinter up. They were clueless. Some of the detectives from Maroubra were telling the head police that we were this full-on organised crime gang, and they got extra money and resources to bring us down.

Never once to this day have we had any meaningful contact with the coppers, and our rules have always been you didn't talk to the cops, under any circumstances.

JAI

JAI LOSES HIS FREEDOM AND LOSES AN EAR, BUT GAINS A VALUABLE INSIGHT INTO A WORLD BEYOND OUR OWN

I never thought Maroubra was ever that rough. I don't know where these bastards grew up. That was just life. It was pretty sweet, the way I looked at it.

For a while there was a homey thing coming in when the American influence was getting big, and there was a bit of trouble then. That was when we started training hard. At first we were just punching and bodylifting, punching, bodylifting. It wasn't like now when it's all kicks and wrestling in with the punching. We had a boxing ring set up in the backyard at Bond Street and it was pretty brutal; no one would be holding back. We got right into it, 'cause you had to be ready in case you got caught one-out.

I used to train a lot with Johnny Gannon. We'd go all morning on the beach and in the boxing ring. Then I'd finish training, have a ciggie straightaway, then walk into the pub and have a bourbon and a Coke chaser. Johnny called it the Jai-athlon. I'm always about balance, bra. You can't be too healthy. I never realised it back then, but that first half an hour after you train is very important. Now I'll put a protein shake straight in, but back then it was a durry and a bourbon. I figured I'd earned it.

We had an ongoing feud with this one family that went on for years. Whenever we saw them it was pretty well on. It was a bad time.

Sunny nearly got killed at Coogee. It was New Year's Eve and I was at this big dance party in the city. It was a night when crew kept coming up and asking me if I was all right. I just felt like something was up. The next morning, sure enough, I find out Sunny is in the hozzy. A couple of them from this family had stabbed him and he'd nearly died. Sunny's chick was pregnant at the time and was really stressed out by it all. I was stressing too. Fuck, bra, how are you supposed to feel when ya brother gets stabbed? Luckily, he came good pretty quick.

I saw the guy who did it in a nightclub soon after. It was a guy Koby had gone to school with. He was just standing there, smiling at me, laughing, so I just hit him with a glass. The glass went through me hand, almost cut me hand off, but didn't do him much good either. He got 180 stitches in his face. Nearly killed him.

That bloke and his family, they were the maddest little soldiers I ever met; they were staunch. I got locked up for it, but the bloke I stabbed never give me up; some other people in the nightclub put me in for it.

That's the only time I've been locked up, apart from the Tony thing. I got a year weekend detention for the glassing but I fucked it up and ended up doing six months' jail and two years' weekend detention, just for not turning up on weekends. Every time you didn't turn up to mow lawns and pick up rubbish, you got two days' jail.

I hate jail. I hate jail more than anyone. Since you were a kid you had it drummed into you that you're gonna get fucked up the arse in there and have the shit beaten out of ya. You hear all this shit, 'don't drop the soap', you know. The first time I got locked up I was only 75 kilos wringing wet, so walking in there I was wondering, 'Fuck, is it all true?' But once I got up there I was okay. There were some good people in there. That's not what I tell the young kids down here, though. I say, 'You wanna be tough? Then you better be ready to get bent over if you end up in there.'

I did okay up at Long Bay, but I was saying my prayers and had no dramas. There were heaps of older Maroubra boys in there. I got classoed, so I made my way down to minimum. It was as good as jail could be, I suppose. It was the worst, though, as it was so close to home. Long Bay's just up the top of the hill overlooking Maroubra. I'd wake up some days, smell that air, and know straightaway what I was missing.

'Fuck, boys, the surf is pumping.'

'How do ya know?'

It'd been raining and southerly for three days, and then ya wake up one morning and it's sunny with a crisp fresh sou-wester. Ya just know it's gonna be pumping down the road. Those days were long days, bra.

I never worried too much in jail. I just hated the screws – copper dogs. I'll handle it wherever I am, I can adapt. I'd slept in the dirt in Third World countries. But it was missing my friends and my girl that got to me, missing my family. And I miss the ocean. There's a famous saying that wraps up jail: 'It's not where you *are*, it's where you're *not*.' That sums it up beautifully.

In Long Bay that first time, that's when I first started believing in God. It restored my faith heaps. That was in '99; I stayed out of trouble for a while after that.

When I got out of jail I still had weekend detention. I was spewing. I'd rather have stayed in jail and done the time. It just seemed like the weekend detention dragged on forever. For two years of me life I couldn't travel. If anything else ever happens, I can never get weekend detention again, because I fucked it up that time. And even if they did give it to me now, I'd throw the chair at the judge to make sure I got jail instead. At least in jail you can adapt. In weekend detention you work two days a week, then go work in your old life for the other five. You can't get used to one life, you can't get used to the other. It puts you in a bit of a spin.

Me ear got bitten off not long after.

I was out in town on my first date with my new girl, Natalie, and we were in a bar up on Oxford Street. The bloke who stabbed Sunny that night in Coogee, the guy I'd glassed, well, I was now having trouble with his brother. It had turned into the full family feud. Anyway, the older brother was a boxer, so he was lethal.

I sat with my back to the crowd, which I normally never do. I don't like to have me back to nothing. I want to sit where I could see the joint, especially in them days, and especially in the city. I'm sitting there and next thing *boom*, I'm on the ground. The guy has left hooked me. I spotted the guy and picked up a chair and ran at him and gone *boom*, but he's blocked it at the last minute. He's there, flexing up.

'C'mon, Jai. Out the front now!'

I'm going, 'Fuck, why didn't that chair just finish it?' He was a machine.

The fight? It was a bloodbath.

He's whaling me, and Nat's going, 'Run! Run!'

'I can't fucking run!' Running would have been worse, trust me.

So I just had to stand there and get hammered. We were out the front blueing and that's where he took the bite out of my ear.

I'm walking off after it'd finished and the cops have pulled us up down the street.

'Mate, your ear's missing.'

'Yeah, mate, no worries. I just caught up with some old school buddies.'

That rivalry was going for a few years. It fully checked itself, though, after a while. It couldn't have gone on like that forever, and we had a mutual respect for each other at the end of it.

One of the brothers is dead now. May his soul rest in peace in heaven. God bless them.

SUNNY

A KNIFE IN THE RIBS GALVANISES THE BROTHERHOOD
FOR AN ACT OF BAR-ROOM RETRIBUTION

I was just coming to, the morning after I'd been stabbed.

I was in hospital on New Year's Day, and I was still drugged up on morphine after they'd operated on me. I was looking up at the ceiling and everything is really blurry. My heart is beating like a drum, my vision is blurred, and all of a sudden the ceiling's pulsing like the surface of the ocean. And suddenly the black hockey puck is back. It's bouncing off the corners of the roof at right angles. I was back in the cot at the house in Randwick. I was having a flashback to the same dream I'd had as a kid.

I've forced myself to wake up. My eyes have focused, and there it was – a blowfly. That's what the black dot had been 20 years ago. It had been a fly. Jai and I weren't allowed to piss in the bathroom at that place, so we had to piss in a bucket in the room, and that's why the flies were there. That's what was scaring the shit out of me in my cot, and I'd turned it into a nightmare.

Me being stabbed that night triggered the full family feud between the Abbertons and the family of the guy who did it. That night was going to lead to all sorts of shit, and it also led to Jai going to jail for taking revenge.

As brothers, Jai and I are prone to the occasional cold war. We're always going to love each other and be best mates, but that doesn't mean we're always going to get along. We can go weeks or months not talking, some stupid little blow-up causing a bit of friction. Just because of the people we are, our day-to-day relationship is going to fluctuate between love and hate, but whenever either of us is threatened or in trouble, the day-to-day bickering doesn't mean anything; we'll be there side by side. It's an extreme kind of brotherhood but we're always going to be there for each other, no matter what.

Growing up, Jai would either be cracking me up or infuriating me. That's his personality. During my first year on tour, I brought back my first Rusty guns from Hawaii. They'd been shaped by Rusty himself, who was regarded as one of the best surfboard shapers in the world. I'd driven down to check Lurline and it was huge. I've gone, 'Sweet, I'm gonna surf my new Hawaiian boards.' I've got back to our place and they were gone. I've figured straightaway that Jai has grabbed them, so I've gone back up to Lurline and looked down near the drainpipe. I see this board come flying up from the bottom of the cliff and landing on the concrete, just dinging the shit out of it. *Jai.* He'd been washed in and was climbing back up the rocks, but instead of trying to climb up with my board in one hand, he was just throwing it up then climbing after it. By the time he got it to the top the board was ready for the dump. And he'd lent out all my other boards to his mates. That was another three months of cold war.

But we've had so many funny times and good trips together that all that stuff gets forgotten pretty quickly. Jai's the best bloke alive at making up nicknames for people. He's the master. He can size someone up in seconds and have a classic nickname for him. If you're out in the surf and some bloke pulls back on a wave, Jai will be into him. 'You want me to wrap you up in cotton wool, Cottons?' So all of a sudden this guy is stuck with the nickname Cottons for the rest of his life.

Jai's hilarious, and we love each other. It's just that sometimes, because our personalities are so different and so extreme, it's hard. You're brothers and you're passionate. It's hard sometimes being with someone who one week is talking about saving the whales and the next week he's threatening to set your car on fire.

When Jai glassed that guy, we were both there in the club together. We were in the middle of a cold war at the time; I can't remember what it was over. We were both there that night, but we weren't talking.

As soon as I saw the guy there I realised straightaway that Jai had seen him too. We'd both spotted this guy. As Jai hit him with the glass, I was moving in on him as well. His girlfriend snapped a pool cue over my head, and from there it turned into the full bar brawl.

Even though at the time we weren't even talking to each other, we were fighting side by side. It doesn't even matter that we're not going to talk later on. And Jai ends up going to jail for it. I was kind of like, 'Mate, I was going to come at the guy anyway with a pool cue. Now you've cut your hand, you can't surf, and you're going to jail.' I was two seconds away from hitting the guy, but Jai has beaten me to him.

Jai has always defended us, though. That's his nature – always looking out for everyone else with no thought for himself.

Part 5
Ride or Collide

SUNNY

IN HIS NEW INCARNATION AS AN INTERNATIONAL
MUSIC PROMOTER, SUNNY FINDS YOU CAN NEVER TAKE
THE WEATHER WITH YOU

It was around this time that I dabbled in the music business.

It all started when we were lobbying Randwick Council to get a skate park built in Maroubra – a process that went on for years. With the help of a local touring company, we organised an event to raise some money for the skate ramp. We wanted to put on some bands, have a surf comp and a skate comp, promote the surf shop, and raise a bit of money at the same time – a full crossover event. We hired this massive skate ramp, put on six punk bands like Toe To Toe, and held a surf comp, all together down on Maroubra Beach. We even made a huge slip 'n' slide running down into the surf for the grommets. We advertised it in the music mags and on pole posters, and 5000 people turned up. It was killer, and it went a long way to getting Maroubra's skate ramp built.

It was so successful that it got me thinking that we could make some money out of this. So the following year Surf Skate Slam was born. I roped in Nath Rogers, my partner in the surf shop, and Matt Goodall, who was running Maroubra boardriders with me, to help pull it off. I approached Randwick Council with the idea of doing a big outdoor concert. Of course, they were fully against it right from the start. But I'd learned heaps from going through that whole process the year before, going back and forth to the council with them constantly saying no. I learned how to get them to say yes … well, at least say yes more often, anyway.

I got a spot on the council's youth advisory group, but it was just bullshit. After listening to them talking for two years, whinging about the kids in the area and all the trouble that was being caused, when we went to them with the idea to put in a skate ramp they immediately said

MY BROTHERS KEEPER

no. Their number one priority for that year was to repaint the local fences. It didn't occur to them that if the kids were skating then they may not need to have the fences painted so often. Trying to get the permits for the concert and getting through the brick wall they put up in front of you was a nightmare. I learned a lot from doing it: how bureaucracies work and how to not take no for an answer.

My idea was to fence in the whole of Byrne Reserve on the beach at South Maroubra and hold a big surf, skate and music festival with market stalls and food. I actually fought the council right up until the night before the event to make it happen.

At the time I was planning Surf Skate Slam, Silverchair was the biggest band in Australia. *Freak Show*, their second album, had just come out, and they were huge. I thought, 'Well, if you don't ask, you don't know,' so I got in touch with Silverchair's management and put the idea to them of playing in Maroubra.

We were still going ahead with the event whether we had Silverchair or not. We had a pretty good line-up – Grinspoon, The Living End, Frenzal Rhomb and a whole lot of other bands – but not enough to get 15,000 people through the door. We needed a big band. We needed Silverchair.

I was living up in Bond Street at the time, and we set up an office in the back garage. I got my mate who worked for Telstra to run some phone lines out to the shed, we set up five desks, and we were away. It was stinking hot, because the garage had no windows. We worked on a concrete floor and it was pretty grungy, but in a way it suited what we were doing. So here we were, trying to book the number one band in the country out of a garage in North Maroubra. I'd got on to this guy, Owen Orford, who was booking Silverchair at the time. We called him and sold him on the whole idea and he went for it, he loved it, but he had to take it to the band and their management.

I was out in the surf one day over at Bondi when I got talking to a girl. As we went on, I found out that she worked for Silverchair's management. Bingo. At this stage the deal could have gone either way, and we had no idea what they were thinking. She didn't know who I was, so I started asking her about what the band was up to and when they were playing next 'cause I wanted to see 'em.

'Well, actually, they're doing a concert over the hill at Maroubra.'

There it was. We'd got 'em. I slept a little better that night.

But the police and the council tried to stop the concert the whole way. It was a full-on nightmare getting a permit for it. They called this big meeting just the week before, because Bob Carr, by random coincidence, was booked to officially open Byrne Reserve the day after the concert. Bob Carr was our local member and the NSW Premier at the time, so it was a big deal for the coppers and the council. Two weeks prior to the date they'd said, 'We're not going to give you the approval because we don't want the park trashed.' Eventually I agreed to pay to have the park cleaned by the time Carr got there, which was fair enough.

So we'd done the deal with Silverchair and signed off on it, but Owen kept asking to come over and meet us at our 'office'. During the whole brokering of the deal, we'd never met face to face. There was no way I wanted him to know the guy he was doing this six-figure deal with worked out of his garage. I kept throwing him off; telling him the office was being renovated. Owen finally got sick of talking to voices on phones, and came out to Maroubra looking for us. He asked some guys down at the beach where I lived, and someone pointed him up to Bond Street. We were in the garage working when we heard this knock on the door. Then Owen sticks his head in and sees us squirrelling away. He surveyed the scene and just pissed himself laughing.

The concert ended up being huge. We pulled it off. We had Silverchair, we had 15,000 people, and we had no real dramas with idiots coming in and causing trouble.

It worked so well that the next year we tried to do it Australia-wide. We approached the new owners of the Maroubra Bay Hotel to let us set up an office on one of the derelict floors above the pub, and somehow they agreed to it. It was too funny. It was the love shack – and that's where we were running our budding music empire. But I was soon to learn a few hard lessons of the game: namely, that while you may win the battle with bureaucracy, you never win the war.

We were gonna do one show in Sydney, one on the Gold Coast, then Coffs Harbour, then Melbourne. We ended up bringing over a heap of bands from America and Europe – Fuel, 59 Times The Pain, Down By Law, No Fun At All and Sprung Monkey. I'd gotten all the council approvals. It had been the same shitfight with officialdom, but because we'd pulled off one show successfully and had runs on the board, it had smoothed the road a bit.

Then I had a meeting with the new mayor of Randwick Council a week before the Sydney show – the first show of the tour – and he's gone, 'Bad luck about your concert.'

'What do you mean?'

'The council voted last night not to give you approval.'

'Mate, I've got a signed permit from you guys here in my bag.'

The council had already issued a statement in the paper that day saying Surf Skate Slam was off. We threatened to sue 'em and there was this huge emergency meeting. They were all trying to shut us down. In the end, they only relented under the threat of a giant lawsuit, and the gig went ahead.

It rained the day of the Sydney concert and we only did 8000 punters.

The next day, when we got to the Gold Coast, our concert site was surrounded by police claiming the event was a money-laundering operation, and I was told half the venue was now off limits. I had to refund 3000 tickets, and on the day of the concert it pissed down again. Next day in Coffs Harbour we got hit by a lightning storm. By this stage we were in a hole. We cancelled Melbourne. The tour had been a disaster of monu-fucking-mental proportions, the scope of which I'd only truly recognise in coming weeks when I was staring at a pile of invoices a foot high and a bank account that covered the first inch and a half of them.

All up, we lost about 80 grand. That was tough. To work on it for so long and have it implode like that in two days was fucked. That was hard, because I owed people money, which I'd never done before. We'd tried to do it the right way and pay all our bills, which we eventually did. It was fucking heartbreaking, and it marked the end of my career as a concert promoter.

JAI

LYING PRONE IN THE BACK TRAY OF A UTE ON THE PRINCES HIGHWAY, JAI EXPERIENCES A CUMULUS REVELATION

Before jail I was more into spiritual bullshit, but in Long Bay I started saying me prayers.

I was in there six months. I had a Bible with me, and I started building some faith. I remember praying, hoping I got out of there no with dramas, hoping I didn't stay there long, hoping I'd just have a smooth run.

When I got locked up that first time, I'd been dealing with a lot, and when people have problems in their lives they go searching for answers. When I was 12, my grandfather, who was like my dad, died; then my grandmother had a stroke and lost her voice. I just had to deal with things, and needed answers, early in life. I needed to know whether there was something else there.

I've seen things, brother, unexplainable things.

One day in '99, not long after I got out of Long Bay, Shane Chappo and I were carpet laying at Berkeley RSL Club in Wollongong. There were four of us and we'd just knocked off for the day. We were driving home in the ute, so we had to go rock-paper-scissors to see which one of us had to lie in the back from Wollongong to Maroubra. I lost. We start driving up the Princes Highway and I'm laying flat on the tray, watching the clouds go past above me. I looked up and said, 'God, if you're true, I'd love to see something.' I closed my eyes.

God strike me down if I'm lying, but when I opened my eyes and looked up at the clouds there was the most perfect lead pencil sketch you've ever seen of a lady holding a baby. The clouds were white, but there was this perfect detail of a lady holding a baby – Mary holding Jesus. I remember it clearly.

God showed me something, but I didn't use it like I should have, I didn't pray. Because when things are going well for you, you forget about it; it's often only when you're in a bad situation that you turn to prayer. It wasn't till all this drama I had later on with Tony that I turned to prayer again.

When I hear people say they don't believe in God, I think they haven't been through much in their life, while those who have strong faith, generally have. At a young age I read Stuart Wilde and other new age books, because I needed answers younger than most other people would. It all led me to God.

God is true. God decides whether you walk out and get hit by a car right now. God decides whether you get shot right now, *boom boom boom*. Everything that happens here, God's pulling the strings up there. Here is only a test to see if we make it to the next life. So people shouldn't be too greedy down here or cut their morals short, because we're here for a flash, but it's eternity in Hell or eternity in Heaven. It's a long time, brother. Fear God.

Me and Koby are both Geminis. But you know what they say – most Geminis spend their lives fighting each other and fighting themselves. If you can find balance between your two halves and get them working together, though, you become powerful. Who the fuck wants to spend their life fighting themselves?

Koby makes out he's not at all spiritual, but when he showed me the tattoo of the Devil he had done on his knee, I went, 'You're fucking tripping, bra. I wouldn't get that on me for 10,000 bucks. You want to even that shit out, bra, you want to even that shit out.'

He makes out he doesn't believe in it, then, *boom*, a week later he's turned up at my place with the biggest cross tattooed in the middle of his back, and now he's got a tattoo of Mary on his arm. He's been listening to God, bra, even if he doesn't know it.

johnny gannon

BLOOD, SWEAT AND BEERS — THE MAROUBRA TRAINING REGIME

Me and Koby used to train a lot when he was younger.

He didn't drink, he didn't smoke, and he was full-on into his training. We'd run, swim laps of the beach and do a lot of boxing. When Ma lived up in Bond Street, we set up a gym with an outdoor boxing ring. We did a lot of sparring, and anyone who rocked up would end up in there whether they liked it or not. We had odd boxing gloves. The ropes were made from leggies, and we only had two mouthguards, which were both full of blood and spit. It was only the bare essentials, but we just used to rip into each other. And that was when everyone really started getting into their training. They were good times, because it really brought everyone close together. No one trained on their own; you always trained with mates. It's how we still try and teach the younger guys today – get 'em into training and keep 'em out of trouble.

It was super-competitive up there. Occasionally it went from fun to serious, especially if an outsider came in and got over one of the boys. But between the boys it was hit as hard as you want. Everyone was so competitive to be the best boxer, or do the most chin-ups. We used to have chin-up competitions every day. Kobe got pretty good at 'em at one stage; he's really competitive. If I did more chins than him, he'd train secretly every day, just doing chins, until he could beat me.

He'd started surfing big waves around that time, and I think he realised that it was his way out – not out of the area, but his one way to succeed at something he loved. He trained so hard and was so fit it was unbelievable.

Jai and Sunny got into the training, but they weren't as full on into it as Koby. They more just surfed and charged big waves.

One day we were on the beach doing some boxing when this Brazilian guy, Alex Prates, come down. In his broken English he asked if he could train with us. We said, 'Sure, no worries.' We did a boxing session, and afterwards he started telling us about jujitsu. We didn't know much about it, so he showed us a few moves. It was unbelievable. He showed us a standing guillotine choke. It's such a simple move and we could all do it pretty well straightaway. We'd all been in that position in a fight before and we thought, 'Fuck, if we had that move we'd be beating anyone.' He's done a few sessions with us, and we were going mad with it. We knew nothing, but were trying to choke each other and crack each other's shoulders. Alex spent his whole time telling us to slow down, 'cause we were going to hurt each other. He said, 'If you really want to learn jujitsu properly, you need to see my friend Bruno.' So Sunny and I and a few others went over to the Police Boys Club at North Sydney and did some sessions with Bruno Pano. Once he found out there were 20 or 30 guys ready to start doing it, he moved to Maroubra and opened an academy here. So instead of us trying to kill each other, he taught us it's about trying to use your opponent's strength against them, instead of using your strength.

Jujitsu is good in a way, especially in defusing situations down in the pub. Instead of walking up and hitting someone as hard as you can on the chin and they fall over and hit their head on the ground and you go to jail, with jujitsu, if someone's being a complete fuckwit – even one of the boys – you can walk up, put a choke on 'em, lie 'em on the ground and they're asleep for 10 seconds. When they wake up they've still got their teeth and you haven't caused a massive scene.

In Maroubra we'll go through phases where everyone's training; it's generally when the waves have been ordinary for a couple of weeks. Once a couple of guys get back into it and start talking, pretty soon the whole crew is back into it. It runs hot for a while then tapers back off when the swell comes back up.

The fitter and stronger you are around here, the more you look after yourself and train up, the more self-respect you'll generate, and the more people look up to you. It sounds a bit Neanderthal, but that's the way it is around Maroubra. It's a good thing as well because, to a degree, it keeps the young blokes out of trouble. We try and push it as much as we can. We got a lot of them into jujitsu. Just that discipline of turning up to training every day hopefully carries on with them later in life when they've got to go and make something of themselves. You've got to work. You're never going to get anything sitting on your arse waiting for something to happen.

KOBY

KOBY TAKES A WEEK OFF FROM HIS CARPET–LAYING GIG TO WIN THE MOST DANGEROUS SURFING CONTEST OF ALL TIME

I'd never really heard anything about the surf in Tahiti before I went there for the world tour contest at Teahupoo.

The Tahitian surfer Poto, one of my favourite surfers at the time, had always said there were mad waves there. With my carpet-laying money I paid for a ticket and headed off, not really knowing what I was letting myself in for. I was only 17, but after doing okay in that Nias comp I knew that if the waves were good I might go okay.

When I got there the surf was three or four foot, perfect little reef waves, and I just thought, 'Unreal, I might do all right in the contest.' The wave at Teahupoo breaks on a reef pass half-a-mile out to sea, under the shadow of these giant green volcanic mountains. The place is so fucking beautiful, bra. We're surfing these fun little coral reef waves thinking, ya know, that we'd found paradise.

I'm doing okay in the contest, making a few heats, when the swell suddenly jumped up to six foot, and the wave is just firing. All of a sudden I find myself drawn in the quarters against three of the best tube riders in the world – Nathan Fletcher, Myles Padaca and one of my all-time heroes, Hawaiian Johnny Boy Gomes. I go to bed the night before the finals thinking, 'How good is this?'

If there is an opposite to paradise, the next morning was it. Before we even leave the dock to drive out to the reef I can see it's *way* bigger than the day before. There's water washing up onto the road. We pull the boat up in the channel as a set hits, and it's 12 fucking foot, easy. It's huge, and really fucking heavy. I'd never seen waves like that before; no one had. We didn't think waves could do what these waves were doing. People were freaking. Guys were running around, panicking.

'Let's call it off, someone's gonna get hurt!'

I'm going, 'What are you talking about? It's on! No argument. I'm scared shitless but we're going.'

No one had seen a contest like this before; not even Pipeline would've been this heavy. These waves were coming out of water hundreds of feet deep and surging waist deep over the coral reef. Crew thought someone was gonna die there that day, and a couple of guys almost did. Before I even jumped out of the boat it started to dawn on me that I was going to win, because I knew I was the only guy who was gonna go these things.

I paddle out for my quarter straight to where I think the takeoff spot is. No one had seen it this big and no one had any clue where to sit. Anyway, it's the first wave of the first heat of the day. I paddle into a 10-footer and just get the biggest barrel of my life and get spat into the channel.

'Koby Abberton, perfect 10.'

I just thought, 'How easy is this?' I paddled back out there and Nathan Fletcher, who became one of my best friends down the track, says to me, 'Did you make that wave? There's no way I'm going one of those things.'

Nathan's one of those deep thinkers, and he had no trouble telling me he was scared that day. He's since told me that that day changed his life, bra. He was smoking and being pretty bad to himself, and that day made him turn it all around. He's now one of the best tube riders in heavy surf you've ever seen. That day changed a lot of people's lives, I reckon.

Anyway I'm paddling back out and here's Johnny Boy Gomes. He'd won the Pipe Masters a few months before, and was regarded as just about the toughest, heaviest guy in surfing. You had to tread pretty carefully around him.

But he's just sitting there. I'm thinking, 'Well, if he's not gonna go, I am,' so I paddle past him. I take off on another one and get a nine pointer to go with my 10. As I've paddled past him a second time I just felt a tug on my legrope. It's Johnny Boy, and he's pissed off.

'If you get another wave, I'm gonna beat the fuck out of ya.'

'Fuck off, mate, what have I done?'

He looped my legrope around his leg so I couldn't paddle anywhere. I'm 17 and about half his size, and I'm thinking, 'What the fuck do I do here?' I look across at Nathan and he's like, 'Sorry, dude, I can't help ya here.'

Johnny Boy's held me there for probably 10 minutes until he's gone to paddle for a wave. He missed it and he's just screaming at himself, wigging out that he couldn't get into one. So he's snagged my legrope again. I'm going, 'Fucking let go of me!' As he's turned to paddle for a wave he's let go of me and I've swung around him on his inside and just stolen the wave off him. That was another nine. As I paddled back out I could hear him from miles away screaming, 'You're fucking dead, bra!' I'm just thinking, 'Yes, I won the heat!' I didn't even think, 'Hey, that massive guy over there – he's really pissed.'

The judges' scoring was all over the place. As the final paddled out, the onshore wind hit, so I've thought to myself, 'I've gotta get the first wave before it gets too ugly.' I got the first one and it's another perfect 10. I've paddled straight back out to the inside and got a nine. I just sat there and thought, 'I've got this.' Then I see Conan Hayes, the Hawaiian, get one … and suddenly I'm no guarantee of winning this thing. Then we're just going at it, trading waves. He got an eight, then I've got one and been clipped and washed in across the reef. As I'm paddling back out I've seen Conan paddle into this monster. He shoulda won; that wave was a 12 out of 10. But you can't score higher than a 10 and they had nowhere to go with their judging scale even though his 10 was better than my 10. But it's happened to me a heap of times since, so I don't care. I can still sleep at night. Conan's a millionaire with his clothing company now and I've got nothing, so it's all evened out.

And so there it was – I'd won. I couldn't believe it; this was the maddest. I'm looking at the 10 grand prize cheque going, 'This is the shit!' Bra, as soon as I went in I started skolling this cheap wine. I got up on the podium and I couldn't even see! I was that fucking drunk I must've come across as the biggest knucklehead. But I didn't care because I had nothing; I was going back to nothing at home. I was going home to lay carpet.

But now I had 10 grand.

Everyone's suddenly going, 'You should come and do the WQS tour, bra. You're coming third on the ratings and you've only done one contest.' So I went, fuck yeah, I'm on. When I got home, MCD sponsored me and I surfed the whole year on the World Qualifying Series. I only needed to finish in the top 16 and I'd be on the proper world tour. I did the whole year, travelling through France, South Africa, all over the place. I had a ball.

But then in November came Hawaii – and shit was about to catch up with me.

KOBY

THE KOBY ABBERTON STARDOM EXPRESS HITS A MINOR SPEED BUMP IN THE GUISE OF A RATHER IRATE HAWAIIAN COLOSSUS

I remember walking out of Honolulu airport and wondering who might be there to pick me up. I pass through Customs and I see my biggest idol ever – Brock Little, the Hawaiian big-wave legend. I'm looking around, wondering who he's there to pick up, and he's walked over to me.

'Koby?'

'Er, yeah.'

We pile my boards into the van and as we drive off towards the North Shore he turns to me.

'What did you do to Johnny Boy?' I hadn't given what happened a minute's thought since Tahiti. Brock goes, 'Bra, *he wants to kill you.*'

I'd been hanging out most of the year with Wink and Matty Gye, a mate of mine who was making surf movies, travelling up and down the coast in Australia, through France and South Africa, partying and having a good time.

The next morning, Matty comes around to my place; he's all rattled.

'Mate, Johnny Boy just slapped Toby Martin because he thought Toby was you!' He thought 'Toby' was 'Koby'; he was slapping Aussie guys whose name even sounded like mine. The news wasn't good, but I started laughing.

'Bra, who gives a fuck?'

Matty went, 'No, *he really wants to fuck you up.*'

I asked around as to where he'd be. I hate hiding. Growing up around Maroubra, when something like this comes up you confront it, then it's over. So I thought I might as well go and see him.

I heard he was at Haleiwa, surfing in the contest, so I get Brock to drive me there. As we pull into the car park at Haleiwa, Johnny Boy is right there. He just starts running at the car; he was the biggest human I've ever seen.

'Holy shit …'

I'm thinking I'm gonna get bashed in the car, so I quickly jump out. He's right there, blocking out the sun, twice his normal size. It's pretty clear he's not happy with me.

'You wanna go, *bwoooy*?'

'Fuck no I wanna go. Have a look at the size of ya!'

He's about 18 stone and I'm 12. He's 30-something and I'm 18.

'Mate, you're Johnny Boy Gomes. You'll kill me.'

'Come here, bwoooy. I wanna talk to you in the toilets!'

So we walk into the toilets and as soon as we get in he just smashes me. We start fighting and I'm just windmilling, trying to save myself, scared shitless. He bashed me up. The biggest rumour ever was that Johnny Boy Gomes got beaten up by *me*. He punched the fuck out of me! But what happened was he threw a huge punch at me; I ducked it and his hand hit the wall. He broke his hand. After that he's gone, 'Enough.'

I had a big cut on my eye and a bleeding nose.

He says, 'Wash your face. I don't want trouble.'

'Mate, I don't tell on people anyway.'

'That's good to hear. You're a man. Not many people are gonna do that.'

I told him I didn't mean any disrespect and that I was sorry. And this is how the whole story about me beating him came about. In all the punches I threw I must have landed one and he had a little bit of blood on his eye. I've got a clean face 'cause he made me wash it. But there's no way I'm gonna say to Johnny Boy, 'Hey, mate, *you* better wash *your* face.' He woulda bashed me again. I just walked out all cleaned up. There's crew outside who knew what was happening inside; they've seen me come out clean and Johnny Boy with a bit of blood on him and gone, 'Holy fuck, he's bashed Johnny Boy!' I've grabbed my board and just gone for a surf. They're all thinking this cunt has gone in there and beaten up Johnny Boy ... then gone for a surf afterwards! And so it's started all over again.

The following year when I've got to Hawaii I'm hearing from everyone that he's after me again. Fucking *great*. By this stage I was hanging out with Bruce Irons and those other Hawaiian guys, so I thought I was safe. Anyway, fresh off the plane I'm riding my bike back home in the dark from Brock's house. It's all muddy, so I get off my bike and push it. I look ahead and I see this guy with his back turned to me, with this huge tiger tattoo on it, with a whole heap of other big Hawaiian guys.

It's Johnny Boy.

I've gone, 'Get fucked! Look what I've just walked into.' I'm walking in the opposite direction with my head down when I hear this loud screeching.

'*Koooooobyyyy!*'

He spots me. Then I look up and I realise they're holding some guy. How's the luck of me: first day back in Hawaii riding through there in the middle of the night and that's what I run into.

'*Kooooobyyyy!* Come here!'

I started riding off in the other direction.

'You coward, *Koooooobyyyy!* Get back here!'

I go, 'Fuck this, I gotta face him.' So I turn around and see that the Hawaiian guys he's with are holding this *haole* and beating him up. I worked out something real bad was going on, but for some stupid reason I walked up to them.

'Hey, boys, what's up?' Just trying to break the ice.

Then Johnny Boy comes flying at me. Suddenly one of the other Hawaiian guys said to Johnny Boy, 'Hey, we got other business here.' Johnny Boy's turned to me and gone, 'Koby, get out of here, you stoopid fucking *bwooooy!*'

When I was in Hawaii last year, 10 years after the Tahiti incident, I heard Johnny Boy was still looking for me.

I'd met Bruce and Andy Irons in Tahiti that same year I won – 1998 – and a year later I was hanging out over on Kauai with those guys and their crew. Lots of the Kauai and North Shore guys were from the same kind of background as a lot of the Maroubra guys, so we got on with those guys right from the start. They'd look after us when we were in Hawaii; we'd look after them when they were in Australia.

The following year me, a young surfer from Maroubra named Mark Mathews, Bruce Irons and Myles Padaca, who's also Hawaiian, were in Margaret River. We're walking along the street and this guy goes past us with a heap of his mates and just looks at Myles and goes, 'Ya fucking black cunt.'

Myles just keeps on walking, because there's about 20 of them. I turned around.

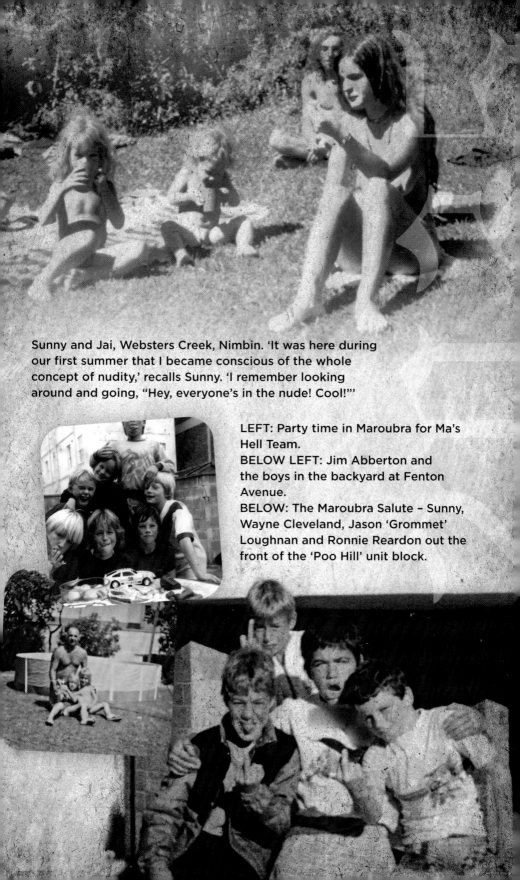

Sunny and Jai, Websters Creek, Nimbin. 'It was here during our first summer that I became conscious of the whole concept of nudity,' recalls Sunny. 'I remember looking around and going, "Hey, everyone's in the nude! Cool!"'

LEFT: Party time in Maroubra for Ma's Hell Team.
BELOW LEFT: Jim Abberton and the boys in the backyard at Fenton Avenue.
BELOW: The Maroubra Salute – Sunny, Wayne Cleveland, Jason 'Grommet' Loughnan and Ronnie Reardon out the front of the 'Poo Hill' unit block.

A young Jai Abberton dropping into the 'Dunny Bowl', where Maroubra's best righthander met the overflow from the Malabar sewerage works.

LEFT: Koby and Jai with hand-me-down board and wetsuit.

RIGHT: Ma's Hell Team clean up at the North Maroubra Surf Riders annual presentation.

TOP TO BOTTOM: Sunny and the NSW team for the 1988 Australian Scholastic Titles at Bells Beach; the humble North Maroubra Surf Riders club tent; Sunny, amongst Australia's best junior surfers at Narrabeen; the motley North Maroubra crew.

At a young age, Sunny took his act from the sands of Maroubra to the world stage.

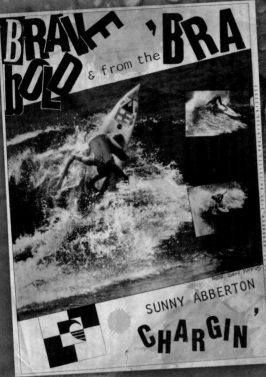

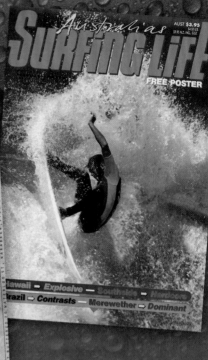

TOP: Sunny, amongst it on the biggest day ever surfed at Ours, June 2007.

BELOW: Sunny with his co-director on the *Bra Boys* film, Macario De Souza

SUNNY ABBERTON

KOBY ABBERTON

Koby, Apocalypse, Java.

Cloudbreak, Fiji, and the wave voted the world's best tube ride of 2005.

Chilling in Bali, Koby's second home of late.

King of the road, heading north.

JAI ABBERTON

OPPOSITE PAGE:
(1) The Bra Boys family photo, 2003; (2) Jay Brown, one of Maroubra's early surf stars; (3) Ronnie Reardon, ready to fight for the Australian title; (4) Maroubra, home of the Australian surfing animal; (5–7) Koby, Ours. 'I couldn't believe it. I'd travelled around the world a hundred times chasing heavy waves, and one of the heaviest waves in the world was just down the road from Maroubra and we didn't even know about it.'

1

2

3

4

5

6

7

The 5th of the 5th, 2005, and Jai, clutching a crucifix and flanked by his family, walks free from the NSW Supreme Court after being found not guilty of the shooting murder of Tony Hines.

Jai, Koby and Sunny celebrate with a beer in the Maroubra Bay Hotel after Koby avoids a jail term in relation to the shooting.

Sunny, Jai and Koby take a sibling bonding trip to Cyclops – the most dangerous wave in Australia.

Jai rolling the dice on his backhand.

Four hours and several litres of blood later, Koby finally makes it to a hospital.

Sunny, about to run out of water on the barnacle-encrusted reef at Cyclops.

DAKOTA ABBERTON

Sunny and Dakota, 2035-ing.
INSET: Like his three brothers before him, Dakota was thrown into the waves of Maroubra at an early age.

ABOVE: Jai, Koby and Dakota with their grandma, the marvellous Mavis Abberton.
BELOW: Blood, sweat, but no tears in the Bond Street boxing ring.
BOTTOM: The new Maroubra, featuring the novelty of green, clean water.

Sunny's daughter, Kiyahna – 'the sea breeze from the north'.

A rare convergence of all four Abberton siblings on McKeon Street, Maroubra.

Koby and Sunny with Russell Crowe at the Sydney premiere of their movie, *Bra Boys*.

The Maroubra entourage after *Bra Boys* won the X-Dance Film Festival in Utah.

Koby: 'I just love being out in the waves at Maroubra and hanging with my mates. Surf some good waves with ya mates, come in, beers on the hill; there's no better day than that to me, you know. My best surf trips haven't been to Tahiti or Hawaii, they've been down the road at Maroubra. It's not always about the waves.'

'What the fuck did you just say?'

'*Ya fucking … black … cunt.*'

I asked him who he was talking to, and he pointed at Myles. I've just snuck my way closer to him, pretending I couldn't hear, and said, 'What did you say again?' then just went, *whack,* and knocked him out cold. Me and Mark ended up getting the shit punched out of us. But then they went back to Hawaii and word got out that we'd helped 'em out, so from then on if anything happened to me I was on Bruce's team and vice versa. When they come to Australia they stay at my house. We're close to the Hawaiian guys to this day … they've stood by me through all the shit we've been through.

Those guys cop a lot of shit for policing the line-up at Pipe, but I think it's good what they are doing 'cause Pipe is so heavy. There's mushroom head rocks underwater, sharp ones. If you get kooks out there dropping in on people, people will die. So if someone steps out of line, if something bad goes on, one of the boys will blow the whistle, which generally means the guy who's dropped in will get slapped. People say you don't need violence, but if they weren't policing that place more people would die. I fully believe it.

I've pulled dead bodies out of the water there at Pipe. I tried to save a guy one year … only I didn't save him. I was sitting in the water and I noticed this guy on a boogieboard way out the back. It wasn't a big day, maybe six foot, eight foot, and he was way way out, Third Reef, half-a-mile out to sea. I was wondering what the fuck he was doing out there. It looked like he was lying on his board, but then he'd bob underwater then pop back up again. It was hard to see him because you'd lose him in between the swells. Even though I don't like boogieboarders, I tried to keep an eye out for this guy because I wasn't sure he was that okay. I pointed him out to some other guys and they were curious as well. He wasn't moving naturally which is what made it seem strange.

Anyway, I caught a couple of waves and eventually paddled in. By this stage it's about five o'clock and starting to get dark. Then all of a sudden I've noticed a boogieboard floating loose through the middle of the crowd. No one seemed too interested in trying to see where the guy who owned it was. Then it clicked that it was the same boogieboard I'd seen that guy on earlier. So I went and grabbed the board and threw it into a wave so it was out of the way. As I've grabbed it I felt weight underneath it, then this arm broke the surface, attached to the boogieboard by the arm rope.

I've pulled the guy to the surface and tried to drag him onto my board, but he weighed a ton and was just bloated and really white. There were no signs of life whatsoever. He was full of water and he wasn't breathing, but I presumed he'd only been under for a couple of minutes so I had to get him onto the beach quick. I managed to drag him onto the beach, laid him out and started to do mouth-to-mouth. He wasn't breathing and he had no pulse. I gave him about four puffs, and every time I gave him one I'd get a mouthful of water – and I mean a *full* mouthful. He was so full of water it was under pressure and it'd shoot back up and go straight down my throat. I thought, 'Fuck, this is heavy.' Then Brock Little showed up and started giving him mouth-to-mouth as well and the same thing's happened. After a minute Brock's gone, 'There's nothing we can do for this guy.' The lifeguards came down soon after with the tube and the mouthpiece and started working on him, but the guy was gone. Turns out he'd been dead for a day, floating around out there.

I was sitting at home two months later and I get a call from one of the lifeguards.

'Are you sitting down, Koby? That guy you rescued had AIDS.'

So much for being a good bloke and trying to rescue someone. That's your reward: AIDS. I'd sucked in about five litres of AIDS water. So I had to go for another AIDS test and wait two months for the results. The wait was freaky as shit. I'd had AIDS tests before, but that time I was scared, because I was a bit older and knew the consequences if it had come back positive. Both me and Brock talked about it, because he had to be tested as well. It was heavy. I nearly fell over on the spot when I got the call telling me it was negative. It was another get out of jail free card.

SUNNY

A BIG WEEKEND WAS HAD BY ALL WHEN YOU WAKE UP ON MONDAY MORNING TO DISCOVER YOU'VE BEEN BANNED FROM AN ENTIRE STATE

Maroubra Boardriders had essentially wound up in the early '90s. For 10 years it was basically just kids, as most of the original older guys had left Maroubra – some of their own accord, some with a bit of heat applied to them by the cops. When the boardriders club was healthy, Maroubra was healthy, so now that I was off the tour and I had the time, I threw myself back into the club to see if we could get it back to its former glory and give the kids something to do.

The presidency of Maroubra Boardriders had been a kiss of death to a number of guys over the years, had sent some of them over the edge, so a few of us decided to run it as a committee with the aim of making it a big social club more than anything else.

Matt Goodall and I did all the administration, while Moff was Murdoch from *The A Team*, because he could put up the club tent, stick the flags in the sand, and have the first sausage sandwiches off the barbecue before the first heat had hit the water.

We just wanted to try and get as many of the guys back to the beach as possible. We'd physically drive around to people's houses on a Sunday morning and wake the grommets up and drag them out of bed and down to the contest. It was surf all day, then beers and a barbie at the end.

It started as a social club, but, being Maroubra, it soon turned really competitive. Jimmy Olsen would come down and lay a book for each surfer, so you could bet five bucks on Koby beating Jai in a heat. You could bet on whoever you wanted. We'd spend the whole day down there laughing and generally being knuckleheads.

We'd rig the finals.

'It's a dead heat, boys, and we can't separate you guys on a countback.'

So when the two guys got back to the beach, the rest of the crew had to decide how they'd settle it. We always carried two pairs of boxing gloves and a big ghetto blaster with us to every contest, and the crowd had to decide how it was going to be sorted out.

Fight for it or dance for it?

If it was fight, you'd have to put the gloves on and fight a couple of rounds for first place. If it was dance, we'd fire up the ghetto blaster, and you got a whole track to bust out your biggest moves. It was also a good way to bring a lot of these kids out of their shells a bit.

Meanwhile, Jimmy was doing his own bit to keep the young blokes off the streets and out of trouble. When Jimmy left school he'd done a carpet-laying apprenticeship with another local guy, Wazza Fox. The two of them are the hardest working blokes in Maroubra, and over the years they've put about 30 kids from the beach on their books and given them work and a trade. They became Maroubra's own version of Centrelink. Jai's worked with him, Koby, Ronnie, both the Kingsleys, Shifty, Balby, Richie, Evo, Beasty, Cory, Trots, Troy Boy, now young Kano. The list is so long. Anyone Jimmy knew was a good kid and needed the work, he'd put 'em on. His carpet-laying business has funded about a thousand surf trips over the years, but at the same time he also taught those young blokes a lot about hard work. Mind you, whenever the surf was good they'd down tools and go surfing.

Maroubra would often surf against other clubs. Apart from the time we trumped Merewether, who were the national champions at the time, it was always more a social, cultural thing for us. We paid heaps of attention to the B-grade guys, because we knew there's no sense in just having the same final out there every week. The real people who make up the club are the guys who get down there early and put in the effort. You've got to make it fun for everyone otherwise no one keeps showing up and the whole thing dies in the arse.

And then came the 2002 Kirra Teams Titles, where I think we became the only boardriding club in history to be banned from a state. The Kirra

Teams had become pretty huge by this stage, and all the best clubs from around Australia would travel to the Gold Coast for it in February each year.

Before we left we advertised in the *Gold Coast Bulletin*, looking for a 'mascot'. Eventually, one of the boys said to us, 'Look, I've got this chick here who'll do it.' We thought she was a stripper, and that she was going to do some dancing, maybe a bit of topless action, put on a show for the other teams ... Anyway, she's said she'd come and dance on the beach all weekend if we paid her airfare up there, so all the boys chipped in and she was booked.

It was a funny trip. We all met at the Maroubra Bay Hotel, which was where the bus was leaving from. It was a 22-seater, and in the end I think we packed 28 guys onto it. Our mate Lopez, the spaghetti guy, just happened to be drinking at the pub when the bus pulled up, which was bad luck for him. Next thing he knows he's on the bus with us. I grabbed him a pair of boardies and a shirt from across the road at the surf shop, and we kidnapped him.

A million joints were passed around on the trip up, 20 cases were drunk. The theme of the trip was: 'Nobody sleeps, nobody gets hurt'. Everyone had razors, everyone had scissors. After hour after hour of drinking and smoking you'd eventually get people nodding off; within seconds their eyebrows were gone and a bald spot buzzcut from their scalp. Lopez fell asleep on the bus floor and we shaved both his eyebrows, and cut every piece of clothing he was wearing in half, straight down the middle. Out of the 28 people on the bus, 20 had their eyebrows and hair mutilated, so to say that we looked like a rough bunch by the time we got there was an understatement.

We arrived on the Gold Coast the next day and the contest was huge. All of Australia's biggest clubs were there with their best guys, huge buses and giant tents set up on the beach. We set up under these pandanus palms at the back of Duranbah Beach with our shitty Housing Commission tent. It had a rusty steel frame with a crappy blue tarp stretched over it. But what we did have was a DJ with a giant PA that blasted to life at eight every morning, we had a dozen cases of piss, which also started at eight, and we had The Mascot. On the first day of the contest, half the boys had been out all night and hadn't slept; they've come straight from the strip clubs in Surfers Paradise to the beach.

The first day at Duranbah was massive. The Mascot was topless by 9am, and as the day progressed the whole thing snowballed downhill at a rate of knots.

That night a couple of our grommets walked over to McDonald's at Greenmount to get a feed and had a run-in with this big gang of guys in the park, who proceeded to beat the shit out of them. They come running back covered in blood, telling us how they'd just been snotted by this group of homeboys. Next thing there's a whole crew of our older guys running down there to confront 'em.

Our mate Corey Adams, whose son had been beaten up, has marched straight up to 'em and gone, 'Which one's ya leader?'

There's about 40 or 50 of 'em there, Koori lads and homeboys, and some big bloke has stepped forward and said, 'Me.' It was on straightaway, this giant rumble. Ronnie had a beer in his hand at the time, and knocked out three guys without spilling a drop. They had a full-on go, but got reasonably sorted out.

The next day our mascot lifted another gear, and it was just one of the all-time days. Somehow we were doing really good in the contest, and from Australia's best 24 clubs we ended up finishing fourth. We had a massive barbie down on the beach in the afternoon which turned into a giant dance-off between the grommets from all the different clubs. Then the legropes came out and it turned into a ritual flogging, where you'd have to see how many lashes with the legrope you could take. It was going mental. Maroubra comes to the Gold Coast. It was just a full crazy, healthy day of surf, sex and rock 'n' roll.

That night we had the presentation. We were all walking down to a local nightclub in Coolangatta, and in the distance we could see this stink starting out the front of the club. As we got closer we realised it was our guys in it. The bouncers ended up retreating into the club, locking the doors, evacuating everyone through the back and calling the riot squad.

There were dogs and police surrounding the nightclub, all because of a punch-up out the front. Nineteen of our guys got arrested. The stuff in the paper the next day included the line 'the Bra Boys threaten civilisation'.

Since then we've been banned from Queensland as a group. The local police said that if we came over the border for the contest the following year they'd shut it down. The Kirra club and the other clubs supported us; they backed us up, saying that there'd been trouble in the lead-up with both the gang in the park and the bouncers at this nightclub. But the article in the local paper the next day ended with something like: 'So as the 19 sit in the cold, dank cells of the lock-up, it'd mean nothing more than a good yarn to their mates back at the Dunny Bowl.' We were banned from Queensland for 10 years. We've only got to wait until 2012 and we're back in.

KOBY

PAID 15 GRAND A MONTH TO GO SURFING AND HAPPIER THAN A PIG IN ITS OWN GILDED FILTH

I think it may have fucked me, surfing that many good waves as a kid. It just meant I had these great expectations every time I left for a surf trip. And when I joined the pro tour we were travelling to spots with a lot of shitty surf. I started thinking, 'Do I really want to do this?' Knowing all those perfect waves were out there while I was somewhere else meant I was losing my mind. I started to realise I'd signed my life away to ride shit waves.

I believed all along I could make the WCT, the Dream Tour, but after three years I was over it. I just couldn't do it. My first year on the qualifying tour, the year I won Tahiti, I finished 40th. My second year,

1999, I dropped back to 60th. In my last year I did it full-on. Halfway through the season all I had to do was make the quarterfinals in one event and I was in. You wouldn't reckon I could fuck it up, but I did. I needed to finish 16th. I finished 33rd. I just said to myself after that, 'I'm not going through this shit all over again.'

I started watching what other surfers around the world were doing, the guys who weren't surfing contests. They were discovering incredible waves, surfing, doing photo trips and being paid to do it. And here I am travelling the world to lose heats in shit surf. I just made the decision: 'Fuck it, I'm gonna do it.' I asked my sponsors whether they wanted me to do the qualifying tour or just go freesurfing, and they said, 'We don't really care.' So I walked away from it and have hardly surfed a heat since.

There was no real plan. I was still getting paid to go surfing, but instead of surfing two-foot shit surf in Brazil and losing to some guy I've never heard of, I was surfing the biggest, heaviest waves I could find, and I had someone there taking photos and shooting footage. Suddenly it just opened a whole new world. It was about the same time that swell forecasting started to get really good, and that changed everything for me.

I had a hit list of spots, all these heavy waves I liked to surf. I'd check the forecasts and see the swell coming seven days out, then I'd just keep an eye on it. Once I'd see a swell building I'd check the forecasts a couple of times a day, because the swell can change dramatically in six hours. I just watch it from the seventh day to the sixth to the fifth. Then I watch it down to day two, and if it's still looking strong and I know it's a groundswell, I just book the closest flight I can get to it. If the swell's hitting at six in the morning, I'll try and fly into the place at 10 the night before. You wait till the last swell update then you just jump on a flight. The full hit-and-run.

My new program worked. During the three years I was on the tour I had one cover of a surf mag, a shitty little two-foot wave from France. Within six months of freesurfing and chasing good, heavy surf, I had four. I had feature stories in mags in America, Australia, and I was in movies all over the place. Made me think why I hadn't fucking done it earlier, bra.

My only problem was that I was so impatient. If I showed up somewhere and the waves weren't there, I'd just leave. I hate waiting around. It's probably not a good habit for a surfer to have, 'cause even though the forecasting sites can predict the swell, it's still the ocean and it's always going to throw some waves at you when you don't expect it. That's what happened in Tasmania. That trip is something I still regret, one of those things that still honestly burns me to the bottom of my soul.

We'd heard a few rumours about this righthander down the bottom of Tassie, but at that stage no one knew anything about it. I'd spoken to Tassie surfer Andy Campbell about it. He'd surfed it, but he wasn't talking it up too much. I now know why: he had one of the world's maddest waves down there all to himself.

In April 2001 we went down to Tassie with photographer Sean Davey to find this wave. There was me, Kieren Perrow, Drew Courtney and my mate from Maroubra, Marky Mathews. We get down to Tassie and it's fucking freezing, the wind is howling, and we're stuck inside for two days waiting for the weather to clear. You couldn't walk outside, bra. Seriously, it was that cold your nose would have just turned black and dropped off. On the third night I was sitting there when Dean Morrison rings me from the Gold Coast and says, 'Kirra's pumping, get up here.' It was six foot and he said it was gonna be all-time the following day. I turned on the TV and on the news I see footage of Kirra just firing. I looked outside and it's about minus 10 degrees with torrential rain. I had a Qantas staff ticket, so I could fly to the Gold Coast for $50, and the next flight left in two hours.

'That's it, boys, I'm outta here. I'm going to Kirra.'

They've all gone, 'We're coming!' but no one could afford the flight. I'd paid for Mark's trip 'cause he was only young, and he's going, 'Take me with ya, please!'

'Nah, mate, you wanna be a surfer, this is what you have to go through.' Like I was some wise old man.

So I left him there and flew up to the Gold Coast. I woke up the next morning and Kirra had dropped, it was only four foot. I surf all day, then later that night I get a phone call from Marky.

'You have no idea what we just surfed! You wait till you see what we just surfed – the biggest, best barrels ever.'

'Get fucked, you're joking.' I'm thinking he's having me on.

'Nah, I'm serious.'

He emailed me a photo the next morning of Kieren in the biggest barrel I'd ever seen in Australia. I just started fully dry retching on the spot. I just went pale; it was instant nausea. The only other time I've felt like that was when I lost 20 grand in one hit in Vegas. I know I would've got a bigger one than Kieren. I'm not the world's most patient man, and it taught me a valuable lesson that I still haven't learned.

At this stage I was doing whatever I wanted and getting paid for it. It was a dream. I had a manager at the time, Wayne Munro, who was the old man of my mate Trent Munro. Wayne was really good, but I just didn't like having to report to anyone. I've never had a mum or a dad to report to, and that's why I'm basically a manager's worst nightmare. I've never really dealt well with people telling me what to do. I'm pretty rude to people who I don't respect. But I just believe I'm doing what I'm doing, and no one's gonna tell me how to do it. 'You haven't surfed 50-foot Jaws, so keep quiet about it and let me do my thing.' And the worst thing – which is bad of me but I don't care – is that I'm blunt. I'll tell 'em to their face in as few words as possible. 'How many covers have you had, buddy? What, none? Well don't tell me how to go and get one.' If a team manager gives me the shits, I just tell him to fuck off and ignore him. That's probably why I've had about 50 different sponsors.

Then in 2002 Oakley came along and offered me a contract. It was like 180 grand a year, so it worked out pretty good. I was stoked; I signed up straightaway. Dino Andino, a Californian ex-pro surfer, made the approach to me from Oakley, and he'd be the same guy who'd sack me a few years later. The contract basically said I could do whatever I wanted … just don't get in trouble, apparently.

It led to a blow-up with Wayne. He'd done a good job as my manager, and I was kinda rude in the way I dealt with it. But I could see that I was going to make some good money for the first time in my life, and I just thought for what he was getting he didn't really do enough. The deal was that when he secured me a new contract he'd get 20 per cent. But the Oakley contract had come through me, not him. They'd approached me directly and I'd referred them to Wayne. So he was going to get 20 per cent for a contact I'd made, which I didn't think was right. I just thought, 'I can get my brother to do this for five grand, not 30.' In the end I gave Wayne 17 grand and I've never had a manager since.

Before I knew it I was over in America doing a photo shoot for Oakley. All the Oakley head bosses were there introducing themselves. They've asked me what I drank, and I told 'em scotch. Within half an hour there's a bottle of Black Label scotch in front of me. Next thing I'm at the photo shoot just throwing my guts up in front of all the Oakley big guns. They're looking at me going, 'Is this the guy we just signed?' I'm going, 'You bring me a bottle of scotch and a thousand beers and you didn't expect me to get drunk?' I ended up hooking up with one of the models on the shoot. The next morning Oakley's US team guy has come and got me at my hotel and he's gone, 'Dude, you were so drunk last night!' All of a sudden the chick has wandered out and I've gone, 'How drunk was I last night?'

Within a few weeks I'd be driving past billboards and here's me head, 50 foot high. It was a strange thing, bra, seeing your head that big. The boys at home reckon that's how big it is all the time. But I was more worried about my hairline in the photo; it looks like I'm losing it, which I wasn't real happy with.

For the first time in my life I had real money. It was 15 grand a month. The first month was party time. Actually, come to think of it, it was always party time when I was on that contract. But I remember thinking, 'I can do something with this money for the family.' So I bought a house up in Curtin Crescent at South Maroubra, two units and a penthouse apartment in Queensland. At that stage property was booming and anything you bought in Sydney was going to go all right.

When I bought Curtin Crescent, me and Jai went and grabbed Ma, because Jai had thrown in some money for it as well, and we all went up there. Ma's walking through the house, and it was pretty clear she liked it. Me and Jai are laughing away.

'Ma, we just bought it. It's yours.'

She didn't believe us at first, then she's just given us the biggest hug. It was one of the best feelings I've ever had in my life, being able to do that for her.

The whole thing was that I was now getting a ton of money to just go surfing and I wanted to ride the biggest, nastiest waves I could find. And by this stage I was getting pretty good at finding them.

I soon went back to Apocalypse; I had unfinished business with that fucking thing. The photographer Jason Childs has rang me and told me we're on; there was a swell about to hit Java. I was in Jakarta the next day, but I got on the piss that night and when the boat went out the next morning I wasn't on it. It's so rare to get this place on that the rest of the boys couldn't wait, so they sailed off without me. I ended up hiring a speedboat for a thousand dollars, got the skipper on the satellite phone and told him I was on my way. I get out there late in the arvo and the swell is peaking just as I arrive. It's smoking, even more perfect than it had been last time. The other boys have been surfing all day – Aussie surfers Dylan Longbottom, Damon Harvey, Asher Pacey, Steve Clements. I paddle out just before dark straight into the biggest wave of the day. Got the cover shot on me first wave, and got two more waves after that which ended up on magazine covers all over the world. Then I said, 'Well, I've had enough, boys,' and went in and drank beers on the boat. That was my trip. Went there, travelled two days each way, caught three waves and come home. Job done.

I was travelling so much at this stage that I was building up a network of mates around the world, but I reckon the one place I loved going to more than any other was Kauai. It's just about the most incredible place in the world, and staying with Bruce and Andy Irons was epic. Staying with those two was like staying with me and Jai in Maroubra … just with palm trees instead of concrete. First, they argue about whose house you're gonna stay at. If you go, 'Okay, I'm gonna stay at Bruce's tonight,' then Andy will come around early in the morning and wake you up to go surfing before Bruce wakes up. Fully comes over to steal you off Bruce. But then you stay at Andy's house and Bruce will do the same – come around and try and poach ya. Andy goes, 'You're coming to dinner at my place,' and Bruce goes, 'No he's not, he's coming to mine.' And I'm going, 'What are you guys on?' It's the same wherever they are; they just argue. Me and Jai will fight, but these two are just at each other all day long.

I almost got killed on that first trip. The surf was massive and breaking at a secret spot near their place. It's like Backdoor Pipe, but 15 foot. It's probably about the craziest waves you can surf, anywhere in the world. It's like a giant Kirra, just breaking over reef.

We've got up this morning and the swell is pretty big. I didn't have a big board, so I'd bought this old 10' 8" for a hundred bucks off this guy at a garage sale on the side of the road. We're getting ready to paddle out and Bruce has gone, 'Koby, you can't wear a leggie out here.'

'Fuck, bra, it's a mile out to sea! There's no way I'm losing me board out there!'

'Seriously, Koby, *no leggies*.'

We've started paddling out – me, Bruce, Andy and Reef Macintosh – and this massive set rolls in, these giant freight-training tubes, and we're fully caught inside. I look across at Bruce and he's bailing, throwing his board.

'What the fuck are you doing, Brucey? You've got no leggie on! You're gonna lose your board!' And right then I've seen the board flip over and there was his leggie, attached to his ankle. He just starts cracking up while I had to Eskimo roll this giant board and hang on to it while I got destroyed.

Bruce had karma coming, though. Half an hour later we're back out there and caught inside again. This time it's even bigger – 15-, 18-footers – and we're fully in the impact zone, about to wear them. We're just looking at each other, and I'm pissing myself laughing as Bruce tries to rip his leggie off to save his life.

I had Christmas over on Kauai with them that year. I don't really have Christmas at home, so I went over and spent a month with those guys. I had a mad time. That's when I met Sanoe. She'd starred in *Blue Crush* not long before, and she lived and surfed on Kauai. We met at a party over there and I hung out with her for a couple of months, which was unreal. She was a really cute, cool chick. She was one of those ones you look back on now and think, 'Did I let her get away?' I think we broke up eventually because Bruce and the boys teased me so much about doing my nuts over her.

KOBY

JUST 200–ODD METRES AWAY AND 200–ODD YEARS AFTER CAPTAIN COOK'S TERRITORIAL PROCLAMATION IN BOTANY BAY, THE BRA BOYS PLANT THE FLAG AT OURS

I couldn't believe it. I'd travelled around the world a hundred times chasing heavy waves, and one of the heaviest waves in the world was just down the road from Maroubra and we didn't even know about it.

Marky had told me about this reef he'd seen in a boogieboard magazine. And you know how sometimes you can tell where a place might be by the colour of the water? Well, I looked at the photo in the mag and instantly I thought I knew where it was. Plus the boogieboarder in the photos was a local guy. I'm thinking, 'That's fucking here, bra. That's just down the road.' Marky goes, 'I think I know exactly where it is.'

It was a really south swell at the time, and we agreed to go and try and find this place the next morning. But the next morning Marky wakes up real early and goes by himself, doesn't he. Just fucking left me out. Thanks, Marky.

He comes back two hours later.

'I've found it. I know where it is … and it's pumping.'

We pulled up just as a set hit.

'Get fucked, *that's the wave!*'

It was so close to the rocks that I first thought, 'That's not surfable; you're going up on the rocks for sure.' But we paddled out there and we just had a ball. We ended up getting some five-foot barrels that day. It was fucking all-time.

I got rolled for the first time out there. I remember coming up an arm's length from the rocks and pushing myself away from them. It's all rocks there, bra, and they're gnarly. They're covered in these long barnacles, as long as your little finger, and the only way in and out is up the rocks.

But that first surf … We had one of those surfs where you don't even contemplate coming in. We were just out there thinking that this was the best wave we'd ever seen. It really is a world-class wave … for the heaviness, the barrel, how deep you can get, how many waves you can get. And it freaked us out to think it'd been there for so long, only a couple of miles from Maroubra, without being surfed.

We just claimed the place straightaway; that's why we called it Ours. No one was really surfing it before us anyway. Pretty soon after me and Marky surfed it, the boys were all over it and it just turned into a full scene. It became a contest: who could take off deepest, who could take the biggest ones. It was typical Maroubra, the boys just pushing each other, trying to outdo each other. Then you've got all the boys on the rocks hooting ya into the sets. You can stand there on the rocks and almost feel like you're in the line-up. It's such a scene, all the boys on the rocks screaming their heads off as you're paddling into waves. The boys would take it in shifts: one group would surf while another sits on the rocks, then swap over.

The surfing that would be going on if we'd known about that wave earlier would be 10 times what it is now. If we'd been surfing that from age 10, the limits would be pushed so hard. Around here you've got all these waves – Voodoo, Suck Rock, Lurline, The Southy, The Pebble –

every one of those waves are pretty heavy on their day, but this was something else altogether.

Someone's gonna die there one day for sure. Because of what that wave is and the way everyone's surfing it, it's destined to happen. Everyone is expecting it. The place is pretty fucked up. When you're flying through the barrel as you come into the last big section, if it bounces you the wrong way you're gonna go on the rocks. A lot of my friends aren't the best surfers, ya know, but they're still charging it pretty fucking hard. Hopefully it's not one of us. Hopefully it's no one.

Everyone thinks there's a bad vibe out there from us and it's all trouble. But you're going to get teased there before you're going to get bashed. If you pull back on anything out there and don't go, you're not gonna get another wave, ever. We don't mind if ya come out and eat shit 10 times in a row, but if you pull back then you're out. I think people are hesitant about going out, not because they're afraid of getting beaten up, but because they're more worried about getting the shit ripped out of them if they don't charge.

We don't feel a sense of ownership of that place. Well, we don't like boogieboarders, to tell you the truth. It's not that they're boogieboarders; it's that they come out in packs of hundreds. We can't even surf Shark Island at Cronulla any more. Where we sit at Shark Island, on Surge, you can't get a wave. It's clogged up with lids. I love seeing surfers out at Ours. If there's other guys out there when we're towing, we'll tow them into waves. I'll come in and say, 'Who wants a go? You're up.' I just don't like boogieboarders being out there. I don't mind 'em being out there early in the morning, as long as they're gone by the time we get there. That's fine.

There are no boogieboarders in the Bra Boys. We've got blacks, whites, Asians, wogs, we've got them all in our crew, you know. We're open to any race, any person in our crew, as long as you're our friend. We just don't have any friends who are boogieboarders.

SUNNY

INSIDE MAROUBRA'S OWN BERMUDA TRIANGLE, WHERE
GOOD MEN BRAVELY VENTURE NEVER TO RETURN TO
MEANINGFUL MAINSTREAM SOCIETY

I was living above our surf shop in McKeon Street when the pub across
the road approached me with a proposition. The pub's business was
struggling at that stage, and the three levels of dilapidated hotel rooms
upstairs had been shut down by the council. No one was allowed to live
in them, but they could technically be used for office space. After we'd
successfully pulled off the first Surf Skate Slam, the pub's management
asked us whether we'd take over the promotion of the pub, booking their
bands and entertainment. They said, 'We'll give you the whole top floor
as an office.' It was a 60 square office, with 10 adjoining rooms off the
hallway. Then there were another two levels of exactly the same thing. So
we lived every Aussie male's dream and moved into the pub.

That was one of the funniest, craziest times of our lives. We had a full
180-degree view of the beach, we had three levels of the pub to run around
in, we had free drink tabs; we had all these hot girls working for us. The
boys would hang out in the office all day, and several moved into the rooms
on a semi-permanent basis. We were living the dream. But it was the cops'
worst nightmare. They nearly had a collective heart attack when they found
out we were booking the bands and running the show at the pub.

Our mate Brook Silvester's band Hated And Proud was the pub's
resident band, and we'd book all these local punk and pub bands. The pub
was going off. It was packed. You'd be down in the pub having a few
beers; then you could just go upstairs whenever you wanted and you
suddenly had your own private nightclub up there. You couldn't dream
that shit up. Crew were in there all the time. When the pub closed we'd do
after-parties and lock-ins that would go all night. If any of our mates from
up and down the coast were cruising they'd just stay upstairs in the pub.

I'd wake up in the morning across the road above the surf shop, and shout out my window, 'Tea party!' One by one these heads would appear out of random windows in the pub, one head on the first floor, another on the third, another in the middle, all wearing coloured clown wigs and they'd reply, 'Tea party!', looking up and down at each other like the fucking Brady Bunch. These random barflies were all our mates, and they lived on and off in the abandoned rooms for free.

The pub is where Maroubra is run from. There's so much history and so many stories attached to that pub, and it's been the second home for Maroubra's surfers over the past 40 years. The pub is the epicentre for the good times in Maroubra; this is what people don't realise about the place. Sure, five per cent of the time there might have been some trouble or fisticuffs, but the other 95 per cent it was non-stop comedy, with guys trying to outwit, out-clown, outsmart each other. It was never that different to any other surf town up and down the coast, just a little more extreme.

We've been good and bad for business at various times, and the publicans over the years have learned to read the vibe of the front bar. They'd know when the damage bill was likely to exceed the bar takings. Often we'd spill back in from boardriders on a Sunday afternoon and the publican would say, 'I'll give you three cases, boys, if you go back up to Ronnie's.'

'Five!'

'Done!'

Back in the mid-'90s, before the pub was done up and it was its old, grubby self, the bistro there was struggling. The food was probably a little too upmarket for both the pub and the area, 'cause the pub was pretty wild in those days. The owners had done a lot of marketing and advertising; they'd been trying really hard to make this thing work.

Okay, it's a Saturday and the boys are on an all-day bender in the pub.

There's a guy named Lopez, and there was a hot barmaid who was working in there. Lopez had been harassing her for weeks, asking her out on a date. For reasons known only to her, on this day she's finally agreed, and he's said, 'Okay, I'll pick you up here at six o'clock when you knock off.'

At lunchtime that day the boys had rocked up to the pub and were fully on it. Full zoo. The pub is going mad. Guys were drinking nude, people were wrestling; the boys were riding down the stairs on plastic umbrellas they'd snapped out of the ground in the beer garden, riding them like toboggans.

So, through a stroke of extraordinarily bad timing, the bistro has finally got Leo Schofield, the *Sydney Morning Herald*'s restaurant critic, showing up for dinner that night. He's turned up and walked in – he said this in the paper the next day – and was greeted by one of the local boys carrying a palm tree above his head, chasing another local, who rips another palm tree out of its pot and swings it by the crown, spraying dirt all through the bistro. Frog and Chappo. And that's Leo's first impression of the Maroubra pub … and it was only about to get worse.

Lopez, meanwhile, has got on the piss with the boys all day out the back bar and has just realised, 'Shit, it's six o'clock. I've got to go and pick up the barmaid.' She'd just knocked off work, and had no idea Lopez had been out the back with the boys boozing and is about 25 sheets to the wind. In those days the publicans encouraged us to drink out the back and not to fraternise with the general public out the front. So Lopez walked out the back of the pub and around the front like he's just walked in cold sober off the street.

'Hi, babe, how are ya?'

'So where are we going?' she replies.

'I thought we might just eat here.'

He's gone out to the bistro with the barmaid, and they've both ordered spaghetti bolognese. She reckoned he had one look at his food and went white, started rocking, and has just collapsed face first in his spaghetti and fallen asleep. First date. She could only laugh, so she's eaten her dinner and got up and left, leaving him there.

Meanwhile, Leo Schofield has gotten past Frog and Chappo swinging the palm trees, and the rest of the boys going crazy, and got to his seat and ordered a steak. His food's just arrived and he's sitting there with his wife, three tables away from Lopez. All of a sudden Lopez has woken up from his spaghetti. He scrapes the spaghetti off his face and gets up. He walks past Leo's table just as his steak arrives. Lopez stops next to the table, looks down, picks the steak up in his bare hands, takes a giant bite out of it, puts it back, and keeps walking.

Leo's review in the paper the next day said something like, 'If you can get past the apes and animals in the bar, and avoid the swinging coconut trees and the clientele asleep in their main course, you might find a good meal.'

The restaurant people had to laugh. They weren't even shattered about it; it was almost comical. They'd finally got their critic there on the worst night possible. But it made them realise this place was never going to change, and they were better off serving chicken schnitzel to the animals than filet mignon to the critics.

Then there was the time the pub got held up. It was in the middle of the day, and a handful of locals were drinking in there when the guys in balaclavas have stormed in. They've gone to the bar and demanded money. Well, no one is going to really get involved in that. They just kept drinking. Then the robber turned on the punters and said, 'Hand over your money!' to the crew drinking in there. Well, there were a couple of the boys in the front bar, and they've just gone, 'No way, mate. Not in this pub.'

Scotty Gunzer ended up wrestling with the guy over the gun. He reckons the guy was trying *not* to shoot him because it must have been someone who knew him, but Scottty got shot nonetheless. The gun's gone off and it got him on the side of the stomach. When he woke up he was in the Prince of Wales Hospital up at Randwick. He just wanted to get out of there. He's ripped the drip out and walked out of the hospital and straight back to the pub, a good three kilometres away.

He's gone straight up, ordered a schooner, and sat back down in the same seat.

Like in any family, there were some heavy times going down in Maroubra, but they were always outweighed by the fun times. If you believed everything you read about the place you'd think Maroubra was more like Baghdad, but the reality was so different. Maroubra was so much fun for us. But it was extreme, Maroubra-style fun … kind of like Disneyland taken over by mental patients.

Whenever the surf was flat everything was spontaneous, and whatever you started you'd soon have 20 people doing it with you – car surfing, street surfing, sewer surfing. But with Maroubra's extreme brand of fun, the line between fun and causing trouble would be pretty fine sometimes. What's fun for us is not always fun for everyone else.

Barbie Mountain, up on the hill at North Maroubra, is a really iconic spot. It was popular around the time when we were getting a bit hassled by the cops. We found this grassy platform above the rocks near the corner of Bond Street and Marine Parade that looked straight out over the waves in the Dunny Bowl. It was about 10 metres below the level of the road, so the cops couldn't see us as they drove past. Any time there was a council clean-up and people left old furniture out on the street, we'd grab it and carry it down to Barbie Mountain. Sofas, rolls of carpet, coffee tables, we'd even take down lamps and bookshelves and set the place up like a lounge room. And from noon on any good summer's day we'd be down there, fairly on it. By the arvo we'd have a big barbecue and beers going, and by the end of the night the lounges would go onto the fire. The lounges that survived would sometimes be sat on top of skateboards and ridden down the hill on Marine Parade.

The real carnage would be further round the headland on the rocks. The older guys used to tell us their motto was 'The rocks are your friends', and from the time we were kids, whenever the waves were too small to surf we played these games around the rocks between Maroubra and Lurline. It was generally super dangerous, but it taught you about dealing with the ocean and the rocks, which is why so many Maroubra guys are so comfortable surfing over reef.

Further north there's a cave we used to swim into; it's right below the jump rock we called Hammerhead. There are a few different levels at Hammerhead. There's a 20-foot drop, a 50-foot drop, and Street Level, which is about a 100-foot drop into the ocean. When you're down in the water in that cave and you hear someone jump from Street Level into the water, it sounds like a bag of bricks. It's a big drop. It's not actually that deep there – you can touch the bottom – so it's also really fucking dangerous. All the boys get into it. We've even got a little mate Tommy who's a midget, and he's right into it. The kid's fearless.

Only certain crew, though, will do Street Level. There are all these classic stories you'd hear about how Lee Stubbs had ridden off the cliff at Street Level on his pushbike, and how Rod Saunders had ridden a motorbike off there once. When we took our Koori mate Billy Barnes there for the first time, he walked over, had one look over the edge, walked back to his mark, then nonchalantly ran at it and did a huge backflip off the cliff. Instant hero status.

frog

JAMIE GORE ON THE CENTRE OF MAROUBRA'S UNIVERSE – THE PUB

The pub was home to us. It was our little clubhouse, our meeting spot. You could always go down to the Bay and there'd be someone there you knew.

We used to do some crazy things in the pub. We'd come back there after our all-night benders in town. The pub would open at about nine or 10am and there was a big beer garden out the back. So if the pub wasn't open we'd climb over and sit in the beer garden, all twisted, until they opened the doors and then it'd be on again. After a big night, if you're still going at dawn you'd go to the beer garden; that's where everyone would regroup.

The night Leo Schofield showed up to review the pub's restaurant I was there bending with a heap of the boys. I don't remember much about that night, only what I've been told. Apparently I was running through the place trying to clean someone up with a palm tree or something.

Then as the *Herald* food critic was about to cut into his steak, our mate Lopez has picked it up, bitten into it, thrown it back on the plate and walked off. I think the review in the paper said the food would be great if you could get past the animals.

It's just that the Maroubra idea of fun is just 50 per cent more than it is anywhere else. We've always had the reputation of being a bit wilder than everyone else, but it comes from the boys pushing each other that little bit further. It's that whole culture of trying to outdo your mate, whether it's in the pub or in the surf, most of which is just harmless fun.

There's a real hard, stern stereotype out there about the Bra Boys, but it's so far from the truth. A good night at the pub and you'd see that. We'd be having more fun than anyone. That's just how we have fun; we rip the shit out of each other. Sometimes it can get a bit over the top, especially for people who are only passing through or who aren't used to hanging with the boys, and I think that's where that whole hardcore thing comes from. But it's been like that long before the Bra Boys were even conceived. The Bra Boys have always been there; they've just been called something different. These days it's the Bra Boys, back in the day it was the Maroubra Republican Army, in 10 years it will be the McKeon Street Elite. It just changes names every 10 years.

I think the papers have given us a reputation that's way, way over the top, and I think some of the boys are trying to live up to that reputation which makes us look worse than we really are.

ronnie reardon

SUPER–FEATHERWEIGHT PUGILIST, MAROUBRA HEART AND SOUL

I was good at boxing, that's what attracted me to it.

I met my trainer, Bernie, through Paul, Dakota's dad. Paul boxed pretty well, he was a southpaw. One day he said, 'You should come in,

Ron, and start training.' After two months of that I ended up going in there with Billy Barnes. Bernie was sitting back in his bedroom in there, 'cause he lived in the gym, and Billy's introduced me to him. I was 16, going on 17, so I was only about three foot tall. I got in the ring and had a spar with Billy, my first time, ya know, and I just kept going for three rounds. Billy's done a bit of boxing by this stage. Bernie has walked out, walked around the ring and watched my last round against Billy. When we finished up he's gone, 'Are you still going to school?' I boxed in his gym every day for the next three months and then had me first amateur fight.

It was out at Bonnyrigg, out with the cows. We didn't go past Anzac Parade in those days, so me and Sunny are driving out there wondering where the fuck we're going. I fought a bloke named Spencer Thompson, this tough Irish-looking guy. We were out in the Cross years later and we ran into him, working as a bouncer at a strip club. I looked at him and he looked at me and we both laughed. 'You were me first fight!' He was stoked to see us. I won that fight, and won all my amateur fights right up until I went to the world championships in China.

Before I went over to China, Bernie said, 'Why don't you live in the gym here?' So I lived in the roof at Sydney Gym. I used to climb up a ladder every night and sleep under this tin roof. Warm? I was fucking sweating up there, it was fucking hardcore. Bracks Berley, who used to hang with Marty and Hinesy, he boxed at the gym as well and he'd made these peep holes into the girls' showers. You'd look through and there'd be sheilas in there soaping themselves up, doing what they're doing. But if Bernie caught ya, mate, you were in the shit.

Bernie made me stop surfing. I was only 17 and loved my surfing. I'd surfed in the NSW Titles a couple of times, even surfed a heat against Sunny. I was never going to be a pro surfer like those guys, but I loved it. I didn't know it back then, but Bernie had a world number two fighting with him – Sharky Raymond – and he'd had an accident in the surf and fucked his shoulder, so Bernie was deadset against it. He brainwashed me against surfing. Whatever Bernie would say I would do; I'd never question him. And now, 15 years later, Sunny is the only person who gets me back out in the water, and every time I do I feel grouse. I missed surfing a lot during those years; it was all about my boxing.

Bernie was from the old school. I got him right in his later years. He was a genius with boxing. Never drank, never smoked; just boxed. He lived in the gym. Bernie had fought Freddy Dawson twice – one of the first black men to come from America to Australia to fight. After me Australian title fight I had Jeff Fenech and all these other guys wanting to take me under their wing. But I'd never leave Bernie. I didn't have it in me; I was too loyal. It wouldn't have been a bad thing for my career, probably massive, but Bernie was me first and last trainer.

Sunny would organise all the boys to come to my fights. Years later, I said to him, 'If it weren't for you, mate, I don't know where I'd be.' But I never knew all these blokes were in the crowd. When I walked into the arena before the fight, it was empty; when I walked out after the fight, it was empty. It was only when I walked out to the ring from the rooms that I got to see anyone. When I walked out for my big one – the Aussie title fight at Newtown – the coppers were trying to take Wayno away. I'm going, 'No, mate, he's with me!' We grabbed Wayno and he come with us.

My Aussie title fight against Ricky Rayner was at Johnny Lewis' Police Boys Club. It was the hottest building you've ever been in. The sweat was condensing on the ceiling and dripping back down onto the crowd. There were a couple of thousand people jam-packed in there. The boys reckon there were rumbles and all-ins going on in the crowd. Hinesy was there at the fight; he was on weekend leave and he got into a stink with someone by the first round apparently. Hinesy and Grommet both did day release with Johnny Lewis at the gym, and they were really close with him.

I can only remember the later rounds of the fight; I'm thinking, 'Fuck, is this still going?' I was looking at Ricky going, 'Mate, would you just lay down!' It was fucking heavy. In the end it was a draw. The scores went 114–116 his way, 117–114 my way, and 115-all. It won the Australian Professional Fight of the Year for 1996.

They were good days. I fought on my birthday not long after, and the boys put a show on for me back at the pub. Five hundred people converged on the Maroubra Bay Hotel. The boys have gone 'Don't go too far, Ron. We've got something for your birthday.' I knew exactly what they had, and it wasn't good news 'cause I had me two grandmothers right there in the front row, I've got my girlfriend who I've only just started seeing, and me mum Tiger was there too.

I'm in the back bar of the old pub and out walk these two strippers. I'm lying down on the ground with my new sheila standing right next to me. The stripper puts a dildo in my mouth and starts squatting on it. I've gone, 'Fuck the dildo!' and just bit her straight on the arse. The stripper's screamed and run out of the room, my girlfriend is going off her head, my two grandmothers are losing it, and my mum's tried to king-hit the other stripper. The place just erupted.

KOBY

A SILENT CACOPHONY THAT SPEAKS OCEANS

The noise is the first thing you notice, bra. Inside a giant barrel the noise is deafening. It's like being in a giant echo chamber, like being inside a plane engine as it takes off. I'm sensitive to noise; I lay awake at night and I can hear people through the walls. So when I get in a 15-foot barrel that's the first thing I'm conscious of – this giant fucking roar.

It's a pretty incredible sensation being inside a *really* big barrel. Your senses are on full alert, 'cause you know if you fall you're going to get hurt. But you look down the line and it's bright blue; it's a perfect day and there's this big tunnel just about to form around you. There's no feeling like it, serious. It's fully alive in there. It speeds up and slows down, expands and shrinks, breathes out and breathes in. Pretty fucking sick, bra. But if I get a wave like that, I don't stop and think about it. I can't even remember most of my best waves, 'cause I'm too busy trying to get the next one.

I only like catching the bombs. Out in big surf I just want to get the biggest wave I can, the wave of the day, and I won't worry about anything else. And I hate it when other people get better waves than me. Fucking hate it. I'm also really loud and hyperactive in the surf, and I like fucking around with people out there. I just like teasing crew and mucking around. It's like a party. I don't sit out there and look at sunsets and think about poems. I'd much rather have a laugh and poke fun at my mates and talk shit than sit there and look at a mountain, that's for sure. There's no romance in it for me, bra. I annoy the fuck out of those guys who are out there looking at mountains.

I reckon I feel so comfortable out in the water because I did so much spearfishing as a kid. Sometimes I'd go diving out off Maroubra on my own and just drift away for hours. When I'd finally stick my head up I'd be two kays out in the middle of the ocean next to the container ships. We had spearguns from an early age, and we'd all be out there spearing anything that moved. It's a miracle we never speared each other, come to think of it. I speared a big jewfish out there, an eight-kilo jewie off Yellow Rock, which was my record as a kid. If you swim out when there's heaps of fish around and take your chances with the sharks, you can nail some big fish.

I'm still looking for the photo of my huge lobster. We were over in New Caledonia on a surf trip when I caught it. It was huge, bra, over 10 kilos, the biggest lobster I've ever seen. When I told my Koori mate Rat about it he bagged the fuck out of me. Rat and his mates are the master divers, and the running joke over at La Per is that I caught a 10-kilo lobster. Whenever we're drinking with the Koori boys, Rat will give me that much shit.

'Hey, Koby, tell all the boys about the time you caught the 10-kilo lobster.'

None of them believe me; that's why I need that photo to show the idiots.

We were out of the drop off on the reef, I dove down real deep, and there it was, looking straight at me. It was like a prehistoric dinosaur. I just went, 'What the fuck is that!?' I went down and tried to grab it. I got two hands around it, holding it like it was a barrel. It's started shaking me off, trying to claw me, so I let it go and swum back to the boat, got the gun and shot it. The thing was fucking huge, bra. Fed 10 of us.

The biggest fish I ever shot was the year after, over in the Mentawai Islands.

There was me, Phil MacDonald and Bruce Irons, and our boat was anchored in the channel at Macaronis. I was diving out near the drop-off and I've seen this flicker of silver. It was a trevally the size of Brucey. The thing was a monster. I've swum up behind it and shot the thing through the back of the tail and it's just taken off like a bullet. It's flying off out to sea, dragging me behind it like I was being towed behind a speedboat or something. I swear I was doing 10 knots, and I didn't reckon this thing was ever going to stop. Then it's dived down over this ledge, 15 metres straight down, and it's trying to pull me under with it. I just thought, 'Fuck, I'm gonna drown here if I don't let go.' But I wanted this fish, 'cause it was huge. I threw the gun and it wrapped around a piece of reef. I've quickly swum back to the boat and gone, 'Phil, quick, get out here with ya gun. I've got the biggest trevally you've ever seen in your life.' He's swum out with me and dived down and his eyes have just bulged. He's shot it and between us we've managed to drag it back to the boat. It was up to my chest, this massive submarine of a GT. It weighed over 25 kilos, and it fed two boatloads of surfers that night.

If you want to really know the ocean, though, and you wanna know yourself, you need to get fucked up proper by a big one. I've had plenty of pretty wipeouts, especially over those couple of years when I was surfing a lot of big waves. But they say it's when you least expect it that it gets ya. And that's what happened to me over in West Oz.

I pulled into this big one and have gone down on it. Actually, it wasn't that big, but it was breaking over this reef in the middle of the ocean, 20 miles offshore, that just dropped off into hundreds of feet of water. The joint is gnarly powerful.

It power-drove me head first so deep, bra; I must've been driven 20 metres down. I'd been driven so deep that I was beginning to worry.

Then I realised that I was still being driven down and it wasn't showing any signs of stopping. I was thinking, 'Shit, I'm going really deep here, proper deep.' This was starting to freak me out. 'How deep am I gonna go?' I was flying to the bottom. I was either going to hit the bottom head first or have the longest swim of my life to get back up.

I kept going down, down, down and then finally stopped. I just went, Sweet; I could now work on getting back to air. I opened my eyes and it was blacker than black. I've started swimming up, then thought to myself, 'Hang on, am I actually going up or swimming back down?' It's so hard to tell with all the turbulence around you. I kept swimming up and up; I stopped and looked and I swear it was even darker than before. I thought, 'I better just wait here and see where the fuck I am.' While I'm waiting it's gone all quiet. I'm just about to get it all sussed when – *wham!* – the second wave hits and just drives me straight down again, another 50 somersaults. Right about now I'm thinking, 'I'm pretty fucked. I think I could drown here.'

I've never really thought like that before.

This was fucking heavy. Second wave of the hold-down – okay, be calm – and I just drifted up. I never felt like I was going to black out, but another wave and I was in trouble. I could feel my eardrums pushing out with the pressure. The noise was indescribable. It felt like my eardrums were outside of my ears, flapping around there like two little balloons. I know from diving that once you're that deep, and have gone down that fast, if you try and equalise the pressure in your ears they'll pop.

I finally broke the surface and took the biggest breath of my life.

I'm staring up into the sun. My head was spinning. It was like I'd just walked out drunk from a dark nightclub at six in the morning, straight into the bright light of day. I swear there were tweety birds flying around me, chirping, my head had been under so much pressure. Where I'd come up was 200 metres away from where I'd wiped out. I'd been washed around the inside of the reef and was almost at the other side.

But you need one of them every now and then.

KOBY

My new Monaro cost me $58,000 off the lot.

It'd only just come out; I had one of the first ones in Australia. I bought a red one. I don't know why; I hated the colour by the time I got it home. And I didn't have a driver's licence. I'm banned until about 2012. I just liked having a good car, that's all.

I think Jai gets his licence back in 2032. It's not fair, bra. I see people driving down the street who can't even drive. I got caught three times driving unlicensed, unregistered, uninsured …. One of those times they said I was trying to drive off and they called it a high-speed chase. I only went 300 metres down the road! I know I'll get my licence back before Jai, though. The way it's going, Jai won't be able to see by the time he gets his back. I'm thinking of going to court with Jai and asking them to give us a break. We haven't had licences for that long that it's hard to have a life.

So, I got me Monaro back up to my place that arvo and called up a heap of the boys who've all come around and drunk beers to celebrate me new car. We were on the beers all afternoon, hanging around the car playing music. I've fallen asleep early that night on the couch watching telly. Jai was asleep in one room; Ma was asleep in the other room.

While we're asleep some fucker has come into the house and taken the keys *out of my pocket*! I was probably lucky I'd had a thousand beers and didn't wake up, because to do something that ballsy the guy would have been armed up for sure. You wouldn't go in there unarmed with me and Jai and the boys all hanging around the place.

The door that backs out onto the road was unlocked, and the cunt has come in and gone through my pockets, stolen my car keys and driven off in me fucking car! I woke up the next morning and straightaway felt something was weird. The door was open, and I knew someone had got into the house. It took me about two seconds to work out what they were after. I walked out onto the balcony, looked around and saw the garage door was open. And I knew. I had it one night and it was gone. It had 80 kilometres on the clock.

I went right back and bought an even more hotted-up Monaro for 88 grand.

I've got a pretty bad track record with jet skis too. I hate getting 'em on and off trailers. It shits me. But there's no way I'm gonna take the rap for launching that ski into traffic on Anzac Parade that day. That one wasn't my fault, bra.

But that wasn't even the funniest thing that happened that day. We'd gone to Malabar to launch the ski. It was a 15-foot swell and the water was surging 20 metres all the way up the boat ramp. There's no way you could reverse the car down without it getting washed out to sea. So I said to the boys, 'We'll take the ski off the trailer, I'll get on it, and when a wave washes up the ramp, you guys push me down the ramp and I'll ride the wave back out into the ocean.' The water was surging up into the car park, and the ramp's really steep, so it was a sketchy manoeuvre. I said, 'Make sure you hold me when the wave comes, otherwise I'm gonna get smashed backward into the retaining wall.' The wave comes up the ramp; I'm sitting there ready on the ski. I look beside me and the boys are gone. Thanks a lot, motherfuckers.

I just get slammed up against the retaining wall. Then the wave has started drawing back out. I'm flying down, trying to hang on as the ski grinds down the ramp when suddenly there's a six-foot wave coming back at me. I knew I had to start the ski and gun it straight into the wave; otherwise it was just going to wash me back up the ramp and into the wall. I've fired the ski up just as the wave fully stands up. The lip throws over me, the ski punches through the wave, and I get coathangered by the lip and go straight over the falls.

That's the thing: if I pay 20 grand for a jet ski, and pay for the petrol, the other guys who go surfing with me like Jesse, Richie Vass and Mark – they put it on the trailer. That's the deal. I'm not paying for it *and* doing all the fucking work. Later that same day, we're on our way home from the surf. We pull up at the lights on Anzac Parade and suddenly this guy on a pushie swerves out of the traffic in front of us. The traffic lights in front of us had just gone red, and my mate Jack Kingsley, who was driving, had to swerve around him to stop. As the car screeches to a halt, we suddenly hear this grinding sound.

Next thing the ski shoots out in front of the car and goes straight through the intersection. The ski got up on its keel, so there was no friction on the road, and the thing went like a rocket. It stayed upright and just flew. It went faster than the car had been going. It just slingshotted off the trailer, because some idiot hadn't tied the fucking thing down. We've looked up and it's gone straight through the lights, and has somehow missed all the traffic. I was laughing right up to the point where we saw the old lady. This old lady hasn't seen it and is walking straight across the road into its path. No one could talk; we all just froze. I'm just thinking, 'Well, here comes jail.' Somehow she stops just as the half-ton ski rockets past, a couple of foot in front of her, then keeps going for another 50 metres up the hill. That's how quick the fucking thing was going. She's just kept on walking like nothing happened. As soon as everyone started breathing again, well, that's when the finger pointing started.

One stupid thing to another stupid thing to another stupid thing. It's great. It's what we are.

KOBY

FROM CLOUDBREAK TO JAWS TO A CAMEO FROM NEPTUNE HIMSELF, IT WAS THE YEAR OF SURFING OUTRAGEOUSLY

The hard thing with what I was doing was that your whole livelihood relied on the waves. You needed epic waves to make a living, and if they weren't there, then there wasn't much you could do about it. But when you got on a roll you can just go *boom boom boom boom*. And that's what happened when we had that golden run – Fiji, Tahiti, Ours, Cyclops, Jaws – all back-to-back.

It started in Fiji. It was June, and we heard there was a swell due to hit Fiji, right in the middle of the pro tour contest when the world's best guys would be there. Me and Marky made the decision to go, and we were on a plane from Sydney first thing in the morning. We dropped the bags on the beach when we got out to Namotu, the island we were staying on, and were out at Cloudbreak surfing 20 minutes later. Our bags didn't move off the beach for the four days we were there; we never opened 'em – that's how much we were surfing. Not long after we rock up, Laird Hamilton shows up out of the blue. I'd never met him before, and it was like having King Neptune on your island. He's the freak of freaks. I've never met a guy who had the same presence. And we were gonna get to surf with him, which was pretty fucking cool.

When we got out to Cloudbreak, it was pretty big, probably 15 foot. Laird's driven over to me on the ski.

'You wanna tow?'

'Er, yeah, okay.' You don't knock back a chance to tow with the best big-wave surfer in the world.

So I've ended up towing Laird into five or six waves, and I'm going, 'Okay, that's enough, isn't it? My turn?' I'd been watching it for a while and had seen these big ones marching through way up the point, breaking way deeper. We've swapped over and Laird's jumped on the ski to tow me.

'You want a small one to start?'

'Fuck no! Tow me into the biggest one ya can find, as deep as you can get me.'

Well, the wave's come, a 20-footer. Laird's driving the ski, yelling out, 'No, you're too deep!' and I've just let go of the rope and got such a sick one. I've backdoored the biggest barrel I've ever been in. I haven't seen a photo that does it justice. It ended up getting voted as the best tube ride in the world that year. It was my birthday, and it was the best present I ever got in my life.

All my best surfs in big waves have been with Marky Mathews. I remember seeing Marky surf for the first time when he was a kid. He was surfing this wave called Honeycombs with his little mate Craig. Honeycombs is over between Lurline and Coogee, a little right reef that we thought was the best wave ever when we were kids. I started seeing him down Maroubra a lot, and by this stage he was surfing really good. I went up to him and asked if he wanted to tag along and surf with us and that was it – he was part of our crew, straight up.

Once I got the Oakley sponsorship and had some money, I gave Mark whatever he needed: paid for him to go to Hawaii, paid for him to go on that Tassie trip with us; gave him boards and wetties and helped him to find a sponsorship of his own. People would say I was helping this kid out, but the fact is he was my friend and I wasn't doing it to be a charity. I just enjoyed hanging out with Marky and surfing with him. Anyway, I knew I wasn't going to be paying his bills for too long, 'cause the kid could surf.

Mark's really smart, too, ridiculously smart. From the very start Marky would know what direction the perfect swell was for every break we surfed, and to the exact degree. He'd know the exact number; he'd carry all that shit around with him in his head. It was never dumb luck with Marky. While we were sitting in a house in Tassie on that trip in 2001, rained in, waiting for the weather to clear, I remember telling him that he could be doing what I was doing easily. He's got a repertoire – he could freesurf big waves and he could surf contests as well. Within a year he was off doing it himself. It's little wonder he's gone on to surf big waves the way he does and make a career for himself.

Over the years there's definitely been an unspoken rivalry between Mark and myself, sure. One day I was speaking to my mate Reni Matua about this. I was trying to get him to sign a contract with South Sydney so he could play first grade at Souths with our other good mate, John Sutton.

'The rivalry between you and Sutto would make you a better player, bra.'

'But I don't have a rivalry with Sutto. He's my mate.'

'Of course you've got a rivalry; it's natural.'

There's not one surf me and Marky have where I don't paddle out wanting to get a better wave than he does. It's not a personal rivalry between me and Mark; it's a rivalry between me and the guy who's challenging me on any given day for the biggest waves out there. And most of the time that guy is Mark, because he's such a good surfer and he and I surf together so much. It's because Mark is always getting the good waves that he's the guy I need to trump. There's nothing personal and there's nothing malicious. I love the guy. When we surf, it's just like two big dogs in a small yard. It pushes us both to go harder. It's not like I hate his guts and wanna see his eyeballs get slashed open on his next wave, ya know. A few urchin spines in the foot, maybe, to keep him off the next set … It's like that with all the guys in Maroubra. There's always a rivalry to trump your mate and outdo him no matter what it is you're doing – surfing, footy, boxing, pulling chicks, writing off – but it's always healthy. It's what drives the guys around here to go that bit further.

That whole year, everything me and Marky surfed just got better and bigger. And it all led to Jaws.

We flew straight over to Jaws from Australia. It was two foot here in Australia and it was 60 foot when we arrived on Maui. It was the day that Dan Moore caught his 68-footer, the biggest wave ever ridden.

We got there and it was fucking huge, bra. I remember coming round the bend in the coast on the skis with my good mates, Maui guys, Tom Dosland, Kalaheo Robinson and Ty Van Dyke and it was big, the biggest waves I'd ever seen. Mark and I had built up this rivalry over the year. I pulled up in the channel next to Jaws and said to him, 'There's no way you're getting the first one out here, buddy. I'm up.'

We've gone out; Kalaheo is driving the ski, I'm surfing. He's the full local and a total maniac out there. First wave he whips me into this thing, and another ski tries to drop in on us. Next thing I know I'm going down the face of a 40-footer and Kalaheo has pulled off the back of the wave and fully T-boned the other ski. They have this full collision, and Kalaheo goes flying over the handlebars.

I'm off surfing the wave, have kicked out on the inside, and there's no Kalaheo there to pick me up. We'd caught the first wave of the set, so I'm now sitting about 20 metres seaward of the impact zone, with another five or six 50-footers heading straight at me. I've floated over the first one, but it was fully standing up as I did. Same with the second one. As I floated up the face of it, I realised that each wave was dragging me a little closer towards the impact zone. I look across and see some kind of drama in the channel. There's about 20 skis and a couple of boats clustered around someone, and no fucker is even looking at me. By this stage I'm almost in the death zone and there's still two or three 50-footers to come in the set.

'Hey, boys, how about me?'

On the very last wave of the set, the biggest one, I just felt myself lift. I'm floating up the face, up and up and up, and I'm thinking, 'This is a 60-foot wave here, and I'm about to go over backwards.' That was scary. It was kind of like the bad dreams you have where you feel like you're falling through your mattress. I remember my heart just about stopping. I had a stomach full of butterflies, and an overwhelming feeling that I should have given Marky the first wave.

I knew that if this thing got me I'm dead. But I was also calm, because there wasn't a single thing I could do about it. At the top of a 60-foot wave, looking back towards shore, I had the full moment where time slows. All of a sudden I can see crabs running on the rocks half-a-mile in shore … I was just fully weightless up there, just waiting to go over. At the last minute I spun around to face the shore, 'cause I just thought, 'Okay, if I'm going over here at least I'm going to dive head-first and penetrate, 'cause if I go over backwards I'm gonna die for sure. I'll probably die anyway, but I'm gonna go in fucking style, bra.'

Well, luckily just then the wind has gusted offshore, and it held the crest of the wave up just long enough for me to float safely off the back of it. Right then Laird spins over from the channel and grabs me, and tells me that Kalaheo has broken his leg. Next thing I know, here comes the chopper to pick him up. My first wave at Jaws, and it ends up in carnage. I saw 15 jet skis go down that day. It was crazy. Three-hundred grand's worth of skis just washed into the rocks and trashed.

Somehow our ski was okay, so we kept towing. I had no tow boards when I arrived in Hawaii, so Makua Rothman had lent me this dodgy twin-fin tow board. It was a terrible thing. It was almost square; it was like a coffee table. I got another wave on it and it was that shaky and that scary that I could just imagine Makua sitting there laughing his head off watching me try and surf it.

Most big waves around the world run off into channels, but not here at Jaws. It was like surfing four-foot Ours, just that it was 50 foot, with 150 guys out there, 90 jet skis, 30 boats and five helicopters. It's a full scene out there. Jaws is a fucking big tube that keeps bending at you. Surfing it is like driving a sports car around a mountain bend at full speed, except the mountain is moving. You get down the bottom and if you fade for more than a second you're brown bread. You're gone. And you could get the flogging of your life.

I wiped out once more on the inside that day, but I was all right. I think you've just gotta let yourself get washed in by 'em when you're caught by a wave that big. Some guys try and dive under it, but I try and stay up high and get washed in towards shore. Why would you want to stay out there and have to dive under 40 foot of white water 10 times in a row?

But I caught the biggest wave of my life that day. I always believe I was meant to do that shit. It's just exciting to be able to surf waves that big. I've always been able to paddle into 20-foot waves, but to catch waves that big was insane. We had a ball. It was like snowboarding when it gets that big, but the mountain is chasing you. It's like having an avalanche coming after you. That day was a bit of an eye-opener. I'm a big believer in 'if you can do it, I can do it'. And there were a lot of guys doing it out there that day. I was watching them thinking, 'You know, I reckon I can surf this place better than them.'

SUNNY

AN INJUDICIOUS PIECE OF PARTY PLANNING SEES A
HUMBLE 21ST BIRTHDAY PARTY BECOME THE SPARK
THAT SETS MAROUBRA ON FIRE

I remember walking into Marky Mathews' 21st. The place was packed.

It was up in the Coogee-Randwick RSL. There was a really good vibe to the room, but the management seemed a little worried that we were there. I didn't know why the guy was doing it at the time, but he just seemed a little over enthusiastic to serve us beer in plastic cups. He didn't want any glass. I said to him, 'We're all mates, no one's glassing anyone. Chill out.'

But it was a good vibe. All the boys' parents were there, their girlfriends. It wasn't just a room full of 20-year-old blokes. It was just like any other normal 21st birthday party.

I remember hearing there was another bar upstairs, and some of the boys had seen a few older crew around the place who looked like coppers. Then a few of the boys started saying that the police were holding a party up there. I initially thought, 'Oh shit,' but didn't give it much thought after that.

Anyway, it was the end of the night and everything had been fine, when all of a sudden there was a bit of a scuffle out near the lifts. I think Richie Vass had tried to jump in a lift full of coppers. I looked over and saw a bit of push and shove outside the entrance to this other bar.

And then it just erupted. Their guys started pouring down the stairs; our guys started pouring out of the bar.

Me and Johnny Gannon fought our way to the front, in between the boys and the cops, and said, 'Boys, settle down, settle down.' Then I saw this huge copper, this massive bloke, just beside me, right in the middle of all the boys. He's pushed one of the boys in the face to get him out of the way then someone unloaded a massive one on him and it was on again. We were right in the middle of it. If you wanted to get out of it you had to fight your way out.

We've tried to break it up, and there were some cops trying to break it up as well. We could all see it was a no-win situation. Usually me and some of the older guys can calm down stuff like this, but so much tension had been brewing between the cops and the boys in the months leading up to this that it became impossible to stop. It just erupted. It was like a full Wild West bar fight: people being thrown through glass windows, people getting stomped on, punches going everywhere. I remember seeing that huge cop throwing haymakers. Then I see this big fat sergeant – one of the guys we'd seen earlier bad vibing us – climbing to the top of the stairs. He's pulled out his badge.

'Stop! Police!'

Someone's just king hit him from the side and he's gone cartwheeling down the stairs. He ended up breaking his leg.

You know when you're caught in a crowd at a rock concert where the whole crowd surges and suddenly you're off your feet? Well, it was like that, except there's four guys on top of you throwing punches at each other. You'd scratch your way up to your feet and start fighting again. And there were some big guys on both sides. Fuck, it was on, completely on.

By this stage it had spilled out onto the street. There were police choppers above with spotlights, and the coppers who'd been called in were batoning people as they came out the door. It was the biggest all-in brawl you've ever seen. I remember grabbing one or two of the guys who I knew couldn't afford to be in trouble and saying, 'Let's get out of here, now.' We bailed out the back door, straight down to my car.

The next day there was a SWAT team on the beach with machine guns, a line of them on the sand. On a hot summer's day they swept the whole beach with drug dogs, up and back on the promenade. They're standing on the storm drain with their Uzis or whatever they've got and looking out to sea. They looked ridiculous; it was pure overkill. People in the local community took our side when they saw the way the cops reacted.

Once the dust settled they targeted our stars, of course. Eight guys were charged including Mark, the birthday boy, Reni Matua, the footballer, and Benny Kelly, who was studying law. Everyone beat the charges because the police had been off duty, and large amounts of alcohol had been drunk by both groups. But if people are going to be charged surely it has to be members of both groups, not just us. The cops come off worst, sure, but no police were charged even though plenty of our guys got hurt as well.

There was so much tension between the two groups that this thing was unstoppable – and that was the night the gunpowder got lit. The party organiser at the RSL should have got sacked for booking us in together. Once we were all in the same building, and both parties were on the piss, well, it just took on a life of its own from there.

Things between the Bra Boys and the police changed that night. For the next three days they were everywhere. They seemed so determined to square up, and they were just searching for a way to do it. You got the feeling that this whole 15-year feud between us and the police was coming to a head – which is exactly what it did in the months ahead.

PLAIN CLOTHED
AND
UNIFORMED
**POLICE
PATROL
THIS
AREA**

NSW Police Force
www.police.nsw.gov.au

INITIATIVE OF EASTERN BEACHES POLICE
AND RANDWICK CITY COUNCIL

Part 6
Like Thunder

JAI

PANDEMONIUM IN DARWIN

I'll tell you what happened. We were fishing for barramundi, that's what.

Hinesy went mad up there. It was in the papers, 'One Man's Wild Darwin Trip'. On a flight up to Bali there'd been some trouble between him and his chick on the plane, so they landed the plane in Darwin and took him off. Next day he bashed this guy with his camera tripod – he loved to take photos – and then he hammered some bouncers at the casino.

So I've gone up there with him for his court case. Tony rang and asked me, saying, 'There might be some mad bush cunts trying to get me up here. Why don't ya come up.'

'Sweet, no worries. You shout the ticket, I'll come up.'

While we were there we went out fishing in the mangroves for barramundi. The guide reckoned the place was infested with crocs and we shouldn't even put our hands in the water.

I was Hinesy's mate, but he could just turn on you. *Boom*, my phone rings. I'm talkin', I'm talkin', I'm talkin'.

'Get off the fucking phone! You're scaring the fish away.'

'Hang on a sec, mate.'

He snatches the phone off me. 'I told ya to get off the fucking phone! You're scaring the fish. I should just chuck you in the water with the crocs.'

'Well, go on then, chuck me in the water with the fucking crocs!' I knew he might, so I said, 'No, fuck that, I'll just jump in.'

So I jumped in. All of a sudden he's there freaking out.

'Get out of the water, ya fucking idiot! There's crocs everywhere!'

I said, 'Jump in'.

He's looked at me and gone, 'Okay', and he's jumped. It was box jellyfish and croc season, and the guide in the boat is screaming his lungs out, just freaking.

'Get the fuck out of the water! *Get the fuck out!*'

We climbed back in the boat and kept on fishing, and soon after we nailed a big barramundi. *I* hooked the fucking barra, but Hinesy had to come over and steal the fucking rod off me. We'd caught a couple of sharks before that, but as soon as Hinesy saw my fish was a barra, he's just snatched the rod out of me hands and gone, '*Boom*, I've got it now.'

Hinesy took a photo of me and him with it.

SUNNY

THE SEVERAL COMPLEX AND INTERTWINING WORLDS OF TONY HINES

When I still had the surf shop, Tony wanted me to design him some T-shirts – he wanted to call it the 'Pandemonium' series.

There'd be four T-shirts in the range, each one celebrating one of Hinesy's infamous trips away. The story of him and Jai in the croc-infested river – that was Pandemonium in Darwin. This would be followed by Pandemonium in Bali and Pandemonium in France, respectively. Each T-shirt would feature a cartoon outlining the pandemonium that happened on each trip.

Pandemonium in Jindabyne … He told me the story behind that one. Him and Tim Vlandis, the snowboarder and an old Maroubra boy, were down in the snowfields. Tony had already beaten up some guy who'd picked on Tim; he broke the guy's jaw. Suddenly all the cops were looking for him. He jumped on one of those tourist buses going back to Jindy from Perisher. Well, there was a footy team on the bus, singing these team songs. After 10 minutes Tony's had enough.

'How about you bunch of girls shut the fuck up.'

Some big bloke got up and said, 'Make us.'

Tony told us, 'After about five minutes of fighting this guy, I said to myself, "Hang on a minute, he's kind of getting the better of me here." So then I thought, "Fuck this," so I hit him with a combo, dropped him, bent down and bit his ear off, picked him up above me head and threw him through the back window.'

Even though our grommet days were well and truly over, nothing had really changed between us and Tony. We'd see him occasionally and he'd hang out with us, but we were always wary of him, just like we had been when we were kids.

One time there was a group of us, including Hinesy, at a restaurant in Maroubra. We're all there having dinner and Hinesy was ripping into Ronnie Reardon something horrible. Hinesy had just gotten out of jail and was 100 kilos, very fit and just scary. Ronnie's only 5' 2", but he had just boxed for the Australian title. We were all drinking beers, having dinner and all arguing, but Hinesy just kept pushing and pushing Ronnie. Ronnie's eventually just gone, 'Fuck you, mate. I'll punch you in the head.' Hinesy kept laughing and playing his games, throwing stuff at Ronnie, just geeing him up. And then Hinesy got up and grabbed Ronnie's hair and gave him a 'frenzy', rubbing his hair and ears real quick.

Ronnie's just clicked. He's stood up and gone, 'Come on, mate!' In the blink of an eye Ronnie's thrown one of his big overhand rights, collected Hinesy on the chin, and just dropped him. Hinesy's legs have gone out from under him and he hit the deck. It was a beautifully timed right that only a professional boxer could throw; he landed it right on Tony's chin and just dropped him straight back through the door of the pizza place. Tony was three times the size of Ronnie; it was the full-on David versus Goliath. We were sitting there just watching this, going, 'Fuck! What's gonna happen here?' We thought it might turn into the all-time rumble.

By this stage Hinesy's recovered and grabbed Ronnie's legs in a tackle; he's got over the top of him and thrown a few. Ronnie had a cut over his eye already 'cause he'd boxed the week before, and Hinesy got his thumb and jammed it in there, opening him straight up. Then suddenly Hinesy just got up, smiled, and that was it. We all sat back down and kept eating.

It was a big moment. No one had ever dropped Hinesy. He was one of Sydney's most notorious by this stage. There weren't too many people who could fire up with him and not end up eating through a straw for six months. But Tony respected Ronnie for doing it. Hinesy was stoked – stoked that little Ronnie had stood up to him. Five-foot-two Ronnie wasn't backing down. But Ronnie also knew he'd been lucky.

We'd always stood up to Tony and Grommet since we were young; we'd spar with them, give them shit. But this was different. We were all now in our mid-20s, we were grown men. But you sensed that, to Tony anyway, the games we played as kids were still going. 'Okay, grommets, you've got 15 minutes until we come looking for you. Let the games begin. Go!' That's what he was still like 15 years later. It was all a big game; a psychological, physical, extreme game.

Tony was such a complex character. He was our friend, but he also wasn't the sort of bloke you rang up on a Saturday morning and said, 'What are you up to, mate?' He didn't work, so he wanted to chase every swell, or come along and hang out. But you didn't ring him and say, 'Hey, mate, what are you doing?' If you got stuck with him, you were there till the end of the ride, which more often than not would end in some kind of drama.

This was your typical day with Hinesy. We'd be in the café down Maroubra Beach and I'd say something to him like, 'Geez, you've put on some weight, mate; you're looking a little heavy.' Then he'd start patting his stomach and going, 'You reckon? You reckon?' Then he'd look around the café and he'd see a hot chick having a quiet breakfast with her boyfriend. He'd go straight over there, whack his shirt up, and go to the girl, 'Do you reckon I'm fat? Touch it. Go on, touch it.' And he's got a big hairy belly hanging out. He grabs her hand and whacks it on his stomach. Then he starts on the boyfriend. 'You reckon I'm fat? You reckon I'm fat?' It was just so intense. You don't know what the boyfriend's going to do; they can see Hinesy's jatz crackers. Anyway, he comes back over and you're shaking your head going, Jesus Christ. Then some old lady's walking past with a little poodle and he goes, 'Come here, precious,' and he grabs the dog and picks it up. 'Oh *precious*!' The dog's licking him all over the face, while the little old lady with the fur hat and scarf is freaking out. He starts licking the dog back, full facial licks, then he goes, 'Precious is coming with me!' He starts taking off the dog's collar. Then the old lady starts screeching, and they both have this full tug-of-war over the dog. He finally puts the dog down and comes over and goes, 'So, what are you doing tonight?' like nothing ever happened.

We were trying to avoid him one night and he turns up at the pub. We're all dressed up because one of our mates has a model friend who's invited us out to a dinner party with her friends. Then Hinesy turns up.

'Where are yas going?'

'Nowhere, we're just going out for a few drinks with a mate.'

'So where are ya going? A mate's party? Who's ya mate?'

'Oh, you don't know him, Tony.'

'Nah, what's his name?'

'Milney.'

'Milney! I know Milney. He's a good bloke. I've got his number right here in my phone. I'm gonna call him. Wait right here. I'm gonna whip home and get changed. I'm coming with ya!'

So we take our chance and get out of there. And I suppose this is our relationship with him. Not many people would say 'Let's get out of here' and leave Hinesy – cold stone backdoor him – 'cause he would want to square up with you. But we had that kind of relationship where we could do stuff like that with him and it'd still be cool.

So we backdoored him. We had to get petrol so we pulled into a petrol station on the way to Coogee, and Hinesy, coming back in a cab from his place, happens to see us. The cab pulls over and he jumps out. We all go silent. 'What are yas doing here? Why didn't you wait for me?'

'Ah, we just had to get petrol.'

So Hinesy jumped in the car and we're off. We had a dinner at Mille Lire, this Italian restaurant at Coogee. There's a whole lot of beautiful girls there. Hinesy rocked up and fully started straightaway; the full charm act, Elvis songs at the top of his lungs – you name it, but he could pull it off. It was incredible to watch. He missed his calling; the guy should have been on stage. He goes over to the table across from us where there's a whole party of American backpackers.

'Where are ya from?'

'Texas,' they reply.

He starts singing 'Deep in the Heart of Texas' at the top of his lungs. He keeps going and going; there's no off switch. The manager comes over.

'Mate, can you be a bit quieter, thanks; there's people complaining.'

Hinesy pushes him out of the way and goes, 'Get out of here. You're spoiling my show!'

He ends up moving all the tables in the restaurant so there's now a runway going straight out to the balcony that overlooks the street awning below. He rips a red tablecloth off one of the tables where some guy and his wife are eating. It's full magician style, except shit goes everywhere. He ties the tablecloth around his neck, moonwalks to the back of the room, then starts snorting, pretending he's a bull. Then he charges full pelt at the balcony and jumps straight over the edge, landing on the awning below. The whole restaurant runs out to see what happened, just in time to see him bolt down the street with his red cape on, disappearing down Coogee Bay Road. He doesn't return.

The next morning I hear he'd climbed up the awning of another restaurant down the road and went, 'Da-nah, I'm here!' and started straight into a set of Elvis tunes at the top of his lungs. Finally, when a bodyguard who was there looking after a client said, 'Mate, can you sit down and shut up,' Hinesy has said, 'Make me.' He grabbed the salt and pepper shakers off the table and smashed the bloke into a coma with them. He's then jumped back over the balcony and disappeared. That's your night out with Hinesy – hilarious and scary all at the same time.

Are you going to ring him the next morning and ask him if he wants to go for a surf?

Tony hated having his photo taken, but he loved taking other people's photos. We've hardly got any photos of him, even though he was around all the time, and the ones we have got are generally of one of Tony's alter egos. I know Jimmy has a classic photo of 'Virgil'. Virgil was a full-on English clubbing eccy-taking geezer. Virgil had dyed blond hair, the gold chain around his neck, the tracksuit, even the accent. Virgil only drank water, and Virgil did heaps of drugs. Tony could stay as Virgil for days. But Virgil overdosed one day and died. Tony overdosed and his heart stopped for a couple of minutes. They managed to bring him back, but from that day we never saw Virgil again. We saw Tony, and we saw that Tony didn't do drugs any more. We asked him why and he said, 'I've never done drugs. Virgil did the drugs, but he's dead now.'

He could become someone else and pull it off flawlessly – the voice, the dress, the music, the sunglasses, the drugs, the mannerisms.

One time, when we were kids, Hinesy bit a guy's finger off. He used to have a couple of professional victims. They hung around with him but they were more like permanent hostages, gimps, ya know. They were hostages on a long leash. Sometimes they got to go home, but other times Hinesy wouldn't let 'em escape for days. Sometimes we'd go around to Ronnie's house on Poo Hill and there'd be people tied up down in their secret basement, wrapped from head to toe in cling wrap with just a straw to breathe through. Who knows what was going on?

Anyway, this guy was one of these professional victims, and Hinesy had bitten off his whole finger down to the first knuckle. The guy's screaming and there's blood everywhere. We were little grommets, hanging out in the street, and Tony and Jason come out and start playing piggy in the middle with his finger, throwing the finger over him and speaking to him like he's a little kid, whingeing for his finger back. One of the shopkeepers has called the police and told them it was Tony.

Hinesy's already wanted for God knows what, and within a couple of minutes there's the SWAT team, there's helicopters, there's sirens. They're coming from everywhere and they've cordoned off the whole block. They're all looking for Tony. I just remember him bolting into the pub. The cops looked for him for hours but never found him.

A few years later I saw him down at the café and I asked him how he'd got away that day.

'Well, first thing I did was I run in the pub and ordered a schooner of water with ice in it. Then I whacked the finger in it and sat it under the bar. When the sniffer dogs came in looking for the finger they couldn't find it. Then I ran out the back of the beer garden and started jumping fences. I got to a block of units, ran up the stairs, kicked down a door and ran in. That's the first thing you've got to know: you've got to kick the door hard enough to bust the lock, but not so hard that it busts the hinges. So if anyone's hot on your tail you can still close the door and it doesn't look like anything's happened.'

'What if someone's in there?' I asked.

'That's why a good gangster should always carry this,' said Hinesy, and he pulled out a big wad of cash, at least a thousand bucks. 'So you say to the person, "Look, I need to rent your apartment for a few hours. Here's the money; remain quiet and don't say anything and everything will be good."'

'What if they don't agree?'

Then Hinesy crosses his legs, picks up his cappuccino, takes a sip and says, 'Then you've got a hostage situation.'

'What do ya do then?'

'You tie 'em up, mask 'em, throw 'em in the cupboard and put the kettle on.'

SUNNY

A LONG LOST VOICE FROM THE PAST PRECIPITATES A DAY TRIP TO SILVERWATER

I was working in our surf shop one day when out of the blue he called.

'Where have yas been? You haven't come out and seen me once!' That voice – it could only belong to one person. Almost 10 years after we'd last seen or heard from him, it was Grommet.

He was angry that we hadn't been up there and seen him at Long Bay in all that time … angry and sad, I think. When Jason went inside he was 18, so his life outside had stopped at 18. When he was 18, we were his mates. We were some of the only real mates he had outside, even though we were five years younger than him, because we were the kids he'd hang with at the beach every day.

He practically demanded that we go out and see him. So Ronnie and I drove out to Silverwater.

We walked into the visiting room, and we were amazed. Here he was. He'd hardly aged a day since we last seen him; he was just bigger, fitter. He was that glad to see us.

'G'day, Grommet,' I said.

'Grommet? Nah, it's Locko now.'

By this stage he was just about the toughest bloke in the NSW prison system. The stories we'd heard were legendary. And the toughest guy in the jail isn't going to go by the name of Grommet.

Within five minutes he was up on the table shadow boxing.

'C'mon, Ronnie, get up here.' He knew Ronnie had turned into a champion boxer, he'd heard all about it, and he wanted to see Ronnie's style. Those visiting rooms are so quiet; they're really sombre, sad places, full of heavy guys with all the screws watching on like hawks. And here's Locko up on the table sparring and laughing. It was pretty clear he could more or less do what he wanted in there. Ron's got up there and is kind of shitting himself at first. He was a bit nervous about having to get up in front of all these gnarly guys, but Locko gave him no choice. Locko used his hands for focus pads, and he called out the combinations to Ron: 'Left, right, left hook! Good, Ron. Good.'

I was watching Ronnie and Grommet boxing away and it was like I was back in Torrington Road out in Grommet's garage. It was like we were back in the car park at North Maroubra again, 10 years earlier. I had the full flashback.

When he got down we started talking, mainly about Maroubra. We told him all about what was going on down the beach, what the boys had been up to, what the surf had been like. Who'd moved away, who'd died. He asked a lot about Ronnie and his boxing. It was pretty clear he missed Maroubra a lot. We didn't ask him much about what was happening inside; I don't think we asked him anything actually.

He told us how years ago he'd started these boxing programs for young offenders out there. Both he and Hinesy were close to Johnny Lewis, the boxing trainer, and Grommet had got in touch with Johnny and got him out there to help him with this program. Johnny loved him too. Grommet got Johnny involved in his program so the younger guys would come and box with them. Grommet could then get in their ears and give them some advice, the stuff he's learned: do your time smart and get out of there.

Before we left he said to us, 'Boys, I've got no other friends on the outside. I was 17 when I got in here. Promise me you're gonna come out and see me again.'

We gave him our word. Then me and Ron walked out of there and went, 'Holy fuck, what just happened?'

He got transferred to Lithgow soon after, and true to our word we went out and seen him. We weren't going to let him down.

It was a few years later when Jason's mum, who we'd always been close to and really loved, called me with the news. I went up to the hospital and saw him in a coma. With only a couple of months to go until he was free, he'd overdosed. He'd already been paroled once, and he'd met a beautiful girl and married her while he was out. They'd even bought a place together. Then he'd broken parole and had gone back in for another six months. He was counting down the days till he got out when it happened.

I called Hinesy, and he came straight up to the hospital.

Grommet never woke up.

There was a full Maroubra crew at his funeral; young and old, they were all there. No one had forgotten the guy, not even during the 20 years he was inside. No one could. He was a full child of Maroubra, 100 per cent. That's why he was The Grommet – The Child of Maroubra – or, as he used to call himself, The Chosen One.

ronnie reardon

BAD NEWS DELIVERED FROM THE INSIDE OUT

I remember going out to see Grommet in jail at Silverwater. That was freaky.

Me and Sunny have turned up and gone, 'G'day, Grommet. How are ya, mate? It's mad to see you.'

And he's gone, 'Grommet? Nah, boys, me name's Locko.'

He was fucking massive, but he was still a good style of a bloke too. It was fucking freaky. I was amazed; it'd been that many years since we'd seen him. When he went to jail we were 14, he was 18. He was in and out of boys' homes then he went to Long Bay. We hadn't seen him in 10 years, maybe. We've walked in and he's gone, 'Where have yas fucking been?'

Apart from his name, he hadn't changed. Straightaway he made me shadow spar in front of the whole jail. I'd fought for the Australian title not long before, and he was keen to see how I went. Mate, I was that embarrassed, having to spar in front of all those blokes, my head was going all red. But Jason missed Maroubra so much. He had plenty of friends on the inside, plenty, but he didn't have that many on the outside. We were kind of it.

I was in jail at Long Bay when he passed away, years later. It wasn't that long before Tony died, actually. Me and my good mate Al were coming back from work at the prison hospital. As we're standing at the gate to get back into our section, this bloke has come up to us.

'Fuck, I think your mate Locko's dead.'

Me and Al have both looked at each other and gone, *'Fucking what?'* As much as we didn't want it to be right, we said, 'You wouldn't want to be having a lend of us, mate, 'cause we'll fucking pound ya.'

Guys like Grommet just didn't die. We rang up and found out he was in a coma. An overdose, they reckon. The bloke never woke up.

The night before, he'd been speaking to the bloke in the cell next to his and he was going, 'This is what we're going to do when we get out.'

He had big plans to run boxing classes and look after some kids, stop 'em making the same mistakes he'd made. He'd married while he'd been out on parole the year before as well, and him and his wife had bought a house. Mate, the guy was only a couple of weeks off getting out.

We just didn't believe it, though. A guy like that, he's like Superman. When he passed away, every jail in NSW had a service for him. He just took the ball up, mate, but he had a beautiful heart too. He had the charisma and the personality and the front, but also had the heart to pull it all off.

JAI

NEW YEAR'S DAY, 2001, AND THE GAMES BEGIN

From the second I picked up the phone I knew it was a bad idea.

I was in bed with my girl Natalie when I got the call from my mate HR.

'Jai, do you reckon you can drive Tony's girlfriend and his daughter out to Silverwater to see him?'

It was pretty early on New Year's Day, I was in bed with Nat and I was hungover, so I wasn't really too keen to do it.

'Go on, mate, do him a favour.' I told him I'd do it.

Soon after, Grommet – Jason Loughnan – shows up at my place and got me out of bed. Grommet had done his 15 years for killing the guy who attacked him in jail, and had just got out on parole. He fucked up soon after and ended up back in there.

'C'mon, mate, get up. You're driving Rachael out to the jail.'

And so I went. I didn't want to piss Tony off, and I thought I was doing him a favour. Jason Loughnan got in the car with me and we drove around to Tony's place. Rachael and Tony's baby daughter got in, Jason got out, and we drove out to the jail.

Tony's on remand in jail at the time for nearly killing a mate of ours, Jarrod*. He'd nearly killed Jarrod after accusing him of sleeping with Rachael. So Tony's in jail after almost killing a guy for thinking he was having an affair with Rachael, and here I am driving out there with her alone. It didn't take much for a guy like Tony to start believing stuff. All the way out I was thinking it was a bad idea, and that's what it turned out to be, bra.

While I was in the waiting room and Rachael was next door with Tony, I started playing with Tony's daughter, just keeping her occupied while her mum and dad talked. I was just trying to make her laugh, and that's when I saw him looking at me, just staring.

'Wait in the fucking car!' he yelled; he just fully turned on me.

I sat in the car and I was just thinking the worst. 'Fuck, this guy thinks his daughter knows me; he thinks I've been around at Rachael's place.' All the way home I was just thinking to myself, 'How the fuck did I let myself get roped into doing it?' I got home and crawled back into bed with Natalie.

A couple of months later, HR calls me.

'Jai, I gotta see ya.'

He's come around to Ma's and said, 'Bra, when you went out to the jail that day, did you sleep with Rachael?'

What!?

'Bra, I was just with Tony, and, mate, he thinks you did. *Do not* go for a drive with him. *Do not* drop the ball. He wants to knock ya. If he says, "Come to my house," don't.'

If his girl was Elle Macpherson and she put it on you, you wouldn't touch her. Too much drama. If she was the most beautiful girl in the world you wouldn't touch her because you know what would happen. There are other girls out there in the world. Why would I go for his chick and hand myself a death sentence?

---

* *Name has been changed.*

I was lucky I got the heads up, though. Tony had just got out of jail, and a couple of days later he pulled up in his car.

'Let's go for a drive to Bondi.'

He was cunning. He'd pretend it was all sweet, just like he'd done with Jarrod. Tony had called Jarrod up and said to come around to his house for Christmas drinks; that he'd forgotten about the whole thing with Rachael. And look what happened to Jarrod – he got beaten with an iron bar and had his arms and legs broken, then he got doused with petrol. If I hadn't had the heads up I would've gone, 'Cool, let's go for a drive.' If I'd got in the car that day I would've been dead, 100 per cent.

The first time he confronted me about it was in Bali, a few months after he'd got out. He showed up out of the blue. I was with a mate and we were walking down this lane in Kuta where all the restaurants are. *Boom*, there's Tony, sitting there eating. I tried to turn but it was too late, he'd seen us, and whistled us over. He keeps eating his nasi goreng and is talking to my mate, asking what we've been up to, what the surf's been like. But the whole time it's like I'm not even there. He's making no eye contact with me. The whole scene is just icy, bra.

Tony got up without saying anything and walked off. I figured I had to set this straight then and there. I walked over to his car. He's sitting behind the wheel, looking straight ahead.

'Tony, I heard you think I slept with your girl, man. I would never do that to ya, bra. I drove her to the jail to do you a favour.' And he just turns around and looks straight through me.

'I don't *think* you fucked my girl, I *know* you fucked my girl. If you admit it, I'll give you an easy death. She's admitted it. If you admit it too, I'll make it quick.'

I just went, fuck, what a situation. He was convinced. There was no way I could reason with him. When he'd asked Rachael if she'd slept with me, he'd strangled her and beat her until she went, 'Yes, I did it,' just to get him off.

'She's admitted it. So you're *not* admitting it?'

'Bra, there's nothing to admit. I didn't do it.' And he just glared at me.

'Then let the games begin.'

I went into hiding for a few days at my hotel. I remember a mate saying to me, 'Fuck, bra, it's a different world over here in Bali. They'll just stab ya in the heart and make ya disappear in the rice paddies.' That's what I reckon Tony had in store for me. I was freaking out. I still couldn't believe what was happening, so I holed up in the hotel. I eventually convinced myself I couldn't stay there forever, so my mate and I went out one night to Double Six nightclub.

Sure enough, Tony showed up. He'd let me see him then he'd disappear again. Wouldn't come up and say anything, but just keep popping up, staring at me. He'd walk towards me as if he was coming over to say something, then turn before he got to me. He kept doing it all night. He loved to fuck with your head. I've gone to my mate, 'Bra, I'm out of here. I'm not relaxing with this guy here.'

We made sure he wasn't following us, and ended up going back to the hotel. We were sitting by the pool on the banana lounges having a drink with some other crew who were staying there when all of a sudden Tony comes charging in. He goes, 'Where's the chicks? Where the chicks?' and then just walks off.

He could go from psycho to clowning around to psycho again like that. You could never predict what he was gonna do, and that's what had me worried, bra, especially over there in Bali.

It wasn't an accident he showed up at our hotel that night. The next morning I moved to a new one. I stayed a few more days then changed my ticket and came home. I didn't want to be in a place like Bali with him around.

He got into some trouble on that trip. He got into a fight with some local boys out at Uluwatu, and they pulled knives on him. He lost it. 'What! Those knives would wanna be sharp! I'll toss ya little monkeys off the cliff, ya hear that! I'll throw ya all off the cliff!' They're all walking round with machetes, and suddenly they've looked at him going crazy and gone, 'Ah, that's not the guy. Sorry.' They knew exactly it was him; they just shit themselves when Tony fired up. When he got like that he was frightening.

That was the beginning of a fucked two years, bra. It went on for two years, from the first moment when he said, 'Let the games begin.' He read that many psychology books while he was locked up, he just wanted to fuck with my head before he killed me, ya know. Every night while I tried to sleep it was all I could think about.

There were times after he said, 'Let the games begin,' when I'd be sitting at home and I'd hear his voice out in the lounge room. I'd walk out and there he was, having a cup of tea with Ma.

'Tony? What are you doing here?' I'd ask.

'I'm not here to see you; I'm here to see Mavis. Hello, Mavis.' And his whole manner was like butter wouldn't melt in his mouth, the full act. Just fucking with me head, bra. That whole two years he made sure I couldn't relax once. Not once.

I bought a caravan down at Kurnell, but I never stayed a night in it. I thought I could go and lay low there, but I never went. I bought the caravan for $2000, but I never ever went out there, never set foot in the thing. After I bought it I started thinking, 'Ya know, how the fuck could I move in there? It's like fucking *Cape Fear*, and he's straight up like de Niro. Fuck, what am I gonna do – move in out there on me own?' So I was spewing. I couldn't go there and move in and next thing it mysteriously burns to the ground one night with me in it.

There was nothing I could do. If I moved anywhere he'd find me. If I tried anything I'd just be throwing my life away. The cops? Never, bra. I just kept saying my prayers, saying, 'Please, God, don't let this bloke get me. You know I didn't touch his girl. Please … don't let this bloke get me.'

SUNNY

AN UNGROUNDED VENDETTA CAUSES
DISCOMBOBULATIONS WITHIN THE MAROUBRA RANKS

When I first heard that Tony was after Jai, I just didn't believe it.

Jai's telling me, 'Bra, it's true.' But why would Tony do it? What was he trying to do? It just didn't make sense. We were some of the few real mates he had, and he was alienating himself to the point where he would have no one. I couldn't work it out.

For a while I'm thinking Hinesy was just playing one of his games and I didn't take the whole thing seriously. That's how he was. Hinesy was always trying to mentor us, and I didn't know if this was just a role play and he was trying to test us. He'd ambush us when we were young. I remember walking down Marine Parade and him jumping out of a doorway and pretending to slash your throat, going, 'Got ya! You weren't ready.' I thought this whole thing could be one of Hinesy's games.

That's what Hinesy and Grommet used to do in prison, too. They'd 'cause these dramas in prison to occupy themselves. Then when they were out of jail they used to do it to us. Grommet would come up to you and go, 'Have you seen that Hinesy cunt? I'm after that cunt. He's a low cunt, isn't he? What do you think of him?' They'd just create a drama. Then they had enemies, then they had victims, then they had drama, then they had a game. They did this kind of thing in prison. When they were out on the street the game continued.

It was our worst nightmare for him to be coming after one of us. I didn't believe it, and I didn't want to believe it for a long time. But then Hinesy started playing his games. He'd turn up at Ma's having cups of tea, sitting out on the porch with his legs crossed, while Jai was there. One night Koby rang me and said, 'Sun, Jai's rang me from Kings Cross and he needs help.' I've gone and got Koby and we've rushed to the Men's Gallery, where Jai and Hinesy were having a full Mexican standoff inside. Me and Koby didn't even stop the car; Jai ran out the front and we just scooped him up and went.

It was all cat-and-mouse games, and Koby and I were now a part of it. This was a Hinesy game, and he set it up, so you were never sure of where you were standing with him. And we knew how to play it. You couldn't show fear because then it's over, he wins, and it usually means you get hurt.

One time I saw him at the Coogee Bay pub. He came over and I had a few beers with him. This would have been about three months before the shooting. I was trying to talk to him about what was happening. It just didn't make sense that he'd go after Jai like that, and I was trying to get a straight answer out of him about why he was doing it. I'd thought about it long and hard, and couldn't work it out. If he had any friends, if he spent any time with anyone, it was us.

So after a couple of drinks, he's asked me if I wanted to come for a joint back at his place, told me he wanted to speak to me about something. It was a bit risky, but I knew that if there was going to be any way to deal with this nightmare, I'd have to confront it and play along with the game. I had to find a way, the best diplomatic way, to bring it up.

We go into his house in Beach Street, Coogee, and I see he's done up the whole place. The last time I'd been in there it was this run-down 1970s style place, but he'd put in new timber floors and these beautiful big windows all around. He rolled a joint. My Brazilian girlfriend Aryena was with us and Hinesy got on really well with her. She was doing a PhD in sociology, so naturally Tony gravitated towards her. In a way I thought it was the perfect time to broach the subject of Jai, although I still thought he'd try and scare me in some way. That was just him.

He'd just been away, and he started talking about his trip. He'd taken a heap of photos, so he got out his photo album and was showing me photos of this Swedish girl and all these mountains. He's eventually got to a photo of him and Jai on a fishing trip, and they were holding up a barramundi.

'Pandemonium in Darwin,' he said, 'back when me and your brother were friends.'

'Mate, you guys will work it out, Tone. You guys have always been friends. It'll be sweet.' He didn't say anything and just kept flicking through the photos until he came to another one of Jai.

'Who do you reckon would win out of a fight between Koby and Jai?'

I said, 'Jai. He's got a lot of heart.'

Tony didn't say anything. Then he got up, walked around a little bit, picked up this remote control and has gone, 'Have you seen my new security blinds?'

He chuckled and hit the remote. All of a sudden these heavy shutters started rolling down. It was then I noticed that the rooms near us all had locks on the *outside*, not the inside. It was a full-on fortress. He'd already done time for rape, and he'd leased out one of the rooms in his place to these two Swedish chicks who he called his 'experiments'.

The blinds start rolling down, and I just start getting this bad feeling. So I played it off, I kept talking like it was all sweet and like I wasn't rattled. I think it was a little test, ya know, it was one of his little games, and when it became clear to him I didn't seem worried, the blinds soon rolled back up again. Going around there didn't resolve anything about Jai, but there was a possibility.

But at the same time, with Tony, you never knew what he was going to do.

KOBY

STANDING, PERPLEXED, IN THE IMPOSING SHADOW CAST BY A FORMER CONFIDANT

I was really close to Hinesy.

We travelled to heaps of places together: France, Bali, Queensland. He tried to follow us to Hawaii once but got turned back by US Immigration. We were close. He'd just come and hang out, surf, travel, party with us ... whatever.

He and I got along great. One of the main things the prosecutors couldn't work out later on was why he was such good friends with me if he wanted to kill Jai. But it wasn't till later on that he started doing weird shit. He was always really fit, and we'd train together; boxing, weights, whatever. He was just a funny guy to be around. You'd see him in the middle of Bondi walking into a café in his cossies singing Elvis songs at the top of his lungs. He'd go up to any girl and start talking to her. He was just amazing; he had that much front. I just liked being around him, just the crazy shit he'd do. I can honestly say that when he was with us we had a good time. But there was always this evil side to him, and you just knew it was waiting around the corner somewhere. We knew how gnarly he was. We'd all heard the stories about Hinesy in the yard up in jail just cruising around in his Speedos in the middle of winter; we'd heard about him terrorising people. It was the one thing about him and Jason Loughnan – they were a two-man gang. How can two guys run a whole jail? It was unheard of, but they did it.

But I think he was lonely. When ya look at it, a lot of his friends were scared of him. I have people coming up to me in the street now, going, 'I was Hinesy's mate', and I just laugh at 'em. I tell him we were his mates; we were with him every fucking day.

One time we flew up to Queensland together and before we left he'd asked me to go see this guy for him. Didn't tell me why. The guy goes, 'G'day. You here for Hinesy?' and I tell him I am. So he gives me this big backpack. I got around the corner and opened it; there must have been hundreds of thousands of dollars in there. I just put me hand in and said, 'Thank you,' took me commission, and dropped it back to Hinesy.

'You look what was in there?'

'Yep.'

'How much did ya take?'

'A handful.'

'Yeah, that's sweet. Let's go to Queensland.'

We're on the flight and we've gone to get some drinks and he's said to the stewardess, 'Me mate's got this one! He's loaded.' He was gonna run me dry of the money I'd taken off him.

There was this one real hot chick I'd had something going with last time I was up on the Goldy. She'd heard I was there and she got a hold of me. I've pulled her and she's come and stayed with me and Hinesy down in Byron Bay. She came out with us to that Rae's place at Wategos Beach; we had four bottles of Dom Perignon, lobsters, all on Hinesy's account.

The guy would have thousands of dollars on him at all times. We never asked him where it came from.

Tony hated the French, and the French didn't know what the fuck to make of him when he turned up in France looking for me. I was surfing a few contests and minding my own business when suddenly out of the blue I heard that raspy voice, 'Hey, Koby!' I was like, 'Oh no, here we go. Hinesy.' We hung out in France and we had a ball, right up until he had a bit of an episode one night. That was the thing with him; he'd either be in the best mood and you'd have a ball with the guy, the funniest fucker ever, or he'd be in a crazy mood and there'd be some stranger laid out cold missing his teeth. Nothing in between. On that trip he fought the biggest French guy at a bar and caused all sorts of drama. I said to him, 'Mate, it's too much,' and I kinda lost him for the rest of the trip. Then he latched on to my mate Bruce Irons, and Brucey and his mates couldn't shake him. Brucey's come and seen me a few months later and gone, 'Thanks a lot, Koby. Your buddy went crazy, bra.'

Hinesy and I had an arrangement where he'd hang around me and my pro surfer friends whenever he wanted as long as he didn't do anything bad that would drag me into it. That was our deal. And you know what – besides him fighting anyone who come near him who he didn't like, I never did see him do anything really that bad. Sure, he was a complete nutter. He'd surf in his sluggoes all day in the middle of winter. He wasn't a great surfer but he loved the water.

But then Hinesy came to Bali looking for Jai, and I was there. That's when it started to get weird. Jai's come back to our *losmen* all freaked out and said, 'I've just seen Hinesy, and he's here looking for me.'

'Don't worry, mate. Nah, he's not.' I was telling Jai he was paranoid. Turns out he wasn't. When Hinesy was in Bali he was renting four villas, which we thought was strange. He was living four different lives over there and you wouldn't be sure what he was up to. He could be four different people, bouncing between four different villas at a thousand bucks a night, living four different lives. He did that kind of thing.

Jai just took off home. That was Hinesy's whole thing – *I know where you are.* Bali's such a radical place that you could probably knock someone and get away with it. Maybe that's what he was thinking. He'd been really close with Jai, but after that trip, after all that shit happened, things changed. It was kind of trippy actually; that was the same trip where I got my tattoo, 'My Brothers Keeper', around my neck.

I still didn't really believe Jai at the time, he can be a pretty paranoid guy, but my mate Wilko has gone, 'Bra, there's something going on here.' I didn't really catch on, but Hinesy was definitely starting to pop up a little too randomly all the time when Jai was there. When Jai said to me in Bali, 'He's gonna kill me,' from that moment I started to sense that there was a different aura about Hinesy.

Tony would be at my house at Curtin Crescent most mornings, and looking back on it, who knows what he was doing there apart from the fact Jai was living there as well. He'd come and try to get me to party: 'Come to Bali', 'Fly me to Hawaii'. Then after Jai said to me, 'Please, bra, don't bring him to the house any more,' I started to watch Tony closely. You could see him trying to intimidate Jai. He was getting inside Jai's head, doing his crazy psychological numbers that he did to people. He could fuck with your brain like no man alive.

I woke up at five one morning up at Curtin Crescent and Hinesy was standing over Ma in bed with a coffee in his hand going, 'Good morning, Mavis.' Jai and I have come in and gone, 'What are ya doing?'

'I just came in to see you boys and give Ma a coffee and some flowers, that's all.'

But he always did weird shit like that. He'd come up to the house just to sing her Elvis songs. You could never really add up what he was on about. But he was a good person when it came to Ma. He'd brought around flowers and food for Ma for years, because Ma had taken care of him his whole life as well. He was one of Ma's kids too, ya know. He did have a sensitive side, it's just it was outweighed by this psychotic tendency.

I was hanging around both him and Jai, and at that stage I started to full-on believe something was going on. There was a subtle change in

Hinesy; you could tell he was up to shit. He was always turning up trying to scare Jai, just trying to fuck with his head. Maybe he didn't want Jai dead; maybe his aim was to send Jai mental. I really think he was trying to torment him. He was an imposing guy. The big thing was that you never knew what he was thinking. You never fully knew what he was up to. He never let you in. By that stage he was being weird. After that time he turned up at Ma's, he's come up to Jai and said, 'I can get into your house any time I like.' I didn't think much about it at the time. Hinesy was really close to me at that time, but he never tried to get into my head like that. Never.

Hinesy used to fully spin when he was on the pills; he used to get real crazy. He nearly died from a coke overdose once. I think the cops tried to get him and he snorted this huge ball of coke to destroy the evidence. Maybe this was what was fuelling his paranoia.

One night Jai rang me from up the Cross; he'd been up at the strip clubs. He was panicking. 'He's following me everywhere. He's planning something. I'm up the Cross and he's here. Can ya come and get me?' So me and Sunny drove up in my car and just got him out of there. We didn't see Hinesy that night. We waited around the corner and Jai just comes bolting around and jumps in and we floor it out of there.

As we're driving away my phone goes off. I look down and it's Hinesy.

'Where are you?'

'I'm with my girl.'

Straightaway he snaps, 'No you're not.'

Somehow he knew I'd grabbed Jai. We took Jai home and he's sat down on the lounge and gone, 'Some time in the next week he's gonna kill me.' Jai was really fucking scared. Jai would have fought Hinesy any day; Jai was never scared of fighting anyone. But Hinesy didn't want to fight Jai, he wanted to kill him. 'Bra, 100 per cent he's gonna kill me.' But that's what Hinesy used to do: he'd fuck with people's minds to the point where they'd want to kill themselves, ya know. He liked the torture. He'd tell people how he wanted to torture them just like he'd tortured other people, just to scare the fuck out of them. And I think that's what he was doing.

I said to Jai that night, 'Why don't you just go away?'

'He knows where I'm going. Everywhere I go, he's there.'

I reckon he knew people at the airport. He had a network. It was around this time that he was dealing with all these drugs and he had these friends everywhere.

I was travelling heaps at that time, so I didn't see what was going on day to day. Then one night when I was home, Hinesy has come up to me at the Beach Road Hotel in Bondi.

I was at the top of the stairs and he walks up to me and says straight up, 'I'm gonna get your brother,'

'Whaddaya mean, you're gonna get my brother?'

'He fucked my chick.'

'He didn't do anything to your chick, mate. He hasn't done anything wrong.'

And we just went into a mad wrestle. I don't know how it happened. It wasn't a full punch-up, but we just started wrestling. Suddenly he's just jumped off me, and as he walked away he goes, 'I'm gonna get him!'

That kind of rattled me, 'cause I knew then it was fair dinkum. I told Jai later, I tried to tell him to go away, and that Hinesy would get into trouble soon enough on his own and be back in jail.

'I can't really go anywhere, bra. I don't have any money, and even if I did, he'd find me.'

Every time I was going away I was worried about Jai, not sure whether I'd see him again. Jai knew that *I* knew the truth, but everyone else thought he was just crazy. If you look at what Hinesy has done to other people he's dealt with over time, you can add it up. You see the pattern. The whole thing was that I don't think he tried to actually hurt Jai for a while, simply because he and I were such good friends. But then I think after we had that altercation and we stopped talking, it twigged something in him and all bets were off.

JAI

MUSINGS ON A TROUBLING TWO YEARS

Me and Nat met down here at Maroubra.

She was a Koori girl who'd come from the country, Wagga Wagga, and I met her when she'd just moved to the city. She was this mad little country girl. But within a month she was in trouble, hanging out west at Bankstown with crew she didn't know.

I spoke to her one day and told her she was too good to be doing that shit, and how those blokes out there didn't give a stuff about her. 'They don't give a fuck about you,' I told her. 'You're a country girl. I remember when you first showed up down here you were all innocent. Now look what you're doing.'

Then, *bang*, we started going out and we both got real healthy. We were a good pair in the early stages. It was love, for sure. But once that honeymoon thing died down, all of a sudden we weren't that good for each other. We almost got too close, and it wasn't good for us. But she's a soldier. She knows my heart and knows I'd do anything for her.

It was when I was seeing Nat that I first started hanging out at Redfern. Nat had relatives up there, and I was training all the time at Mundine's gym. When I got locked up back in '99 most of the pods I went to were full of Koori boys, so I became pretty tight with them. I'd been mates with the La Per lads since I met big Rat that day out at Voodoo when I was about 12, the same day Koby surfed it with us when it was huge. The armrope had snapped on Rat's boogieboard and he was nearly drowning and I come and grabbed him. He was going, 'Bra, I was nearly gone if you didn't come and grab me.' Me and Rat have been heaps close ever since. He's the gemest of gems. I love my Koori brothers as much as I love my boys here in Maroubra; they're my second family. Redfern and La Perouse became my second homes. I just love 'em 'cause they're real people. And with Tony shadowing me, I was doing a lot of time up in Redfern to avoid him.

It wasn't that long after I got back from Bali when Tony found me again. I was at the beach at Maroubra one day and he came up to me.

'Get up. Let's go for a walk.'

He wouldn't do anything if there were people around. He wasn't going to risk going back to jail again. We started walking along the promenade.

'I've come up with a little solution to our problem. If you give me Nat while you watch, I'll wipe the slate clean.'

'What?!'

'You fucked my girl; it's only fair I fuck yours.'

Fuck that. Fuck that. 'No way, mate.'

But he was already walking away.

I couldn't fucking believe it, 'cause Nat was now in it as well. Fucking hectic, bra. That whole two years was fucked. It fucked with me and it fucked with Nat. We just tried to avoid him. We didn't go out that much, and when we did we went to places where he wasn't likely to be. We just tried to avoid the bloke. I'd see him occasionally at the café down the beach where all the Maroubra guys would hang out. He'd talk to the other guys, but he wouldn't make eye contact with me and wouldn't say a word to me. You could just feel the tension. During the day around other people you wouldn't worry; it was at night when he could isolate me and Nat that we had to worry. The worst nightmare would have been to end up at his place. That was where he got Jarrod. It was like a jail, and once I went in there, bra, I wasn't coming out.

He almost got us one night in Bondi. Me and Nat shouldn't have even been there, 'cause he hung at Bondi a lot. We were at the Regis and he spotted us and come over. With Nat and other crew there, he acted like there was nothing going on, but both Nat and I knew. I said to Nat when he went to the bar, 'We've got to get out of here. Let's go.' Nat and I bailed, and he followed. Nat was walking in front of us and he's grabbed me.

'Remember what I told you? Remember? Give me Nat and you'll be fine. Just do what I say tonight.'

We hailed a cab, got in and he's jumped in after us. Straightaway I knew I had to stop this cab going to his place, so I've just gone, 'We're going to Coogee Bay, mate.' When the cab's pulled up out the front of the pub I've gone to the cabbie, 'I got it.' I was going to pay the fare. Tony jumped out, and as soon as he did I've just gone to the cabbie, 'Go, mate, go,' and we drove off. We left him there.

Nat went through a lot during that time. Even though the bloke never got her, you've got to understand how powerful this guy was in the head. You've never met a guy as powerful in the head as him. But he was using it for the wrong reasons.

He got under Nat's skin. Nat was never the same girl again after he started shadowing us. Fuck yeah, that lead to us breaking up. The last six months I was with Nat, she'd wake up in the middle of the night screaming, 'Get him off me, get him off me!' Hectic nightmares, shaking. It was just the pressure of him after us. It spun her out. I'm only scared of God, but Tony was scary – scary for a bloke, let alone for a girl. And she knew, 'cause people were telling her all the time, 'Jai's got to watch out, man.'

It took its toll. It was bad for Nat and it was bad for us, and we eventually broke up. There was one night after we broke up where he almost got her, though. It was at the Regis, and I was there drinking with Koby and a few of the boys. Nat was there, but she wasn't with me; she was hanging over the other side of the room. We were both drunk and we'd been fighting that night. Not long after, I looked over and saw Tony talking to her. Fuck, bra, here we go again. He walked over and pulled me aside.

'Well, well, fighting with Nat, are we?'

He was fully playing it up in front of everyone. He bought round after round of sambucas to the table, and he was making out like nothing was going on between me and him. That's the way he was. But I kept an eye on Nat. She was on the other side of the club but he wasn't going near her, so I thought, sweet, all cool. But then me and Koby have gone down the stairs to leave and he's come over to me and gone, 'Come on, you're coming out for a drink with me.'

Koby's gone, 'Mate, there's no way he's going out for a drink with ya.' I think by this stage Koby had already confronted him about what was going on between me and him.

'I promise I won't do anything to your brother. We're just going for a drink.' He was just laughing Koby off.

But Nat was still there, and she was really drunk. It was the kind of night where something could happen, ya know. I just wanted to get him away from Nat, so I jumped in a cab with him and we went up to the Cross.

The cab ride was okay, a bit of tension, but I knew I was in a bad spot. We went to the Men's Gallery and had a couple of drinks, and the whole time I was thinking of a way out of there. Then the phone rang. It was Koby.

'Are you all right, bra? Has he tried anything? Where are ya?'

'Bra, it's not really all right. I shouldn't have come up here with him.'

Koby ripped into me for going up there with him then I hung up. Tony was right there next to me.

'Who was on the phone?'

I told him it was no one. By this stage he had turned dark, bra. He'd had a lot to drink. That's when he brought up Nat.

'So, what about my ultimatum? Remember what I told ya? So where's Nat? Where'd she go? Maybe you should get her up here.' He was into me for a couple of minutes and it was heavy. Then the phone rang again. It was Koby.

'Bra, where are ya? I'm coming up to get you.' I told him where I was, and then it kept getting heavy with Tony. He was freezing me blood, bra; just keeping on about Nat. He was getting scary.

Koby rang again; he was out the front with Sunny. I knew Hinesy wasn't gonna let me go, so I had to bullshit.

'It's Nat, she's out the front. I'll go out and get her.' I knew the only way he was gonna let me go was if he thought that I was going to bring

Nat in. I had to play along with him. As I've got up he's grabbed me by the arm.

'You're lucky, 'cause if she didn't show up you were going out to Botany tonight.'

That was his way of saying I was dead. I ran out to the car and jumped in.

'Let's go. Fucking quick, bra.'

We drove past the Regis on the way home to make sure Nat wasn't there. I was worried about him coming back and finding her. That was the end for me and Nat. I still loved her, but I was watching her breaking down. This guy was in her head, and it was too dangerous for her to be near me. It hurt me that we broke up, bra, it really did, but at least I knew that she was going to be safe. I just wanted Hinesy to get off Nat's case, 'cause, fuck, it was a lot of pressure for her. Because of my drama I could full on see her changing before my eyes.

A couple of months later Nath Rogers had this big party at Bronte, and I met a girl there, BC*. She was cool. She was telling me she loved me after a few weeks, which was all a bit quick for me, but we had fun together. When I hooked up with this new chick, it was just some fun. She was coming over, picking me up all the time, getting around with me saying, 'This is my new boyfriend.' I didn't mind, because it was getting back to Hinesy that I wasn't with Nat any more. I thought it was making Nat safe and it was putting an end to all our problems.

But I never for a second thought this girl was going to get in trouble in Nat's place. I never wanted this girl to get in trouble. Never. I just thought he'd see I'm not with Nat any more, he'd take off somewhere and it'd all be forgotten; it'd be sweet.

I never expected he'd go after BC in place of Nat.

And I never expected to bump into him that night in Coogee.

_____

* Name has been changed.

JAI

THE FATEFUL EVENING OF 5 AUGUST 2003

I shoulda been dead that night, bra. It shoulda been me.

When he pulled the gun back I went for it, and when I went for it it's just gone off. If it had a safety or had been a different gun or hadn't gone off that easy, it'd be me dead now, not him. That's why I believe so much in God. I was praying that whole two years before, asking God to protect me from this guy, and God just looked after me that night. He didn't let that bloke get me.

BC, me and Ronnie Reardon had just driven over to Coogee to get an ice cream. After that we went to grab a beer. Ronnie wanted to go and see Hair Bear in Coogee, so me and BC thought we'd go and have a couple of casual beers in the Coogee Bay while we waited for him.

I remember walking into the pub and seeing Hinesy.

'Fuck, he's here.'

But the thing is, during those two years I'd been in a lot of places with him, and if there's people around, he's not going to do anything; I was pretty safe. You know what I mean? He was cunning. So I just thought I was with this new chick, we'll have a quick drink and then we'll fuck off. I hadn't told her anything about what had been going on between me and him; I didn't want to say anything about him and scare her.

There were no problems until I've gone to the dunny. I've come back and he's there next to her, going, 'What's your name?'

Killing me was too easy. He wanted to rape one of my girls. So he's gone up to her and introduced himself. I ended up grabbing her, pulling her aside and saying, 'Look, this is dangerous. Stick close to me. This bloke, he wants to kill me, and he'll hurt you to get to me.' He was pretty pissed by this stage, and was starting to look dangerous. I said, 'Finish this drink and we're gonna fuck off. I cannot explain how dangerous this is. I can't even begin to tell you how dangerous this is.'

Well, she's never seen me like that with anyone. She's like, 'Okay, let's go then.' Before we could, Hinesy pulled out a heap of eccies and handed 'em out. He's had his, and BC has gone to wrap hers up in the plastic off her cigarette packet. Hinesy wasn't happy.

'It's not a takeaway.'

He made BC take her pill, but there was no way I was gonna take one. Not with him there. I had no idea what he was gonna do. He's standing right there watching me, telling me to take it, so I crushed it up on the table. As I pretended to snort it, I kinda flicked it off the table. He didn't see. He'd lose it when he took pills; he was trouble on 'em. We needed to get out of there pretty quick.

I waited until he wasn't watching, then I grabbed BC and we've just gone. We walked out of the pub and up to her car, which was parked up the street. I'm thinking, 'Sweet, we're out.' I just wanted to be back at her place and go to bed and forget about what had just happened.

We get to the car and look back. He's there. He's followed us out. He's followed us out without us seeing. Ronnie was there as well. I was freaking out, 'cause this is the last thing I wanted. I've gone to get in the front seat and he's just leaned forward and gone, 'Get in the fucking back.' And it wasn't even what he said; it was how he said it. The tone of his voice, it was just venom.

So BC's driving, looking at me in the mirror, just tripping, thinking, 'Jai's just told me how dangerous this situation is and here's the guy in the front seat with me.' When he said to me to get in the fucking back, that's when it struck me that he must have something on him. If I had a gun like they reckon I did, I woulda told *him* to get out of the fucking car. But I didn't.

The vibe in the car was fucked. I'm stressing out thinking, 'This is hectic … *this is hectic.*' I've been to his house before, and he's got it all soundproofed, so I didn't want to end up back at his. I just thought, 'Fuck, what am I gonna do?' My mind was going in a million directions, trying to think of a way to get out of this. I thought, 'Well, let's go have a drink somewhere else.' I needed to go somewhere with other people around. I didn't have any money, so I told BC to drive to my place and

I'd get some money. He's gone, 'Yeah, he owes me some money. Let's go to his house.'

The thing was, he respected Ma, he respected no one but my grandma, and she was living with me and Koby up at Curtin Crescent. I was just thinking of going into the house and coming back out and going, 'Tony, Ma's crook and we've got to stay here with her. Me and BC aren't going out.'

When we got to my house I got out of the car and walked into the lounge room, heading for Ma's room to go and wake her up. But as I was walking through the house I had a feeling I wasn't alone. He followed me straight in, straight in the door behind me. He spins me round and he's got the gun.

'You're not getting away this time. We're fucking Ronnie off and we're going back to my house and we're scotching her.'

I've just gone, *fuck*. I couldn't believe the situation. I was feeling sick at the thought of this guy raping the girl. I'm just going, 'All right, all right.' He's got a gun on me; I got no choice. There was no way I was going to let this guy rape her, but I had no idea what the fuck I was going to do. I was starting to think there was no way out. I turned to walk out and saw a fishing knife next to the boards. I thought, 'Well, looks like I gotta do me best with this.'

We jump in the car and I'm just thinking, Oh no. 'We're scotching her.' Oh no. As we're driving back to Coogee, back to his place, I've gone, 'Let's go the Coogee Bay for another drink.' I was thinking of anything that might get us out of this.

We stopped at the lights on Malabar and Maroubra Roads. I looked over and Ronnie had gone. He'd jumped out and I hadn't even noticed. As the car's started moving I've said again, 'Let's go to the Coogee Bay, let's go to the Coogee Bay.'

Hinesy's seen that Ronnie has gone, and *boom*, that's when he pointed the gun at me. That was him saying we're not going to Coogee Bay, we're going to my place and we're doing this. I just saw it and went, 'Get it the fuck off me.' I just went for it as he pointed it at me. I just went for the gun with both hands. We've wrestled with it, and it's just gone *bang*. It all happened in half a second. I just remember going for it to get it away from me, and it's turned in his direction and gone off and got him in the head. I remember just thinking, 'Fuck, how did that just happen?' All of a sudden I've got it in my hand; he dropped it. I remember looking at it and it was like it wasn't real. Everything was in slow motion and in a strange colour. I remember looking at him and he's started rubbing his head. I'm thinking maybe it's missed him. Did it get him? I just thought, 'Fuck, he's gonna be angry now. We're as good as dead. He's gonna kill us. He's gonna kill us for sure.' I just shut me eyes and just kept pulling on the cunt, *boom boom boom* … just thinking if he gets up he's gonna be awful angry.

It was hectic. BC was driving as the gun's gone off. She stopped the car on the other side of the intersection, jumped out and started screaming. I jumped out of the car, thinking that the cops are gonna come. There are houses everywhere. I didn't even know whether he's dead or alive.

'C'mon, just jump back in the car.' I jumped in the driver's seat, going, 'C'mon, the cops are gonna come.'

She jumped in the back seat, just screaming. I didn't know what to do, and next thing I know I'm at the cliffs at Maroubra. All I can remember is her saying, 'Get him out, get him out!' I didn't know what I was doing. He was falling onto me while I was driving and I'm thinking … fuck, ya know, I wasn't thinking at all really.

I just pulled up at the point and I'm thinking, 'How did it come to this? How did it come to this?' She's still screaming, 'Get him out! Get him out!' We ended up in front of her place on the point and I've just thought, 'Fuck, what am I gonna do?' I opened the door and he fell out onto the road. The only thing I could think of was throwing him over the edge. I just wanted this situation to be over.

Bad situation.

I stood there on the edge for a while and stared out into the night, stared out to sea. It was windy, and the rain was coming in sideways. I listened to the surf raging against the cliffs. The surf was huge.

I turned around but BC had already driven off, so I pulled the hood of my jacket over my head and ran home in the rain.

JAI

A PRE–DAWN STROLL TO CONFIRM THAT LAST NIGHT'S NIGHTMARE WAS IN FACT OF THE WAKING VARIETY

I didn't sleep a wink that night. I didn't sleep for a week. I got out of bed before dawn and went for a drive to the point.

Originally I just walked over to the cliff because I'd remembered that I'd grabbed this fishing knife from the house at Curtin Crescent, and now I couldn't find it. I'd dropped it somewhere, so to start with I just went back and retraced my steps to see if I'd dropped it on the cliff top. I also thought that maybe I could clean up a bit of the mess where we'd parked the car – not that you could really clean that kind of mess up.

So I went to find the knife, and while I was there I stopped and thought, 'Ya know, I wonder if he's in the water? I wonder if he's dead? I wonder if he's still there?' I wasn't sure. I hadn't seen anything the night before; it was too dark. He's one of those guys who you think will survive anything. Imagine that, if he was alive … I wouldn't be here today, that's for sure.

I just thought I'd better go and have a look. So I walked up and looked over. He's on a little ledge a few feet down. I climbed down and checked his pulse. There was nothing. Then I just sat there looking at him.

The swell was massive. There was a huge swell running. Nature was angry. The swell was just smashing on the rocks, the wind was howling and it was raining. It was like something out of the Old Testament.

Once I tossed the body off the cliff I thought, 'Well, how do I go to the coppers now?' At the time, if I'd gone and handed myself in and just told them what had happened I might have been all right. But we just didn't trust coppers. You're not going to go to the coppers when they've got it in for you anyway.

The next morning I started getting rid of some stuff, trying to make it all go away – clothes, the gun, the car. I still wasn't sure it was all real. I wasn't sleeping so I wasn't dreaming; the days just all blurred. It was a strange, shitty feeling. It was like it wasn't real, but it was.

The morning after the shooting Nat rang me out of the blue. I hadn't talked to Nat for months, hadn't said a word to her, because I was seeing BC. She rang me up the next morning and asked if I was all right. I lied to her.

'Yeah, I'm sweet.'

'No, you're not. Where are you?'

'No, I'm all right.'

'You're not all right. Where are you?'

I went and seen her the following day. I didn't tell her anything about what had happened, but she knew something had gone down. She's psychic. Nat's Koori – she feels things through the land. She senses things about people close to her. She can feel things in the wind, can listen through the trees. Nature talks to her. Something told Nat I was in trouble. Yeah, she's a good girl, Nat; she's a soldier. After the shooting the cops would pull her aside and try and get her to turn against me: 'He doesn't care about you. The night it happened he was with another girl.' But she stayed solid the whole time.

The next morning I told BC to go home. I told her I was sorry for dragging her into it. I told her she should go. I said, 'If anyone asks, just say I threatened you with a gun and made you help me drag the body.' And that's what she said in an original statement to the cops. She said, 'Jai threatened me, threatened me to help him drag the body.' I was trying to make sure she was all right. She wanted to stay with me and help, but I said, 'Nah, you'd better get out of here.' She was freaking, but she really wanted to stay and help me.

When she was in court she said, 'I've never been as scared in my life as I was when I was in that car.'

The prosecutor asked, 'Who were you scared of? Jai?'

'Not at all, I was scared *for* Jai.'

She just told it how it was, the aura of the bloke, how she'd never felt anything like it. 'Jai told me to leave. I just wanted to stay and make sure he was all right.' She saw it for what it was. She said, 'Jai was always a gentleman to me.'

The next few days were hectic. Did that really happen? You'd sleep for an hour and wake up and you'd realise that this won't go away. It was the worst feeling ever, brother. This situation is not going away. Going to sleep, you could think it didn't happen, but every time you woke up your first thought was, 'Yeah, it happened all right.' The worst feeling you could have. Knowing there's this trouble hanging over you, this cloud, it's a fucked feeling. It's fucked when you're in trouble and you know you have to go to jail even for something minor, but then *this*?

It was a long two weeks. But as those two weeks went on I felt more like I wasn't to blame for this. This guy put me there. This guy stalked me for two years and he nearly got me a couple of times. He put himself there, he made it happen. I wasn't happy he was dead, but I was happy I was still alive. It was him or me.

I knew by that stage that I'd be handing myself in the next day. A mate come and visited me.

'God used you, bra. He's not going to leave you in jail.'

I went and handed myself in not long after. You never expect you're going to be in a situation like that, but suddenly you are and you've got to deal with it. You've got to face up to it. You're never going to knock yourself, so you've just got to deal with it. You've just got to wait and see how it all unfolds. Maybe the court would see it the same way I was seeing it.

I wanted to have one last surf. Who knows, it could have been my last surf ever. It almost *was* my last surf ever, bra, because I rolled one of the skis out at Bear Island.

We had a barbie up at Jed's that night, 'cause I knew it was going to be the last time I saw the boys in a while. They didn't know anything about what had happened – we made sure of that – but they might have sensed it. I don't think the boys really even knew that it had been me in the car that night. No one spoke about it anyway. From Jed's veranda you could see the road blocked, you could see the coppers down the hill circling like sharks.

The next day we organised the whole family to meet before I went and handed myself in. That was heavy. Ma was there. That was a bad scene, with Mum and Ma there. I was just fucking thinking, 'How did I get into this situation?' You live your life and probably expect some dramas here and there, in and out of trouble, but something like that? You never expect that extent of trouble. Fuck, how did I get here? But you've got to deal with whatever's in front of you. I was ready to face my problems, but what made it hard was seeing how it was affecting everyone around me. I had no control over that. Seeing Ma, the best of the best, who has always done everything to keep us out of trouble ... it was heavy to see how it affected her.

It was real but not real at the same time. I do have recollections of those 10 days, certain things are as clear as if they happened yesterday, but other bits are hazy. When you've got something that heavy hanging over your head and you know there's no way you're going to escape it, you can't relax. I knew it was inevitable. The blood on the road, the car; of course I knew it was coming back to me.

By the time I handed myself in I was glad. I couldn't have stayed like that much longer. My lawyer said to me, 'Look, it's better off you just come down and hand yourself in.' I remembered all the shit going down at Maroubra Police Station, so I said, 'Nah, I won't go in at Maroubra. I'll slide in at Surry Hills.'

It was the biggest relief when I walked up them stairs at the police station and handed myself in. After I threw his body in, I thought to myself, 'Well, I'm gone forever more or less.' But then once I had time to sleep and to settle down and think about it, I thought, 'Fuck, he followed *me*. He fucking followed *me*, ya know. I tried to get away. I didn't ask for this sitcho.'

Then I went and prayed. I didn't ask for this, God put me there. I didn't ask to be there. God will decide whether I'm supposed to spend the rest of me life as a free man or spend the rest of my days in jail. Once

I had time to sleep and think about it, I realised God would decide whether I deserve my life back. God overrules the judge.

God kept me alive that night for something. God kept me alive through those two years for something. He wasn't going to leave me there in jail.

KOBY

WITH A SUPERMODEL IN ONE'S BED AND TROUBLE ON ONE'S DOORSTEP, WHAT DOES A MAN DO?

I wake up and Jai's in my room showering. I could hear people in the lounge room, maybe two of them, freaking out, but I didn't know who it was. I couldn't even tell it was Ronnie and BC. I just yelled out to them to shut up 'cause I was worried they were going to wake up Ma. I didn't think anything of it. I just thought Jai had brought some people home from the pub and they were partying. It happens a bit.

Jai would always come into my room to shower when he was pissed, 'cause I had an en suite and the other bathroom was right next to Ma's and he didn't want to wake her. But he was really banging around in there and I could hear crying outside. I just assumed Jai was fighting with his chick. I stuck my head in the shower and told Jai to shut up. As I did, I caught a glimpse of him just scrubbing himself and wigging out. I didn't take much notice of it at the time.

After a while I've got the shits and come out of my room. I've gone into Ma's room to check on her and I said, 'Ma, it's all right. It's just Jai, he's drunk, don't worry.' As I walked back to my room it was pretty dark – there weren't many lights on – and I could kind of see Jai's chick walking out of the other bathroom. She was crying pretty hysterically by this stage, but it wasn't out of the ordinary for Jai to make his girlfriend cry. It wasn't out of the ordinary for an Abberton girlfriend to cry. But I still didn't add up what had happened.

Walking back to my room, I cross Jai in the long hallway. The look on his face said it all.

'Something bad's happened, bra.'

'Do you want any help?'

'Nah, go to bed. I don't want to get you into any trouble.'

It was dark, but I could see he looked like a ghost. His face was white, and every time I've seen that before it's never been good news.

I just went back to bed with the girl I was seeing at the time, Elyse Taylor, the model. She asked, 'Does he usually come and jump in the shower?'

'All the time. Just go to sleep.'

I kinda thought he might have been in a fight. Jai was always fighting, so I just thought he must've been in a really bad fight, maybe a fight with bouncers, which is just classic Jai. So I didn't think much of it and went back to sleep.

The next morning he wasn't there – no one was there – and I didn't see him all the next day. I thought, 'Fuck, where is he?' I usually just make coffee for Ma in the morning then walk back to bed. As I was making the coffee I looked down and saw a car out the front I didn't recognise. I thought, 'Who the fuck owns that car?' I guessed it must've been that BC chick's car. I drove around in my car to try and find Jai down the beach but couldn't, so I went home, grabbed my board and walked down for a surf.

When I got back BC's car was gone, and my car was gone as well. I lost my shit, bra. Jai hasn't got a licence to start with. I was ringing Jai's phone, I was ringing BC's phone. That's where all the police intelligence came from. They thought I was in on it but it was just me leaving messages on Jai's phone trying to find out where the fuck my car was.

'Jai, where's me fucking car!? Call me when ya get this, bra, straight up!'

The more I rung him, the more it looked like I'd given him the car to go and dump stuff and I was in on the whole thing. I finally got on to him.

'I got the car, bra, I got the car. Don't worry.' Then he hung up on me.

And I'm thinking, fuck, he's got my hundred-thousand-dollar car – 'cause the new one I got was the hotted-up version of the GTO which was $88,000. But as I've gone to say, 'Fuck off, bring it back,' he's hung up on me. I rang him back and his phone was off. I rung BC and she's just gone, 'Something bad's happened,' and hung up on me as well. I've just gone, *what the fuck*!

Then I started ringing Ronnie, who's Jai's best mate. I sent text messages to Ronnie going, 'What's going on?' and then I sent a message to BC. Finally Jai brings the car back and it's all right, but I still couldn't find out what was happening. He kept it dark. He kept it real dark.

That's when they were ditching the car. It wasn't until there were helicopters flying around Maroubra that I started to suspect something. I didn't really know until I drove down the beach. I've seen all these helicopters buzzing the cliffs, and police dogs on the corner of the point and it's dawned on me, *boom*, that's what's happened. Whatever has happened here, Jai's got something to do with it, and considering what had happened over the last couple of years, it probably involved Tony.

I'm thinking, 'Where's Jai?' By this stage Jai was hiding out. It's taken me a while, but I've found the house he was hiding in.

'Fuck, bra, what happened?'

He told me the whole story. I knew they were looking for him, so I'm thinking, 'Fuck, what do I do?'

I remember thinking things were bad. But Hinesy was gonna kill Jai, so you'd rather spend 10 years in jail than forever in the dirt. That was the whole thing at that stage. I didn't think about the future or myself, I just thought about Jai.

SUNNY

DUELLING POSSES AT NOON IN THE COOGEE BAY SALOON

The day of Tony's funeral was heavy.

We'd heard that a few of the older Maroubra guys were in town for the funeral, some of the guys who'd looked after us a bit when we were younger. Marty Lee came down from Queensland and was staying with another old Maroubra guy. We heard he was there for the funeral, and me and Jed and a couple of the other boys went down there to see him, just to say to him, 'Look, it's a sad thing, it was never meant to happen like this. It's just a tragedy.' We were trying to be respectful.

Marty was really quite freaked out that we showed up. He turned white, pale as a ghost. I asked him, 'What's wrong, mate, what's wrong?' He told me that he'd just been down to the funeral and the wake; he said, 'They've got guns. They're coming for ya. There's a posse.'

I finally got it out of him that there was a revenge party plotting, and they were down at the Coogee Bay. They were armed up. That meant a number of things. It meant we were in trouble, but it also meant Jai was sitting in jail by himself. Hinesy was so connected in there and we didn't want Jai looking over his shoulder the whole time. So I told Jed, who was up at Marty's with me, 'We need to get down there straightaway and speak to these blokes.'

Me and Jed drove straight down to Coogee and walked into the bar. Who knows how heavy that situation was? It was a heavy bunch of guys: Hinesy's prison mates, his connections, four of them. But none of them had known him as long as we did. We were trying to be respectful, but we wanted to say to these guys that we're not going to be hiding from anything. I approached the guy we thought was the ringleader and asked him, 'Do you know who's looking for us? I hear there's guys down here after us.'

'Nah, mate.'

We found out later he was one of the guys who had the guns on him.

'This is between friends. This is between Jai and him. And if anyone can sit here and say they were a better friend to Hinesy than we were, then stand up. We'll pay him respect, but this was between Jai and Tony.'

There was nearly a blow-up with one guy, but we made our peace and it didn't happen. It didn't erupt. Mate, anything could have happened. The boys could have been going to *our* funeral the following week. Me and Jed walked out, just looked at each other and said, 'Fuck, how heavy was that?'

I still can't believe we got out of there in one piece; it was by the skin of our teeth. I woke up the next morning and thought, 'What the fuck did we do last night?' Too many tequilas. But, mate, if we didn't confront them, it would have kept simmering. And it still got pretty heavy. One of Tony's mates turned up at one of the boy's places and pulled a gun on him. The whole situation was strange. Fuck, what do you do? Jai didn't want anything to do with it. It was Jai or Hinesy. And Hinesy had made it happen, not Jai. It was a bad situation from the start, totally unfathomable. It only had destruction as an ending. That seemed to be what Hinesy was pushing for: his destruction or Jai's. When you look at it all, and I've thought about it a lot over the past five years, how could Tony possibly benefit from this? He couldn't. It was like he was on a full self-destruct mission.

KOBY

THE CAVALRY RIDES INTO MAROUBRA AND PROCEEDS TO TURN THE PLACE UPSIDE DOWN

I shouldn't have gone to Bali.

But I just needed to get away from all the shit at home. I'd had this trip planned for months, but to the cops it looked like I was getting the fuck out of there because I had something to hide. In retrospect it was pretty dumb; I shouldn't have gone anywhere. On the upside the surf was good, and one of the boys pashed a *banchong* at a nightclub one night which was the first time I'd laughed in a couple of weeks.

The day I got back I was straightaway taken by the coppers for questioning. I walked into my house at Curtin Crescent later that day and the whole place was covered with this white shit. The whole place had been fingerprinted. I picked up the newspaper and it had a huge story saying they'd found Hinesy's body. I phoned Jai.

'What are you gonna do?'

'Bra, I just gotta hand myself in.'

We arranged for the whole family to meet at the Hotel Hyde Park – me, Sunny, Jai, Mum, Dakota, Ma – and we all just said our goodbyes to Jai. It was pretty fucked up actually. Jai knew what had happened, but dumping the body and trying to dump the car made it look pretty bad. Jai just said, 'Guys, you know the circumstances. If I go away forever, I'm sorry.'

The main thing Jai was really worried about was Ma. She was his main concern, along with Dakota. He told everyone he was sorry and that he never wanted his life to go this way, but to remember that God works in mysterious ways. We all left. The coppers were waiting for him at Surry Hills, so Jai walked up to his solicitors. Next thing we get a phone call from his lawyer asking where he is.

'Isn't he with you?'

He'd asked to go to the toilet, and he'd jumped out the window and done the runner. Turns out he ended up going and making amends with his old chick, Nat. He was still in love with her. He went around and told her he was sorry. Then he went and handed himself in to the coppers.

It wasn't until two weeks later that the coppers called me in. I walked into Maroubra station and they said to me, 'If you don't give us a statement, we're gonna charge you anyway.' So I went in there and made a pretty much bullshit statement I should never have made. I didn't tell them that I seen Jai at all that night. I didn't tell them that I saw anything, which wasn't actually that far from the truth. What I should've said was that I'm saying nothing. But because they said they were gonna lock me up anyway – which was a complete lie – I made up a bullshit statement which was eventually the only charge they had against me that stuck. They had nothing else. Next day I was charged as an accessory to murder.

The cops came and took me down to Maroubra Station. They charged me and put me in the cells. They picked me up late in the afternoon so that I'd have to stay the night before I could make bail. The next day a whole heap of Koori lads I knew were put in the cells with me. And they said, 'Fuck, it's all over the news, bra. We heard.' Then what the cops did was take me at four o'clock in the afternoon up to Surry Hills where the holding cells are. They fucking took me there at four o'clock so I couldn't get another court appearance until the following day. This was fucked. I'm walking in and I just know they're gonna throw me in the worst cell. There's a big holding cell with five pretty big guys in there … five big Aboriginal guys. They thought they were throwing me in a cell with the five heaviest guys they could find. One guy was there on manslaughter, another on assault … and one of them was my mate Joe, and another was a bloke called Doy, a mate of mine from school who I surf with all the time. And as the coppers pushed me in, they thought they were killing it.

'Have fun in there, buddy!'

Before they'd even closed the doors, my mate Doy jumps up.

'Koby, cha! Whacha doing, bra?'

I just looked back at the cops and said, 'Suck shit, boys.' I hung out with those guys for two days. Because they'd thrown me in there on a Friday afternoon, I had to stay the whole weekend.

Come Monday morning, I met with my solicitor and we fronted court. Because we owned all these houses, I got $25,000 bail. I walked out of court and there were a thousand photographers and cameras in my face, which pissed me right off. Luckily my mates were waiting for me. They threw me in the car and we drove away.

At the time I felt my situation was pretty bad. I was worried about sponsors and all that sort of shit, which I was right to be because they did end up dropping me. But it's not something you're thinking about when your brother is facing life in jail. Fuck, Jai got me photo in the paper and a weekend in the cells with me Koori mates? So what. You're not thinking like that when your brother's life is in the balance.

I was never really that worried about my situation, though, because deep down I knew I hadn't done anything wrong. I didn't *really* lie. I didn't see a body that night, I didn't see Jai with a gun; I never did anything that helped Jai shoot Hinesy. I never saw blood in the shower that morning; I never saw blood in the house. I never saw the bullet holes in the car. It didn't really worry me. I just thought they were putting heat on me to buckle Jai because he's got such a strong sense of family. I never went to see Jai when he was in jail, even though I could have. If I went to see him they'd just say we'd been corroborating our stories.

I had to report to the cops every day of the week at Maroubra Police Station. I couldn't travel for three months. I needed to be home for a while to deal with this anyway, but eventually I just went, 'Look, I've got to travel because I'll be sacked if I don't surf. I can't do a thing.' So my lawyer said, 'Let's get to court and see if we can do something about it.' Luckily, I had a really good judge who recognised that I had to earn money so I got my passport back. I wasn't suffering from a lack of exposure anyway; I was on the cover of both *Tracks* and *Waves* that month. But I just didn't like it at home; I didn't like the frame of mind I was in and the way I was feeling. There was just too much heat.

We'd tried to shield Ma from what was going on, but she's too smart. She knows all our tricks. Ma was really happy that I was free, but my whole family got worked over. The shooting was the excuse the cops had been looking for to put some pressure on us all; they'd been waiting for that for a while.

The NSW Crime Commission busted in the door at Curtin Crescent at, like, five-fucking-thirty in the morning. They always come in at stupid hours. They barge in and wake up Ma.

'Boys, can she just stay in bed while you guys search the rest of the house? It's five-thirty.'

'We don't care, get her out here now.'

So they dragged her out and made her sit on the floor on the cold floorboards. A 78-year-old stroke victim. I said, 'Mate, can she sit on the couch?'

'Nah, but she can make us a coffee.'

'I tell ya what, I'll shit in your coffee if I'm gonna make it.'

Then I walk out into the kitchen as the cunts are trying to make coffee and did a big loogie in the kettle.

'Enjoy your coffee, boys.'

The way they treated Ma just stunk. It was disgusting. One of them comes over to Ma and gets in her face and says all cocky-like, 'Looks like we got both of them now, hey, Mavis?'

I just went, 'Are you fucking kidding! Boys, she can't talk, she can't walk, she can hardly move. How tough are you blokes? The lady's a saint; she's spent her whole life looking after other people. Do you blokes feel good about yourselves?'

You could see a couple of them felt bad, but a couple of others sat down on the couch.

'You don't sit down on my couch if we can't.'

I called the main guy out.

'I swear to God, I'm gonna lose my brain if they're gonna make my grandma sit on the ground, if they think they're gonna sit on the couch and drink fucking coffee. Get 'em off my couch!' It got pretty close to a full-on fight.

They took all the records and every little pay slip. They found these fake licences, all these gold licences with my face on 'em, and I get charged with them as well. In *Waves* mag I'd said in an interview that I didn't have a licence so someone had sent me these perfect, duped copies. On some of them I had glasses on, some I had my hair parted down the middle. I never used 'em, or I would have really been fucked. It came out in court that those licences were actually perfect forgeries, which didn't look good for me.

Then they seized the house. We weren't evicted, but they seize all your accounts so you can't pay anything. They froze our accounts for six months, which coincidentally is the time it takes the bank to foreclose when you haven't been able to make any home loan payments. They just hung me out to dry. The bank foreclosed six months later and sold the house in Curtin Crescent. They even seized my cars. When it comes to your brother and you facing jail, though, money is just money. You can always earn more. It sucked, but the only thing I was worried about was Ma. We now had to find somewhere for her to live.

The NSW Crime Commission don't answer to anyone. When they take your shit, they take your shit. You can't argue with it. There was 80 grand found in Curtin Crescent. The $80,000 had nothing to do with any of the trouble that we were in, but they felt we were an organised crime gang. I mean, they said we were selling guns, racketeering and extorting money from local shops. They believed that the 80 grand was from that, which was bullshit. They said to me, 'We know you've got $175,000 cash somewhere. We want it or we take your house.' We had to pay the 175 grand, we had no choice; we had to sell the other family properties as well. Before Hinesy died he had to pay $250,000 to the Crime Commission – cash only. You can only pay them in cash, nothing else. They cleaned us out, bra, left us with fuck all.

And it wasn't limited to the Abbertons; the cops were putting heat on all the Bra Boys. The harassment was worse than ever. Now they actually had something on us. They were pulling in and questioning anyone they could think of. Ronnie should have never gone through it. Ronnie did nothing wrong. Ronnie jumped out of the car, you know what I mean. They knew he had a criminal record and a tough upbringing like us, and had no money to support himself, but they thought they might as well put the heat on him and send him broke paying for lawyers.

Then other people were being dragged in – *bang bang bang*. In a way they were trying to drive a wedge through everyone and break us up by doing that shit. Saying to Ronnie, 'Jai said this', and to Jai, 'Koby said this'. I never talked about one person but me.

It's one thing I've never understood, bra. I was at home asleep in my own house, minding my own business. It was dark, I couldn't see any blood on him; I couldn't see any blood in the shower. I had no idea what had happened. I just woke up and told everyone to shut up, because Ma had been sick that week. That was the extent of my involvement. I told 'em to get out and they left. There was no blood anywhere, no signs that anything had gone down, no one said anything, and *I* get busted? They got all that evidence against me, and I was just at home minding my own business. It was fucking ridiculous.

They were trying to break the boys apart with all this shit that was going down, but it was only bringing us all closer together. It was pretty soon after the house got raided that the Snickers contest was held down at Maroubra.

It was a big WQS contest, the biggest surfing contest ever held at Maroubra, with $100,000 prize money. And it was held right in the middle of all this shit going down. I was given a wildcard into the contest. Someone caught wind that I had it and there was a campaign to get it taken off me. I was just like, 'If they're gonna deny me the wildcard, we might deny them the beach.' I didn't say as much, but that's what I was thinking. Then it came through. You know how it is: something goes from being trivial to being on the news in a heartbeat. What made the news bigger was that Kelly Slater was there. If I wasn't there and Kelly wasn't there no one would have given a shit about their contest.

Kelly had rung me after I'd been arrested, and said, 'If there's anything you need, just give me a call … character reference, whatever. If you guys need any help just let me know.' He was behind us, really supportive and not judgmental in any way. And I was lucky, 'cause a lot of my surfing friends did the same. I had Bruce and Andy Irons call … Kai Garcia, Brock Little and Eddie Rothman and all those Hawaiian guys.

I thanked Kelly for coming down to Maroubra. He said he loved it here. He knew it was only a small comp – he hadn't surfed a WQS event for years – but he knew it was a big thing for Maroubra that he was there. I've always been pretty good friends with him because he hung out with Sunny, but he was really supportive and he was really stoked to be there.

And of course, I drew Kelly in a heat. What were the odds? You've never seen more hype over a stupid WQS heat in your whole life. I hadn't surfed a contest in years. I went out the night before, a Friday night, and didn't get home until four in the morning. Our mate Chooky Silvester organised a big night at the Seals Club, the Maroubra Idol night. All the boys had to get up on stage with an act. My mate Chappo has got this character, Laurie Krahn – Laurie the bouncer. Because Chappo's fought so much he's got no bone in his nose, so he puts an elastic band round his head and squashes his nose flat, then he takes his teeth out and does the full impersonation of every bouncer who's ever kicked him out over the years. I think he won.

Everyone was out, it was huge; all the Maroubra boys and my Hawaiian friends were there as well. Everyone was in a good mood. I think we all needed a night like that. When I got home at four I wasn't worrying too much about surfing my heat against Kelly in a few hours. Like, it's Kelly Slater, you know what I mean? There's not much you can do against him, so there wasn't much sense in being tucked up in bed at eight o'clock. Even when he has a bad surf he generally wins, so I figured I might as well go out and have some fun.

It was a massive day. It was sunny, there were chicks everywhere. They reckon there were 20,000 people on Maroubra Beach. I was stoked. As we walked down the beach, me and Kelly went past a line of 50 coppers. Kelly said he was a bit worried by surfing against me, worried about what might happen if he beat me. I told him he didn't have much to worry about, the boys would behave themselves. Then I looked up on the hill; the boys have set up a DJ and a keg overlooking the beach and are all straight back on the piss.

Despite still stinking of beer and surfing on two hours' sleep, I won. I beat Kelly. It was one of those things: because it was Maroubra, I knew exactly where to sit and catch two waves in the Dunny Bowl. So I just sat there and got two good rights, then tried to sit on Kelly and stop him getting a good one. I just got better waves than him. It's not like I outsurfed Kelly Slater, I just got better waves. It was the only time I've ever beaten him; he'd beaten me about four times before that. It was a four-man heat, and first and second progressed to the next round, so I got first and Kelly got second. The next day, Kelly surfed through and won the contest.

Kelly surfed that contest for us. He never said so, but he's that sort of person. He likes to bring attention to causes. I remember he said something pretty cool at the presentation the next day after he'd won. It was something like Maroubra is a pretty unique and special place and that there'd been a lot of stuff being said about it in the papers. He said the place was worth fighting for. He'd rung a couple of times during all the court drama just to see how we were all going. It kinda caught me off guard a little bit, but was really cool at the same time. I haven't heard from him since. I think he feels that when he has the chance to do something good he'll pick his moment and help you out.

A month later, I was in Tahiti. I was supposed to be in court over the fake licences, but chucked a sickie, said I had glandular fever. I surfed in the contest and made my heat on the first day. Mandy McKinnon, the Aussie lady who was handling the press for the event, wanted to ask a couple of questions to send back to the *Daily Telegraph* in Sydney. I said sure, no worries. The next morning she's come up to me and gone, 'Koby, umm, you're going to be really, really angry at me.'

'What do you mean?'

'You're on the cover. The paper nailed you.'

The paper had run a photo of me on the cover under the headline: 'Bail Out'. They were having a go at me for missing court and going surfing in Tahiti. I was never about to skip bail, I was just going surfing. It's what I do for a living, so I wasn't too worried about it all. I laughed at it. I'm the sort of person who knew it for what it was – it was just the papers trying to gee it up.

But as much as I went through it all, the boys went through it with me. Dragging the Bra Boys through the papers with all sorts of gang stories was unwarranted. The papers had no real idea of what was really going on. The boys were all totally behind us. They'd look after Ma and drop her up food, as did everyone in Curtin Crescent. It was cool like that. The more pressure the cops put us under, the tighter the Bra Boys, and Maroubra, became. If anything, my crew were almost too supportive, to the point where they'd come up every day and ask if I was all right. It was kinda like, 'Thanks, but can we give it a break?'

SUNNY

WITH THE FAMILY DOMINOES FALLING AROUND HIM, THE ELDER SIBLING CHOREOGRAPHS BEHIND THE SCENES

We wanted Jai to have one last surf as a free man.

There was me, Jai, Jack Kingsley and Flopper, and we took my jet ski out to Ours. The wind was a bit onshore, but there was a lot of swell and Bear Island was breaking. We got out there and I lent Jai and Jack my ski to go and tow surf it. They both got big stand-up barrels, and then Jai has rolled the ski. For reasons known only to him he tried to get barrelled on the ski and the thing has been rolled across the reef. It almost killed the ski and it almost killed Jai.

The next day was the last day of his freedom, the day before Jai was going to give himself up. We had a big barbecue up at Jed and Jack Kinga's place with all the Bra Boys. There was a warrant out for Jai at this stage, and the cops were driving around the place, beeping their horns and waving and yelling out, 'We're gonna get him.' Personal stuff, rubbing salt into the wounds. Jai was out the back with us and we're all like, 'Yeah, well let him have a couple of beers first.'

The whole family met the next day at the Hotel Hyde Park – Jai, Koby, Mum, Ma, Dakota and me. That was really heavy. We had lunch and then he went in to give himself up. We hadn't really spoken to Mum for 10 years, so there was a little tension and the conversations were short. It was emotional, but also a little awkward. Me and Koby got together and spoke to Dakota, told him it would be all right; we spoke to Ma and told her we knew Jai would be okay. It was, like, here we go. We're going into battle. We knew from here it would never be the same again. Jai's going in, and now the battle starts to get him out.

I was telling Jai not to say anything, and that we'd be there to look after him. We knew that no matter what we said, the police would do anything they could to prove us wrong. We knew that the press was going to fully blow it out. We knew it had started and our total focus was now on one thing: a not guilty verdict.

A friend had put us on to a solicitor, Barry Watterson; he's Maroubra, he's family, so Jai met with him in jail. I became the middleman between Jai and the lawyers – and the one who had to guarantee they were gonna get paid. We were trying to work out what sort of money we'd need up front; how much a 12-week trial was going to cost. We knew we were going to skip the pre-trial; we were going straight to trial because it was all we could afford. And for that we had to raise money and scrounge whatever we could.

We knew from the start that we had more than a chance; we knew we were gonna beat this. I really did believe it. If certain things went our way, if everyone who had information about the whole event came forward, and if we could get them all to tell the truth, then we were going to beat it.

When I went out to see Jai at the jail, detectives would try to talk to me, giving me their cards. We'd had pretty constant surveillance and phone taps the whole time. We were aware they were watching us. It was really obvious: undercover cars doing figure-eight surveillance, the same two cars, going back and forwards in the street. They'd been doing this sort of stuff, calling us extortionists and drug dealers, for so long; it was like, 'Come on, you've got to come up with some evidence eventually.' And that was the scary thing: what if they planted some evidence at Curtin? It'd been 15 years and they'd got nothing … less than nothing. You start to get a bit scared at how personal it all becomes. I've got more faith in justice than that, but it was just their whole attitude. They were stoked they had Jai, which gave them leverage over the rest of us because they knew we'd do anything for him.

Jai was positive when I first went out to see him at Silverwater. That's the hardest thing about prison; you see the whole scene out there – the junkie parents with the prams, the sad faces. It's a really depressing scene. The amount of control the guards have over them, it's just terrible. It's a depressing, bad environment. I hate it.

We were doing jujitsu on some visits. Jai was psyched on juey, and we were doing some moves during visits. Koby wasn't allowed to visit Jai; it wasn't a good look when they were both facing charges. Dakota and Mum visited a few times, and I even drove Jai's old girlfriend Nat out there a few times.

When Koby was arrested things went to a new level. Suddenly I was managing Koby as well. I was liaising with his solicitors, I flowed him some money; we were juggling his mortgage, his car payments, his contracts. When he signed his contract with Oakley he'd said to me, 'I want to buy a house. Can I use the family flats as collateral?' They'd only let him buy Curtin Crescent if we put one of the units solely in his name. We'd said of course. Now if Koby lost his contract he'd miss mortgage payments, they'd foreclose on Curtin, the dominoes would fall and we'd lose the units as well. So there was a lot at stake. Everything was at stake. Although, with Koby, sometimes you wouldn't know it. Koby wouldn't even read his court files, he wouldn't read his statements. Koby largely didn't give a fuck. He just hated dealing with the whole judicial process: the cops, the courts.

Then, in a perfect swift strike from the powers that be, soon after Koby was arrested on accessory to murder charges, the Crime Commission raided Curtin Crescent and froze all Koby's assets, which essentially froze our assets because they were all linked. We couldn't go to the bank and ask for an overdraft to pay for our loans or our lawyers. There was no escape. They had us over a barrel. They only got involved via a loophole because Koby hadn't paid taxes for three years. I knew they weren't going to find much when they searched Curtin Crescent. But from that moment it was on. We hired Sydney's best audit accountants; they went through all Koby's accounts and proved there was no suspicious money. We walked into a meeting with the NSW Crime Commission, and the lead guy from the Crime Commission gets up and says to our accountant, 'You might be holding all the aces, Mr Charlton, but we're winning this hand.' And they did. They're the toughest cops to deal with; they just go by their own rules. They can do whatever they want. We negotiated a deal with the Crime Commission where we could sell the units and pay back the bank, but basically we lost everything. We lost the three units and Curtin Crescent … and that was before we paid solicitors and barristers to keep Jai and Koby free. We lost almost $3 million all up.

All our fates were lassoed together – Jai's, Koby's, mine, Ma's, the house, the units I'd been battling for eight years to pay off. But what do you do? It's your brothers and their freedom. It's your grandmother's house and everything she'd worked for. It's Koby's career, and it's everything we've all worked for to get to where we were.

It was while all this was going on that I met Gina. We used to rent out the apartment next door and she'd come around with one of her Spanish friends who was looking for a room. I ran into her again at the Basque club in the city and we hit it straight off. I'd always had a thing for Spanish girls.

Gina was great, a really down-to-earth chick, and we had a great long distance relationship going for three years. When we first started seeing each other, we were having breakfast at the Tropicana Café on Coogee Bay Road one day. I'm flicking through the paper and I open to a double page story about us, none of it good. At that stage we were being tagged everything from rapists to white supremacists, and I'm wondering what the hell my new girlfriend is thinking about us. It was just the worst feeling ever. But Gina wasn't fazed and saw it for what it was; during that whole time she was great. Whenever the pressure got too much with the pending court case and all the shit surrounding it, I'd just jump on a plane and fly to Barcelona and see Gina. She'd organise these two-week surf trips up and down the coast for us, and we'd just chill out and have a ball. She really helped me stay together during that time, and the two of us really fell in love.

The Bra Boys were getting a really hard time in the press. Up to that point there wasn't much out there that got it right. Most of it was all speculation, and a lot of it was bullshit. And that's the thing; we never spoke to the press. We used to say to the boys, 'You're not allowed to take photos of the Bra Boy tattoo. Don't talk to the press.' So, left to their own devices and with no one speaking to them, a lot of the stuff the press came out with was so far off the mark it was laughable.

It got to the point where we had to do something; that's when we decided to do the ABC's *Australian Story*. That was a bit of a risk for us. It was the first time we'd trusted anyone in the mainstream media with our story and we didn't know how it would turn out, but we needed at least the chance of a fair hearing in the media before Koby and Jai's trials. There was so much shit out there; we needed to balance it. It was risky, but we had to give it a shot to tell the truth. We couldn't assume people were reading between the lines and getting it right.

With these sorts of projects you never know when someone is going to take the wheels from underneath you. But I watched the episode that night and it was good. It was fair, which is all we could ask for. For the first time a lot of people started to see that there was another side to the stories they'd been reading in the paper. Russell Crowe was one of them, and a few days later he called Koby.

Watching our lives and our home beach boiled down to a half-hour episode, I began to get a feeling that this was all meant to happen. It was destiny. There'd been dark times, we were in dark times, but as the credits rolled I could sense a fairytale ending. We were meant for this whole journey; this whole test of faith for our family and our brotherhood.

But first we had to get Jai out of jail.

JAI

JAI DOES 20 MONTHS IN SILVERWATER PURGATORY, AND WITH HALF THE JAIL LOOKING FOR HIM HE FINDS FRIENDS IN HIGH PLACES

You're usually in the police remand centre for about three days. They kept me in there for 10, so I had plenty of time to think.

Maybe I wasn't looking at that much time, considering the circumstances, considering Hinesy'd brought this on himself. I grew up with the bloke, I'd known him since I was a kid and he'd played a pretty big part in my life. I was in there thinking that surely the courts, Hinesy's mates in jail, would see it for what it is.

When I was there for 10 days I figured something was brewing. The officers kept coming to me saying, 'You have to go to protection when you get to Silverwater. You know who you killed, right?' But no way in the world would I ever go there. I'd rather die than go into protection. It's just that I got me own morals. That's how we were brought up by Tony and Jason: you die before you go into protection. But then it got me thinking: why the fuck are the officers saying that?

I got moved out to Silverwater on a Sunday, and after 10 days with no sunlight I'm wondering if I'm ever gonna see the light of day again. When I got to Silverwater the officers were spinning a bit.

'We don't know what to do with him. Fuck, he won't go into protection.'

I was thinking, 'Come on, it was between me and him.' It's none of these blokes' business. It's got nothing to do with anyone else.

Darcy is the part of the jail where you get processed at Silverwater. It's like the reception centre, and you're there for about a week until they put you into a pod. I'd been in Darcy two days when 'I' came down to see me. I was the Koori delegate at Silverwater. I didn't even know who he was at the time, had no idea of the respect the guy had.

So I get a visit from big I. He's about 120 kilograms, just a machine, but a true gentleman at the same time. He took his seat across from me and started looking at me real funny.

'You're Jai, ay?'

'Yeah.'

'I've been waiting to talk to you.' He starts looking me over. 'You're not real big, are ya? You know there's a bit going on here. A lot of people are talking. You know half the jail's waiting for you here? I'm here to tell ya that we're with you 100 per cent. Any bloke wants to go you, we'll stand beside you. If we have to go to war, we'll go to war. That's why they're putting you in the yards, because I told 'em all it was between you guys. He was trying to get your girl for a couple of years, so good onya, you protected her. You protected our Koori sister. Look after yourself, but we're with ya.'

Before I got locked up, when I was seeing Nat, I was hanging at The Block at Redfern a little bit, hanging with my Koori brothers. So I started going up there every now and then to see Nat's cousin; just boxing with them, hanging out. The last couple of years I was up there a lot. Going up there to say g'day, go out to nightclubs with 'em, have street parties with the ghetto blaster blaring. I used to drive my Skyline up there and just park it right there on The Block. Most cars wouldn't last five minutes there, but all the boys knew my car. They always treated me like one of their own.

Some of those guys became a couple of my closest friends, you know, brothers. I also had good Koori friends from La Per and from growing up in Sydney. I had a lot of good Koori brothers. When I went to jail, them coming to me saying 'we'll be with ya' was huge. At the time I didn't really know what it all meant, but when I think back I reckon they saved my life. I'll love them till the day I die, mate. They're like family. They looked at me like one of their own and made things a lot easier for me in there.

They knew Tony well. That was the other reason they backed me: they knew what I'd been through. They knew there was just something about him and women. You'd never trust him near your woman. You know Tony's serious, he's good for it. It's as serious as you're ever going to get. So I, he's a legend. He made me feel heaps better. We're still good friends to this day and I'll always love and respect him.

But I was still concerned, fuck. I'd carry something on me every day. I looked after myself. Even though the brothers were with me, people are still going to do what they want to do. I was strong about it. I believed Tony put me in a fucking bad situation. It could have so easily been me going over that cliff. What did they want me to do – just sit there and let him shoot me?

Bra, I was his friend, and I was sad that a friend had put me into that position. Anyone who knew Tony well enough to stand up and kill me for doing it would've also known that I was his friend. We were his friends. Jason was his best friend. And he turned on me and Jason?

When I moved out of Darcy I ended up going into a cell with HR, one of the boys from down Maroubra, one of the boys I grew up with. That made the first few weeks a lot easier. God bless him, he's such a good-hearted bloke. His whole family are legends.

On the Sunday I got to Silverwater, my mate says he's going to church. I thought, 'Yeah, I'll go to church, sure.' I walked in late, just as the priest was delivering his sermon. The first things I've heard are the first three verses of Psalm 27.

I was in a spin. I might have walked into jail knocking myself and wondering whether I was ever gonna see the light of day again, but here was God saying, 'He came for you, and he stumbled and fell.'

'Pick yourself up.' God spoke loud and clear to me. Why, the second I walked in the church, did I hear those words?

That was God saying he was with me, and that's all that mattered. Then God picked the best barrister. I had God in the courtroom with me. I'd sit there on the stand and think, 'I hope these words come out of this witness.' And those words would come out. God was opening up the witnesses. He ran through the whole situation. God was there that night. He could've turned around and gone boom boom boom, but God was there.

I had a pretty sweet run at Silverwater. I'd get up in the morning and read the Bible, go to church on a Sunday.

You'd have good days there: you've trained twice, eaten good, had a laugh with some good people. But it's not where you are, it's where you're not. You're not lying in bed with your chick, you're not eating a Big Mac, you're not getting barrelled.

I was getting a few visitors. My mate Quinny was out to see me all the time, the legend. I could never thank or repay him enough for what he done for me during some tough times. Nat was coming out too. The guys from Maroubra Christian Surfers were there all the time. They're champions, those guys. Steve Bligh was my scripture teacher at school in Year 7. When I was locked up, he just rocked up not long after of his own accord. He'd keep coming out and saying g'day, giving me Bibles which I'd read for hours.

Then I got moved from Silverwater out to Parklea. I was hanging with the Koori boys at Parklea. In Silverwater the Koori boys had looked after me; I was training and eating with them, living with them, and that was all cool. But Parklea was different; the Kooris had dramas out at Parklea. But after being so close to those guys at Silverwater, there was no way I was going to pretend I didn't know 'em when I got to Parklea, just because they've got dramas.

At Parklea the Kooris pretty much get attacked as soon as they get off the truck. The prison's more or less run by the Asians and the islanders, and these guys fight hard with the Kooris, ya know. There was drama at Parklea. I'm fucking coming up to me trial, trying to concentrate on me trial; it was near the end of Chinese New Year and the place was going mad.

There's three pods in 5 Area – 5A, 5B and 5C. One morning we hear, 'Boys kick it off! Kick it off!' Bang, all the Kooris in 5A get hammered; all the Kooris in 5B get hammered. I'm in 5C and I know what's coming. They're going, 'Look out! Look out!' We turn around and there's 20 Asians flying at us with iron bars taking on five of us, the full tsunami hit. We're just dodging, trying to do our best.

At the end of the day, not one of us got hurt and we hammered one of them. If it was 20 of us flying around with iron bars it would have been a different story. It was then that I realised this was hectic; this was the first big war I'd been in while I was inside. But like I said, I wasn't going to hang with the Kooris at Silverwater and not hang with them in Parklea, just 'cause they've got shit going on.

They moved me out to Parklea two months before me trial; I think they did it just to fuck with me. When my court date came around, every day I had to get up at 4.30 in the morning, go down to the cells and wait. Then I'd get the truck to Silverwater, wait in the cells there, then get another truck to the court in the city. I'd spend the day in court, then come back at 4.30 to Silverwater, wait there, then get the truck back out to Parklea. If I'd been at Silverwater I would've been waking up at six or seven in the morning, 'cause the truck goes straight from there. I was getting back to Parklea no earlier than 10 o'clock, midnight some nights, then getting up at 4.30 again the next morning. I was getting four hours' sleep a night for six weeks and my life was at stake. It was just to fuck with me.

I said me prayers and God just carried me home. Me mate gave me this little prayer called Footsteps, and I carried it with me while I was in the truck. It's the one where a guy who's been walking with Jesus has been in trouble, and he looks back and sees only one set of footsteps. He asks Jesus why he abandoned him when he needed his help. Jesus replies, 'I didn't abandon you; I was carrying you.'

JAI

SEEKING LIGHT AND SALVATION, JAI ABBERTON CRIES HALLELUJAH AS HIS DAY OF RECKONING COMETH

Court was hectic, but after two years in jail waiting for my day, I was ready for it.

The room was tiny, bra. You could've cut the air with a knife. It was a heavy scene. I had Mum, Dakota, Sunny and a few of the boys there for support. Ma was too sick to be there, but I was thinking of her the whole time.

And I just knew I had to keep my head.

They said that the prosecutor they pulled out was the trump of all trumps. That's how much they wanted to sink me, how big a case it was in the media; they wheeled out this big gun. They wanted to win this case real bad. My barrister, Graham, did everything the other guy did, matched him fully, but was tenfold the gentleman. He was a fucking legend, bra, as was Barry, my lawyer. We wanted a not guilty verdict by way of self-defence. That's what I pleaded. If God wasn't looking after me that night, it would be Hinesy being tried for my murder, no doubt about it. And I knew that as God had got me this far, he'd let me walk out the doors a free man.

Fuck, bra, I prayed hard every day in court. You've got about an hour in the cell on your own before you go upstairs to the court, and I just prayed for every witness to open up, and it worked.

Graham was a gentleman and he just opened up the witnesses, all the Crown's witnesses, as well as my witnesses, and made them speak the truth. It was important for the story to come out why Tony was coming after me. The Crown had Tony's girl, Rachael, up there.

Graham asked her, 'Did Tony ever ask you if you'd slept with Jai?'

'Yes.'

'What did you say to Tony?'

'I had to tell Tony that I slept with him.'

'Why would you tell this maniac you slept with Jai when you didn't?'

She broke down in tears. 'He was strangling me.'

It was that hectic in there, but Graham Turnbull is my king, I respect him. The Crown was arguing that Hinesy never had a gun on him. Only one person at the pub had seen the gun on Hinesy, and the Crown was saying the bloke was pissed and had imagined it. When Graham was summing up, bra, he talked all afternoon to the jury.

'So think,' he says, 'this bloke, two years he's after you. This guy is one of the scariest guys ever.' Then he's walked over in front of the jury and he's gone – bang – and pulled the gun out – the gun from the night. He had Hinesy's gun down his pants from lunchtime until late in the afternoon, and no one even noticed.

'Now think what Jai felt,' he said. 'He had to go for it. He had to go for it. And once it's gone off, as if any one of you isn't going to keep firing.'

Hinesy's girlfriend was a Crown witness, and she said, 'Tony strangled me until I told him I'd slept with Jai. I've never slept with Jai.' She was a Crown witness, not even ours.

BC was a Crown witness. 'I've only ever known Jai to be a gentleman. I was so scared for Jai the night he got in that car. After Jai told me this guy was out to kill him, I've never been so scared in all my life.' These are Crown witnesses, and they were all supporting me.

Then, when things were looking okay for us, the Crown brought out this bloke who reckons I'd told him it was a set-up. He said that when I was staying at Nat's cousin's place at Redfern after the shooting, he'd gone there and I'd told him I'd set it up. I'd never even seen the bloke, bra. Never fucking seen him. He was in jail, and was gonna get his time cut in half to testify against me. No matter how good things were going for us in the trial, you were always worried.

I never knew what the jury was thinking. They were just the most normal people, and for them to come into this thing with the blood and the drag marks was pretty heavy. There was a kid there who looked like he was fresh out of school, 18 maybe, ladies, mothers … just average people.

There's 12 on the jury, and on the second day this bloke's got up and asked one of the security guards, 'Why isn't Jai Abberton in a cage and in shackles?' Well, luckily the screws told the court. They called a big meeting. I coulda sacked the whole jury and got another one, because he'd already made up his mind. But I said, 'Nah, let's keep 'em.' So I only had 11 jurors … and 11 is one of my lucky numbers. So then I had seven women and four guys, and I needed women on the jury. What I'd done that night I'd done to save that girl from being raped, and I hoped they'd see that. Then the judge just really drummed it into them: 'This is a long trial. Don't even think about making up your mind until the last day, not until you've heard all the evidence.'

The second last day, bra, the day before the verdict, a lady in the jury starts crying. I'm just looking at her and wondering what she's crying about. They've called a recess and the judge has said to wrap it up for the day, because there was some heavy stuff going down. On the truck back to the cells I'm thinking, 'What is she crying her eyes out for? Why is she crying? Is she crying because she's sending me to jail for 20 years?' I couldn't sleep a wink that night. I had no idea what they were thinking.

The next day, a Friday, the trial finished after lunch. I waited down in the cells and prayed. Barry and Graham are telling me to stay positive, but also not telling me that they reckon they're gonna find me not guilty. An hour later and the jury is back. It was only an hour. Even I knew, without Barry or Graham telling me, that it was either really good or really bad. But I walked up them stairs and I knew God would be there for me.

They read out the verdict.

'Murder: not guilty. Manslaughter: not guilty.'

That's all I'd seen in my head a million times. I'd played that scene in my head a million times, *a million times*. I didn't expect anything else. When they came back with *not guilty, not guilty*, I didn't cheer. I just looked at them and said, 'Thank you.' Some of the jury were hugging me in the end, crying.

Graham is hugging my mum; she's in tears. Then he turned to the judge.

'So, your honour, my client has been found not guilty. Can he leave the dock?'

'Yes, Mr Turnbull, he can leave the dock.'

The prosecutors have gone, 'But we've still got jail charges pending against him!'

The judge goes, 'You've got 30 seconds to produce those charges or he's walking out the door.' Thirty seconds later I was walking out the door. They had no fresh charges, they were just being cocksuckers. Suddenly the door's right there, the street's right there, my family and friends are right there.

I've jumped straight into a cab – me, Sunny, Mum, and Quinny, just tripping. And then I've grabbed the phone.

'What's doing, bra?'

Koby's freaked out. 'Where are ya?'

'I'm in a cab, brother, I'm comin' home! I'll be out the front in a minute!'

He just screamed.

That was the maddest day … the maddest day ever. We went up to Ma's, straight to Ma and the biggest hug I've ever had. It was the best moment of my life. She was crying. I hugged Ma and she felt so delicate. I could feel that she was sick. She'd just waited. She was meant to die.

Two-and-a-half years before, they gave her three months to live, bra, and she was still here, waiting to see me. Waiting for me to be free. Without being able to talk, you could hear what she was saying: 'I can rest now, my boys are out.'

I could have been killed that night in the car. I couldn't *not* believe in God. I walked out of jail on the 5th of the 5th of the 5th – one number before the Devil's number. Tony Hines was born on the 24th of December, the day before Christ. In our society, the Devil's got henchmen here, and God has his people too. I could have got killed that night, but God decides everyone's fate. He's got it all mapped out. If you're sweet with him, you're sweet. It was Tony's time that was up, not mine.

barry watterson

DEFENCE LAWYER, FAMILY FRIEND, WRONG ENDER

I was travelling in Cuba when I heard.

I've got a big thing for Latin music, and I'd thought I'd go over before Fidel died. I was there when I received an email informing me that Tony Hines had been shot. It was followed later by an email telling me that Jai Abberton had been arrested, and I was asked if I would help prepare Jai's defence case.

When I came back, a lawyer who I did some work with, Paul Harden, was already involved in Jai's case but was struggling to get much information and to work out what was going on behind the scenes. Because I had such a strong link to the area and knew most of the people involved, I was brought in to the case to help smooth barriers and to help get the information we needed to mount the right sort of defence.

I grew up surfing Maroubra from the time I was 12. My older brother Neil was in the MSA in the '60s, I was in the MBA in the '80s, and it just carried on. You had the North Enders, and we were the Wrong Enders, we hung at the wrong end of the pavilion.

I knew all the Abberton brothers; I'd grown up surfing with them. They were always around; they were always out the front of the pub while we were inside listening to the Radiators on a Sunday afternoon. And of course my nephews, Luke and Jack Kingsley, were good mates with them, so our families are connected in a lot of ways. It is Maroubra after all, and everybody is connected to everybody else and knows everyone else's stuff. It can be a small place.

First, Hinesy was always going to go over a cliff somewhere. If you caught him in a private moment he would say two things. The first thing he'd tell you was that he was going to live forever, and then in the same breath he'd tell you, 'No, I'm gonna get knocked.' He was just not sure by who. But Tony lived his life the way he did, he knew what he was doing, but I don't think he saw the circumstances of his demise as they played out. He would never have picked trouble coming from Jai. Before the police found out anything about Jai, a local detective was interviewed on TV and asked who he thought might have shot Tony Hines. The copper picked up the phone book and said, 'Take your pick.'

I was one of the first to actually discuss with Jai, out at remand, what had happened that night in the car. Jai was trying to come to terms with the fact he had shot another person and also with where he was. That's a hard thing for human beings to understand about themselves, when they have to take an action like that. He was also trying to get his head around the law in that area.

You don't see a lot of self-defence cases. Most people who use that defence either get found guilty of murder or of the lesser charge of manslaughter. You can go to trial facing a charge of murder and still be found guilty of manslaughter. An acquittal by a jury? Well, you're really rolling the dice, but in Jai's case we thought we had a good chance.

Life wasn't easy for him, but there were times when Jai – and his goofy good nature – saw gold in everything.

'I got to sweep the floors this morning, *woo hoo*!'

But it was very tough, being in jail for 20 months, particularly when you believe that you haven't done the wrong thing. He was up and down a lot. Jai spent almost two years away from the ocean, and away from his support system, his brothers and his Maroubra friends.

There were times I'd go there and have nothing really to tell him, but I'd just go and see him, try and keep his spirits up, have a chat … make sure he knew he wasn't forgotten. We'd talk about surfing a lot, what's been happening in Maroubra. For Jai, because I knew him, it was more of a holistic approach because he wasn't someone who was going to like being caged.

As it went on he started to read the Bible, because Bibles are everywhere in jail. Whatever your beliefs, in certain circumstances religion gives you a structure. Jai started to take on some of that structure and put a lot of faith in it. So he started to bless me as I left. His strengthening faith manifested itself in jail, but that's not unusual. It gave him a basis for hope outside of my surf reports.

Outside we'd meet up with Sunny and talk about how things were going. Of course, we had to try and find a way to fund Jai's defence. Sunny was trying to keep it all together, because by this stage Koby had been charged as well in relation to the matter. Sunny was trying to manage his brothers' and family's finances, trying to keep their heads above water.

The police really believed there was a full-blown gang down there at Maroubra, and they wanted to dismantle it, starting with Koby and Jai. They didn't like the idea that there were all these people down there, working together in unison to make a better life for themselves.

But we also felt that they thought they had the conviction in the bag, and that worked for us. We hit the streets and talked to a lot of the people they nominated as witnesses for the prosecution. The prosecution is obliged to bring all the witnesses forward to the defence, even if the witnesses do their case no good. The statements from their witnesses were essentially in favour of their case, but they didn't follow up on some of them and we did. We dug a bit deeper, and it was able to give us a much clearer picture of what happened on the night and in the aftermath.

Murdering another person is considered the highest crime, so all murder trials are held in the Supreme Court and presided over by a Supreme Court justice. The courtroom was part of the St James courts, which are in the original beautiful old sandstone building from the 1800s. The rooms are a bit pokey and a bit uncomfortable because they're so old, but it's a beautiful old courtroom with the judge perched high up above everyone.

In America they seem to know everything about their jurors; their names, what they do, their political preferences, all that sort of stuff. Not here. You get a pool of people, and you don't know who they are or where they come from. All you do is look at how they're dressed, how they carry themselves. You don't get to question them. Then you can either say yes or no to them as their number is called out. It's a pretty important day, because these are the people who would be deciding if Jai would walk free or spend 20 years in jail. You don't always get the jury you like, but, by the look of them, we got the jury we were hoping for. They turned out to be a very committed, very aware, very tight jury, which is what our case required.

Everything that had been written about this case was negative, and there was no background to what had happened, the history with Tony and Jai. They'd only seen one side up till that point. The only thing we could do was start highlighting some of the aspects of the case that hadn't come to light yet.

Day one was jury selection. On day two we lost a juror. There was one guy who we sort of thought was oddly placed in the make up of the jury. He asked one of the sheriffs why Jai wasn't behind bars or bulletproof perspex in the court; he was worried Jai was going to jump out and attack him. Obviously, he was let go. So the jury was down to 11, but we decided to keep going. We could have made an application for a new jury, but no evidence had even been presented.

In his opening address, our barrister, Graham Turnbull, espoused Jai's innocence and asked the jury to go into it with an open mind. 'Wait until you've heard all the evidence before you start making up your mind.' The prosecutor was one of the most senior guys they have, a fellow named

John Kiley. He's an older barrister, very highly regarded, exceptionally good at his job, and a lovely fella. It was obvious they'd brought out the big gun for this case, so we knew they wanted Jai pretty badly.

There was tension at times, mostly in the gallery. A lot of Jai's friends were there, a lot of the Bra Boys, and they may have even been on a roster to show up. Some would be there every day. But, particularly in the first week, some of Tony's friends turned up to show solidarity with their friend. At one stage when the main prosecution witness was giving evidence, BC, the woman driving the car that night, repeated what Jai had said to her after dumping the body about Tony being a maggot, something along those lines. Tony's mates had been staring at Jai for days, and when they broke for lunch after BC's testimony, they had words with Jai; the guys threatened him. It was a worry.

The trial eventually went for five weeks, but at the end of the first week we believed it had gone about as well as it possibly could. Every witness they'd put on the stand we made some ground on. I remember walking into the Crown Hotel in Elizabeth Street, where a lot of lawyers gather, and a few of them asked us how Jai's trial was going. We replied, 'It's going pretty well. We think we've a shot at this.' And then they've said, 'From what we've read, you guys have no hope whatsoever!' That was important in a way, because although they'd listened to industry scuttlebutt, they'd also read what the jury had read. It did give us perspective that there was still a long way to go to get this done. We couldn't let up.

We always think long and hard before putting a client up on the stand. We don't have to. We're experienced with how prosecutors ask questions, but defendants generally aren't, so they get up on the stand, they say things they think are okay, only to suddenly look nervous and open another door for the prosecution. It was a gamble, but we just felt that we had done so well in the previous four weeks of the trial that the jury might want to hear the story from Jai. State of mind is all important. Whether your actions at the time were reasonable is connected to how you were thinking. It's what's in your mind, it's subjective, and we had to put Jai up there so they could hear from him why he thought he had to do this thing, what Jai knew about Tony, and all the things he'd gone through in the past years.

When Jai took to the stand he stuck to his story pretty tight. His story didn't waver. Some things came out that Jai hadn't told us – he'd never told us he'd hidden the gun after the shooting – which caused a few heart flutters, but at least it fitted in with the rest of the story.

Jai was up there a day-and-a-half, two days. We got to ask our questions first, followed by the prosecution. They showed footage from the Coogee Bay Hotel and were asking him, 'What are you doing here?' Then they froze a frame and asked, 'Is that a gun in your pants?' The prosecution was really pushing the idea that the gun wasn't, in fact, Tony's, and instead that it was Jai's. Then they show a frame of Tony leaving Coogee Bay, and they were saying, 'Well, there couldn't have been a gun on him. Look, here's a picture of Tony walking out with his jacket open, and where's the gun?' Jai was up there a long time, and I was so relieved when he finally got down. When your client is on the stand your arse is puckered.

It was on my recommendation that we had gone for Graham Turnbull as our barrister. He's enthusiastic, he works hard, and he has a sense of the theatrical. When it came to closing addresses, Graham knew that the gun, and whether Tony Hines had it on him at the pub, was an issue for the jury. So at the lunch break Graham grabbed the actual gun and put it under his own belt and covered it with his little vest. He spoke about the gun for 20 minutes, right up until he got to the point where he said, 'And then Tony Hines pulled out the gun!' And as he said it, he's reached into his belt and pulled out the gun in front of the jury, who were only a metre away at the time. They were just aghast. They hadn't seen the gun on him, and they'd been sitting there that close to him for the last 20 minutes. Even I was surprised. That told the jury that you can't necessarily see a single image and draw a conclusion as to whether there's a gun there or not. It was a very telling point.

It's always hard to read what's coming from a jury, but you always like to think the best. Our jury seemed attentive, conscientious; they seemed settled, very close. In some ways we would take our cues from

Jai, because he actually sat right across from them. Occasionally he'd tell us, 'I think that lady at the back smiled at me.' But all we hoped for is that they were listening.

By the last day we were getting confident, thinking we may have done enough to get over the line. There was one incident on the second last day where the foreperson half broke down and we had to finish early for the day. She expressed how hard it was to go through this process. Someone had been shot; no matter what their reputation was, someone shot them, and we just don't do that sort of thing. There had to be a very good reason for them to say to Jai, 'okay, you're all right with this one'. Even though we saw that she had to leave the courtroom, the rest of the jury sat there very tight. So either they were all very happy with us, or they were all united against us; it was one or the other.

The jury retired after lunch on a Friday afternoon. During the deliberation Jai was taken down to the cells. We spoke with him, trying to keep his spirits up, preparing him for a long wait. The end of trials is all about waiting. Sometimes juries are out three weeks, so all you can do is wait. Jai was a bit skittish. He was talking about God a lot, his faith, all those sorts of things. He told us we'd done a wonderful job and had given him every chance, which was appreciated. We all got very attached during the case. It doesn't mean we treated Jai any differently to any other client. Sometimes you're doing a job as best you can, but we got emotionally attached with this case. Jai's a likeable guy. I was thinking that this had certainly been the most interesting trial I'd ever been involved with and, if we got the right verdict, it would also be the most satisfying.

We analyse juries to death, but the reality is that you can't. We were hopeful with the verdict, and that was about as good as we could allow it to get. When the jury returned after only 90 minutes, we knew it was either going to be very good news or very bad news. There were three possibilities: Jai would be found guilty of murder, he'd be found guilty of manslaughter, or he'd be found not guilty by reason of self-defence.

The jury came out and took their seats and the foreperson started reading the verdict.

'Not guilty of murder on the grounds of self-defence.'

'Not guilty of manslaughter ...'

For half a second I'm waiting for the third one; then I realise, hang on, there's only two. That's it. He's free.

There was a lot of emotion. It was an extraordinary afternoon. The jury ran into Jai in the hallway, and half of them hugged and kissed him and were trying to organise barbecues with him. They were waving to him from across the street. It was a very strange trial in that everybody became connected. The jury definitely felt empathy for Jai and his situation and for BC and her situation.

Walking into the Abbertons' house that night for the party, I told the other lawyers, barristers Graham Turnbull, Craig Evans, and the principal solicitor, Paul Hardin, 'Guys, hang on, it might get a little rugged in here.' Coming from Maroubra I had a fair idea it was going to be a big night. We walked in the door and all the boys put up a guard of honour for us. They really did think we'd done a good job, and they appreciated our efforts.

The party actually wasn't all that raucous. The room was more relieved than overjoyed. It was just a big night at the Abberton house, and it went on and on ... midnight ... the next day ... the next week I think.

SUNNY

A FAVOURABLE VERDICT AND AN EXHALATION
OF RELIEF

We were really worried about the Bra Boy stereotype in that courtroom, so we had to make sure our heaviest looking guys stayed at home. Frog, for instance, couldn't come in. Frog's built like a brick shithouse, and we had to make a rule that anyone remotely intimidating couldn't come in, regardless of how calm their demeanour or how close they were to Jai. It was all about perception. If you didn't come in well-dressed and looking like a respectable citizen, we appreciated your friendship, but you're not coming in, sorry. It was so important, with all the bullshit the media were saying.

We weren't expecting a verdict that day, but the jury made up their mind straightaway. Usually on a murder trial it takes anything from six hours to three weeks for a verdict. The jury went into the room for an hour and a half, and then suddenly they're out.

I was absolutely shitting myself. They were certain one way or the other. They were so certain, and I wanted to believe they'd made up their minds that Jai was not guilty, but at the back of your mind you can't help but think, 'What if they think he's guilty?' It was the scariest 10 minutes of my life, waiting for Jai to come up from the cells. I can't even begin to think how Jai was feeling.

The judge asked the jury foreperson, 'Are you sure?' Even he was quite shocked they were out so quickly. The foreperson had become so emotional that she started crying. The judge said to her, 'Look, I'll give you another half-hour to go back and make sure you're happy with your decision.'

They went out and it was in that half an hour that Barry, our lawyer, started to say, 'Look, I really think this is going to happen.' He rang a couple of our people, Koby included, and said, 'I've got a good feeling.'

And then the jury came back a second time.

The judge said, 'Are you sure? It's rash to make a decision so quickly.'

'No, we're ready.'

I was sitting with my mum, Macca De Souza and John Sutton. The trial had been going for six weeks at this stage, and no one was expecting a verdict that afternoon. We thought maybe the next day, which would have been the Monday. So it was only really a skeleton crew who was there when the verdict was read out that afternoon. Our mum was there, I was there, a few of the boys were there, but that was about it.

We were all shitting ourselves. We were petrified. There's no other word for it. Just that feeling ... knowing he's either going to walk out and it's going to be the biggest adrenaline rush, or they're going to take him away for 20 years. There was such a chasm between them, and we had no idea which way it was going to go. Unless you've lived through something like that you can't understand the gravity of it. It was total panic, like nothing I've ever experienced.

And they came back out and there it was: not guilty.

We all just grabbed each other and screamed – me, Mum, the boys. I looked up and Jai is holding his cross, head bowed, kissing it. He was pretty calm, actually, way calmer than us. Then they let him walk from the dock, and me and Mum and Jai just grabbed each other and hugged tight, all bawling. I can't even remember what we said; we might not have said anything. Then I just kept saying, 'I knew, I knew,' and Jai just kept saying, 'I had faith, I always had faith,' and there were 'I love you's going out all over the place.

Jai has just gone, 'Get me the fuck out of here, bra!' We've run straight out and he was set upon by the media scrum. They've started asking some heavy questions about how it felt for him when Hinesy pulled the gun and stuff like that, and he just charged through it, kissing the silver cross he was clutching in his fist.

There just happened to be a cab pulling up outside the court; we've hailed it, jumped in and then we were off. It's gone from this absolute madness and now all of a sudden it's dead quiet. We're all in there – me, Jai, Mum and our mate Quinny. It was like a dream. Once we got in that cab and drove off everything stopped, silence. We all just looked at each other and laughed. The whole lot of us just broke up laughing. *How was that!*

That's when we called Koby. When Jai was released a lot of people didn't understand why Koby wasn't there for the verdict. Koby couldn't be there because he was directly involved in the case and he still had charges against him. He couldn't be there, so he was back at Curtin Crescent with Ma. Jai just picks up the phone and dials Koby.

'What's doing, bra?' He just breaks up laughing.

Then we came flying down Marine Parade past the beach at Maroubra, getting the cabbie to beep the horn, everyone hanging out of the cab. We drove past the pub and there were already people out the front cheering.

We drove back down to the pub soon after and bought 10 cases and bags of ice, and told all the boys, 'Party back at Ma's house, six o'clock. Spread the word.' It was like a wildfire from there. There were hundreds of people out on the street on Curtin Crescent, right through the house and spilling out into the backyard. The boys, parents, grandparents, kids; the whole street was there. Koby had only bought the place just over a year before and yet everyone in the street pretty well was there with us to celebrate. No one put in a noise complaint that night, and they'd been bringing over chickens and wine and dinners for Ma while we were all in court to make sure she was okay. That night reignited a whole lot of spirit in the Maroubra community. Everyone felt it. It was powerful.

The place broke up cheering and crying as Jai walked in. Jai's such a personal kind of guy that it was a long entrance. He stopped and hugged and talked with everyone as he walked in through the crowd. But just the whole vibe of the room was incredible, the smiles, the laughs. And then whenever they showed the news story on TV with Jai walking free out the front of the court, everyone would gather round the telly and just go crazy: 'He's out again!'

All the TV news crews showed up in the street thinking there was going to be a riot. We went out and saw 'em and said, 'Guys, we'd rather you respected our privacy here and didn't film.' To their credit they said, 'Fair enough,' and they didn't film.

Then Steve Bligh and the Maroubra Christian surfers rocked up, guys who'd been there day in, day out for Jai. Danny Boyd took six weeks off work as a carpenter to help look after Jai during the trial. We gave all those guys standing ovations as they entered. And when the lawyers – Barry, Paul and Graham – showed up, we made a guard of honour from the front of the house into the lounge room. They'd never seen anything like it either. They said they've been to plenty of celebration drinks in their time, but they were usually sitting over in the corner instead of getting treated like rock stars.

We had a couple of quiet moments later on in the night with Ma; a big group cuddle with Ma, me, Koby and Jai. There were a lot of moments of reflection. It was a huge weight off everyone's shoulders, just a massive release for everyone. Had Jai been found guilty it would have confirmed all this bullshit the media and the cops had been saying, not only about Jai, not only about our family, but about the whole suburb. So it was the release of having Jai out, but also the relief from all that scrutiny. The dark cloud had lifted.

You could feel it in the air for a week after, every time you walked down the beach. Everyone was seeing each other in the street and hooting. The party lasted four or five days. These spontaneous parties would just break out for the next couple of weeks at different houses. I don't think any of the boys went to work for a week.

Jai, meanwhile, moved in with me up at the flats. Life was good again, and it was time to go surfing.

KOBY

IN EXILE AT CURTIN CRESCENT, KOBY RECEIVES A PHONE CALL TWO YEARS AND A MILLION DOLLARS IN THE MAKING

I didn't go to any of Jai's court dates.

We didn't want me to be tried first and have the prosecution use parts of my evidence to incriminate Jai in any way, so Jai went first. What the coppers were trying to do was charge us together as the co-accused. If they'd tried the cases together I would have done 10 years, no worries. That was the main worry and the main fight for a long time: getting separate trials and getting Jai into court before me.

Jai was in court for a couple of weeks and I had to sit it out. I wasn't

MY BROTHERS KEEPER

allowed near the courtroom; that was part of the strategy. So I had to keep asking everyone how it was going, and they said, 'Mate, it's fucking looking good. The cops are coming off looking like real dicks for the way they've handled it.' I was at home in Maroubra during Jai's court dates. It was a hard time for all of us, and I didn't want to be anywhere on my own. I wanted to be around family and friends.

My mum had moved into my house at Curtin Crescent and I'd moved out. I moved up the road with Jed, into a unit that overlooked the beach at North Maroubra. I'd bought Curtin Crescent for my grandma. I knew she didn't have long left in her, and we wanted her to have a house with a backyard and a front yard and everything. But then I got busted and it was kind of hard. I had all this shit to deal with, and Ma was there telling me I couldn't bring a chick home or drink a beer at lunchtime. I said, 'Come on, Ma. I'm paying the mortgage here.' We started fighting and I just had to say, 'Look, Ma, I'm going to have to move out.' She was really angry and upset. In retrospect I wish I'd toughed it out, because I would've spent a lot more time with her. It kind of burns me a bit now.

When I moved out my mum moved in with Dakota, Mum's friend Annie and Annie's two kids. So there wouldn't have been much peace and quiet for Ma anyway. Mum paid a bit of rent, and looked after Ma while I was dealing with these charges and trying to still earn a living at the same time.

Even though I still couldn't live under the same roof as my mum – that'll never happen – the family became a lot closer while we were going through all that shit. There was a feeling there for a while that the family might come back together, but there's just too many hotheads in our family for it to ever happen. Everyone always believes they're right in their own way. I mean, it's not that everyone doesn't love each other; we just haven't grown up normal so we're never going to be a normal family. Me and my mum probably get on the best we ever have right now, but it still doesn't mean I respect her.

I was just hanging around waiting for a verdict. I spoke to Jai on the phone a couple of times during those weeks. When you speak to prisoners on the phone the police record the conversations, so I knew that no matter what I said they would hear it. But I was happy for them to record it, I wanted them to record it, so they could never say we'd collaborated or concocted evidence. Jai would just say to me, 'Koby, I need you to stay positive. I didn't do what they're saying I did, and if there's a God he will prove that I haven't done anything wrong.'

I couldn't be near the court, and as Mum went to court every day for Jai, I'd go and spend the days with my grandma. We knew that Friday was the last day of the trial, and that the jury would retire and make their decision. It was just Ma and me there, waiting for the phone to ring while not expecting it to, 'cause we knew these things can take weeks. An hour later, Jai's lawyer rings and said they'd called everyone in; they were going to announce the verdict.

'What do you mean? It's only been an hour-and-a-half?'

'Mate, I'm amazed. It's either really bad, or really fucking good.' Barry might have even swore. 'But I don't want you to get excited. I don't want you to get anyone else excited, but we've had a good week and we're looking okay.'

I told Ma, and I'm sitting next to the phone with Ma for 10 minutes before it rings again. I pick it up and I'm just shaking. The phone's kinda gone silent.

'What's doing, bra?!'

I've screamed. Jai's started crying. All he could say was, 'I told ya, bra! I told ya, bra!' I asked him when he was coming home.

'Right now! I'm in the cab, I'll see ya in 10 minutes!'

I just got off the phone and looked silently at Ma. I kept a real straight face. She's watching me, watching me. She's figured something was going on. I'm just sitting there all quiet, just playing it up, and she starts going, 'Hey! Hey!' I'm geeing her up and she starts whacking me in the side of the head. I start smiling.

'Not guilty.'

She just burst into tears and we hugged for a couple of minutes. She was stoked. She was so rapt. But in that moment I almost felt a bit of her leave, right then and there. I honestly believe that she was hanging on waiting for us to get off before she died. And I reckon if we hadn't ended up in trouble she would have died two years before. It was like the court case made her hold on for another two years. I honestly believe that after I let go of her that day, in that moment I saw her turn a little paler and look a little sicker. But she was so happy, and when Jai walked through the door, Ma, me, Sunny, Dakota and Mum have all just grabbed him in a huge hug, all laughing and crying.

Within 10 minutes there were 500 of the boys at Curtin Crescent. Everyone was partying like crazy. The whole street turned up, all the solicitors turned up and everyone chanted them in. It was an incredible feeling. Jai can be a bad person occasionally, but he has a heart of gold. All his friends and family know that, and that's why they were all there for him that night.

It was a good feeling to have the family together, even if it was only for that one afternoon. We're not the sort of family that's like that. Even though we're close from time to time, we fight more than any family alive. But when it comes down to it, if there's any problem, I know Jai and Sunny will be the first ones there for me. We need trouble to bring us together, which is kind of sad. But to have everyone there and everyone so excited, even if only for that brief time, was incredible. We're talking about going surfing again, we're making plans, we're drinking and we're laughing.

Part 7
Rollercoasting

SUNNY

The day after the party we went down to the Dunny Bowl for a surf.

Jai hadn't been in the water in almost two years, so a big group of us headed down to Maroubra with him. I think we all wanted to be there when he finally got wet. We were all so stoked, all smiling, a big group of us. It was a beautiful, crisp autumn morning, but there were no waves. The ocean still looked unbelievable, especially to Jai I suppose, so we all jumped in the water and swam out. Jai doesn't like to do anything half-arsed, and I don't think he wanted his first surf to be in two-foot waves so he's just dived into the ocean and we all followed him out. I don't want to think how many times he'd dreamed of that moment, but I remember him being really quiet and just soaking it up.

Straightaway we just wanted to chase waves. That was the big talk that night during the party up at Curtin Crescent: where were we going surfing? For the whole time Jai was locked up we couldn't plan anything; all our lives were on hold. We simply didn't know how it was going to end. Now with Jai free we could go wherever we wanted, the further away the better.

A few days later we made this spur of the moment decision to head down to the bottom of Victoria. A swell had come up, and we thought it might be perfect for this heavy left-hand reef down there, Luna Park. After not surfing for two years Jai wanted the heaviest wave he could find for his first surf back. We made the decision at lunchtime to fly down to Melbourne and chase it. We organised flights, cars and skis that afternoon, and by midnight we were driving the Great Ocean Road.

Koby had been speaking to some of our mates down that way to organise some jet skis, and word had got out that we were coming down and bringing a camera crew. The guys who live down there don't like anyone filming their waves, and have put the heat on a lot of crew in the past about it.

We're heading down the Great Ocean Road in the middle of the night when Koby's phone rings. It's one of the local guys and straightaway he started threatening us about coming down there with a camera crew. After all the shit Jai's been through, it was almost rude for them to call up and say they didn't want us down there. Who cares about them being staunch and protecting their local spot? This went beyond staunch, it was just plain rude. Koby took the call. It was hilarious.

'Me brother's just been released from jail; we're coming down, and we're going surfing. We've been down here before. We've never told anyone where it was. And, mate, you don't even surf the place! No one surfs it.'

Then the guy on the phone basically said, 'If you turn up with cameramen we'll smash ya cars and smash ya cameras.'

'Fuck off, mate,' said Koby. 'Jai hasn't surfed in two years. It's two in the morning, we're coming down and we're gonna go surfing. If anything happens to the cars or the cameramen, we've got our army with us. You bring your army, and let's do it.'

We'd been respectful every time we'd surfed the place before, made sure it was never named in magazines, and never even gave away the fact it was in Victoria. And who's gonna surf it anyway? It's a full death slab and only a handful of guys in Australia are really up to it.

So Koby has said, 'So, we'll see ya there tomorrow, then?'

The guy goes, 'Oh, I won't be surfing; I've got a sprained ankle.'

Koby's just started pissing himself. 'You've got a sprained ankle, have ya, mate? What – that flares up every big swell, huh?' All in the full sarcastic tone, like only Koby can do. The whole lot of us have just broken up laughing. He's finished up by saying, 'I'll see ya tomorrow ... and I'll bring an extra hat for your second head. Beat it.'

We got there at four in the morning and dropped the skis in the river in the dark. The sun was coming up and it was really magical. The place was amazing. There were these beautiful big ochre and orange cliffs, and these big red rocks. It had been an ochre pit for the local Aborigines. The place had this energy to it. On one side of the lake the whole cliff face and the eucalypts came right down to the river, and on the other side just farmland with rolling green hills and mist.

The river was mirror glass and we were flying out towards the river mouth doing about 90 kays on the skis. We finally came around to the beach. It was low tide, and the river mouth was blocked by 50 metres of sand. We couldn't get the skis into the open ocean.

So Koby has said, 'Okay, if I get a run-up we can drive the ski across the sandbank.' It was 50 metres of dry sand between the river and the sea, and Koby, the brains of the operation, has gone, 'I reckon I can get up enough speed and gun the ski across the bank.' We saw the keel mark of another ski that had crossed the day before on the high tide, and that was enough for Koby. He didn't say a word. He just jumped on the ski, headed back up the river to get a run-up, then turned around and gunned the ski at the bank, doing about a hundred kays. Just before he's hit the sand, though, this little channel has grabbed the keel of the ski and made it veer to the right. And there it was straight in front of him – this big rock ... the only rock within a hundred metres of us.

The ski has just collected the rock at 30 kays and bounced off. Koby was pitched off it and gone flying through the air over the handlebars. Jai and I just dropped to the ground in hysterics; then we bolted over to survey the carnage. Koby is laughing his head off as well, but at the same time going, 'Fuck, what have I just done?' We gathered around the ski – which we'd borrowed off a guy from Torquay – and there's the hole. So boofhead – Koby – says, 'Do you think it's going to sink?' The four of us – me, Koby, Jai and a mate from Torquay – dragged it back into the lake to find out.

It was almost impossible to drag across the sand, but as soon as we got it into the lake we looked at it and went, 'Fucking oath, it's gonna sink. We need to get it back to the ramp before it does.' Then Koby just turns around and just takes off on it without saying a word. We needed him there to help us drag the second ski across the sand, which was gonna be a mission with four guys, but almost impossible with three. I suppose he just felt partly responsible for fucking the first ski!

The three of us had to drag the second ski across the sand. If it wasn't for the fact that it was Jai's first surf we wouldn't have bothered, but we gathered all this driftwood and logs, lined it up and made a little road to push the ski along. It was hard yakka. It took us an hour to get it halfway, by which stage we were ready to turn around. But we kept going and after another hour we were fully rooted, but the ski was finally in the surf.

If Koby hadn't fucked off, it could have been me, Koby and Jai together for Jai's first surf, but boofhead had taken off. So our mate from Torquay, me and Jai took off towards the left. When we got there the swell had dropped, it was only about eight foot, and there were about 20 boogieboarders out there. We just thought, 'Okay, let's go for a drive and see what else is out here.' We had two boards with us on the ski, so we found this big, perfect left beachbreak back up the coast and we towed Jai into a couple. It was so much fun. And Jai finally got his surf.

We surfed for an hour then drove the ski all the way down to the Twelve Apostles. We were right underneath them … looking up, circling around and catching waves off them. There was this one rock that came out of the water like a big hourglass, with these womanly hips. We drove right up and parked alongside it, just reaching out and touching it. There were dolphins everywhere, just an energy. We were out in the elements, there was no one around for miles, and that coastline is so raw and the ocean is so blue. Jai was euphoric. He was placing his hands on the rocks, taking everything in. He was used to concrete, not this. He's such a spiritual guy that this was a real moment for him.

Not long after we got back from this trip, I got a call that Oakley wanted to have a meeting about Koby's sponsorship. At that stage we didn't quite know what they were thinking, whether they'd stick with him or not. We flew down to convince Oakley that they needed him, because we sure as hell needed their money. We were broke, basically.

We lost the sponsorship. I flew down and listened to half an hour of negativity. I said, 'Look, you guys hired him to give your label some grittiness, and the bottom line is he creates publicity. Do you guys want the publicity or don't you? He's controversial, but he gets tenfold the publicity of any other surfer.' I tried to get them to believe, but they didn't want to. They were saying, 'But old ladies ring up and complain about him.'

'I'm not going to lie to you – Koby will still be Koby, and old ladies will keep ringing up and complaining about him. But the bottom line is he is going to get publicity.' They just couldn't see it, and so that was that. The contract money was gone at a time when we really needed it.

In a way that almost spurred us on, so the next trip was to Cyclops. That was just insane. That was the full adventure. The place is super remote, down the bottom corner of West Oz. There was a local guy down there who was supposed to pick us up from Albany and get us to the beach, ready to launch the skis at dawn. We drove into Albany about one o'clock in the morning. We'd spoken to him that arvo and said, 'We'll call ya late tonight when we get in and organise the rendezvous. We're looking good. See ya then.'

We got there and his phone is turned off. So we drove east in the direction we thought Cyclops was. We knew it was somewhere on this 100 kilometre stretch of coast, but beyond that we knew fuck all. All eight of us stayed at this little pub. We woke up at three o'clock in the morning after a couple of hours of shuteye. Still no answer on this guy's phone. We drove to the first all-night petrol station and started asking directions. We narrowed it down a bit, but by eight in the morning, three hours later, we were lost. Totally.

It's stunning country down there, all white-gold sand dunes and wilderness. We'd drive down these 4WD tracks for half an hour, stop, look at each other, and go, 'Where the fuck are we? Where does this road even go?' We followed all these dead ends. There was a bit of finger pointing going on. Me and Jai had the map, and Koby's screaming, 'Ya got the fucking map upside down, you idiots!' And we're like, 'We know, you idiot!'

All we wanted was a track that got us onto the beach, because then we could launch the skis and find Cyclops from there. We knew it broke around an island a couple of kays offshore. But the place is just wilderness, and there's nobody around to even ask.

It was almost 9am by this stage, so we were desperate. We knew Cyclops was pumping, and here we were fucking around trying to find the place. We saw this big farmhouse, so we thought we'd drive up and ask for directions. We got to this barn and started yelling out. A lady came out in her overalls, followed by her husband carrying a pair of shears. It's a big barn full of sheep and they're halfway through shearing them.

'We're looking for the beach. Can you help us?'

They were just laughing at us by this stage.

'Well, there's no beach here, but there's a river just down the road that probably leads to the beach.'

So we're like, Sweet, and that's how we eventually found it. There was a dirt track that followed the river all the way to the beach. When we came out we were in the western corner of this sweeping 10-mile beach. There was a rock point there, and the waves were pumping, six to eight foot. Any other time we would've just stayed there and surfed what we had, but we'd come all this way to surf Cyclops, so the search continued.

There was a sheltered section in the middle of the bay with a big rip running out, and in the middle of it was a huge pod of whales. It was deadset like Waterworld, without a trace of mankind. I've never seen anywhere as beautiful and untouched in my life. It was paradise; islands everywhere, headland after headland, the ocean just alive with fish. We let the tyres down on the cars and drove along the beach looking for somewhere to launch the skis. As we drove along Jai climbed out the passenger window, onto the bonnet of the car and started doing belly spins on it. It was hilarious. We drove for another two hours until the tide came in so far we couldn't drive along the beach any more. So we decided to launch the skis and try to find Cyclops on them.

Jai and Marky Mathews launched one ski, and they took off okay. Forty minutes later they still weren't back, so I went, 'Fuck it, I'm going looking for 'em on the second ski.' I checked out four or five islands, all about three kays offshore, before I finally saw Jai and Mark. They had their fists in the air, pointing towards an island down the coast. They'd found it, and it was big, scary and smoking.

Jai and Koby just drove straight around the backside of the island, didn't even scope it out, didn't see a set, didn't know where to sit, never surfed it before. We saw sets on the horizon and suddenly Koby has dropped blind into this monster. I swear, he's pulled into the biggest, bluest, angriest barrel I've ever seen. He didn't come out, and he got fully smashed. It looked like the start of an action movie; you could have played 'Ride of the Valkyries' to it. It summed up everything about Koby's surfing – reckless, fearless, spontaneous – and it set the tone for what was to come.

We had no idea where to sit or what the fuck we were doing. And there was so much water moving out there. Koby got his next wave and got smashed up against the reef. Right away we knew he was in trouble, because he was holding his hand straight up in the air. By the time he got to the channel he'd wiped his hand across his face, and there was blood all over it. He looked like he belonged in the full horror movie. He'd sliced two veins in his wrist which was now pissing blood. We're all looking at each other going, 'What the fuck are we gonna do here?' We're hours from anywhere, even longer from medical help, but the surf's pumping and it's been such a mission to get out here.

We were worried about the blood in the water because the place was incredibly sharky – the island is home to a seal colony, and the waters around it are full of great whites. We looked at Koby's wrist and realised he wasn't gonna die any time in the next hour, so we all agreed we'd get three waves each then bolt and get him to the hospital. As Jai towed Mark into a bomb, we made a tourniquet around Koby's arm with a legrope to slow the bleeding. Mark got a bomb, a 10-footer, and then he got the next set as well. Then Jai got a good first one, a nice barrel on the end, but then he got a dry one on his next wave and got rolled across the reef. There was no water in it. I went next. Jai, who's just been washed across the reef and wanted revenge – on someone – goes, 'Righto, I'm gonna tow you that fucking deep, mate!'

I got a good one. The water was moving so fast up the face that I felt like I was going backwards. Then I got another good one, and Jai was like, 'Fuck you, mate!' On my last one he's towed me *so* deep that when I let go of the rope I was on the other side of the reef. I'm dropping into it and literally only a few feet in front of me the whole reef has gone dry. I've just bailed off my board, waiting to feel the inevitable reef. It was like getting rolled down a flight of stairs covered in barnacles. I got flushed into deep water, surprisingly still in one piece, but my board had disappeared. Jai's picked me up on the ski and we searched one side of the island – no board. We searched the other side – no board. He ferried me up to the island, 'cause I thought the board must have been washed up onto the island itself. The island was shaped like a turtle shell, and there was nowhere you could climb onto it. It's a scary place, like one of those islands you see in wildlife documentaries where seals slide off the rocks on their bellies and the sharks are waiting for them in the water. So Jai's dropped me off the ski and I'm swimming there next to the island. I didn't want to stay in there too long, so when the first wave surged in I've just swam with it up onto the island. I latched onto the barnacles with my fingers as the waves drew back out and just crabbed it up the rocks. I walked around looking for the board but it had totally disappeared, gone completely, no trace. The island had swallowed it.

Four hours later we were driving home. Koby has his arm all bandaged, but it was still leaking a lot of blood. His knee is in a brace too, because he'd torn ligaments a few weeks earlier. He was a mess. As we're flying down these straight, long dirt roads, Koby has spotted this big snake crossing the road up ahead. He just screamed to stop the car. He's got out and hobbled over to it, already looking like he should be in intensive care.

'That's a tiger!' he yelled.

I've gone, 'Mate, no!'

And he grabs the thing by the fucking tail. He's thinking he's Steve Irwin, and 30 seconds later he was almost as dead as Steve Irwin. The thing has swung around to take a snap at him, and Koby can hardly move because of his knee brace. Luckily it was the middle of winter and the snake was a little sluggish. If it had been summer the thing would've bitten him on the balls and then we'd really be racing to the hospital. Koby'd lost a lot of blood by this stage, and was starting to get cold and sleepy and white, but the idiot still wanted to play with a deadly snake.

The next morning when we went and checked the surf, the swell had completely dropped. We started asking each other what we were going to do. Koby's gone, 'Why don't we hire a chopper and go film Cyclops?' The choppers were too expensive, so we found Bob's Rent-a-Plane. We rang Bob and told him there was six of us and we wanted to go up and fly over the coast in his little Cessna.

He's gone, 'I can't take ya all, mate, sorry. It's a small plane, and I'll lose my licence.'

We hung up and gone, 'Okay, boys, someone's gonna have to sit it out.' We all put our names in the hat. First name out is Jai. We go, 'Nah, we're over here because of him. He has to go up.' We draw again and it's Jai again. We draw a third time: Jai. Jai's so superstitious that he's kinda freaking out by now, like it was a sign that he shouldn't go up. So we rang Bob again and said, 'Look, we really wanna go, but we don't want to leave our mate. It's up to you. There's six of us, but we're all pretty small guys' – just bullshitting him.

Bob's relented. 'Okay, I'll do it.'

We pulled up at the airport and cruised over to where his plane is and the thing is tiny. We're pissing ourselves laughing at how small it was. Jai's going, 'Wheeeeeere's Bobbyyyy? Wheeeeeeeere's Bobbyyyy!?' Out comes Bob, and he's a big boy. He's like two of us put together, and we've already bullshitted and told him we're all small guys. We were laughing, but shitting ourselves at the same time, thinking this plane's not getting off the ground.

But we got up no worries and big Bob flew us down the coast, doing these swooping turns over the islands and the beaches … just sweeping tracts of untouched emerald coast. There was a bit of turbulence on the way back, and we'd kinda had enough by that stage. The joke was over, Jai was going green, and we were hoping Bobby would get us back down safely, which he did.

We got out and we were all that pumped. Jai was joking with Bob, going, 'You shoulda been paying us, Bobby!' We were walking back to the car, mucking around, when the phone rang. It was Mum.

'Ma's gone into hospital. The doctors are worried.'

JAI

JAI SWAPS THE CONCRETE OF SILVERWATER FOR THE GRANITE OF CYCLOPS

I swum out at Maroubra on the sixth of the fifth. It was cold, bra, I remember that.

I just jumped straight out into the salt. You miss the salt, you miss the water. You can be anywhere when you're underwater. You just close your eyes and *boom*, I'm back in Indo. When I was in the shower in jail I'd just shut my eyes and I could go anywhere. I'd dream I was in Bali about to go out at Double Six, I'd dream I was out at big Voodoo, I'd dream I was in the best hotel in Bali, stepping out of the shower about to put me robe on and order a beer. I'd dream I was having an outdoor shower in Hawaii after getting out of the surf at Pipe. I'd dream about walking up the beach in Indo with my chick waiting there for me. Just dream myself anywhere, you know. The ocean's the best. That's what I was missing.

It was such a weird feeling, bra, that first surf. I was scared I'd lost it. At first I couldn't do anything at all. We'd gone down to Vicco to surf that big left, but ended up towing this beachie up the coast, which was eight foot and fun. But, fuck, I couldn't even stick to the wave. It was like I was surfing in someone else's body, ya know. That was beautiful down there, though, bra. Buzzing around on the ski checking out the coast was incredible, although all I saw for most of that trip was Sunny's fat duck arse wobbling on the ski in front of me.

The desert was good. That was a fun trip, Gnaraloo. It was the best feeling, bra, being up in the desert with Koby and the rest of the boys. Jail's no place for anybody, but especially surfers who've tasted the ocean. Just to get up there in the middle of nowhere with desert on one side and ocean on the other was sick. We watched Gnaraloo closing out from the bommie all the way across. Fully closed out; it was way too big.

It was 10 foot in the morning when we got up, and it kept getting bigger all day. We paddled out but we were sitting too deep. We didn't know you had to sit on the Tombstone; we kinda blew it. We were just getting worked and rolled over the reef every wave, wondering what the fuck we were doing wrong. We didn't know the takeoff spot was 50 metres further in; we just kept paddling each other all the way up the reef. We got a couple of good ones, but by the time we worked it out the wind had gone onshore.

That Cyclops trip, though, that was mad, brother. I'd been locked up for two years, and I reckon that was the trip I'd been dreaming about. I was so stoked to see how far Koby had come in a few years. He wasn't scared at all. I hadn't surfed that much with him for about four or five years even before I got put in jail – I was just off doing other fucked-up things – so I had no idea how far he'd gone on with it. Not until he jumped off the ski at Cyclops, going, 'Get me the biggest one ya can tow me into!' I'm going, 'Yeah, bra, that's how we do it.'

When we went down there we had no idea where it was. We had a map, and one local bloke goes, 'I think it's off that island there.' That's all we had to go on. We drove our hire car along the beach until we couldn't go no more. All we could see were a couple of islands. We got the jetties off the trailers and into the water, and I've taken off with Mark. We'll find the cunt. We're driving around these islands looking, going, 'There's a wave here, there's a wave there.' Then we spotted this thing out the back. We got out to this right and we've seen this thing go *boom*, just turn itself inside out. I just went, fuck me! I didn't know a wave could do that. We'd found Cyclops.

We've gone out there and, bra, if we'd had our boards with us right then, we'd have said, 'Fuck off, we're not surfing it.' It was a bit onshore, the water was so dark it was almost black, and there were seals on the island. There was a pod of dolphins and I remember seeing an albino dolphin, a full white one in the pod. But the place looked that sharky. It was like we found it, but fucked if we wanna surf it. Then the sun started coming up, the waves cleaned up, and it started to look almost surfable.

Koby and I have come around the back of the island on the ski and seen this 10-foot set steaming in. Then Koby's just jumped off the back of the ski with his board.

'Koby, don't you wanna go round the front and have a look at it, bra?'

'Just get me the biggest one you can tow me into.'

'Fuck yeah, Koby, fucking oath, bra.'

I've towed him around and gone, 'How about this one?' It was a pretty big set too, and he's gone, 'Nah, too small. Not big enough.' But I just didn't like me brother lying there in the water. What would I do if a great white came up and grabbed him, ya know? I was seriously worried about him. I just wanted Koby to get a wave so he wasn't lying there in the water. Well, the one he's ended up going – the thing was just mental. It was *soooo* fucking big. But he only got two more then he cut his hand and had to go to hospital.

Marky got two gems, two bigger ones. One of 'em ended up being on the cover of *Tracks*. The bigger ones are actually safer there; they miss the reef. Eventually we've swapped over and Marky's towed me into one. I got him a couple of gems then he's towed me into one that's breaking on dry rock! I hit the bottom and got rolled pretty badly. Fuck, I swear to God. If my mates are being towed I wanna get 'em the biggest and best waves they can get, but these guys don't want you getting a better one than them. It's a bit of a shit go when the cameras are around. Then Sunny's got a couple, but by this stage there's so much blood in the water from Koby cutting himself that we're all getting a bit nervous. We knew we had to get Koby to hospital.

That flight with big Bobby the next day was hectic. We had one too many people, and we asked him, 'Have ya ever had that many people in ya plane?' And he goes, 'I dunno, but we can try.' That little plane was pretty heavy; it was struggling to get off the ground with all the weight. I'm just looking at all the gauges and they're going crazy, spinning around, and I'm going, 'Fuck, this thing is a lawnmower. This ain't gonna get up.' Well, we get up in the air and a couple of the boys are looking sick, green as frogs. I was just scalloping them in the side of the head 'cause they're looking all pasty and sweaty, grabbing 'em in headlocks, laughing at 'em, 'cause I never get seasick or planesick. Then on the way back we hit some turbulence and suddenly it's me who doesn't feel so good. I'm usually sweet flying, but I was going pretty green on the way home, shitting myself in that little thing. The boys are straight into me, bagging the fuck out of me. I was never happier to feel the ground under me feet when we landed, I'll tell ya.

That Cyclops trip made me realise how lucky I was. That was a mad trip; I'm still stoked as. Some guys whinge, but we still got two arms and two legs. I'm not in a box or behind bars. Doing that two years was the best thing that ever happened to me. I never appreciated anything before that. Doing that time was the best thing that ever happened. It wasn't the *best* thing, but I sure know one thing – it really, really made me appreciate being here.

KOBY

OUR INTREPID HERO SAYS HELLO TO 40 TINS OF SPAGHETTI AND GOODBYE TO A SIX–FIGURE SPONSORSHIP

The whole of our lives the Abbertons had never done a surf trip together any further away than Voodoo, 10 minutes down the road. Not one. We don't do trips together because we fight a lot. We're all pretty tetchy around each other, and it don't take much for us to trade punches. Have us three in the same room for too long and you're gonna get a fight. But with Jai out of jail this was different.

We went down the coast, to this left down the bottom of Victoria, Luna Park. There was me, Jai, Sunny, Mark and Jed. I was still with Oakley at this stage – not for much longer it turns out – and they helped us out with the trip, including lending us a couple of skis. Anyway, it's kinda in the middle of nowhere and you have to launch the ski in the river nearby. I jumped on one of their skis and was ripping up the river on it, and come flying round to the river mouth. Now, normally the river flows straight to the ocean, but because it was some weird tide there was a 50-metre gap that was sanded over between the river and the ocean. I thought I could skid the ski across the sand, so I've just tried to hammer it as hard as I could to get over it. As I got close to the bank I realised it was way shallower than I thought. Someone had dragged a ski across the previous day and had dug a rut in the sand. Well, my ski has got caught in it, and suddenly my ski is like a train on a track, can't steer, can't do nothing, then … *boom*! Straight into this big rock. I rode it out – the captain never abandons ship, bra. Fuck it was funny. I told the boys, 'I might have smashed the jet ski, but I didn't abandon ship, boys!' It totalled the ski.

The first surf trip together with me and Jai and Sun was insane. I still had charges against me, but Jai was free and that was all that mattered. The brothers were back together. Jai was so stoked to be down there with us. He's such a good surfer and he loves it. You could see he was thinking the whole time about what might have been, ya know, what he'd just come from. He was telling us stories about his time in jail; he said it just sucked. Jai said it's no place for a human, especially the way he did jail. He always had it tough, always in fights. They were putting him in solitary for three or four months at a time, putting him in a dungeon with no one there, no TV, no books. He didn't talk about it too much, but he just said it's good to be with you boys.

It was on that trip that we got that photo of the three of us together. Me, Jai and Sun were standing on the hill up above that lefthander, and Justin Crawford asked if we wanted a photo of the three of us together. You can see in that shot how stoked we are. It was also probably one of the last photos ever of us three together. I don't think you're gonna see too many more, bra.

We come home and jumped straight on the next flight for Gnaraloo, 'cause there was a huge swell hitting West Oz. There was me, Jai, Evo, Richie, a sick little crew up in the desert. The first surf we had was like

12 to 15 foot Tombstones – it was pretty fucking big. The first wave Jai paddles into is just this big massive drop. I'm paddling over the wave yelling at him, 'Go, you faggot!' He goes and he gets annihilated, and just paddles back out screaming his head off.

We had a mad time up there. I'm not a clean person; I'm not the kind of guy who needs to have two showers a day. I stayed in the same clothes up there for a week. I love fishing, I love diving. It was mad fun up there, especially with all the boys there … nothing but laughter.

It was towards the end of my Oakley contract. It *was* the end of my Oakley contract pretty well. I was doing Mitch Thorson's head in by that stage. Mitch was the Oakley team manager. He's given this budget to take us on trips, and he turns up at the camp at Gnaraloo with 40 tins of spaghetti. I looked at everyone and I knew they were going to torture him. Out of everything he could've got, he turns up with this?

'What are we going to do with 40 tins of spaghetti?'

From that moment we pretty much tortured Mitch the whole time. Jai was standing at the campfire; he'd just got out of the surf and he's wiping his balls and his arse on Mitch's towel, doing the pull through. Mitch couldn't believe it.

'Mate, that's my towel!'

Jai's just gone, 'Cool.'

It was that funny. When there's all the boys together we can't help ourselves; we just end up picking on the odd guy out, giving him shit. On this trip it just happened to be Mitch.

Mitch would go, 'Okay, we're grabbing the photographer and going down the beach to go surfing.'

I'd go, 'Mate, that's where *you're* surfing, not me.' He wanted me to go and surf this beachie to shoot photos instead of getting 12-foot stand-up pits out at Gnaraloo. I can be pretty rude to people, I'm a team manager's worst nightmare, big time. Not long after that trip Mitch rang up and said, 'I quit. I've had enough. I can't handle it. Koby's out of control and won't listen to anyone.'

I think we might have got a lifetime ban from the Gnaraloo camp somewhere in it all, too. We got kicked out of the camp. Jai was driving through all the gates and fences. He hadn't driven in five years and we couldn't keep him out of the car. You'd ask, 'Who's driving?' and before the words had come out of your mouth Jai was in the driver's seat revving the engine, telling you to get in. There are a lot of rules in the camp up there, which is weird. You're in the middle of nowhere; there shouldn't be any rules. And we're not real good with rules, full stop. We got up there at three in the arvo and we just wanted to get straight out there for a surf; we'd been driving for a day and there was only two hours till dusk. We came up to the lady at the camp and asked her if there was a site for us. She said, 'Well, you never said hello to us so there's not.' I said, 'We're surfers, we're not say hello-erers. We're trying to race out for the late.' It got the trip off on a bad note, so we got a little wild from there.

That trip psyched us up. We went to Cyclops soon after and scored. That place is really scary. We were driving out to it on the skis. Jai was towing me, and the boys all just sitting there watching, wondering whether it was surfable or not. I've just gone, 'Fuck this, tow me into one.' So Jai's towed me around the back of the island and the back of the wave and straight into a massive one. It was a 10 to 12-footer and I fully got on the foamball of the thing. I fell but luckily didn't get hurt. I got another huge one, but on my third one I hit the reef. I knew straightaway I'd cut myself. When I looked at my arm I knew it was pretty bad, 'cause it was pissing blood. But I didn't want to be the guy who ruins the trip and makes everyone go home so I lasted another hour before we had to head to hospital.

On the drive to the hospital I've seen a tiger snake on the side of the road. I've gone, 'Whoa, snake, stop! I've gotta go and get it.' I was getting all dizzy from the loss of blood by that stage – it'd been about four hours – so I probably wasn't thinking that much. But I've always loved snakes, I love catching them. Whenever I'm driving in bushland I've always got my eye out for snakes. I had my knee in a brace because I'd busted the ligaments the week before, and I was bleeding out of my arm, but I jumped out and grabbed the snake by the tail. He whipped around and tried to bite me, had a go. It was only like a four-, five-footer, a small snake, but probably big enough to kill ya for sure.

SUNNY

Ma was really sick.

She looked really weak when we got to the hospital; even her hair seemed a couple of shades whiter. She used to go and get a weekly rinse through her hair. Shirley, the lady up the road in McKeon Street, used to cut and colour it. When Shirley sold the shop she still lived upstairs in her apartment, and Ma would go and get her hair done there every week. That's the first thing that struck me when I saw her: she looked old.

Ma had told us she didn't want dialysis, so she knew she'd deteriorate. But she was such a trooper that you didn't how long she'd hold on for; it could be weeks or it could be a decade. But after Jai's trial, I think she was ready, ya know. She'd even said it herself. We tried to talk her into dialysis, but she kind of just waved us away as if to say, 'No, what's going to happen is going to happen. All you boys are okay, everything's okay. I've had enough.' She didn't want to keep fighting in hospitals, hooked to machines, being less independent. She'd never be able to handle that.

One thing that was really good about those few days was that all the boys visited her in the hospital. I think they sensed it too – that it might be the last time they saw her – and they all got to say thank you. We were sending her off, and she was acknowledging it. She would squeeze their hand and nod as they talked to her. That was something really special – seeing all the boys filing in one by one to say their goodbyes. There would have been 20 of them at least, and every single one of them left Ma's room in tears.

But she was in a lot of pain and was having convulsions that were buckling her over. The doctors didn't want to increase her morphine dosage, but we blew up and said, 'Mate, just do it, she's dying in pain.' So they did and after that she was out to it; she was breathing, but that was about it. As the days progressed she got worse and worse. She could understand, but she'd drift in and out and she was losing her strength.

Mum was there with us. One night we'd slept in the hospital and the next morning we drove down the road to get something to eat. We'd been doing shifts for those past few days to make sure one of us was always there. We hadn't gone that far when we got the call from Mum.

'Come back, quick.'

Ma had passed away as we were driving back.

The next day we heard that one of the Twelve Apostles had collapsed the previous day, and it was the one me and Jai had touched that morning down in Victoria. It was the one we'd hugged; the one Jai had his arms around. Ma had passed away at exactly the same time the Apostle had fallen. That was really symbolic to me and Jai. She'd been our rock, and to us it was no accident that the rock had fallen at the same time as Ma.

KOBY

FLASHES FROM A LIFE DEVOTED TO HER VERY OWN HELL TEAM

Ma was the best ever, but she was pretty hard to live with.

She could be pretty demanding. She was an old lady, she couldn't speak, and she had trouble walking. It started off me living in her house, but when she had the stroke and needed some care she came and lived with me. I lived with Ma for 10 years, and it was pretty hard.

When we were going through court, she was upset about it and stressed. It was tough on her. Everything that was going on, the whole environment, wasn't good for her. But at the same time, it also made her fight harder; she wanted to hang on to see us all free.

The boys will tell you they could talk to Ma with hand signals, but I was the one who could talk to her the easiest. We had the code. She'd hold her hand above her head and that meant Sunny, head height was Jai, shoulder height was me and chest height meant Dakota. Tallest to smallest; her four grandkids. 'Aaaargghh': that was Mum, 'cause she'd caused Ma a lot of headaches. Jai was 'Aaaaaaaaaarggghh', 'cause he'd caused her even more.

It got to the stage where she could tell me about stuff that happened to her in 1970. I knew what she was talking about. She'd point over the hill and I'd say, 'Clovelly'; she'd make a wavy sign with her hands and I'd say, 'the rocks at Clovelly'. Then she'd start rubbing her arms and I'd say, 'You're rubbing cooking oil on yourself while you're sunbaking on the rocks at Clovelly. Ma, that's why you've got all those holes in your arm!' She'd had a lot of skin cancers cut out. She'd go, 'Aaaarggh,' and wave her hand dismissively, like, 'who gives a fuck?' Ma had these holes all over her body. Her leg had a giant crater in it the size of a cricket ball; a crater here, another there, five up her arm. They were all over her body except for her chest and her back.

She was tough. She'd be walking down the street with a 10-centimetre gash on her leg with a Band-Aid holding it together. She needed 15 stitches that day. I took her up to hospital and they asked me about it. I said, 'I think she's had it for five days but hasn't told anyone.' I used to do all her washing for her; the only reason I knew something was wrong was that her pants were covered in blood. She'd cut herself and just marched on like nothing had happened, wiping the blood away.

She was stubborn too. This one time there was no food in the house and without her saying a word I could tell she wanted to go up to Eastgardens shopping centre. It was early morning and she was pointing, she's into me, asking me to drive her to the shops.

'Okay, Ma, I'll take you, but I'm just going for a sandwich down the beach. I'll be back in half an hour.'

'Arrgggh' … pirate-style.

I went and got a sandwich and came back 15 minutes later to take her, and she's gone. I thought she might have gone to the local shops, but she liked Franklins, which was miles away. Four hours later, I'm driving down Bunnerong Road and here's Ma stuck in the gutter trying to push a shopping trolley. The shops are five miles away! But that's what she was like: 'screw you, I'll do it myself'. I pulled over to pick her up and she wouldn't talk to me, wouldn't even look at me. She walked home on her own.

But Ma also had a wicked sense of humour. I was seeing this chick, Elyse Taylor, for a while, and we were fucking in my bedroom one night up in Curtin Crescent and Elyse was being really loud. We came out in the morning and Ma was there.

'Ma, this is Elyse.'

They shook hands and Ma started grunting, going, 'Aah, aah.' I started crying with laughter. Ma starts laughing as well and just walks away. So rude, but so funny. I'd walk into the house with a girl and introduce her to Ma; she would look 'em up and down and hardly acknowledge them, bra.

I'd give Ma 200 bucks for Christmas, and 10 minutes later she'd give me 200 bucks for Christmas. For her birthday I'd give her a hundred bucks, and for mine she'd give me a hundred bucks. If I walked in the house late or came in drunk, she'd scream. One time she was into me, I said to her, 'What are you going to do, Ma?' She just loaded up and whacked me across the face. I started laughing. She couldn't help herself and started laughing as well. She was no pushover; even once she'd had the stroke you could never get away with anything.

But Ma was getting really sick. The whole court trouble me and Jai were in was taking its toll. Soon after Jai was acquitted, my mum rang me and said she thought Ma was getting worse. Then every time I'd go up there, because she loved seeing me she'd light up. I was like, 'Nah,

Mum, I think she's sweet.' But it was only because every time us kids were there, it'd lift her spirits.

Then I heard she didn't have a bath one night. She'd bathed every night I've known her. I said, 'Check her into hospital, *right now*.' She went to hospital and slowly started to deteriorate, just slipping and slipping. Every time I'd walk out of there I'd say, 'Bye, Ma,' not knowing whether I'd see her again. I'd tell her to hang in there and she'd smile, but after a couple of days I think we all knew.

A few days after she went to hospital I was out with friends when I got a phone call from Jai. He said, 'Bra, you better get down here.' Her heartbeat was getting slower, she was getting sicker, and by the time I got there she was almost gone. The whole room got really cold all of a sudden. If you've ever felt a person who's on the verge of dying, they're freezing cold. We all just gave her a hug and a kiss and said our goodbyes. Everyone was crying hysterically. I was crying my eyes out. But when someone's that sick, and you know that their time has come, you can't really do much.

I would've hated for Ma to have pulled through that – she would have suffered. And she was pretty religious too, although she used to shut the door in the Mormons' faces when they came knocking. But we knew she was happy to be going to a good place. If there was one, she was going to her God.

And then that was it. She passed away. She was gone.

The first thing I think of now when I think of Ma is her funeral. That's why I hate them. All I can remember about the funeral is Ma in the casket. All I can think about now when I think of Ma is her lying there in that white box. Everyone was there; it was a massive turnout. All her boys were there; not just her four grandsons, but all the kids she looked after at Fenton Avenue. All of them were there to a man. Every one of those guys knew what she had done for us as kids.

You've got to respect someone who gave up her life for you.

JAI

MA'S BOYS ATTEMPT TO REPAY A LIFETIME OF LOVE WITH A DONATED ORGAN

Ma passed away about three months after I got out.

I remember it well. Saddest day of my life. Ma is the soldier of all soldiers. Two years before she died, we went to the doctors with her. She was sick. They tried to put her on dialysis; her kidneys had gone. I remember me and Koby saying to each other, 'We'll give her one of our kidneys, sweet.' But the doctors wouldn't let us for some reason; it turned into this big argument. Why can't we just give her one of ours?

'No, she's too old. It's not going to work,' they said, or something.

'We don't care how old she is. We want to give her one of our fucking kidneys!'

They fully wouldn't let us; they didn't even test us to see whether we were a match. It was because Ma couldn't talk. The pricks, I don't think they thought she had long left anyway. They thought, 'She's had a stroke, she's old'; they just thought we should accept her fate. And Ma being Ma, she just shook her head when they offered to put her on dialysis. It was like she's gone, 'I don't wanna come in here every day to be hooked into a machine.' So she just walked out of the hospital and rode it out.

I remember going to the hospital on the morning she died. I walked into her room and she was just about gone. I just thanked her for everything she'd done for us, gave her a hug, and began to pray. I prayed to God, asking him to take her to Heaven, please. She didn't believe in God but she had so much goodness in her heart, he couldn't not accept her.

It made me wonder. What happens when someone like Ma, who is so good, dies but they don't believe in God? And what about someone who believes in God but doesn't do good things with their life? It left me questioning. But on the same day Ma died, one of the Twelve Apostles down in Victoria fell. That was God telling me, 'Of course I took her. Of course. She's one of my trumps.'

KOBY

They dropped the accessory to murder charge on 1 April, which was fitting because it was a joke.

I got charged as an accessory to murder; they held that over me for a year, then on day one of court they dismiss the charges. They knew all along I wasn't an accessory to shit, but they just kept pushing. The way they went about it wasn't right. In the end it was proved that the way they went about it was wrong because they lost. They made so many mistakes and were so keen to see us go down that the judge could see through it. He knew they really had it in for us. My whole family got the blowtorch. When Tony turned up dead and they charged Jai, that was the excuse they'd been looking for: they put the pressure on all of us. They'd been waiting for that chance for a long, long time.

I still had a lesser charge of perverting the course of justice hanging over me, which could have 14 years attached to it if I went down. I knew what I did was wrong; I should have just pleaded guilty in the end. I wasted a lot of money fighting it. I wasted another hundred grand. Then Jai is out and everyone else is getting on with their lives, and I'm left there wondering 'Why the fuck am I the last person still going in a court case?' You know what I mean? Why am I still spending $3000 a day? I was the one home asleep, for fuck sake, not the one throwing a dead body off a cliff.

But all the way through the case I found myself fucking up. I was just getting pissed off. The whole time I just wanted to say, 'Fuck, my statement wasn't exactly right, okay. I saw Jai that night, but I had no idea what had happened.' I was just getting sick of it, and the judge could tell.

'Mister Abberton, do you even care?' I'd be sitting there drawing waves and these weird little surfing creatures, and the judge would say,

'Mister Abberton, can you please stop doing that!' And I'd be, like, up to the colouring-in stage and so engrossed in it I wouldn't even notice he was talking to me. *'Mister Abberton! Can you please stop that! Do you even care?'*

I was so tempted just to say, 'Err, no, actually I don't.'

But the worst thing about court was missing out on the surf. Mate, between hearing about swells in Tassie and Tahiti, it was killing me. You wanna know something? It could be a week before court and there'd be no swell anywhere; I'd say to the boys, 'Boys, watch this. There'll be swell Tuesday next week, the day I go to court, guaranteed.' My court day would come round and *boom*, mystery swell would appear, every time. The court swell. *Every* time. I'd be sitting in court listening to some judge just waffling, watching his mouth move, and all I'm hearing him say is, 'Tahiti Tahiti Tahiti.' I'm just going, 'Get me out of this fucking joint!'

I was lucky that I got such a sympathetic judge. If I hadn't, I'd be in jail now. He could have hammered me. But the judge took it for what it was, and I think my answers told him that I knew I was wrong. I think he believed the cops had put me in a position where I had to say something, and what I'd said was largely bullshit. When you're questioned for so long, it just comes out of your mouth. Then after hearing about our childhood experiences, the judge knew why I was gonna lie for my brother; he added it up. I'd been put in a position where I had no choice. I think he'd also taken into account that we'd lost everything we owned. By that stage I just wanted to get out of court. 'Either send me to jail or send me home; I'm just over it.' Going to jail didn't scare me, I wasn't worried about it. I've been in worse places than jail, I think. I more hated the thought of being away from friends, family and my girl.

Then came the verdict. There was about 30 seconds of hell, because the first thing the judge said was, 'Koby Abberton, I am going to sentence you to nine months' prison.'

So there I am thinking, 'All right, this is it. I'm going in and I'll just have to take it on.' You know when you get bad news and you have about 88 thoughts in one second? I thought, 'Fuck, okay, nine months. That's fucked, but it could be worse.' That 30 seconds of silence felt like an hour. Then the judge goes, 'But I am going to suspend that sentence.'

I'm like, out the side of my mouth to my lawyer going, 'What does that actually mean?' And that was it; I was free. After three years of mental torture I couldn't believe the judge still wanted to play with my head for another 30 seconds! But I understood it. I understood it was his intention to scare me and make me realise how close I was to going inside.

And after three years for us, that was the end of it. We were all finally free.

The whole thing made me realise that life can be taken away from you so easily. It really can, with the turn of any day, if you're gonna position yourself around certain things and certain people. If you care for your life as you like it, just be careful where you take that next step. Watch the company you're with, and no matter what position you're in, know when to walk away.

And the worst thing about going to court? I started smoking durries. I started having a smoke at night after getting home from court. Next thing I'd wake up and start smoking in the morning before I went, then I started to get a bit anxious when I didn't have one. Next thing I'm necking a pack a day. Still can't shake it. A fucking life sentence right there, bra.

KOBY

AS PHILOSOPHICAL AS ONE CAN BE ABOUT LOSING A SEVEN—FIGURE SUM AND TRAVERSING THE STAR—GUTTER CONTINUUM

Sure, I wasn't in jail, but I owed a million dollars. Not a good fucking feeling, bra. I wouldn't recommend it.

It was over, but it *wasn't* over. I'd lost the family home; we'd lost everything we owned. I had to declare myself bankrupt. When I was earning a lot of money the family signed everything over into my name, so when we got fucked we all lost the lot. We owned three units up in Bond Street which were worth $350,000 each, and a penthouse apartment in Burleigh that cost me $650,000. The house up in Curtin Crescent cost me $780,000, and that went. I had two cars, one worth $88,000 and another worth $40,000. Both gone. Between the Crime Commission bleeding me dry, the lawyers' fees and the bank, I owed a million bucks. Once I got declared bankrupt and they had a fire sale on all my shit, I still owed 200 grand to the Crime Commission which would take me another three years to pay off.

But I didn't really give a shit about money. What gives me the shits more is some guy in a suit telling me, 'you owe this, you have to report to this guy, you can't take a shit without signing this form'. Fuck off. I don't wanna sign your papers and I don't wanna report to you. Stop telling me what I've got to do. I hate that shit. Just let me go surfing.

And while I'd lost everything I'd owned, I'd also lost my income. Not long after I'd been found guilty, Oakley pulled the pin on my contract.

They dropped me at the end of the year, didn't renew my contract. They hung in till the year was over and my contract was up, which was fair enough. You could imagine the arguments going around the boardroom: 'Is he worth it? Are we putting the company on the line? What about our *image*?' They have to cover their own arses. I understood them not renewing the contract, but I didn't like the way it was handled, the way they blamed it on each other. I was not going to get angry if someone had come up and said, 'Look, we have to let you go because I'm worried I'm going to lose *my* job as well.' No worries. I understand. But I will get upset if you blame someone else, who then goes and blames someone else, who blames someone else. That's what happened. I ended up just sitting down and having a meeting with them all in the one room and telling them they were a bunch of cowards. At least have the balls to stand up and tell me the truth. I think they realised how much they fucked up by letting me go, because a couple years later they signed up Clint Kimmins who'd just done jail time.

So I was starting again. I knew it that day I walked out of court. It comes down to one thing: I come from nothing; I can go back to nothing.

I know how to live without money and if I've got to do that, then so be it. I know what it feels like. When I was a young kid I pretty much lived on the street with nothing. As long as I got something to eat I don't care. People were saying to me, 'But you were making good money the last five years; it must be hard.'

I didn't really give a fuck. I had a good run. You can take what I've got, but I'm still me. People asked me how come I dealt so good with losing it all. I just told them straight, 'Fuck, me mum left me when I was a kid. I loved her the most in the world. Once that happens, who cares what else happens? Take me fucking house. Do you think I care?' Do you know what I mean? They can't beat me that way. So that's it. I didn't really care. Take it, they can fucking have it. I hope it makes 'em happy. I'm a pretty bad punter, I'm used to having a bad month on the punt, so to suddenly be without money wasn't that strange for me. I used to spend me pay cheque in a day or two. I'd get a 15 grand pay cheque for the month and blow it in two days. I was used to it.

And the Bra Boys, they'll never let you starve. The boys knew I didn't have much cash, so there'd be phone calls going, 'Let's go to dinner.' Now that I look back on it, I probably lived better than a lot of people do. I might not have had any money, but I'd still go to good restaurants. I could sulk about it and feel sorry for myself, I might have lost everything, but I still had my mates there and they were always going to look after me. Jed was a big part of that, Jed and Greg Winter. Jed would make two grand a week tiling, and he'd go, 'Here's a thousand bucks.' I'll never forget what the boys did for me. I still owe Jed 10 grand today, which I've got down from 25. Every month I'll try and give him a grand. I owed Sunny 50 grand. And Marky Mathews spotted me all these surf trips, doing for me exactly what I'd done for him when he was a kid. It's the way it works here.

But the money was nothing. At least I was free; at least I could still go surfing. I thought, 'I'll just get some more photos; there'll be other contracts.' As much as a shit fight as it was, the whole thing brought me to the attention of a lot of people in the wider world and it opened a lot of doors. I didn't have any money to go anywhere, but I could find it; I knew it would come back. I just wanted to do what I've always wanted to do, what I've dreamed of my whole life: I just want to ride the biggest wave I can. I was never worried about bouncing back, but I think I just needed some time and space before that was going to happen. The past three years had just been too claustrophobic, ya know.

But what was really getting to me was the attention. Everyone was meaning well, but patronising the fuck out of me. I hate it when people ask me questions all the time. You know when you get sick and everyone's so apologetic and nice to you? I can't stand that shit. I'd rather everyone just pretend it's not even happening and everything is normal. I just hated it. Everyone would be walking up to me saying, 'Congratulations.' Everyone was talking about me, and to me – talking about my problems. It was just driving me mad. I just needed to go surfing and party.

I was living up at North Maroubra in a rented flat overlooking the ocean. I was surfing a lot at the time, but I just wanted to be by myself. I was using the money I was borrowing off Jed for rent mainly and I took the lease out on that place on my own. I don't like sleeping in beds, so I was paying 500 bucks a week rent and sleeping on the floor. I love being around my friends, but at that time I just wanted to be alone, so I just hung in the house a lot and did my own thing.

Then the boys got together and organised a benefit night for me at Randwick Racecourse. It was Wayno, Wayno's girl Melissa and Hair Bear mainly, but a lot of people chipped in. There were 500 people, all my friends. I've never seen a turnout like it; it was fucking incredible, bra. Russell Crowe turned up and played with his band, which was pretty cool. Everyone was in beautiful suits, the girls were all dressed up and everyone was spending cash. Willie Mason, Reni Matua, Willie Tonga and Sonny Bill Williams spent $10,000 at the auction on a surfboard. It was a pretty humbling experience. Half the money raised went to charity; half went to get me back in the black.

Everyone was together, having a good time, all different walks of life. It was a big night. But to be honest, I couldn't enjoy the night. I didn't give a fuck about being a charity case, but I just didn't feel comfortable with everyone asking me questions. Even though my whole career revolves around it, I hate being in the spotlight. I can't stand it. Especially when the only subject everyone was talking about was the situation I found myself in.

The whole experience of going through the courts and losing everything I had just made me want to go harder in my surfing. It made me see that life is short. It made me worry a lot more about the kids around here. It made me realise how easily life can change living in a place like this. If it wasn't for surfing I'd be in jail now for sure. I know that now. In jail or dead.

SUNNY

CRONULLA'S ILLS SPILL DOWN THE HILL

There were a few things that led to the Cronulla riots ending up here in Maroubra.

When the whole thing started with the lifeguard being bashed, it was painted as surf culture under attack. A few kids rang up talkback radio, saying, 'Why don't you send 'em over to Maroubra? They'll sort 'em out.'

I think that was what led to the newspaper calling Koby and asking him for a comment. We really thought the media were trying to spark up the cultural differences. Because the Lebanese had been in a fight with the lifesavers, the media were trying to flare the whole fact that this was an Australian institution under attack. What Koby said was that he didn't stand for gangs of youths coming to Maroubra and attacking people indiscriminately. But it didn't come across like that in the paper. Vintage Koby.

We were in Cronulla the Sunday the riots went down. We went over there to film, as I'd begun work on a documentary I'd always wanted to make on the tribal nature of Maroubra Beach. It was a movie on beach culture and beach tribalism, and here was this major flare-up one beach south of ours. We had to film it. Groups of youths coming to the beach to attack people was what had been happening in Maroubra back in the '90s. On the day we were there filming for the documentary, we asked questions no one else was asking, like, 'Are you worried about retaliation attacks?' The people we asked were like, 'Retaliation? Whaddaya mean?' We just didn't expect it to be retaliation attacks against us.

Once we got into Cronulla it was scary. There were thousands of people. Straightaway we went, 'Fuck, what's going on here?' By the time we got up to the beachfront we could see thousands of people all with Aussie flags and signs. There were a few barbecues up on the hill and a street party, but by the time we got 500 metres into the crowd it started to get ugly.

Four or five Middle Eastern guys happened to be walking along the promenade. That was the general fear that day; the press had built up this big showdown between the Lebanese and the Australian communities. So these five kids are walking down the beach minding their own business and someone yelled out, 'Here they come!' and everyone has started booing. Before they knew what was happening, the guys were being attacked. The cops had to run in there and scuttle them into the surf club. I think the guys may have even been Italian or Bangladeshi; I'm certain they weren't even Lebanese. Then it just erupted. It was a chase and a showdown. Everyone was yelling, 'They're coming! We're under attack!' It got crazy.

Behind us this little hotted-up car was being attacked. A full can of beer flew straight past our heads. People were starting to run everywhere. It was getting hotter and hotter and the pubs hadn't closed, the bottlos hadn't closed. Over those next two hours the crowd geed itself up until finally they ran to the train station and there were a heap of indiscriminate bashings. When I saw a thousand blokes chanting 'Anzac, Anzac!' attack five guys, I just felt disgust. The Anzacs attacked Gallipoli outnumbered 1000 to 5, not the other way around. Those blokes would be turning in their grave seeing this shit. A thousand people dogging five guys – that's not the Aussie way.

That's one thing we'd learned a long time ago: if there's a bunch of 20 guys coming to the beach looking for trouble, regardless of whether they're Lebanese or islanders or homeboys or whatever, then you give 'em trouble. We never allowed the tension to build to the level it did in Cronulla, and that definitely seemed to be the problem. There'd been so much unfinished business and so much shit simmering that it built up to the stage where it exploded. It wasn't dealt with as it was happening.

I don't want to say the Cronulla guys should've done what we did, but what we realised, after years of warring with crew coming into Maroubra, was that it would go on for years unless you opened the door and welcomed some of these crew in, got them to embrace the culture of the place, and develop a bit of respect for what's there.

When the Lebanese fish shop was sold, the new Lebanese owners came down and introduced themselves to the boys. Soon after Leon and his family took over the shop they'd had a few problems with the local kids, which I'd sorted out for them. Leon came down one day and asked me if I wanted to sit down and have a coffee and a chat with him. We sat down and talked; it was good and it smoothed the road. They wanted to be seen as part of the community here, which we thought was great. It was all in the approach, and suddenly there was a relationship between us and them. And it turned out he was very connected with the wider Lebanese community.

But there's always been a sense in Maroubra that race never really matters. Look at the Bra Boys – as well as white Aussies there's islanders, Kooris, Greeks, even a few Brazilians and Lebanese. Race has never really defined that much with us; it's more a love for the beach and for Maroubra. And over the years, all those little networks within the Bra Boys have prevented a lot of that shit happening here.

But it wasn't enough to stop what happened the day after Cronulla.

We drove straight back to Maroubra from Cronulla that afternoon. On the grass next to the surf club the Maroubra Boardriders and Maroubra Gracie jujitsu academy were holding their combined Christmas parties and a big Brazilian *churrascaria* barbecue, because a lot of the local boys are in both boardriders and the jujitsu class. It was getting dark and

I was starting to tell 'em what was going on at Cronulla when we got the first phone calls.

Our mate Herbie had just driven through Maroubra Junction, a mile up the road, and he said there were hundreds of people on the streets and they'd just trashed his car. A minute later another mate called and said that it was heading this way. It was then that I turned to everyone and said, 'Okay, boys, they're coming, 150 guys heading our way.'

No one believed me at first.

'Boys, I'm not shitting ya. They're coming down Maroubra Road.' I kind of addressed the group. 'Okay, guys, you're either with us in this or you're not. If you're not, get the girls out of here and get into the pub.'

The boys immediately started ripping out fence palings and poles and anything they could use as a weapon. Just then a big police riot truck pulled over on Marine Parade. This was strange; we'd get told later on that the police had no idea about this attack on the beach, but here they were. The truck skidded at the crossing on Marine Parade outside the pub and four cops in riot gear got out and ran over to us.

'There's 150 guys headed your way. Get out of here!'

'Where are we gonna run, mate?'

'Drop your weapons and run.'

'We're not going anywhere, mate. Where are we gonna go?'

And they've run back to their van and bolted. We didn't see 'em again the whole night.

As the boys started breaking out the fence palings, I asked the Brazilian jujitsu guys what they wanted to do. To a man they straightaway all said, 'We're with you.' And they grabbed the steel kebab skewers from the *churrascaria* and all of a sudden we had 12 swords.

It was just about then that we heard the sound of them coming down Maroubra Road. We just heard breaking glass as they trashed every car on the side of the road. I'll never forget the sound. They'd been attacking cars and stabbing people all the way down Maroubra Road. They'd shot at cars, they'd axed cars, they'd stabbed people. By the time they'd got to that corner, smashing everything, it was scary. We're thinking that if these guys get to the main street and to the pub, what was going to happen? Our girls and a lot of the older crew were in there. We had to defend the pub at all costs. There was that real sense of defending your territory. It was war. We were defending our home and our loved ones.

Then we saw them. They started running down the hill from the roundabout at North Maroubra towards us, the first 50 of them. Frog was in the pub with a few of the other boys and had come out and seen it. It's all happening so quick at this stage. Frog has run out of the pub, unarmed, on his own, and just ran straight at 'em. It was the ultimate kamikaze act – and only a bloke as big as Frog could contemplate it. We looked across and hear the first wave of guys laying into Frog on the ground with baseball bats. You could hear the thud as they hit him in the back.

And that was it. About 30 of us, with fence palings and whatever we could pick up, have just charged at 'em. They were about 20 metres up the hill from the pub when we met 'em. My fence paling was about twice the size of me, and it was way too long to be of much use. I remember running straight at this one guy, just looking him in the eyes. You can imagine what it must have been like in all those ancient battles with thousands of people, but as you charge you're just looking at one person. And I was looking at this big guy with a baseball bat. He's taken a swing at me and missed. I swung at him with my fence paling and missed. Then we've both swung and our bats and palings have clashed. There were one-on-ones everywhere on the street. It was on.

We had big Andre the Brazilian – this giant guy who's got long curly black hair – and he was running at these guys with a three-foot metal skewer, screaming his lungs out. One of the Brazilian guys got stabbed in the stomach. One of the other boys got baseball-batted pretty badly. But we managed to drive them back up to Poo Hill, about 30 metres.

They stopped at the roundabout, about another 100 metres up the road. There were five cars parked there that had dropped these guys off. With guys still piling in, two of the cars have tried to do a U-turn at the same time and blocked each other, as well as blocking the other cars behind them that were trying to get out. All five cars were trapped in there, and the boys got to those cars and smashed 'em to pieces. I saw a fence paling speared straight through the driver's window of the first car.

It was at that stage that I first realised the cops were actually there. They'd been watching the whole thing. One of the gang cars came flying around the headland from North Maroubra on Marine Parade, and came straight at us from behind, trying to run us over. It was one of the convoy cars. As we dived out of the road I saw out of the corner of my eye three policemen do exactly the same. We got asked the next day whether we'd defended police that night, and that's where it must have come from. A handful of cops weren't going to do anything among all that. We didn't even know they were there, didn't even notice them. They had no control of the situation. It was like a battlefield.

Some of the cars got out, others didn't, and a couple dozen of the guys had to run on foot back up the hill and out of there. There were about 40 of us chasing the last of them back up the hill. Once we got to the top, we stopped, and the boys all let out a cheer. They'd trashed Maroubra, but we'd repelled them from the beach.

Then we run back down to the pub. We were still getting calls that there were more guys coming in, and we assumed this wasn't going to be the end of it. So we rallied all the blokes out of the pub, and everyone armed themselves with whatever they could – sticks, chairs, whatever.

That night there were skirmishes all over Maroubra. Late that night we were getting reports from the police scanners that there was another convoy on the way down. The younger grommets had a team of scouts throughout the area, and there were still convoys of guys cruising around looking for crew to attack. The young guys would hide in the shadows, wait for the cars to cruise past, then throw bricks at 'em and disappear again over fences. That went on all night.

But the important thing for me that night was that half the guys who'd defended the beach with us were first or second generation Aussies. Some weren't even Aussies at all. All these guys had joined us, because we'd been open to them and their cultures. It shows that not only will they embrace our culture; they're actually willing to fight for it. The Lebanese guys who attacked us that night were fighting us because they thought we were racist, but they were attacking islanders, Aussies, Brazilians and even other Lebs.

Once it quietened down a bit, I got on the phone. I rang my mate Leon, the Lebanese guy I'd had coffee with that morning years ago, and arranged to meet with him and two senior members of the Lebanese community that night. We organised a meeting at one in the morning in Maroubra, which had quietened down a bit by then. They drove into Maroubra, and I met them down on Marine Parade. I walked down McKeon Street with these three Lebanese guys. The street was quiet and the pub was closed. We went under the shopfronts across the road and sat down on the ground. By that time there were 20 of the boys there, and I had to cool them off and tell them these guys were sweet. Our peacemakers had nearly copped it, which would have been a disaster.

I just told these guys we had nothing to do with Cronulla. We didn't want to get involved in a race riot. It wasn't our fight. It wasn't the way we were. We're one of the most multicultural beaches in Sydney. No one here had incited it. I said, 'Can't you guys see what this is? The cops are trying to take two of Sydney's most hated minorities and play them off against each other. We've got nothing to do with this. They're trying to make us go to war. They arrest the lot of us, we all go to jail, and we're all off the streets. You see how full-on the cops have been here in the last few years: the raids, the sniffer dogs.' We really felt like they wanted tanks on the street. We really did. We felt they were trying to play us off to get rid of us and to get more police powers. 'Why were there no cops there trying to stop it?' That's what I said. 'We're being played here, guys.'

And those guys saw it too.

On the second day, the Monday, we heard Maroubra was being targeted for retaliation attacks. There's so many different divisions within the Lebanese community – religiously, geographically, politically – and we realised that just talking to one guy wasn't going to stop us being attacked. We had to speak to a number of them, from religious leaders to the people who the kids on the street were going to listen to.

The next morning there were hundreds of people in the street, people from Maroubra, people from all over the eastern suburbs really. There were crew from Maroubra, La Per, Malabar, Coogee, all floating around seeing what was going to happen next. Word was going around that they were coming back that night and everyone had agreed to meet at six o'clock on the beachfront.

Those two guys I'd met the night before were part of the Auburn boys, so the next day we met with a couple of different factions from other areas. We first met with Keyser Trad, who's a vocal Muslim leader. Koby and me went and met Keyser outside the Channel Nine studios where he was being interviewed. We had a meeting with him about our thoughts on how we could slow this thing up. He agreed to meet with us the following day, and I organised through Johnny Gannon's mate at Channel Nine to get us on the *Today* show the next morning. We met with another Lebanese leader that afternoon.

Jai was freaking out by this stage. He was worrying that we were going to be seen as the face of racism and not the face of peace. Here we were, we had nothing to do with the riot, and we're on one side and the Lebanese are on the other. He thought the more interviews we did the more it would seem like we were the other side of the problem, which was probably true. We were trying to play a role, just not too much of a role.

By the Monday afternoon there were 600 people on the beachfront in Maroubra, a lot of them armed. The police had closed off the beach from Fitzgerald Avenue to Maroubra Road. They locked down the whole suburb, and you had to show your driver's licence with your address to get into Maroubra. The police had moved in from both ends of the beach, asking everyone to drop their weapons and move on, although no one was really interested in doing so. 'You didn't protect us last night. Why should we move on now?' The whole suburb was ready for another attack, and this time it was more than just the Bra Boys, it was the *whole suburb*. In the laneway next to McKeon Street, the wooden fence had been kicked in and the whole lane had become an arsenal of weapons: old house bricks, metal pipes, four-by-twos. At seven o'clock we agreed to disperse the crowd. We didn't want to inflame the thing, but we also wanted to show that we're not going to let crew come in and randomly smash the place up. We wanted a show of strength and solidarity from the community, but we didn't want a race war.

I was still on the phone trying to speak to various Lebanese leaders, but I soon realised I needed to speak to the guys out there who the kids on the street were going to listen to, and that was the Comancheros. They've got a lot of influence in the west, but they've also got a Lebanese leader. They're an Australian bikie gang with a Lebanese leader. So I met with him – his name was Mick – and I told him the same thing I'd told the other guys. It got a little bit heated when I first got on the phone, but he eventually calmed down. I said, 'Mate, we've had nothing to do with this. Can't ya see what they're trying to do? They're trying to play us all off. They want us at war. They want to jail us and they want us off the streets. They want new powers. Let's not buy into it.'

'All right, I'll tell ya what, we'll meet tomorrow morning at 11 o'clock. You organise the press and I'll be there. I'll tell my boys we'll do it, shake hands on the street, and it'll be over.'

We met down at Marine Café. We asked the press to move away so we could talk face-to-face first and get a few things sorted out; then we went over and faced the media. It was pretty bullshit, a bit of a stunt, and it was a bit awkward. But it worked. They came down with a solid team of 20 guys. There was me, Jai, Koby and a few of our senior guys, and it was surreal. It was like a war truce. There was still a lot of tension, but it was the end of hostilities.

But it was my friendship with Leon Habibi – *habibi* means friend – over that two years and learning a little bit about how each other's side worked that had helped put all this out. It all started from there. Later that afternoon he and I went over the pub at Maroubra for a beer. He was the first person I had a beer with that afternoon and we both tried to work out what the hell had just happened.

frog

Mate, I didn't really run out on my own, ya know. That's been talked up a bit.

I was in the pub having a beer when someone's got a call.

'There's a hundred Lebs coming down the street with baseball bats!'

I've thought, bullshit, but then I've looked around the pub and everyone's phones are going off.

'I'm serious! They're coming down Marine Parade!'

I've still thought it might be bullshit, so I've walked out the front of the pub to have a look with a dozen or so other guys. I got out on the road and had a look up the hill from the median strip and, sure enough, there's a hundred blokes with bats and sticks coming at me. Then I've looked back and all of a sudden I'm standing there on my own. One of those situations where you volunteer by staying still and everyone else moving back.

I've just thought, 'Fuck, what am I gonna do here?' I'd had a few beers, so I just went, well, I'm not gonna run back into the pub and hide, so I've just gone and ran straight at 'em on my own.

In hindsight it probably wasn't the greatest move of my career, but when you've been out since the night before you're not thinking too clearly about anything. And I didn't even have time to think 'cause by the time we got out the front they were only 50 metres away.

I knew I was gonna cop a hiding, but I thought I was gonna try and take as many of these guys with me as I can. I knew when I was running that Sunny and the jujitsu boys were down at the surf club and would be in behind me. As I was running up the hill at 'em I could hear Sunny yelling out, 'No, Frog!' And I've just gone, 'Yes! Come on!'

And me doing that got the boys into action. They were all a bit shell-shocked at the time. From what I can gather I went down, got batted a bit, and Jack and Benny Kelly have pretty well run straight across and thrown themselves in on top of me, they've covered me up. I was up there for a couple of minutes on my own, but that was about it.

It was a strange time. The boys were all in battle mode. There were kids sitting on top of the shops here with rocks and bits of wood, waiting for it to happen again. It took me a couple of days to recover 'cause I copped a couple of big hits to the head with bats, but when I come out four or five days later I wasn't that surprised to see the kids had sticks on every corner, stashed away, just waiting.

The way we seen it was if they're coming once, they're coming again. It's not if, it's when. My biggest worry was that it was going to be one of the kids walking down the street on their own that was going to cop it. I think we ended up with a good result, 'cause it could have got really ugly and people could have got killed quite easily.

And then it could have carried on.

Luckily none of that happened. We still have a strained relationship with the guys who came in that night, but we do our best and we hold no grudges against anyone.

It was pretty well Koby and his big mouth that got us into trouble. He just doesn't know when to say nothing. He's always got to say something. I know he was taken out of context, but out of everybody he should know not to say anything to the papers 'cause it keeps getting him into trouble.

KOBY

A FEW ILL-CHOSEN VERBS DOWN THE PHONE LINE
ARE RECIPROCATED WITH THE MILDLY UNNERVING
PING OF GUNFIRE

It was something I said that got quoted in the paper that brought the riots here that night. I said to a newspaper reporter, 'Maroubra Beach

MY BROTHERS KEEPER

isn't like Cronulla, because the Bra Boys police the area, but everyone's still welcome. We have a big multicultural background here and we welcome people to the beach who respect the area. We've got Maoris, we've got Lebanese, we've got Kooris, we've got Samoans, we've got white guys ... the Bra Boys are multicultural.' The only thing that gets printed is 'the Bra Boys police the area'. We *police*? I couldn't think of anything worse to say than I *police* anything. I hate the police and it's a word I should never have said. I read it the next day and I thought, 'Fuck, that's pretty bad on my behalf.' But what happened that night I never expected. I rang the journalist.

'Mate, what happened to the rest of it?'

'Your phone must've dropped out.'

'What do you mean my phone must've dropped out? You reported the bit before it and you reported the bit after, but your tape cut out during those key words in the middle?'

'Well, sorry, mate, I didn't hear it.'

'Mate, 200 cars just got smashed because you left off the end of a sentence.'

I was staying four houses up from where it all happened that night. I could hear all this commotion and all these alarms going off. I was wondering what the fuck it was. The boys were barbecuing down on the beach; it's lucky the boys were there. They fought 'em, Frog got in there first on his own into a group of a hundred of 'em. I couldn't go down. I was still on charges, and I would've been straight back in jail. And anyway, they just would've killed me.

I was the one they were looking for.

They were ringing me that night, shooting guns down the phone line. 'Hey, Koby, we got something for you, bra ... *bang bang,*' down the phone.

These were guys who I was friends with before it, and guys who I'm friends with now. But when their race gets challenged, they believe in shit; they believe in their religion and race more than the everyday Aussie. So even though I was their friend, they were pissed off. They'd heard somehow that I was down at Cronulla the day before which was bullshit. The newspaper story didn't help.

They thought we were coming out there to get them. I don't even know where Punchbowl is. I'd spoken earlier in the day with a group of Lebanese guys to set up a meeting to sort it out peacefully before anyone got hurt. So the voice on the phone that night goes, 'Are you coming down?' And, thinking it was the guys I was meeting with, I said, 'Yeah, of course I'm coming down.'

'You are? Well this is what you're gonna get! *Bang bang.*'

I looked at the phone and went, 'Get fucked.' It was the wrong person. It was a big misunderstanding.

Then we heard they were coming down in carloads, so there's crew here carrying guns and knives and bats and axes. There were petrol bombs set up on all the roofs so that if they came in they'd get bombed from the roof. It'd be like a war.

To see that in Australia … Once I saw all that happening I said, 'Fuck, we gotta stop this shit.' The guys at Maroubra were the only ones who were gonna fight – no one else was gonna fight – which is another reason they ended up coming here. It's the only beach that's gonna go the distance, and that made us more of a target. In the end it was the police and the media hyping the whole thing. Every night on the news, Channel Nine, Seven, Ten, they're showing a Muslim guy being bashed in Cronulla, then an Aussie guy getting bashed in Maroubra; just fuelling the fire. I seen 16-year-old kids on a roof with 50 petrol bombs lined up, and kids in the street with axes and guns. It was like, whoever doesn't die tonight will be going to jail forever. It would've been a bloodbath. And because I was in the middle of it and because I knew how both sides were thinking, we were either going to see a lot of Australians die – and when I say Australians I mean *both* sides – or we can use a bit of our pull and stop it.

What happened in Cronulla was the most cowardly thing I've ever seen. A thousand people beating up four blokes? Then all those kids getting arrested and locked up and going straight into protection? They caused that whole thing and then not one of them came out of their house for two weeks. In the end I had people ringing me up from Cronulla going, 'Can you say sorry for me because you're the face of it now?'

'How am I the fucking face of it? You say sorry yourself, mate. You deserve everything you get. If I had four friends beat up by a thousand people I'd be attacking yas too.' It was such a weak thing to do.

But I think it's brought awareness to everyone. As fucked as it all was, I think it was a good thing in the end. You can't go around agitating people 'cause if they get pushed, no matter who they are, they're gonna react. It brought racism onto the agenda. It made people realise there is racism here; it put it in people's faces. And it made everyone realise we've got to live together or we're all gonna kill each other.

KOBY

ROB A MAN OF HIS SURFING; PARACHUTE HIM INTO THE EYE OF A FOUR-DAY SNOWSTORM AND HE'S BOUND TO DO JUST ABOUT ANYTHING

When I busted my knee I started partying like a nutcase. I couldn't surf, so there was no sense even going to the beach. I didn't want to tease myself with what I was missing out on.

I'd blown my knee out while surfing Red Sands. It was a pretty big day, and I was paddling into a 10-footer, a thick one. I was paddling, paddling, paddling, when the thing has doubled up and the offshore wind started howling into my face. I couldn't see a thing. I'm in the lip, but I thought I could drop into it late, land it, and pull up into the barrel. So I went late, late, late, and I'm thinking, 'Yeah, I've got this, I'm gonna make it.' I landed at the bottom of it and shut my eyes. As I've pulled up under it, the lip has just gone *wham*, landed straight on top of my head and pushed me down through my board. The board snapped in three spots. When I floated to the surface I could feel a tweak in my knee, but it was in the middle of winter, a really cold day, so I couldn't really feel much of anything.

I've taken off on the next wave and gone to do a cutback and my knee just buckled. I knew straightaway it was gone, I'd done ligaments.

I couldn't surf for six months. I was hating the world. If I'm not going to go to the beach I might as well wake up hungover. I couldn't surf, I couldn't do anything. Jai had a broken leg for all those years. For two years Jai didn't get in the water because his leg was so bad. I reckon it really affected him, that time out of the water. It robbed him of his surfing and Jai was a guy who lived to surf. As a surfer you can't imagine what you go through if suddenly you can't surf for two years. It changes the people you hang out with, because all your mates are still off surfing. You see guys who it happens to and they start partying, they start hanging out in different circles. They don't see sun so much, and they get tempted into bad shit.

My average week was out every night, Tuesday to Sunday. Seriously. Tuesday night was half-price drinks at the uni; Wednesday nights Goodbar; Thursday night Beach Road at Bondi then on to Goodbar; Friday night Ladylux till all hours of the morning; Saturday night was Saturday night – everywhere; Sunday night Ravesi's and Sapphire and Hugos. Monday night sleep or just party it right through. For a year, bra, easy, that was my week. Just partying hard. I didn't have much money, but I didn't have to. Wherever I'd go I'd get free drinks, free coke, and there was just an endless supply of people to party with. That time out of the water changed me.

I was doing a lot of drugs at the time, doing things I swore I'd never do, and it's no wonder I eventually tried to kill myself. I was doing a lot of coke, and the night it happened I'd been four days without sleep. I was just completely scattered, the full coke psychosis. In that four days I did a lot of bad shit that I didn't respect myself for. But I just hated myself for the fact alone that I was doing coke, after all the shit my family has been through. I felt like, fuck, what's happened? I'd become the person that I hated.

I didn't feel like I *had* anything, didn't feel like I *wanted* anything. I just felt hollow. And it was a time when I should have felt like the king of the world. I was free, my brother was free. I'd lost a lot of money and the family's house, but that never bothered me. I don't give a fuck about material possessions. Things should have been great for me. But I felt right then that I had nothing.

I came home on my own late one night to my flat at North Maroubra. It was day four of my bender. I walked into the bathroom and just had a massive mirror moment. I was sitting there looking at myself and I hated what I saw.

I gave it a good go. I'd just grabbed the knife and went for it at my arm. I must have been that angry with myself that I figured I deserved it. Not really sure what happened then, but if my mate Chappo didn't walk in at six o'clock the next morning I wouldn't be here today, no doubt. He walked in and found me passed out on the lounge. He said the whole floor, the whole house, was covered in blood. He reckoned I must have been walking in circles, 'cause there was a giant blood circle in the lounge room.

Apparently there were coppers all over the landing and in the room, but I didn't see one of them. They just found me in the corner carrying the knife. The coppers couldn't get near me. Chappo had to talk me down, but I don't remember any of it. Apparently he was saying, 'Don't let them see you like this. Is this what you want?' You know, you're a bit twisted and fucked up if there's a room full of people there and you didn't see one of them.

I woke up in the hospital so embarrassed that I wish I didn't wake up at all. Like, did I just try and knock myself? I had a shocker. It took 160 stitches to fix. You can see the scars under the tatts on my arms. The doctor came in and told me I had blood infections. It wouldn't have been a pretty scene to walk into. It wouldn't have been a heroic or dignified way to go. But after all that, not one word got out. There were so many coppers and paramedics there I can't believe it never got out. That's one thing I really respect those police for.

Hair Bear was there at the hospital. He's a Bra Boy, a mate, and a professor of psychology and about a thousand other things. He was the only reason they discharged me from hospital and didn't put me in a mental asylum. He vouched for me and told them he wouldn't leave me until I was better. Ya know, when it all went down, I kind of would've rather been in a mental home for a while. I've always thought that since. I had a friend who done it; he'd gone through the same shit. We were talking about it and he's gone, 'The whole time, all I wanted was just some space. I didn't want the phone to ring. I didn't want people asking if I was okay.' He said, 'The mental home is full of nutcases, but it's the rest you need.'

I know why it happened when it did – when things were going well for me, and not a year before when everything was going to the dogs. If you do a four-day bender and put as much shit into your body as I did, you're going to come down real hard. When you take cocaine for four days, it gets you paranoid and it gets you thinking strange, bad shit. Then you realise that you've become what you've hated.

Jai knew about it. He come around and sat with me for a couple of days. He was really upset. I don't know if Sunny knew or not; I think he might have been overseas. I don't know which of the other boys knew. But Jai come and sat with me and cried with me. He wanted me to fix whatever was going on, stop doing the shit I was doing.

It's when you're doing really good, when you're up there flying, that the drugs happen. They come along with it. Everything was going so well for me. I was free, I had my mates, I had waves. I wasn't thinking straight and it was the drugs that did it, nothing else. To get to that point was just a shocker. I might not respect my life but it doesn't mean I don't respect myself so little that I wanna kill myself.

I think I needed to get through that stage to get to where I'm at now. I'm a lot happier. I think I had to know where the bottom was to know which way up was. I see now that I do love life, and I love the life I have; I just don't respect it. I'm not even sure myself exactly what the distinction is. But I'll never allow myself to get like that again. It happened and I fucked up and it's life. I've thought to myself in the years since: 'Wow, is that what it happened over? Four days on the woof?' But I still look at sharp knives today and I think about that night.

Part 8
Beyond
Happy Valley

SUNNY

A VALIANT ATTEMPT TO SECURE THE THUMBS UP
FROM MAXIMUS

The movie took four years to make. The contract we'd signed said two.

But with the shooting and the court case still going, there was no way we could finish it. I still had total creative control over it, so although I wasn't being paid for the last two years, I wouldn't put the thing out half-arsed. I wasn't gonna sign off on the movie until it was ready. And every time I thought it was ready, some other shit would go down and the cameras would keep rolling.

I was spending my rent money on video stock. I had some savings, but I'd already spent all of that. I'd spent $55,000 on Jai and Koby, so we were all on the bones of our arse. Jai had been locked up, Koby had been arrested, we'd lost three properties ... but through all this we were still pushing on with the film. It was all falling apart around us, but the film kept rolling. We had no money, I was driving a shitbox car, and it was frustrating. I was lucky in that my co-pilot on the movie was a guy named Michael Lawrence, and he really supported me through those years. I'd gone to school with him at Maroubra Bay High, and he'd become a successful businessman. We'd stayed close over the years, and when I pitched the movie to him he signed straight on as the executive producer.

But when I began telling other people about what I was trying to get across with the movie, I never felt anyone got it. I'd been researching the history of Maroubra, and it struck me that its whole history has been about class struggle. I went to the library and spent days reading. I read about the local Koori tribes and how they'd been treated once the white man got here. I read how a shantytown called Happy Valley had sprung up behind Maroubra in the early 1900s. I read how the missionaries had banned all the Aborigines from swimming in the surf. I read about how

MY BROTHERS KEEPER

the police had banned the lower classes from swimming in the surf and how they'd formed a group called the Sun Club to defy the coppers. I read about the first surfers at Maroubra being banned from riding surfboards. And the more I read the more it became clear that the Bra Boys were just another Maroubra tribe in a long series of tribes who've been locked in this class battle with the powers that be. And it hit me: *that was the story*. That was the movie – the whole class struggle, the struggle of the Maroubra tribes culminating in the Bra Boys today.

I was trying to get the message across that even though the Bra Boys' story might be unique in what's happened to us, it could also have happened to any one of those past generations and tribes in Maroubra. And in a lot of ways it did. We were just the latest incarnation, the latest tribe. A lot of those guys in the RIP section at the end of the movie were from those past generations; they were guys who didn't make it – surfers and chargers who didn't come through the tunnel. Maroubra got 'em – jail, drugs, suicide. We knew it would be controversial, we knew people would be confronted by it, but we also hoped people would be moved by it and understand what was going on underneath, the social undercurrents that flow through it. We hoped they'd see the positivity through the struggle. And after the utter negativity and lies being spread about us, we had to tell our side of the story.

I was originally going to feature another family's struggle to illustrate what living in Maroubra can be like. I didn't want the Abbertons to be the focus of it. But then the shooting brought the focus squarely on to our family and we had no choice. From there the movie took its own course; it played out in real time in front of us. We lived it. We tried to end the movie about half-a-dozen times, and each time something else would crop up – Jai being acquitted, Koby escaping jail time, Ma passing away, the Cyclops session, the Cronulla riots. We were just rolling with it as it all happened. We had no idea where it was going to end.

I knew even three years before we finished that we'd get Russell Crowe to work with us on the movie. When I was writing the story I imagined a voice narrating it, and that voice was Russell's. We were trying to break out of the surf market. We thought the story was worthy of a wider audience, and we knew we needed someone like Russell to help us do it. The producers were screaming at us to finish the film – and everyone wanted us to show it to Russell. I said, 'Russell doesn't wanna know anything about a half-arsed film. We've got one shot at it.' I wasn't about to show him anything until I knew it was ready.

Early on, we'd told John Sutton, who plays for Russell's football team, the South Sydney Rabbitohs, that we wanted to pitch the film to him. I went overseas for a month and while I was gone the producers got onto Russell and sent him a shitty rough trailer that I hated. I spewed that they'd showed him. Sure enough, Russell said he hated it. I thought that was our one shot and we'd butchered it. But Koby and Michael Lawrence said to Russell, 'Look, wait till Sunny's back from overseas. He really wants to speak to you.'

I got back and called Russell, grovelling, trying to get an audience with him. He goes, 'I'll give you half an hour in the morning. Bring your running shoes.'

So at 6.30 the next morning we were running around the Botanical Gardens, me pitching him the movie as we went. He'd read most of the typical press on the Bra Boys, but he'd also seen the *Australian Story* on us, and that was what interested him enough to take our call. He knew there was a little bit more than he'd read in the papers.

Anyway, I'm pitching, pitching, pitching, and it just wasn't working.

'Russ, I don't think you understand the movie I'm trying to make. It's about *the struggle*.'

I told him about the 1890 law that banned swimming on Maroubra Beach between the hours of 6am to 6pm because those hours were supposed to be reserved for those 'in meaningful employment and not scoundrels who chose to shamelessly bathe in the surf instead of working'. He stopped in his tracks. That was the line that got him.

'Hmm, now that sounds interesting.'

He's kept running and hasn't said much. We went up into Darlinghurst, had a juice, and he said, 'All right, it sounds good, but I want to see it when it's finished.' So he'd showed a little interest, but I knew we only had one more shot at getting him involved.

When it was about 90 per cent finished we organised a private screening for him. We'd never asked Russell to narrate it, and we're not sure whether he twigged that that was what we were really after. We'd tried three or four narrators by this stage, including Brendan Cowell. He was actually a little bit *too* good; we had to cut him because we were sure Russell would never narrate it while Brendan was doing such a good job. We deliberately used a mix of four narrators, so it sounded a bit disjointed and it'd red flag the narration when Russ watched it.

So there we were. It was me and Russell in a cinema all by ourselves, with Macario De Souza – my co-director – and Koby a few aisles back. Russell watched the whole thing and didn't say a word. Not a thing. Didn't flinch, didn't blink; no expression at all, totally impassive. It was like sitting next to Maximus. It was fully uncomfortable. I'm sitting there watching him and he's like a statue. Did he like it? Did he hate it? Was he awake?

Anyway, the film's got two endings: there's a false ending, then the multicultural part follows where some of the Bra Boys talk about where their families have come from. The film ended – the first ending – and without saying a word Russell gets up and starts walking to the aisle. Even though I knew there was more coming, I get up and follow him and the next bit of the film starts. It's awkward, as we're both standing in the aisle watching it.

As we walk out I go, 'So, whaddaya think?' I was just holding my breath, dying.

He says, 'Let's go get a coffee.'

He was really stringing me out. As we go outside I've got this big smile on my face, trying to mask the fact I was shitting myself.

'So, Russ, whaddaya think?'

'The good news or the bad news?' Then he smiles and goes, 'Nah, I love it.' We yakked about the movie for an hour.

But I know there are windows of opportunity in life that present themselves at a time and a place, and we really didn't give him a chance to say no. I asked him about bits of the movie and his opinion. Then I asked him what he thought about the narration.

'Shithouse.'

Without even drawing a breath I fired it out there.

'Will you do it?'

'For sure.'

We knew we had one chance and it worked. And Russell was so good after that; he gave us so much advice on how to go with distribution, how much we should control the film ... everything to the speeches on the opening night. He fully mentored us. When our movie wasn't doing well in Melbourne, he even spent 20 grand of his own money on pole posters and marketing down there. It was cool.

He ended up buying the rights of the documentary to make a feature film. We really trusted him. It was because of the whole way that he presented himself; and everything he said he would do, he did. He helped out with Koby's benefit night, his band played; he didn't charge us for the documentary. He really believed in the project and he wanted to try and make it work.

It's still a bit surreal when your phone rings and occasionally it's Russell Crowe. But he's a normal bloke, and the more normally you treat him the more he likes it. One afternoon he and Peter Holmes à Court called in to the Maroubra Bay Hotel and had a beer with us. The night the Rabbitohs got back into the NRL, he got us all a limo and got us out to the ground. We really tried to give him that working-class support which is the Rabbitohs' bread and butter. He's a knockabout bloke who loves the battler story, and he could see we were very much part of that culture. He's a guy who doesn't like to take shit and he's a guy who's big on mutual respect.

The night before the premiere, I was lying in bed thinking about all the shit that had happened – the shooting, court, the swells, the riot, the whole rollercoaster ride – and how surreal it was that we were going to be at the State Theatre at this huge, star-studded premiere. I imagined us up on stage in front of everyone, and then someone comes out of the crowd and walks up and shoots me. And I swear to God, I thought it'd be a fitting ending. I really did. Shot down on stage. It didn't scare me; I thought it'd make sense ... and it wasn't out of the realms of possibility. It'd make a sick bonus feature on the DVD.

I woke up next morning to a phone call from Michael Lawrence asking me to meet him for breakfast. When I got there he tells me there'd been a hand-delivered death threat dropped in to the State Theatre. It said that if me or Koby got up on stage we'd be killed. I kind of just laughed. I was blown away by how in tune I was with my ending. In what was then an ironical turn of events, it was the police now trying to protect us. They demanded the security be upgraded; they wanted metal detectors on the doors, and they wanted us to wear bulletproof vests. We stressed that we didn't want to make a big deal of it. The last thing we wanted to do was scare all the celebrities from turning up. But because the threat had been hand delivered and not phoned in, they thought it was fair dinkum; they saw it as a serious threat.

We told them we wouldn't wear bulletproof vests. We figured if someone really wanted us dead it'd be a lot easier to find us down the beach at Maroubra rather than to pull a gun in front of a thousand people. But it certainly added to the adrenaline of the whole night. With all the police warnings about it, and police advising celebrities not to show up, it was as if the powers that be were intent on us not succeeding.

I remember being nervous before reading some of the first reviews. The movie meant so much to me that the thought of it being publicly picked to pieces rattled me. But we got a standing ovation at our first press screening, and the first reviewers all really liked it. Margaret from *The Movie Show* gave us four stars, while her offsider David hated it and gave it one star, which I thought was classic. I tried to not watch anything or read anything, not get caught up in the hype. It was a bonus that people liked it, but I was happier that people understood it and got the message we were trying to get across. It even made the Govinda's list. That's when I knew we'd really made it. You could now watch the *Bra Boys* while eating a vegetable korma served by the Hare Krishnas.

We woke up from the Gold Coast premiere super hungover then drove down to Byron where we were screening that night. When we get into Byron, there was the biggest line of people stretching down the main street. We go, 'Fuck, what's on?' Then we realised they were there for the movie, in *Byron* of all places. I couldn't think of anywhere more different to Maroubra, and yet there's 700 people there to see the movie. That was the third screening, and that was when it really hit us that this thing was taking off.

For me, the movie was about everyday people dealing with real-life struggles. I just tried to show it for what it was. We got some criticism that it was one-sided, but it's all there. What really shit me about the claims that we weren't being objective was that we weren't even talking about all the harassment we've endured over the years from the cops. It could have been so easy to nail them, turn the movie into a vendetta, but we just stuck to our story.

We tried to see through all the bullshit, and see what was really special about the community here, and that was the bond of friends and the brotherhood in the area, and the fact that it's had a long history of it. The Bra Boys just didn't grow out of the sand on Maroubra Beach one day; they're the evolution of the groups of surfers who have been calling Maroubra Beach home for decades.

We've had so much bullshit from the press and the establishment over the years that here was our one chance to actually say for ourselves what we really are. It might have seemed one-sided, but could you blame us? There's so much bullshit floating around out there about us, so much insinuation, that anything new just gets referenced against all that same old shit and keeps perpetuating itself. This was our chance to break that cycle. When someone can look at the story and see it for what it really is, hopefully they'll get the message. The movie's not made for film critics and uni professors in tweed jackets with suede elbow patches; it's for the people who grew up like us. And many people have come up to me and said, 'The movie has inspired me.'

It's encouraging people from tough backgrounds to bond together to make their communities more liveable. It's about not judging. Ma told us not to judge someone by how much money they had in their pocket or by the way they look. From a very early age it was expected that because we were the kids of heroin addicts, kids from the housos, that we'd perpetuate that cycle. That's always been expected of us. We were trying to show that there's a way out.

And the only way the story was going to get told right was if it was told from the inside out.

KOBY

THE DAY HOLLYWOOD CALLED AND WAS POLITELY TOLD TO GET FUCKED

My phone rings. 'Koby, it's Russell Crowe here.'

'Yeah, sure you are, buddy. Get fucked.'

I thought it was one of me mates fucking with me, so I've hung up on him. Then I got an email a couple of days later saying, 'Koby, it's Russell Crowe here. Give me a call.' I wrote back, 'Whoever this is, stop fucking around with me!' Then Johnny Sutton, a Bra Boy who plays for Russell's footy team, South Sydney, sees me down the beach.

'Bra, Russell's been trying to contact you. He says you've been telling him to get fucked.'

'*What!*'

We were filming the documentary at the time, and we started seeing quite a bit of Russ. There'd be 50 of the boys in the pub going mad and he'd just sit there sucking schooners with us, talking away, hanging out. Mate, he's just like one of the boys. He was risking big money and his reputation hanging out with us, but he's one of those people who can walk into any conversation or any situation and be comfortable with it.

Me, Jai and John Sutton went up to Russell's farm at Coffs Harbour. We had a lot of fun. We turned up to Sydney Airport, got on his private plane and *boom*, we're up there in 40 minutes. He's got this beautiful big piece of land. There's 20 dirt bikes, so we're just ripping it up on them. He's also got 10 Harleys. As soon as we get up there he sets out the ground rules.

'There's only one rule out here, and that's don't ride the Harleys. They're my pride and joy.'

Next morning at seven o'clock I'm on the best Harley in his collection, just fanging up the road. He comes out screaming.

'Get the fuck off that bike! How many times have I fucking told ya!'

'Sorry, bra, I couldn't help it.'

He just smiles at me and goes, 'Just get the fuck off it.'

The next day we went riding out in the mountains on the dirt bikes with Peter Holmes à Court, who co-owned Souths with Russ. We didn't know what to think of Pete at first, because he comes across a bit dry, so we thought we better test him out. We're coming up the top of this hill and I pulled over and flagged him down.

'Fuck, Pete, I've broke me leg! I've broke me leg!'

He goes, 'Holy shit!' He gets off his bike and goes, 'Where?'

'Down near me ankle!'

And as he bends down to look at it I just gun the bike and give him the biggest mud shower. Everyone looks back and we're pissing ourselves. Then we get down the bottom and he's disappeared. I'm riding past and I hear, 'Koby!' I look around and he throws a big handful of mud straight into me face. Then it's on: we're chasing each other, trying to knock each other off. Russ had given us a warning: 'Don't ride into the paddocks, you'll scare the horses.' All of a sudden I'm flying around in the paddocks, and because they were wet I was doing these big 360s. Then the front wheel has grabbed and I've gone straight over the handlebars and landed on my head. I look up and here's Russ.

'I told you not to go in the fucking paddocks!'

I'm just on the deck laughing, going, 'Sorry, mate, couldn't help it.'

Russell had a big family dinner that night. His whole family live on the farm – his brothers, his mum, his dad, his uncle – and he has a chef who cooks all day long. We played bocce, we rode horses, motorbikes, quadbikes. It was mad fun. There's that much land up there, bra. It's like Maroubra to La Perouse. Big mountains, big hills; it's such a beautiful place. The surf's only 15 minutes from there and he's got 20 surfboards.

He's got everything, everything you could imagine. We're just guys from Maroubra, going, 'How good is this?'

JAI

WHY 2035 IS GREATER THAN 90069 AND A BAMBOO FLOOR WILL ALWAYS TRUMP A RED CARPET

I used to have Sunny's name tattooed on me arm, but I took it off with a lighter and a knife.

He spoke pretty loud and clear to me in that movie of his. I hardly seen him when I was in jail. I seen him at the start, then I didn't see him after that. But I saw him in court when he had his camera. It's not my style, but he spoke loud and clear to me through that documentary of his.

For me, bra, it was a lot to get on the TV and be interviewed about that night for their movie. I only did it because they'd lost their precious houses. I don't care about houses or money.

They lost their houses so I thought I'd do it for them, get on their documentary and try and get some money back for 'em. Then Sunny didn't even come to me and say, 'This is what I'm running. Is this okay with you?' If I'd signed off on it, do you think I'd be so angry?

Bra, I could get knocked on the street in a heartbeat for getting on telly and talking about that night. I wanna stay out of trouble, but who knows what's gonna happen in the future? The cops hate me. There's a big chance I could walk back into jail any day. It's been three-and-a-half years since I got out and I haven't gone back yet.

What's good for Sunny isn't always what's good for me. I'm the loyalest person in the world. For me to turn my back on you, it's for a big reason. I just guess some people put money before morals. I'd much rather be back where we were before all this happened. I'd rather not have any of it. Leave me out of it.

And when his movie got big and they turned into celebrities, I didn't want nothing to do with it. I headed the other way. Koby was into me, going, 'Come to Hollywood with us.' What have I got in common with those people over there? I'd rather be up The Block with my Koori mates. What am I gonna talk to Hollywood people like Paris Hilton about? I'd rather be sleeping on a bamboo floor in an Indonesian village. I'd rather be with the real boys in Hawaii, Redfern, Wreck Bay or the Bra.

Hollywood? *Please*.

KOBY

SHOOTING WILDEBEEST WITH JOHN SINGLETON REMINDS OUR HERO THAT HE'S NOTHING MORE THAN A SURFER

John Singleton rings me up the other day.

'You want to come up the farm and shoot some *wildebeest*?'

I had no idea know what he was talking about, but he's always ringing me up with crazy shit like that. We're as crazy as each other I reckon, so it's no surprise we get on. I'll ring him up and say, 'What's doing, Dad? When are we teaming up?'

'Where are ya, son? What are ya doing, ya little poofter?'

John's got a stable of kids, but he's a full father figure to all these people around him as well, me included. They all love him. He's a gem. You don't get many people like that, and I was lucky to meet him.

When we were doing the *Bra Boys* movie, he was bringing out Bondi Blonde beer around the same time. I think he was curious to meet us. He's pretty good at spotting a diamond in the rough. Not saying I'm a diamond or anything, you know what I mean.

Johnny Gannon used to train a mate of John and Jack Singleton's, and Johnny passed on the message that John and Jack wanted to meet us.

I knew John as the bloke who shouted the whole racecourse beers when he won. Everyone knows John Singleton. He's an Aussie icon, the larrikin advertising millionaire.

We went to meet him at his offices in the city. Me, Johnny Gannon and Frog walk in; there's no one there, so I go straight to the bar fridge, grab a beer and start skolling it. John walks in.

'Ya comfy there, mate? Can I get you anything?' Straight into me.

'Nah, mate, all good. I found the fridge. Nice view from up here.'

We were pretty well mates straightaway. We had a talk and he's pegging us with some questions, just starting a bit of conversation to get a feel for whether he liked us or not. But it all went pretty good. We talked about the movie, and he talked about his beer, and then as the meeting was coming to an end, he goes, 'Koby, here's my number. Call us whenever ya like, mate.'

A couple of weeks later I did.

'What are ya doing? I'm down at North Bondi Italian. Come down for this Bondi Blonde party we're having,' he says. It was a launch for the beer and all the owners were there. So me, Sunny, Frog and Johnny all rock in just as he's doing his speech. He's just being a ratbag, pretty much classic John, and we get on the piss together. The boys left and John goes, 'Let's go upstairs to the RSL and go for a punt.' He's a mad punter, and he's got $10,000 on this horse. He's saying to me, 'Let's go halves.'

'Nah, look, John, I haven't got the money.'

'C'mon, ya little poofter, grow some balls.' The horse was the fourth horse in a quaddy. He'd won the first three races, so he needed this horse to win to clean up a lot of money, and he was trying to cut me in on it. The final horse was only paying a dollar fifty, so it was always going to win.

'Look, you can pay me back.'

'John, that was a tough bet. I'm not gonna come in and take ya winnings.

'Whatever ... ya poofter.'

We walked upstairs into the RSL club, carrying our beers in with us from downstairs. When we walk in the door with these beers, this young guy comes flying over.

'You can't bring your beers up here,' he says.

John goes, 'Mate, I can bring my beer up here if I want. I'm not hurting anyone.'

'You can't bring your beer up here.'

The guy had no idea who Singo was – one of the most famous Australians going round – and at that stage even I didn't know that Singo owned the fucking building the RSL is in. John just goes, 'You're fucking kidding, aren't ya?' Then all of a sudden the bloke gets shirty with John.

'Mate, you're gonna have to leave and take your beer with you.'

I'm just looking at John going, 'Don't worry about it, mate. Let's just skol our beers and walk in.'

As John starts skolling his schooner, the guy reaches over and tries to take the schooner glass out of his hand. I'm skolling mine meanwhile, just following John. The guy goes to John, *'I told you, mate!'*

John kind of looks at me as if to go, you got my back here? Then he turns to the guy.

'You know what, mate, I got one good fight left in me I reckon, and you're going pretty close to being it!'

In the end we broke it up. We went in and we're watching the race and John's muttering, having a little blow-up.

John's horse got up and he ended up collecting $190,000. He'd tried his best to cut me in on a certain 95 grand, which kind of blew me away. It blew me away even more that I'd knocked it back. But I think John secretly liked the fact I did. It showed him I wasn't hanging around him to get anything; I was just there as a mate to watch the race with him … and stop him trying to fight bouncers.

About half an hour later the guy from the door comes over and looks at John.

'I'm sorry about that, Mr Singleton.' Someone had obviously pulled the guy aside and said, 'Bra, you almost fought John Singleton, the owner of the whole place.'

John goes, 'Yeah, well you were lucky, 'cause I would've given it to ya!'

The guy's like, 'I'm sorry, mate, I was having a bad day.'

I said, 'Mate, there's a way to do that stuff. Just tell us we can't take our drinks in but don't get in our faces about it.'

John goes, 'Shut up, Koby, ya wimp.' He turns to the guy and says, 'Mate, what sort of job would ya like?'

'Well, err, I'm just cleaning and picking up glasses at the moment.'

'Well you pick a job here you like and you can have it. I like your style.' John promoted him for trying to stand up to him.

That was my introduction to the world of John Singleton.

John's pretty loose with his contracts; it was a bit of a gentleman's agreement between us with the Bondi Blonde gig. He just said, 'We're gonna have some fun with it. We want ya to be there. It's more of a piss-up than a job.'

'I'm in.'

Shooting the Bondi Blonde ad was fun. We shot it down in the corner at South Maroubra. I ride this big wave all the way to shore, pull off in the shorebreak in waist-deep water, someone throws me a beer and tells me how much I'm ripping. Then the chick, Jamie, comes up from underwater where me cock is, I skol the beer, and at the bottom of the screen scrolls, 'Nothing goes down like a Bondi Blonde.'

It was all done in good humour, but it got banned within about five minutes. I wouldn't say it was distasteful. There are worse ads out there, for sure. I think Singo just wanted to get it on TV as a laugh. It would've been the best ad in the history of ads.

As part of the Bondi Blonde campaign, they ran a Miss Bondi Blonde bikini contest, and they invited Paris Hilton over for a week as part of it. I kind of chaperoned her around, hanging out, partying, having a good time.

On the day of the Miss Bondi Blonde contest, I'm hanging at Icebergs with John. Me and John are blind by midday, skolling beers. He starts getting pissed, I'm pissed. At lunch I'm eating a plate of spaghetti. John reaches into my spaghetti and grabs a handful and just mashes it into his mouth. Bra, it's hot, and he's got spaghetti sauce all down the front of his shirt.

'Fuck, John, what are ya doing?'

I take my jumper off and give it to him. He just pulls his collar out and walks off like nothing happened. What a legend. After we've been drinking all morning, he gets up on stage for the press conference. As you'd expect with Paris there, there's a thousand press, and the first question he's asked is, 'Why did you pick Koby?'

Without missing a beat he's gone, 'Why do ya think? I rooted his mum. *I'm his father!'*

The place has just gone nuts. I can hardly see through the tears. I'm thinking right there this is the best bloke I've ever met. I'm crying, thinking, what is he gonna say next?

He taught me one thing that's stuck with me: if you're serious, every little stupid thing you say is gonna be quoted to make you look like an idiot, but if you act like an idiot, every serious thing you say is quoted. If you're too serious the silly things get quoted, if you're too silly the serious things get quoted. I'm thinking, 'Fuck, here we go; that quote's gonna be all over the papers the next day.'

Not a word of it. He said, 'Koby, son, the more you say the less that gets written about you, because they all start to think you're a complete and utter nutcase.'

We had a mad day after that. I hung out with Paris that night, but I didn't fuck her like some people thought I did. When her boyfriend Stavros turned up a couple of days later, I gave them some boards and we all went surfing.

John was having a ball with us for that whole week as well. I get on really well with John's son, Jack, too, He's a good bloke. And John's daughters and his whole family are cool. When you hang with John it's always a big family thing; he's on the phone the whole time to his kids. I wish he'd adopted me when I was five instead of adopting me when I was 27.

He's the dad I wish I had, an absolute fucking legend. But he's a ratbag. A full larrikin ratbag like no one I've ever met. He's a 20-year-old stuck in a 60-year-old rich businessman's body.

He's been bankrupt six times and bounced back every time. When I was declared bankrupt I rang him and asked him what I should do.

'Grow up, ya little girl. I've been bankrupt six times. Stop ya whinging and move on.' I just laughed. He says, 'Koby, you've got to focus. The times I went bankrupt I was trying to be something that I wasn't. Koby, you're a surfer. Don't get caught up in all this movie shit. You will go bankrupt if you try and do something else. You've been given a gift; don't fuck with it.'

And it was so true. The times I was going no good, like when I stabbed myself, was because I wasn't focused on my surfing. Singo said to me, 'I always thought of myself as the second best ad person in the world, after my mate. The times I went broke were when I was fucking around doing other things and getting off the path. You're a surfer and I make ads.'

In the years after I met him and when I started getting a bit of a profile, I noticed that his words really came into play. He's like, 'Never lose focus on what you are and what you do.' And those words really helped me. After the Bondi Blonde ad, things took off for me. I'd be walking down the street and all of a sudden someone would be trying to take my photo. I'd go into a club and there'd be 90 people trying to talk to me. Sometimes you can get a bit ahead of yourself, but I always remember what John told me.

'You're just a surfer. That's all you are, buddy.'

SUNNY

TWENTY OUT, THE BRA BOYS FRANKLY GO TO HOLLYWOOD

Our whole plan was to get to the States.

Our plan was to pick up a distribution company that would give us the clout and publicity in Australia to take us on to America. We're just lucky that it actually worked. We got picked up by Berkela Films, who are basically the leading action sports film distributor in the US. The owners of the company, Sal Masakela and Jason Bergh, both also cross into the celebrity scene. Sal hosts *E!* and Jason is a music video director who's made clips for everyone from Justin Timberlake to Wolfmother. What we were trying to do was cross this surf film over into a bigger pond. Sal's a surfer as well, so not only did they have the connections to take the project where we wanted it to go, but they believed in it as well. They came from a skate and surf background; that's why we went with them and that's why it all worked. They were on our level.

That first trip to the States was wild. We jumped on a plane and it was all systems go. We really wanted to keep the thing snowballing. It was daunting, taking this pokey little backyard flick to the States, but we found that you can't underestimate yourself over there. Any signs of weakness and you'll get eaten alive. They can give you that feeling that you're the Aussie bumpkin, the country cousin, and take advantage of that. But that can also work in your favour as well, ya know. I think that's why Aussies do well over there; they're down-to-earth, and they just want to get the job done and have a cold beer afterwards.

The Huntington Beach Film Festival was our first screening. I've seen the movie a million times by this stage, so I can't really watch it all, but I knew there's a couple of trigger points in the first five minutes of the film where people will laugh or gasp. I was dying to know how this was going to go, and sure enough the American audience laughed and gasped in exactly the right spots. I went out to the bar and had a few drinks on my own and came back in for the last five minutes, and people were laughing and cheering and we ended up with a full-on standing ovation. We won the festival.

We were living in Santa Monica for the first part of our time in the US. There was me, Koby and his girl Tahyna renting a two-bedroom apartment in the heart of Santa Monica. By the time we had our first press screening, we had 19 guys staying in there. We organised for all the Maroubra boys to come over, partly to say thanks for all their help on the film, but mainly just to go mad over there. We wanted a big crew. I think it's a bit easier to make an impact 12-out instead of one- or two-out.

We hired the Polaroid House, right on Malibu Beach, for the after-party for our first press screening. It was the happening mansion. It's two doors up from Paris Hilton's place, where we'd been hanging in the week before the screening.

We'd met Paris in Australia while she and Koby were working on the Bondi Blonde beer commercial a few months before. She and Koby had become friends and had been texting each other. Jason, our distributor, his missus is a Playboy model and is best mates with Paris, so before we know it we're all kinda hanging out at Paris' house for the week, which was sweet, but just a little surreal at the same time.

One day Paris said she wanted to learn how to surf. There were only little waves, so Koby and I got the boards out and took Paris and Tahyna surfing. We'd seen the paparazzi and stuff lurking outside her house, but it was a real eye-opener to see first hand what those stars go through. The paparazzi just surrounded us. Koby was the main one giving her surf lessons, but I pushed her into a couple. She took off on a couple of full-on shoredumpers. We were pushing her onto these waves and she was going face-first, neck-first, into the sand. Paris had asked me to take a photo of her on a wave. Koby pushes her on a wave and she goes face-first into the sand. She comes up with sand all over her face and her bikini top around her waist. So I've taken the snap. There was a photo in *OK!* mag where I looked like this mad, creepy paparazzo who'd just come out of the water to get the tit shot. Hanging with Paris Hilton was like we were on another planet, but we were just running with it, laughing at it. She was such a cool chick, really mellow, and the whole week was a lot of fun.

The Polaroid House, where we had the after-party, is double level, with three giant party sections. It was black tie service, five-star catering, lobster, prawns and cocktails. We had this full-on beach party, and it was just rocking. There was a biplane flying overhead trailing a sign that read 'Malibu welcomes the Bra Boys to America'. There were half-naked chicks everywhere, random glamours, celebrities. It wasn't quite Friday night at the Maroubra Bay pub, but it'd do for now. Here we are, guys who've grown up together in the streets of Maroubra, and we're all just looking at each other going, 'What the fuck! Where are we again?' Hollywood types all walking around, and us all tatted up in boardies, drinking beer.

It started getting a bit rowdy. Brandon Davis was there, the oil heir. He's a really funny guy, but later in the night he started paying out on some of the chicks. He was being hilarious, but at the same time also being the full chick repellent. By this stage there were only 20 girls left in the place and a heap of guys, so we said, 'C'mon, mate, take it easy. The chicks are leaving.'

He's still carrying on like a pork chop. It was all funny, but he just kept running with it. We were going, 'Brandon, chill out, mate. You're scaring the chicks away.'

It started getting a bit raucous. One of the boys told him to pull it up, and Brandon just laughed in his face, so next thing he's choked Brandon out. Put him to sleep. All the Hollywood crew are like, 'Ahhh, you've killed him!'

We're like, 'It's okay; he's just having a little sleep.'

Brandon was lying on the ground; then his eyes opened and he looked up and pointed.

'Aren't you the guy in the movie?'

We all cracked up. We pulled him to his feet and kept drinking with him.

That night we stayed there, and around 10 o'clock the next morning the estate agent has come in and gone, 'You guys have gotta leave.' I'd just ducked up the road; when I come back, everyone's packing up to leave. I just went, 'Where are you guys going?'

'We're being kicked out.'

'Whoah! We're here at Malibu in a mansion full of beer and food, and you wanna go back to Koby's apartment with 19 of us on the floor? Boys, we're not going anywhere.' So we refused to leave. The owners were trying to kick us out, and we're going, 'You're gonna have to build a bigger fence than that!' That became our motto for the whole American tour. Anyway, we stayed to about nine that night before they finally got us out of there.

After the opening we did a whistlestop tour of the States with 12 screenings, east coast to west coast. We had these big vans to cruise around in and we went to so many different, un-Maroubra kinds of places. We still didn't know how the movie was going to be received in places like New York, though. We thought that the idea of brotherhood would be pretty universal but we didn't know if people were going to understand it in Australia, let alone America.

New York was super cool. We ended up doing something underground in New York; me and Koby introduced the New York premiere to a full mix of people – old, young, black, white, none of them surfers. One of the promoters who had a penthouse in Trump Towers organised this barbecue for us with 50 models, the most beautiful girls I'd ever seen. Where are we? But the really sad part of it was that we had to walk away from it. A room of 50 hot chicks and we're like, 'We've got to go home, we're on *Good Morning America* in the morning.' Everything was so tightly packed that parties blurred into interviews which blurred into premieres and more parties.

We did *Good Morning America*, which was really nerve-racking, and the next morning we were booked to do a radio spot on ABC. Apparently it's got nine million listeners or something ridiculous. We'd turned into pumpkins the night before, dragged ourselves home by midnight because we knew we had to be up early the next morning for the interview. I went home but Koby escaped and stayed out all night.

That morning when we went and picked up Koby he was still blind and he stunk of stale piss. I said to our publicist Nancy Carlson, 'Look, I think you should scratch Koby from this interview; he's not up for it.'

'No, no, we want him there.' She was fully adamant.

The interview was a little more highbrow, socially and politically, and in the state Koby was in he was going to be lucky to remember his own name. When we picked Koby up the first thing he does is wind down the window and chunder. We pulled over and got some water for him, let him clean himself up a bit, and he's going, 'Yeah, I'm sweet.' He now stunk like stale piss *and* spew.

Our giant limo pulls up out the front of the studio and we walk up the path to go in. As we get closer to the doors I'm getting stuck into Koby: 'Come on, mate, this is serious.' Nancy's going, 'Come on, Koby, this is serious.' All of a sudden I look around and Koby is as white as a ghost. He's gone, 'Hang on a sec.' We're out the front of the studio and he's got a bottle of water, tipping it over his head, blowing snot out his nose. Nancy's going, 'Shit, I hope no one comes out.' We're at the door to the studio, about to be interviewed in front of nine million people, and Koby's stopped and fired the biggest projectile spew you've ever seen, right outside the foyer, then backed it up with two more spews. I've seen him spew a lot, big projectile chunders, but these were in a new league. Fuck knows what he'd been drinking.

After we'd cleaned him up we went in to the studio. The lady interviewing us was quite serious and straight. They put us in a booth on our own for the interview with headphones on, which might have had something to do with the smell of Koby. Anyway, Koby has mumbled and slurred and burped and stuttered through the whole interview. I had to cut in and save him on about 20 occasions. She'd ask him a question, he'd get halfway through some kind of answer and then forget what he was talking about, and go, 'What were we talking about again?' Thankfully the interview wasn't live. The next day the interview goes to air; we're in Berkela's office waiting to hear it. The interviewer goes, 'I'm here this morning with Sunny Abberton from the Bra Boys ...' They'd completely wiped Koby out of the interview – luckily.

We partied a lot in New York, and it was good to cut loose with Koby, even if it meant he was a nightmare to deal with the next day. We got taken to this club called The Box, which is the coolest, strangest club I've ever been to in my life. It was kinda like Moulin Rouge meets *Hustler* meets New York performance art. It's like an old cinema with different levels in it. When we walked in the place was pumping. They run three shows during the night. In the first show there was this black guy with dyed blond hair, this weird, shirtless, androgynous guy, and there's a queen size bed with five beautiful, topless blondes all kissing and fondling on top of it. Meanwhile the guy has started delivering this monologue on sex. All of a sudden this big lump has started rising up out of the bed; then the sheet gets thrown off and it's a midget. He jumps out and starts chasing the girls around the stage. Then this girl comes out and gives birth to a rubber baby. Another girl comes in and chews through the rubber umbilical cord with her teeth and dropkicks the baby into the crowd. It might have been because we came from Maroubra, but we couldn't quite work it out. Then they asked for a volunteer. There were 10 naked girls up on stage. We pushed Koby up there and he's had this massive pillow fight with all these topless chicks. It was the coolest, most artistic, fucked-up club I've ever been to. We spent 15 grand of the film company's money in there that night.

From New York it was back to California for the Surfer Poll Awards. It's kind of like surfing's Oscars, the biggest night in the surfing world. We had a heap of the boys from home with us, 'cause we were nominated for six awards.

The day of the awards we went surfing with a Californian mate of ours, Jesse Billauer. Jesse's a paraplegic who runs his own foundation to get people with similar injuries back in the water surfing again. The guy can fully surf. He lies down on his board and cruises across the wave, turning, getting tubed, but he just needs someone to paddle him into it. It was unbelievable watching him, so inspirational.

With us that day was this Canadian motocross rider who'd recently been left a paraplegic after a crash. His dream was to go surfing. He'd been hooked up with Jesse and here he was, ready to go. Jesse knew we were in town and asked us to come down with them and take this guy surfing. We were all there; there was me, Johnny Gannon, Jack Kingsley and a whole lot of our crew. We're almost at the beach when Jack gets a phone call from his mum. She tells him that his old man has just passed away. We got to the beach and the whole lot of us are almost in tears, 'cause we've known Jack and his family since we were eight. We asked Jack if he wanted us to go back to the hotel and he said, 'No, we're going surfing. Let's not let this guy down.'

The feeling in the water was so powerful, the emotions full on. Jesse and the other guys didn't know what was going on with us, but we all swam out, Jack included, and took this guy surfing. The look on his face on that first wave was something I'll never forget.

We'd had this really emotional day, and the awards were that night. We got a 20-seater limo to pick us up from Koby's place in Malibu, and it's full of Bra Boys. We get there and it was the full red carpet. We get into this massive hall with the whole of the surf industry there, and they've put us right at the front of the stage. There's three reserved tables with 'Bra Boys' on 'em. Normally we're at the back – if we even get in – and here we are in front of Kelly Slater and Andy Irons. When me and Johnny went to get a drink, we ran into the girlfriend of the Canadian guy we'd surfed with that day. He'd got tickets through Jesse, but was sitting right at the back and couldn't see anything. We said, 'No worries, come up and sit with us.' We walked down the aisle to our seats and sat him in front of the stage, the full rock star seating.

So the award night starts, we're right at the front, and my old mate Benji Wetherley along with our US agent, Sal Masakela, was hosting it. The first award was Best Wipeout. Richie Vaculik was nominated for a wave at Ours that had nearly ripped his head off and should have killed him. Rich had already bailed home for his mum's birthday, but we had a young Maroubra kid, Jesse Pollock, with us. Koby has gone, 'Jess, if Richie wins this award, you're going to go up and accept it … *in the nude.'* Richie is a committed nudist and will lose his clothes after two beers no matter where he is; it's what he would have wanted. They announced the winner.

'And the Best Wipeout award goes to … *Richie Vaculik.'*

Jesse's stood up and strutted to the stage completely starkers apart from a pair of sneakers and socks. What we'd told him to say in his acceptance speech was, '… and by the way, I'm looking for a clothes sponsor'. But the poor kid has got up there and looked out over the crowd, which was going off by this stage, and it's kind of dawned on him that he's nude in front of 3000 people and about 300 cameras. He started shitting himself. Half the crowd was cheering and half were stunned into silence. We won three awards that night: Best Documentary for *Bra Boys*, Richie got Best Wipeout, and Koby won Biggest Barrel for the one he'd caught towing with Laird Hamilton in Fiji. When we won Best Doco, all three tables of us got up on stage to accept it, including the Canadian guy, who we carried up. We ended up dedicating the award to him.

Then we jumped in the van and headed up to Utah for the X-Dance Film Festival. The X-Dance is part of Sundance, and it's for action sports movies. We were even on the back page of the Sundance program, a full-page story on the movie, which was huge. You couldn't pay a million bucks for that kind of publicity.

So we've gone from Planet Malibu to Planet New York to Planet Sundance. They've got these huge 'gifting suites' there, and if your movie gets invited you get a crack at it. So here we are in line behind Jack Black and Danny Glover waiting to get our photo taken. Then we got sent upstairs; you go into the gifting suites and they give you all this free shit. I got a GPS, a DVD player, a phone, shoes. I was just flabbergasted. I didn't understand how it worked. 'So, err, we get to keep this shit?'

And we won. We won X-Dance. Here we are on stage being awarded the trophy from Tony Hawk the skateboarder. That was a big affirmation moment for us. Our little backyard movie that was originally funded by my rent money was the biggest sports movie of the year. That was quickly followed by the biggest party of the year.

Our crew went berserk. They said it was one of the biggest crowds they'd ever had at an X-Dance, and the party that we held after was insane. Macca De Souza got up on stage and rapped; it was the most insane party. We ended up hiring two penthouse suites back at the Americana Hotel and had an after-after-party full of topless chicks.

And the party train kept on rolling, right back to LA. It was only just starting. We'd met Ian Thorpe back at our Sydney premiere. Koby's girlfriend Tahyna is really good friends with him, and we hung out with him in LA quite a bit. When we got kicked out of the Santa Monica flat – with 19 of us in there, who knows why – we had nowhere to go, so Thorpey has gone, 'Why don't you guys go and stay up at my place?' He owns a place up in the Hollywood Hills that used to belong to John Lennon. After promising we wouldn't have 19 guys staying there, we moved in.

It was surprisingly cool being in that scene for a while. What I think has given us a bit of an edge is that we always treat people pretty much the same as we would anyone we met down the beach or in the Maroubra Bay pub. We've never really been intimidated by the rich or powerful or the famous, we treat them no different to anyone else, and I think people in that position appreciate it.

That town is so wild, just who you can bump into. One day I was on Rodeo Drive with my girlfriend Gina and she sees this guy walking down the street wearing a black tracksuit with a giant rabbit on it. She's like, 'Sunny, that guy's got a Rabbitohs jumper on.' All I can see is a scrum of paparazzi. He's coming over in our direction, walking straight up to us, and I go, 'That's got to be Russell.'

'G'day, Sunny.'

And there we were having a chat with Russell Crowe in the middle of Rodeo Drive. He goes, 'Here's my number, give us a call and come round for dinner tonight. Hoo roo, mate.' Stuff like that was constantly happening; every night there'd be something on.

We were going to the best nightclubs, hanging with the Hollywood brat pack. We were going to Les Deux a lot. You don't get a booth there unless you're paying for a $1500 bottle of Belvedere vodka. It was such a blow-out to see it all in action. Here we were – we'd won awards, we were in the biggest nightclubs, everything was for free, we were drinking $1500 bottles of vodka. We couldn't believe it. The film company was saying to us, 'We want you and Koby to come to these parties, but we can't take 12 guys.' And we kinda said, 'Well, it's all of us or none of us.' By the end, everyone got on with everyone and we became the life of the party wherever we went. We must've been like a circus sideshow to them, and that whole scene was like a circus sideshow to us. The boys we were all pinching themselves. When you're in a private booth with Paris Hilton, the whole nightclub surrounds you. We're just looking around like we were on another planet.

We knew we were lucky to be there, but we also had this feeling that it was all supposed to happen. Our lives have been so up and down that I suppose this was just another one of the ups, just a little more surreal than previous ones. We'd seen fame before as professional surfers, but never sniffed air like this. But we knew not to take it too seriously, get too caught up in it, or believe it was gonna roll on like that forever, 'cause we knew it'd be lucky to last five minutes. We were just rolling in the moment like pigs in shit. We were just enjoying this good run and making sure the boys did too 'cause it may never happen again in our lives. I don't think I stopped smiling for 18 months.

After the movie tour ended and all the boys went home to Maroubra, I spent a month in LA by myself, staying up at Thorpey's house in the Hollywood Hills. Every afternoon as the sun started to sink I'd kick back on John Lennon's veranda, drink a cold beer, look out over Hollywood and laugh.

'What the hell are we doing here?'

KOBY

LOVE, LUST AND LUNACY IN LA LA LAND

It was through John that I met Tara Reid, who I was seeing for a while.

She was in Australia doing some promo work, some shoots at one of John's resorts. John calls me and goes, 'Koby, I reckon you could hook up with Tara if you play your cards right. I know I would've in my day.'

So he sends down a chopper for me. I get up there and John and I are doing beers at 11 in the morning, just having a ball.

He goes, 'I bet you can't hook up with Tara.'

He flew me up there just to bet me, bra. We're on the piss, hanging out; we had a mad time. He's got all the moves for an old bloke, and he's gone from betting against me to trying to set me up. It became a full game. He'd be looking at Tara, pointing at me with his thumb, winking. Then it'd be something like this.

'Koby, remember that time you surfed the 80-foot wave?'

Tara would go, 'Did you surf an 80-foot wave, Koby?'

And I look over Tara's shoulder and John's got both thumbs up, nodding his head, laughing.

'Koby, what about that time when you won $60,000 on the tables at Vegas?' We had a ball, and sure enough I've won the bet and ended up hooking up with her. Tara and I hung out for a week before she flew home to California.

A few weeks later, me and one of my best Maroubra mates, Jay Boy, flew over to California for a week. I'd been signed by Analog clothing by this stage, and I was there to put in an appearance at the SIMA surfing trade show. Tara's found out, and I said, 'No worries, we'll drop in.' She thought she was fully dating me at this stage, but I thought the arrangement was a bit looser than that. Tara's a nice chick, but she just lives the party life, and that's exactly what I was trying to avoid at this stage. Anyway, we have a couple of nights together hanging out; then she comes up to the trade show with me.

I've spoken to Paris in the meantime and organised her to come along as well. Our limo with the tinted windows pulls up out the front and the whole trade show's wondering who it is, and we jump out. We're walking through with Tara Reid and Paris Hilton, walking through the place like rock stars, just killing it.

Soon after I got back to Australia, I met Tahyna.

It was a pretty heavy story. One of my good mates at the time really liked her. He and I were hanging around together a fair bit at the time, going out, hooking up with chicks, having a ball. One day he says to me, 'I really like this chick, but I'm kind of stuck for words around her. Can you come over and get a bit of conversation going?' He knows I can talk to any chick. When I met her at lunch I went, 'Holy shit, she's the bomb!' It was Tahyna, the girl he was chasing at the time.

A couple of days later my mate's invited me out to dinner with them. Tahyna's mum and dad were there as well, so I was talking to them, pouring on the charm and we're all getting on really well. Then my mate asked me out with them *again*. By this stage I'm thinking, 'What are you doing? Anyone would think you're trying to set *me* up with her.' Eventually Tahyna has gone over to his house and he's tried to make a move on her. She's backed off, and gone, 'Look, sorry, we're only friends.' Later he asks me, 'What am I gonna do? I've been hanging around with her for five months and she won't kiss me and says we're only friends?'

'Well, I guess it sounds like you're only friends, bra.'

On New Year's Eve we were all partying. I saw Tahyna again and it just kind of struck me: this girl is *beautiful*.

We went out for a couple of lunches in the weeks after that, and I told her so. 'But look, I'm not like my mate. I'll tell you straight up, I want this to go somewhere.' My usual direct self. I took her out to dinner, but I was sensing nothing. There was no real spark there. I started thinking, 'Well, I'm not going to drag this along for months if it's not going anywhere.' We met up again; this time it was different, it was just like we were friends. I think we'd both put the idea of us ever dating out of our minds. We went out as friends and it was really, really cool.

We started hanging out and having a good time about once a week for six months or so. It was about then that I hooked up with this model, Saskia. She was hot. I had photos of her and I showed them to Tahyna, going, 'Have a look at my new chick. What do ya reckon?' It was all in the game plan.

'Yeah, she's really nice, Koby.'

I was hanging out with Saskia, but I never really felt much for her. Tahyna had already heard about Paris, Tara, Krystal from *Big Brother*, and she was a little suss on me, thinking I was just a player. Good girls like bad boys I suppose. You know, come to think of it, I went through a good run there for a while.

Tahyna and I had become really good friends by this stage. Then she got a call to go back to America to do some acting work in New York. While she was there she was ringing me every day. Out of the blue one day she said to me, 'I really miss you.'

She came home for a while and I caught up with her down at Cronulla. She's telling me how she really liked this other guy. It was weird. When I come to think of it, she may have been doing the same thing to me that I did to her with Saskia. 'What do you mean, you're *trying* to get him?' I said to her. 'You could have any man on earth.' But Tahyna hasn't dated a lot of guys; she's not a player. She's really choosy, which was the complete opposite to me. When she told me about this guy I just said, 'Well, your dream man is probably standing right in front of you and you don't even know it.'

'What?'

'Your dream man could be standing right in front of you.' We both started laughing about it.

Then she went back to New York to work again. I missed her so much, and that time apart really got me thinking about her. The *Bra Boys* movie was finished by this stage, the premiere was a couple of weeks away, so I rang her up and put it on the table.

'Look, I've fallen for you big time. I want you to come back and be my date for the premiere. I'll put you on a flight.' She was missing home and wasn't having a great time in New York anyway. She was reluctant at first, but she came home the following week.

Just before the premiere I was having a suit fitted at Peter Morrissey's and I've put it on, walked out and caught Tahyna checking me out. That was the moment I knew it was on, for sure. It was the way she looked at me. I could sense it, 100 per cent. It was different.

We went to the premiere and I hung with her the whole night. We still hadn't kissed. I was pulling out all my tricks that night. At the end of it we were on the stairs, away from everyone, and I pulled her aside and said, 'It's been a pretty special night for me, and it means so much that you're here. You could make it even more special if you gave me a kiss.' I was doubly glad I didn't get shot that night, because she kissed me.

At the time Tahyna and I started dating, I was having a hard time at home. I just needed a break from the scrutiny. I wanted a break from Maroubra, a break from the questions. It really got to me. I just needed some space from Australia. I'd hate to know how Russell Crowe or any of those stars feel. I'm a D-grade nobody, or whatever I am, and I can't get a moment's peace. I go out at night and I can't stand it. I get people coming up to me, talking about their drug-addicted parents. Taj gets surf groupies, I get mental people. It's either normal people who think I'm crazy or crazy people who think I'm normal. But when I'm drunk I get everyone coming at me. I just didn't want to keep talking to people and answering questions and having photos in the paper. I just wanted to be a nobody again for a while.

And by this stage I had a taste for America. Tahyna was back over there, and I'd been signed by Analog, an American company, so I had a lot of work over there. I'd already tried to kill myself at home, doing a lot of drugs and partying and doing things I didn't respect myself for. I thought, 'You know, that's not me.' At that time when all that shit converged, I just woke up one morning and said to myself, 'I'm done, I'm outta here.'

I packed a bag and jumped on a plane to LA that day. When I moved out of my unit I left all my stuff there, including most of my artwork. I also left two plasmas just sitting there, a bed, all my furniture. I didn't even tell the real estate; I just went, I'm done, and I moved to America for a year.

California was great. California was good fun. I was surfing a lot over there. Because I'd moved there during the Hawaiian winter, there were always waves nearby, so I was going back and forth to Hawaii a lot to surf. It was only a 200-buck flight to get to the North Shore.

We moved into Santa Monica. It was just me and Tahyna, but we had plenty of friends dropping in. It was quiet mainly, and I was just able to cruise and go surfing. I'd wake up every day and check the waves. If there were no waves, I'd go to the gym, go and see sponsors, magazines. Cruise down the street. But it just felt good to not be recognised for a while.

We went and lived in New York for two months. New York is a big party town, but it's a fun place and it gets you motivated. Everyone is in New York for something, trying to be something. It made me start thinking about working on my clothes and my designing and wanting to be something. It was a good eye-opener; it was one of the best motivators ever. People were going to me, 'But there's no surf there!' and I was like, 'I don't give a fuck. My head's not in surfing at the moment.' Eventually it made me miss and appreciate surfing, but it also made me think about doing other stuff, opening up to a whole different world. In Maroubra people are just happy to rock up to the beach every day. My surfing is only going to last so long, so I needed other things in my life that meant something. My trip to New York led directly to me signing an international deal with my label, My Brothers Keeper.

The movie had opened in the States by this stage, and it was good to see all the boys again. I had 16 of them on my floor when they came over for the Californian premiere.

But the release of the movie reignited all the publicity, which I wasn't so comfortable with, especially as I was just getting used to a nice quiet life again.

The other good thing was that I finally had money again. Between Analog, Bondi Blonde and the movie, I was back on my feet, which, considering my proximity to Vegas and my love of a bet, was a dangerous thing. I think I went to Vegas 10 times the year I was in California. I found that as fast as I could earn money, I could piss it away. One time I was in Vegas with my mates and we were just partying it up, having a ball. I walk in with $6000, put $3000 down, win another $6000. Put $6000 down and win 12. So I've suddenly got 18 grand. I'm thinking, 'How good is this?' We got a limo and went to the strip clubs, then at 11 that night we go to this nightclub next to the casino we were staying at. We walk in and the guy goes, 'It's $150 each to get in.' I thought, 'Fuck that; I'm not paying $600 to get into a club out of principle.' But I looked at all my money and thought, 'What if I run back into the casino and just win another $600? It's not coming out of my pocket then, is it? I'm paying them with their own money, aren't I?'

I walk back to the table thinking I'll put a thousand on and win the money for the door, I'll show this bastard. I lost my thousand. Put two thousand down; lost it. Put four thousand down; lost it. Put eight thousand down; lost it. Put the rest down; lost it. Eighteen grand gone in five minutes. Five rolls and not a cent left. The casino had given me a room when I had won earlier. I woke up the next morning and put together what had happened and just started dry retching. I had to borrow $20 off a guy in the street to get petrol after having 18 grand in my pocket six hours before.

Out of all the Hollywood people we met, Paris was the coolest. She's a legend. When I'd go away surfing to Hawaii, she'd take Tahyna to the movies or shopping. Tahyna didn't have a lot of friends in LA, and here was Paris Hilton, the biggest star of all, going, 'You wanna do stuff?' Just making time for her.

To see the life they live is unbelievable, though. Paris is a girl who's become famous for smiling for the camera. Everyone bags her, but she's made money out of smiling for the camera. She'll be walking down the street and she'll just stop and pull this mad pose. All these guys just materialise with cameras and start blazing away. It's bullshit. When we go to her house there's an army of photographers on the beach in front at all times and another 50 at the front door. When they see her some of them will even yell out, 'Paris, ya slut!' just to get a rise out of her. But she's really cool. We got along really well and she invited all the boys to the parties at her place. She's just an everyday person really, just maybe a little more out there.

Hanging with Paris had its perks. Tahyna and I went to a party at the Playboy Mansion with Paris, Nicky, Fergie and their boyfriends, and my mate Jason Bergh and his girl. We all go to the Playboy Mansion in our undies. The party was their biggest one of the year – the Pyjama Party. Every Playboy chick is nude, with their underwear painted on.

It was free everything. It was all you can drink. Being an Aussie, I'm thinking the free piss is gonna run out in five minutes, so I'm just double-fisting everything, thinking the booze has got an hour at best. I'm power drinking, and pretty soon I'm the drunkest person in the Playboy Mansion.

I was talking to this chick, having a full-on conversation with her, just this six-foot-two craziest Miss September bomb model, and it occurs to me that she's talking to me completely naked. I look down, then up, refocus and do it again.

'You're naked.'

'Yeah, I've been naked all night.'

Fuck. Then I look around and at that second it dawned on me that out of the thousand people who are there, I'm one of about a hundred who actually have any clothes on. The rest of the chicks at the party were nude. Most were bodypainted, some were on rollerskates, but they were all nude and all very fucking hot.

Then they'd jump in the pool. At the Playboy Mansion there are spa baths in the bedrooms that are all linked up. You can swim between rooms, from bedroom to bedroom. The pool snakes through the whole bottom level of the house. You swim through it and come up inside a big monkey cage, then dive under again and come up in another bedroom. I'm in the pool just doing laps around the house, just fucking around, being a drunk lunatic. All the chicks are in the pool with their painted undies and the water's turning green 'cause their undies are washing off. You couldn't dream this shit up, bra. Then they just get out completely nude, walking around the party. Seriously, girls dancing away on the dance floor wearing high heels and nothing else, hundreds of them. Real freaky. Then Hugh walks up. I high five him, introduce myself and thank him for putting on the show. He goes, 'No worries, Koby, anytime you wanna drop by, I'll get you on the door list.'

I've had a couple of moments over there when I've seriously questioned whether I hadn't entered some other fucked-up parallel universe. One night I was in New York with all these models that Tahyna knew. I was sitting there in this club called Butter, one of the biggest nightclubs in New York. I've got 15 bottles of alcohol on a table in front of me, every type of spirit you can possibly think of, and Miranda Kerr, Gisele Bundchen and all these Victoria's Secret models were clustered around me. I'm the only guy on the table.

I look around the table and go, holy shit. I've got this tattoo on my wrist that says, 'Wish you were here'. I remember that night in the club looking at it and thinking of all my mates back home in Maroubra. Quentin Tarantino walks past, there's Jay-Z, P. Diddy, the redheaded guy from *True Romance*. I looked around and went, 'Holy fuck, have a look who's around us.'

One other time, my Maroubra mates Richie Vass, Evo Faulks and Macca De Souza and I were in Vegas for the opening of Nicky Hilton's club. We couldn't get in and we were spewing. There's 300 people lined up out the front. It's like you're going to a music festival and they're all trying to fit through the front door of a house. I'm walking back and suddenly I see these cameras flashing and all these people parting. I'm thinking, 'Fuck, I hope I know who this is.' We're cruising through and all of a sudden, *boom*, it's Paris. She sees me and says, 'Koby!' and runs over and jumps on me.

'What are you doing?'

'We can't get in.'

'You can now!'

I look around at the boys and just claim the moment: Paris Hilton has just got us in. We go in and she takes us straight up to the heaviest VIP section ever. There's Mike Tyson, LL Cool J, the heaviest crowd. I have to stop Richie from wanting to fight Tyson.

'I just wanna get knocked out by him!'

'Richie, he'll kill ya.'

'But it's my dream to be knocked out by Mike Tyson!'

Richie cage fights at home, and his all-time idol is Tyson. So Rich goes over to him, just stands in front of him and stares. Tyson goes, 'What are you looking at?' It was the funniest shit. Pretty soon he was hanging out with us. He comes over and goes, 'Hey, what's up,' in the funniest squeaky voice. At the end of the night we're on the tables – me, Rich and Evo – just dancing up a storm. The whole party's looking at us, going, 'How much fun are those guys having?'

Tyson's just sitting there watching us, thinking, 'Who the fuck are these guys?'

Part 9
Tough Love

KOBY

THE INKY HAND–SCRIBED ROAD MAP OF ONE MAN'S MORTAL COIL

That Mother Mary on my arm here, she's just praying away down there.

After all the shit I went through in the last few years, I realised I needed something in my life other than myself. I'm not going to say I'm a Catholic. I'm not going to say I'm a Muslim, a Buddhist or anything. Sometimes you need to look for something higher. After all that shit happened – trying to kill myself, stabbing myself in the arms – I knew I needed some help. And she covers up the scars pretty well, too.

Below Mary I've got Mavis and Scotty's names on my wrist. My ma and Scotty Linford – two of the most important people in my life who aren't here any more. Rest in peace.

'Wish you were here'; I look at that one a lot when I'm away somewhere really nice, places like Tahiti, Hawaii, the Playboy Mansion. I think about my friends and wish they were there sharing it all with me.

'My Brothers Keeper', around my neck. One day in Bali, me and Jed and Jai all got 'My Brothers Keeper' tattooed. We got home and everyone's gone, 'That's sick,' so we just made up some hoodies and T-shirts for ourselves. All the boys started going, 'They're mad, where can I get one?' So we made 100 jumpers for the boys and they disappeared like that. We started doing more and it turned itself into a business, MBK.

The Devil on my knee … I like the picture. Jai didn't; he freaked when he saw it.

Now I've got the army rising sun on my hand, but it's not like I want to go to Afghanistan and shoot the Taliban, bra. I just like what it stands for and I like the look of it. Just because I've got a big cross on my back doesn't mean I love Jesus. I just like the cross.

'Abberton' on my other leg; self-explanatory. It just reminds me of who I am.

The ones on my feet I did myself. I didn't do the tiger, but I did the wave and the sun myself.

Then I got 'Maroubra' on my feet, and '2035'.

I tattooed my own cock for a laugh one time in Bali. My friend Kane and me were in one of those raucous moods. We'd been drinking arak all day. We'd just turned into knuckleheads and decided to get a tattoo. We got in the shop, grabbed the gun off the guy and decided we'd tattoo each other. Kane tattooed the inside of my bottom lip – 'Bra Boys motherfucker' – then he started tattooing his own mouth.

'Fuck this, give me the gun,' I said. 'I'm gonna tattoo me cock.'

Then he's gone, 'Fuck that, I'm going to do it too!'

I've gone, 'Watch this!' I've got me knob out and started tattooing it. I ended up with 'Bra Boys' and some lightning bolts and black love hearts all over me knob. It didn't *hurt*; wasn't a lot of fun, though, I can tell ya that. But if you're in the mood to tattoo your own cock you're generally not going to be feeling anything.

The cross on my arm – that's just the bit of religion I've got in me but I don't really know what it is yet.

The Australian flag; I'm a proud Aussie.

'Bra Boys for L' with the heart: Bra Boys for life, Bra Boys for love.

The sacred heart; I like this one. That's me old chick's.

'Bra Boys' tatt on me back. That one's me favourite. Every time I look at it I wish it was bigger. There's 16-year-old kids with their whole back covered in 'em, three times bigger than mine.

It's only skin; I don't give a fuck about it really. It hurts to get 'em done, but it doesn't *hurt* hurt. Mental pain is way more full-on than any physical pain.

KOBY

BROTHERLY LOVE AT 100 KAYS ON THE WRONG SIDE OF THE ROAD

This is how easy me and Jai fight.

We were driving down the coast to Red Sands not long after Jai got out of jail. Marky Mathews is driving his little green car, Jai's in the front seat, I'm in the back. There was plenty of swell about, the winds were good and the tide was dropping.

Jai's going, 'You can't surf Red Sands at low tide.'

I said, 'You *can* surf it on low tide, Jai; you're tripping.'

'You can't surf it on low tide, ya fuckwit.'

'Jai, you *can*.'

'Fuckwit, ya *can't*.'

It started getting heated.

'Jai, it's just *you* who can't surf it on low tide. The rest of us can.'

That was it. I see him about to jump over the back and punch me, so I've just gone, *whack*, and hit him first, straight in the eye. He reached over the back and is just smashing me.

Next thing, we're going around this corner at a hundred clicks and Jai's reached over and just yanked the handbrake up. Straightaway we start spinning down the hill, 360s straight over onto the other side of the road into oncoming traffic.

Marky has managed to stop the car, and it's sitting on the wrong side of the road in the dirt. Jai's not finished. He jumps out of the car and runs around the side, trying to get in my door. I'm yelling at Marky, 'Fucking drive!'

But we're on the wrong side of the road; we would've been driving straight into oncoming traffic.

'Fucking drive! Leave him here!'

Jai's kicking the car going, 'Get out, cunt!' I'm winding all the windows up and locking the doors to keep him out. He's trying to kick the window in on this tiny little car, and the thing wouldn't break. I'm screaming, 'Go, Marky, go! Let's leave him here.'

Then all of a sudden a cop car turns up. Here's Jai booting the windows with a big black eye; I had a bleeding nose and a fucked-up mouth. The copper goes, 'What are you guys doing? What's going on? Why are you on the wrong side of the road, and why is your mate kicking the window?'

Jai goes, 'We just slid out. We were only mucking around.'

The cop points at me and goes, 'That guy's got a smashed-up mouth and you got a black eye. Don't tell me you were playing.'

I backed Jai up and said, 'Yeah, we're just mucking around.'

The cops walk off, Jai just jumps in the car and we drive off and go surfing, just pissing ourselves hysterically.

We got to Red Sands. It was dead low tide and I surfed it, no worries.

KOBY

FUNCTION AND DYSFUNCTION AND AN UNFLINCHING FAMILIAL DEVOTION

You couldn't get a closer set of brothers than us.

I mean, it shows with what we went through in the courts. I'd do it again all right now. And I'd take the 14 years that went with it if it meant keeping my brother out of trouble.

We've always been pretty close, the four of us, but when you get to a stage where you nearly lose your brothers a lot changes. We became really close there for a while. *Really* close. And it was a good feeling.

Everyone was getting on really well – still fighting and arguing and shit; that will never change for us – but it was a good feeling in those months after Jai got out. There was a lot of love there, and Ma being really sick and dying soon after pulled us in even tighter.

The peace lasted about a year, I reckon. Jai didn't like the *Bra Boys* movie, and that's where his feud with Sunny started. The feud's still going today. Jai doesn't like the way Sunny did the doco without consulting him, and that's what the whole thing's about.

It's the way we are: I don't believe in something Jai does, Jai doesn't believe in something Sunny does, and because we're so fiery, we don't talk about it, we fight. Most brothers would think, 'You know, I don't like what he does but I'll keep it to myself.' We'll just have a straight-out fist fight then hate each other and not want to talk for a few weeks, but then come back together even tighter than we were.

Jai will do anything to get a better wave than Sunny. They both surf as hard as they can when the other one's around. It was good to watch the two of them surf together 'cause they'd always push each other. They still do. And it's why they became so good. Without their rivalry, they'd probably both be fagging around on boogieboards today instead of being world-class surfers.

The year Jai got out of jail, we all had Christmas lunch together for the first time in 15 years. We were over at Bondi at the Swiss Grand. Jai and Sunny are sitting there and they just grab each other's throats over the table and it's on. Whatever it was about was bound to be really silly. I think it was Jai smoking at the table. Then Jai and Sunny jumped the table and were wrestling, food's going everywhere. They hadn't even had a beer.

Who knows if they're ever going to get along; they're both pretty stubborn. I'm not stubborn at all. If you do something pretty bad to me, I'm gonna get ya for it, but I'm not gonna be sour for the rest of me life with my brother. We've been through too much. They both think they're right, so how do you get a resolution out of that? I hope they start getting on again, but I'm not going to lose any sleep over it.

Me and Sunny both love and respect each other. We're good brothers. If Sunny does something to me, or we have an argument, we'll have a verbal, but we've never had a punch-up. Not like me and Jai, who have 'em every five minutes.

I see Jai every day I'm at home, speak to him 10 times a day on the phone. Me and Jai have always been the closest. Sunny travelled a lot when we were going through really hard times when we were young. It's hard to say 'closer', but it's definitely like Jai was there for me more when it mattered. I don't blame Sunny for being away; it's just the way it was.

We're a lot alike, me and Jai. We're both Geminis, so we're hot tempered. Jai is the best person ever; just don't doublecross him. He can be real fiery, but he has a heart of gold.

Jai's problem his whole life has been that if he's got 10 bucks to his name, he'll try and give you 15. When he made $25,000 off the movie, he gave Mum $5000, Ronnie $7000, his ex-girl $7000 and he kept the rest. That's what he's like. He's too generous for his own good. And then a week later he'll say, 'Can ya lend us some money, bra?'

I don't worry about Jai. When he's on the level he can more than look after himself. I do worry about him a bit when he's upset, and I really worried about him when he was taking drugs. I didn't respect that. But drugs just have that pull over people where they can't stop it. I know; it's happened to me.

At the moment we're not really the closest the family has ever been. When we were young, we were inseparable. But we're not a picture perfect family, don't kid yourself. You know, come to think of it, I think I don't actually get on with my family … but they're still my family and I still love 'em. I don't need to hang around with Jai and Sunny, go out to dinner and give each other birthday cards for them to know that I love them. We're not a normal family, and we don't show that we love each other in a normal way.

This Christmas just past, we had another go at a Christmas family lunch. Me and Tahyna hosted Christmas lunch up at our place. There was me, Tahyna, Sunny, Jai, Dakota, Mum and Kiyahna, and it went great, bra. Tahyna put on some grouse food, everyone behaved themselves, no one got thrown off the balcony. Jai sat outside on the balcony, Sunny sat inside on the lounge. They'd swap every half-hour and didn't say a word to each other, not even when they passed in the hallway.

SUNNY

AN ABBERTON FAMILY CHRISTMAS GALA

Those first few years away from Dakota were hard, but we'd had to cut ties with Mum and Paul altogether. We just couldn't be around them. Paul left her when Dakota was about three. But even with Paul gone, the way we felt about Mum, there was no way we could have been around her. It would have been really bad for Dakota. It would have just confused him. But we've built a great relationship with him in the years since. We've all lived with him at certain stages, and the more we've seen of him over the years the better it's been with Mum. He's been a bridge back to her. You wonder what our relationship with Mum would have been like today if he'd not been here. Maybe we'd still have nothing to do with her.

My relationship with Mum has only just got back on the rails in the last five or six years, Koby only in the last two. Jai's remained pretty close to Mum, especially through his time in court when Mum was there for him every day. But we wiped her from our lives for well over 10 years, hardly a word, so it was never going to be an overnight reconciliation.

I'd taken Dakota and Kiyahna up the coast surfing right before the shooting. We took the jet ski up and had a mad week. And that's what was hard about the court case. It had finally gotten to a stage where we were comfortable with our lives and we could start to relax. We'd really planned to do a lot with Dakota, 'cause they were important years for him. He was about 12 when it happened. We wanted to take him to Bali and on surf trips, and we wanted to train with him. He was surfing and showing some promise. He had a lot of ability in big waves because he doesn't show any fear at all. Koby towed him into a wave at Ours, a 10-footer, and almost killed him. Dakota didn't flinch. He popped up a minute later and there was no expression on his face. He was fine.

Most kids would never go near the water again but his pulse rate hardly even changed. He's got that thing that both Koby and Jai have got, that fearlessness, and at certain times he even *looks* like a cross between Koby and Jai. His eyes and the bridge of his nose are exactly like Koby's, his nose is kind of like Jai's, and he's got my chin. It's like the three of us in one person. What a combination. We all try and influence him in our own way and he just sits back and takes it all in without saying too much, which is the sign of a really powerful person. Dakota's got a bit of personality from all of us. He's a quiet thinker, which comes from his old man. He's quite spiritual, which comes from Jai, and he's ambitious and a bit cryptic, which is Koby. He could be the trump. He could be the one.

We left school early but we saw the value in education. It's hard to keep a kid on the straight and narrow around here, though, and Koby was unreal at that. I was really proud of the way Koby played a role when Dakota was playing up at school. It was good for Koby to do it, too. It was the same role I'd taken with him when he was young. Koby would take Dakota up to school and make sure he walked in, and if he caught him wagging school he'd make Dakota run laps of the beach with him and torture him, just to make sure his day off wasn't too enjoyable. He'd make Dakota train until he puked, and suddenly school looked a whole lot better. It's tough love.

Looking back, when I left home to follow the pro tour, when Koby was only 10 or 11, it must've hurt him a lot. He must have been really angry with me, because he seems to have blocked out our whole relationship before that. But we were really close. Jai would always pick on him and bash him and I'd have to step in, but he doesn't remember anything up to 12 years old. The only thing he remembers is me not being there.

I know what Jai and I did with him – we helped guide him to become one of the world's best surfers today, just each in our own way. Koby and I are really close now, probably the closest we have been for a long time. Maybe he sees it all a lot clearer now and has more of an understanding of the role I had to play.

Even though Jai and I have a few problems at the moment, we've always had our ups and downs. Jai didn't think the movie would be so popular, and because he hates publicity and hates the limelight he's never been comfortable with it. Hopefully he won't feel like that in years to come when he's in a better place.

We always want the best for our brothers. We've always had that and it'll never change. It doesn't matter that we haven't spoken to each other for two years, it doesn't matter that I've just towed you into a wave and almost killed you, it doesn't matter that we just punched each other at Christmas dinner. We're always gonna want the best for each other, because that's the only reason we've got to where we are today.

The Christmas just past, Kiyahna organised for the family to get together again. For a 12-year-old, she's got a really strong sense of family and she wanted us all together, the whole family. The Abbertons hadn't been under the one roof together since the Christmas at Bondi when Jai and I had the fight, and it would never have happened without Kiyahna insisting on it. So we had Christmas lunch up at Koby and Tahyna's place. Dakota and I bought Koby a new barbecue for Chrissie, and we had the full barbecue seafood lunch. Tahyna cooked up a storm. It was unbelievable. It's always a bit of a diplomatic nightmare trying to get us all together, 'cause Koby's not talking to Mum and I'm not taking to Jai. But Kiyahna got us all there and we actually had a ball. Jai and I didn't talk, but we didn't fight either. We both knew how important it was to her.

Kiyahna really looks up to her uncles. Loves 'em. She's taken up surfing, and we were driving home from a surfing weekend not so long ago when out of the blue she says to me, 'Dad, do you ever think me, you and Uncle Jai and Uncle Koby will ever be inside a really big barrel together one day?' Not only is she imagining herself surfing inside this giant barrel, but then she looks around and her dad's in there and her uncle's in there with her, hanging out together. I just melted when she told me.

KOBY

YOU CAN'T TURN YOUR BACK ON A BABY BROTHER WITH A PREDILECTION FOR INK

I speak to my mum, but I don't have any feelings for her really.

I'm not going to give her a hug and tell her I love her. Because when I was 13 that's what I needed, and I never got it. I'll never give Mum the satisfaction of me ever loving her again. People say it's not good for me, but I don't care.

As the years went on she was always in the background in my life. What ended up happening was that Dakota's dad left Mum about three years after Dakota was born. Then, you know, she had nothing. She was out on her own. But after Paul left Mum, she started to realise that she could live by herself and that life was actually better. She cleaned herself up and she changed a lot, which means she's looked after Dakota a lot more than she looked after us. Mum took up nursing, and has been doing that for 20 years, so in that regard she got her life together.

She's my mum and, yeah, I speak to her because my little brother is there. I mean, you're a 13-year-old kid and someone picks drugs over you, then you get told to get out of the house and get hit by a baseball bat? That's a big crossroads in your life. There's no going around the roundabout on that one and coming back, bra. She's sorry for it and she should be, because she ruined everything we had.

It just shows you what a hold that shit gets over people, how weak it makes a person. And no matter what happens, no matter how many times an addict says they're straight, no matter who it is, you can never really believe them. It'll always be lurking in there somewhere.

To her credit, Mum was really supportive throughout court. Even though she knew I never wanted her to come near me, she'd turn up all the time. She's my mum by name, that's all she is to me, but it meant a lot to Jai to have her there, and so, in that way, it meant a lot to me.

These days I think my mum has her heart in the right place. She just caught a disease somewhere along the way. After what happened to me – stabbing myself after four days on coke – I'm beginning to understand how it could happen.

I never think about my parallel life, the life I might have had. I don't think about what I'd be like now if I'd grown up in Bondi with two parents who were there all the time. I don't need to. I've grown up perfect. I've grown up being able to talk to anyone, travel in different circles, be a loving person. I think I've been brought up well. Better than most people.

I see Dakota pretty much every day. He left school in Year 9. Dakota's pretty reserved. He's like the quietest out of all of us, by far. Now that he's getting a bit older – he's 18 now – he's opening up a bit more, but you never know what he's thinking. Dakota doesn't let any of his emotions show. I remember when he had a broken arm and I squeezed it because he didn't go to school that day. He didn't even flinch. He just stared at me.

I did what I could to keep him in school. I used to take him up the school and walk him through the front gate, then say to him, 'If you leave I'm gonna bash ya.' I'd be driving down the end of the street and my phone would ring and it'd be the principal telling me Dakota had just walked out of class and left. I just don't think the Abbertons are school people, to tell you the truth. I just wanted Dakota to have the basics nailed. I didn't care if he left school before Year 10 as long as he was reading and writing properly. It was hard for me to lecture him about staying in school, though, when I left in Year 8.

We get along pretty well, though. He's just cruising and doing his thing. He's exactly like his dad. I lived with Paul for eight years and I reckon I had seriously five minutes of conversation with him in that time. I had nothing to say to him, he had nothing to say to me, and that's how

MY BROTHERS KEEPER

it was. You have to reckon it was exactly the same for Dakota, and that's probably why he never has a lot to say.

Dakota doesn't surf much, but when he gets out there he's a real natural surfer.

I almost killed him not long ago. I towed Dakota into a 12-footer at Ours and watched him go over in the lip. Him going over worried me more than it would if it was me going over the falls. I looked back and I thought he was doing a floater on the lip while trying to pull off, then I've just seen him pin drop and land on his back on the dry rocks. Straightaway everyone's gone, 'Get him, he's gonna drown!' Luckily he's come up a minute later and just sucked in this huge breath.

We almost lost him another time, bra. The boys drove down to surf that left in Victoria, Luna Park. That wave is pretty full on. We've driven down there a few times, a day's drive each way, and not even surfed it because it's been too heavy. I just wanted to take Dakota on a trip, he said he wanted to come, so I said, 'Jump in the car with the boys, drive down with the skis, and I'll fly down and meet you there.' We get there and we score. I get a cover and a couple of photos out of it. It's a heavy reef that one, and I think it might have scared the shit out of Dakota 'cause he was only young, but he got a couple and had a good time, I think.

I had a bad feeling about the car while we were driving back up the Great Ocean Road. It just didn't feel right. When we got to Melbourne I told Dakota to jump on a plane with me and fly back. Richie was driving on the Hume Highway about six hours out of Melbourne when a tyre blew out and the car flipped a half-dozen times. No one was hurt, but the car and the ski were totalled. And where Dakota would have been sitting in the backseat was fully crushed flat. There's no way he would have survived.

There are still a lot of lessons Dakota has to learn, and I reckon travel is the best way to teach him. I like taking Dakota away 'cause he really livens up. I'm happy for him to be in Maroubra and work and do what he wants, I'm not going to pressure him about that, but I always let him know that if he ever wants to go on a trip I'll shout him. I took him and his mate Jesse Pollock to Bali with me last year. For about three years I've been going to Bali to get healthy. It's kind of a retreat for me. I won't party over there. There's no way I'm gonna die in Bali when some crazy Javo lets off a bomb. If you come to Bali with me I won't let you go out and party. You're gonna surf and eat good food and you're not gonna go out. When Dakota and Jesse were there with me we'd go for a surf in the morning, come back and eat some brekky, go to the gym, come back and hang out for the afternoon.

Then one night they told me they were going out to get some food. Tahyna and I are sitting at home waiting for them to come back. I don't like them being out over there and I knew they'd be right in the middle of something. After two hours Tahyna's gone, 'Where are they?'

'I know exactly where these little fuckers are.'

I'd been flowing them money that whole trip but never getting any change. It dawned on me, ya know, they're saving it for something. Jesse had told me his mum hadn't given him any money, so I rang his mum.

'No, I gave him 800 bucks.'

I jumped on my motorbike and knew exactly where they'd be. I come around the corner and here's Dakota standing in the middle of the street, smoking a cigarette, drinking a Bintang, his whole arm covered with this giant tattoo. I've just gone, 'Get fucked. What have these kids done?'

Then I walk into the tattooist and here's Jesse getting the biggest, ugliest tattoo you've ever seen in your life. He's getting 'My Brother's Keeper' in giant block letters three times the size of mine across his chest. I just said, 'Jess, I would have took you here and you could have got any tatt you wanted, but I'd never have let you have a tattoo that fucking big.' It was half done, no turning back, so I grabbed the gun and started colouring him in.

I don't care if Dakota's covered in tattoos from head to toe; the main thing for me is that I never want him to think life's a free ride. He is a little bit different to us when we were growing up, thinking he is going to get the good life without working for it, just because he's seen me with it, you know. When I was kid I never seen anyone doing any good. I made myself what I am through knowing that if I didn't make it for myself, I would never get it. I just want to drum into him that there's no free ride.

Growing up, I looked up to Sunny and Jai more than anyone else, and still do, but I never wanted to *be* them. I wanted to be *better than* them.

SUNNY

THE MAROUBRA WHIRLPOOL

Remember that movie *Fantasia*, where Mickey Mouse gets sucked down the well?

'Mr Wizaaaaaard! Help me!'

There are a lot of people who come to Maroubra and just get flushed away by it. The place just swallows them whole; they never get out. You've got to be careful of it. I've even spoken to some of the crew who used to hang around with us in the early days who disappeared off the scene. One of them, Cootie, said to me, 'I never really thought about why I stopped going to the beach, but one day it hit me – the whole scene was just too much. The constant testing was just too full on.'

When you've grown up in it, and know how it works, you know what to avoid and how to keep your head above water. But you see a lot of guys come in and they don't know how to get out of it; they don't escape the whirlpool.

There's energy in the air here that's really positive, but there's also tension, intensity. Some handle it, some don't, and the ones who don't either get drawn into trouble or they just pack up and leave. A lot of those top surfers, the guys in the generation before us, they left. We were the first generation to say, 'We're staying, *we're not leaving.*' A lot of the generation before us couldn't handle the intensity of living in Maroubra. But they had to face it all individually, whereas we banded together.

A lot of crew leave Maroubra but a lot of crew have also come back. There are guys who've left only to come back a decade later. I think Maroubra crew, once they've grown up here and lived all their life here, find it hard to move away and live in wider society. As hard as it can be to live here, it can also be harder to leave.

But I don't want to paint too bleak a picture, because we had the luckiest experiences growing up here. The place has turned us into what we are, and living here has been a full-on adventure. It was like the last frontier, the last frontier of city surfing. It was ignored and left to its own devices for decades. But our generation was under so much more scrutiny. There were more cops, more media. There's nothing we did that the older guys here at Maroubra wouldn't have been doing and vice versa – they were more full-on, if anything – it's just that there was a hundred cops down here all day watching us.

It's the siege mentality. You could never relax. From day one, Hinesy, Grommet, Marty and their mates would drum it into us: *be ready*. It's like we were in that mode for 15 or 20 years. And that's why people moved out. How long could you live like that? It's only the fact that surfing got us away from it occasionally and allowed us to see the world and see the bigger picture that kept us sane. The places we were going were so completely opposite to Maroubra. But being ready all the time did also help you in certain ways.

It keeps you pretty level, living here. You never know who the next Tony Hines is. Or if that little bloke is another Ronnie Reardon, who's five-foot-nothing but punches like Tyson. It makes you humble. It doesn't pay to showboat here, 'cause your chip will get knocked off pretty quick.

You hope the next generation understands what they have to do so they can bring *their* kids up here one day and feel safe. Isn't that what any community wants? And that's where a lot of my conflict lies. Don't we want the same things any other community wants? I'd love to see Maroubra become a culturally alternative area, a surf town celebrating a rich history, an area that's not glamourised like Bondi or gentrified like Bronte. An area that's home to a mix of incomes, an area that's not the preserve of the rich.

Five years ago we demonstrated against the installation of parking meters in Maroubra. What you've got to remember is that there's been no infrastructure money spent on Maroubra in over a decade. There were never any trees in the streets, nothing but pollution. So the council voted to put parking meters in. Our argument was that a single mother with three kids wasn't going to bring her kids to the beach if she suddenly had to pay $4.50 an hour for parking. Then they said they'd be able to buy a certificate that says you live in the area and you can park for free, but that's gonna cost you $80. The parking meters started at Bondi and spread south until Coogee. We were the last beach with free parking. We just saw it as another attack on the culture, and another way of stopping the poor kids getting to the beach. The beach should be free for everyone and not just the domain of the rich.

I think the movie influenced heaps of kids. I think people really got it. The battlers – stoked on it. The Kooris – stoked. The migrants – stoked. The property developers in the area – not so stoked. But who cares about them? They're only thinking about one thing right now: if we were to ban all the kids from the street it'll be another Bondi in five years and we'll make a killing. But Maroubra would lose its working class community and its surfing culture.

It's all so connected. Since the decline of the boardriders, the Sunday afternoons on Barbie Mountain have declined too. Jumping off the cliff at Hammerhead; taking a carload of guys to Voodoo to surf – all that stuff has slowed up in the past few years. It's got a bit to do with us getting older and having responsibilities. But you'll still get a random Friday afternoon down at the pub and out of the blue all the boys will file in, some from overseas, some from just up the road, and suddenly it will be like 15 years ago all over again. Those days are getting rarer, but they're magic when they happen.

Why Maroubra? Maroubra has always been a juncture between black and white, rich and poor. Jake Trotter, one of the Bra Boys, his ancestors were convicts aboard the First Fleet in 1788, and another Bra Boy, Matty Page, is a Koori, and his ancestors met them on the beach. Two hundred years later they're in the same tribe. We're the descendants of those homeless people who lived on the beach, the shanty town in Happy

Valley; maybe not in blood, but certainly in spirit. I read a story about a police constable in the early 1900s who'd been dispatched to check on reports of scores of larrikin men swimming in the ocean on the beach at Maroubra. He walked over the dunes and the Happy Valley crew were on the beach drinking, swimming, partying. The copper has asked his Aboriginal guide, 'Who are those people?' The guide's just gone, 'Him Maroubra, him too much.' I don't think I've ever heard a better description of the guys who live here.

I like the dual aspect of Maroubra. It's a concrete jungle, but you can walk two minutes to the southern end of the beach and you could be on the south coast. You walk through the bush and there are horses on the range and you can't see a trace of man, but then you look north and it's full of apartment blocks. You can get a sense of what it would've been like before white fellas got here. To us it's a beautiful beach and we've always fought to try and keep a natural feel to it. The city deserves a bit of breathing space so you can be reminded of how it once was.

Maroubra is alive; it breathes. I think it was always a really powerful place for the Aborigines. That's why they called it Maroubra, 'place of thunder'. It's just got this feel to it. It's got an energy that brings its people together, and as successive generations come and go this energy is passed on. What's the rule of energy? It can't be created or destroyed, it just changes shape.

JAI

WATER FINDING ITS OWN LEVEL

I was just happy to be free.

I appreciated life a lot more after seeing the other side of the coin. I realised how lucky we were. I was just trying to get in the water every day and get heaps closer to God, reading my Bible every day.

I had a few close mates from jail, and some top Aboriginal mates from Redfern, and I'd go and hang out with them. Me and another of my brothers got a job together as removalists. We were keen to work, but there just wasn't much work on at the time.

Mate, I've had non-stop court and been trying to stay out of jail ever since I've been free. It just seems like I've been reporting to the police for years. I know some really strong people who've had court hanging over them and it does their heads in. Nothing comes without a cost.

I was doing Sunday church, but I went to Lakemba mosque last week. That was the first time I'd gone out and prayed like that, and it made sense to me. I've just been checking out all denominations. I like it because the average Muslim will fast for 40 days at Ramadan, and won't eat or drink between sun-up and sundown. Christians can't even eat fish one day a year. What I like about Islam is the discipline. I respect it.

Right now I'm as much a Muslim as I am a Christian. I read the Koran and the Old Testament now, both of them. I read what Moses says, I read what Jesus says, I read what Mohammed says. They're all prophets; they're all saying the same message.

I was driving down to the snow with Dakota and his mates a few months back. We're getting close to the snow, and I go, 'Here, boys, touch the book for good luck.' I had my Bible with me and they all touch it. We pull into the car park, which is totally full, and *boom* the closest car park to the lifts is empty. We can snowboard back to the car we're so close. Touch the book again, *bang*. We'd bought dodgy lift tickets on the first day, and here comes the inspector. He gets to Dakota, turns away and goes to the next person like Dakota isn't even there. The grommets are looking at me going, 'Fuck, this book of yours has got some power, bra. Your book's on fire today.'

I met Kiri playing the pokies at the Coogee Bay Hotel. We got introduced, but we'd always thought about each other, I swear to God. It just felt like we knew each other. We only talked briefly that night, but I couldn't stop thinking about this Maori girl I'd met, and she says she couldn't stop thinking about me. We hooked up on New Year's Eve. I never believed in love at first sight till I met Kiri. God sent me the most beautiful angel alive.

Kiri and me went over to New Zealand for a while, over with Kiri's people. New Zealand is the coolest place. We went down to Christchurch, and I remembered the place straight away from being there as a kid; I hadn't been there in 25 years.

And then we went to Hawaii. The Hawaiian boys couldn't look after us enough. Kai and Kala, Makua and Eddie, the legends, they gave us the mansion to stay in. 'Jai *bwoy*, you see this house? I want you to feel like it's your house while you're staying here, bra. You and your girl, you do whatever you want.' The house was out the front of Eddie's place at Sunset Point, and it was incredible, bra. Those guys just took me and Kiri under their wing. They were true gentlemen. We were just surfing and training and hanging on the beach.

We got Phantoms on at 20 foot, and I caught the biggest wave of my life this year, bra. The biggest wave of my life at 34.

From there I went to Thailand. I got mates over there in the fighting camps. The discipline is so gnarly, but it's what ya need, bra. I'm thinking it'd be a good place for Dakota to spend some time; it'd be good for him.

But I went broke real quick 'cause once a day we'd give something of ours away. I'd walk past this poor kid in the street and *boom* I'd give the kid some money, but then I'd run back on the sly – *boom* – give him some more. Run back on the sly again – *boom* – give him some more. Couldn't help myself, just gave all me money away. I eat every day, I've got a roof over my head; I don't need nothing. These poor cunts are struggling. I've never chased a dollar or put a dollar before my life. If you've got faith in God you've got everything.

I've learned a lot in the last few years, I'm a lot more accepting now, especially with my mum. I realised that what happened with my mum, well, that kind of thing happens with people. I just don't think it's much good hating. That shit happens and that's life. Hating isn't going to help me little brother. Living with hate only hurts yourself.

My mum's really cleaned her act up and I'm so proud of her for doing it. She never would've had a house like she's got now. She's got a job, she's got food in the cupboard. She's turned around. And she was there in court for me every day, bra. Every day. That meant a lot to me.

It's taken me a while to warm to her again. We trusted her as kids, so when you lose your trust for your mum … We had to deal with a lot of things from an early age. I was going to knock myself when I was younger, just because I'd had to deal with so much. But then I found some books – like *The Celestine Prophecy* and some Stuart Wilde books – and they helped me deal with things. You deal with things or you let them crush you and you die.

I drove past the old Astoria Circuit place last week with Dakota and said, 'That's where you were born, bra.' The old block is gone now. They've pulled it down and made townhouses.

Dakota is the best kid. He's a little rock. Dakota's only got one emotion. I've seen Koby tow him into some double suckers at Ours, 10-footers, getting him hammered, and he pops up exactly the same as he went in. If you put him in a bad situation and tow him into a death wave it doesn't faze him too much. His heartbeat never changes. He's just content and quiet and cruisey.

I think me and him are closer than he is to the other two. He knows if he gets into any trouble he can ring me and I'm there for him. He's a good kid and he's been through a lot. He's got a good head on his shoulders. He wants to meet his dad. Paul was a top bloke, never touched my mum in 10 years; he was mellow. That's why Dakota's such a quiet kid; he's got it from his old man.

Dakota is going really good. There's a couple of his mates who are writing off and being a bit stupid. But we've got 'em together and we train with them when there isn't surf. I care about every one of Dakota's mates, so I'm really just trying to look after them and train with them. I'm really proud of the effort they've been putting in. Dakota's going to be a fighter. Dakota's got a warrior's head; he's got thick skin above his eyebrows and he loves the kickboxing.

I remember when we first had our tatts done. But it's fucking lost it a bit, the Bra Boys, you know what I mean. It was bred into us you never tell on anyone, you never bail, and if ya go to jail ya never go into protection. But this telling shit to everyone, it just seems like it's been blown out to be a bit of a wank, if you ask me. It's lost what it was.

My Bra Boys tatt's still there, and Koby, Dakota and Ron's names are still there too. Ronnie Reardon – me best mate back then and still me best mate to this day. My true friends know me, God knows me, and the rest of the world doesn't mean shit to me.

Maroubra will always be home, but I need to get out for a while. We've always said since we were kids that we're going to get stuck in Maroubra; I'd get out of here next week if I could. Maroubra's still the grouse, but I'm looking where I could live that's cheap enough. Somewhere that would put up with us.

I think everyone finds life hard, but life teaches you things. If you've come this far and you haven't learned anything, then it's probably your own fault. If you're going to sit there and beat yourself up, just remember you've got two arms and two legs. People get around worrying about all the shit they haven't got, instead of thinking themselves lucky for what they have got.

I just want to get married, have kids, do the right thing by my family. That's a real man. I'd never leave my wife and kids. I just figure God will put me where he wants me. He's carried me this far. I don't need a stack of money. Don't get me wrong, it'd be nice to be comfortable and have the grouse things, but I used to do stupid things for money. I'll never put money before my life again. You can't take it to Heaven with you … if I'm privileged enough to make it there.

KOBY

FROM ATOP THE BROOM STREET HILL, KOBY ABBERTON SURVEYS THE FUTURE OF HIS BELOVED MAROUBRA

It all started when we printed a T-shirt with Mary on it.

Jai had said to me, 'Bra, you should put Mary on a T-shirt.'

'No worries, Jai, I'll do you a Mary shirt.'

A lot of the designs I do for My Brothers Keeper have got religious icons in 'em, so that's nothing unusual. So I printed these shirts up that had Mary holding Jesus with dollar signs in her eyes and 'Mary had a little scam' printed across the bottom.

Jai's come into the office a few days later.

'Hey, Jai, do you like the Mary shirt I did?'

He's seen it and just froze for 10 seconds then he's started going red. There are about 20 shirts in the pile and he's just grabbed 'em and started ripping them up into a thousand pieces with his bare hands, screaming that he was gonna kill me. He was more angry with the Mary T-shirt than he was with the Devil tattoo on me knee. And the thing was, I didn't even print the shirt to stir him. It was a fucking good shirt, bra. That's just Jai, he does these weird things.

I suppose there's going to be a few arguments, doing our own clothing line. I'll want Mary crying blood or pictures of skulls, Jai wants Moses or sunbeams or some shit. We have our arguments, we'll argue over designs and it gets a bit hard 'cause I'm away so much. I'll get back from a month in California and see a pile of hoodies sitting on the ground gathering dust. I'll say, 'Boys, the reason those 200 jumpers are sitting there not selling is because they look like shit.' I do most of the designing for MBK. I've always been able to paint, and I think I've got a pretty good eye for art and design. I just don't know how to use computers. I can email, but that's about it. But I know what looks good and I know what's gonna sell. Now I just go in there with an image and go okay, this is what we're gonna do with it. I can go design 10 cool shirts in an hour. And I reckon I've got a good idea of what My Brothers Keeper is and how to sell it without looking like a thug or an idiot.

We started doing our own label because I hated the big surf companies. There's no loyalty with most of 'em; it's just like a big machine chewing guys up and spitting 'em out. And at least with our own label we can steer it where we want. And MBK has been killing it, bra. We're big in America, Italy, Israel, all over the place.

I've been digging having a job to go to. That shit's new for me. I wake up in the morning and check the waves, and if the waves aren't good I go straight to work at the MBK office. And I'm working with my mates, too. We're all in it together – me, Greg Winter, Jed, Jai, Sunny. It gets a bit fucked up at times, but there's nothing better than working with your mates in a business you own yourselves.

I've missed some good waves in the last couple of years promoting our *Bra Boys* documentary. I've got to be here doing this, there doing that, and I've missed a lot of good swells. 2005 was my last year of really good uninterrupted waves … uninterrupted by court, the movie, my fucked knee. I'm still scared to do a turn on my bad knee now. I can't surf as much as I used to, so I'm not going to go out when it's one or two foot and try and do airs and have a cunt of a time. I'll just wait until that one big day when the surf is big and good and perfect and I'll surf all day long, three days in a row, break 10 boards, get some magazine covers.

There's nothing I hate more in the whole world than missing good surf. I remember seeing Marky Mathews on the cover of *Tracks* last year at Ours, and I missed that day. I was in California, locked into doing other shit, and I was fucking spewing. A month later I seen the next swell forecast for the Australian east coast and it looked big. I was in California but there was no way I was going to miss it.

The morning I flew in to Sydney I drove straight out to Ours and the swell was big and getting bigger. There was only one guy out, John Dwyer – Bones – but the wind was north-west, which isn't that good for Ours. Then all of a sudden I saw Bones get a 12-footer, the sickest one I've ever seen out there.

'Boys, this bloke's making us look stupid! *And he's from fucking Bronte!*'

Marky's like, 'Just wait a little bit, Kobe. It's gonna get good.' Mark's a freak like that. Wind changes, swell direction, swell pulses; it's like he's fucking psychic, bra. By this stage it was noon, and it was the shortest day of the year so it was gonna get dark at 5.30, so I said, 'Fuck this, we're out there.'

Me, Jai and Jesse Pollock went out and started getting a few, then Mark comes out half an hour later and the second he gets out – the *second*, bra – the wind swings perfect south-west.

It was one of the best days of surfing I've ever had in Australia. It was just good to be back in the water again. It's the only thing that keeps me sane.

I get really bored with my surfing these days. I don't really enjoy surfing unless it's big or it's somewhere I haven't surfed or it's a huge deep barrel breaking in front of rocks. I think even as a kid I was like that. I'd go and ride dirt bikes or be a ratbag and go on thieving rampages; I had more fun doing that. When I was young I thought I knew all about it and there was nothing for me to learn. I notice I find myself thinking the same thing now: 'Do I even like this shit?' But ask me after I've had a week of 15-foot surf in Tahiti and I might tell you I'm in love with surfing again.

I don't surf Maroubra that much these days. But when I do, I don't get all nostalgic and trip down memory fucking lane, though, bra. I don't think about memories of good surfs and good times. I can't remember most of 'em to start with. I just love being out in the waves at Maroubra and hanging with my mates. Surf some good waves with ya mates, come in, beers on the hill; there's no better day than that to me, you know. My best surf trips haven't been to Tahiti or Hawaii, they've been down the road at Maroubra. It's not always about the waves.

There are not many beaches where there's such a big group of guys who are so close. And that's where it's from – it's from 25 years of the Bra Boys hanging out together and surfing and partying and going mad. You'll get on the beers at the pub and mates you haven't seen in weeks will grow out of the carpet next to ya, some kind of chaos will go down. That's generally the way it happens.

That shit is starting to mean more to me these days, 'cause it isn't happening as often. We'll have Australia Day beers on the hill at North Maroubra. At Christmas when the waves are flat and everyone's bored we'll start a fire and we'll barbecue. We'll do the occasional Friday arvo in the pub. No boardriders trips or fancy dress parties any more. We're banned from the Seals Club and the surf club. We're banned from Queensland. And after the last few years everyone's slowing it down.

What we got will never go away, though. The Bra Boys gave me a family that I didn't really have. To me it's family, and if it wasn't for the Bra Boys, I could be anywhere, I could be in the gutter. I look at Sunny and Jai sometimes more like Bra Boys than brothers. They are my blood brothers, but I love my Bra Boy mates just as much as I love Sunny and Jai.

The Bra Boys were here 10 years ago and they'll still be here in 10 years' time, for sure. There'll definitely be Bra Boys, whatever they're gonna be called.

Maroubra's a rich suburb these days, but with dark corners, really dark corners. Stay in the light and you'll be all right. You hear a lot about how Maroubra has changed, how it's becoming like Bondi and Coogee, but you look out the window and in every direction there are Housing Commission units. Until they get rid of the Housing Commission estates, you can have the front two streets full of beautiful new apartments, but you're still going to have the same people living here. That's how the developers deal with Maroubra: they fix up the beachfront and bluff people into thinking they're in Bondi, and just hope no one goes for a drive through the back streets. Bondi and Bronte, they're fashion, partying, money, whatever. People come and go. But Maroubra is still about surfing and hanging down at the beach and families.

I'm happy for Maroubra to stay Housing Commission. It's what makes it Maroubra. It's not just for the rich people, it never has been. If you're a Housing Commission kid and there's this whole beautiful beach in front of you, then you can't complain there's nothing to do. At least the kids have something to do here and somewhere to go. The beach here at Maroubra is like childcare anywhere else.

If you hang at the pub or the beach, every day there's a drama; there's a fight every week. You just get to the stage where you think, 'Do I really want another fight? Do I really want the cops looking for me for some trivial thing?' It's just too much. I guess people get to the stage where they think the only way to avoid jail is to just move away. You know, even just living up in Broom Street on the hill half-a-mile from the beach, you realise how much quieter it is and how much easier it is to stay out of trouble.

I've never considered living anywhere else, but I'm feeling something different lately. There's just too much trouble here. There's a lot of shit that goes on, Maroubra street politics. You can still get in trouble here easily and the last thing I want is to ever go back to court again.

I swear to God, I'm gonna say no to fighting. But living here in Maroubra there's a big chance it's gonna happen again. There's a fight every weekend and it's hard to avoid. And if someone picks on me I'm gonna fight, so I have to be away from those situations.

But then again, this is where I live. This is where I've always lived. Hopefully I can work something out. I'm sleeping on a mate's couch at the moment, and I'm happy, and if I'm happy I don't really care. I just wanna have a nice house, I wanna be doing my clothing label; I just want to hang with my girl and surf. But I don't plan. I never have. If that stuff happens, it happens. Plan all ya want, then one day trouble walks in the door and your plans are down the shitter. One night you're lying in bed with a supermodel in your own house minding your own business, and next thing the door opens and Maroubra's got hold of ya again. It happens here.

My little surfing mate Jess Pollock is banned from the beach at the moment. He's not allowed anywhere near Maroubra Beach, he's not allowed near any of us, just like they did with me when I was his age. And you know why? For swearing. *Swearing*, bra. Can you fucking believe it?

The police presence is still all about breaking the boys up. More than ever. But it seems the more they do it the tighter the boys become. They still haven't learned. They're just like the developers: they want the kids out of here so Maroubra can become just like everywhere else in Sydney. You walk down the beach and there'll be a copper on the beach, there'll be two in a golf cart; they'll be on horses. That's why people leave. They're at you until you go to jail, and then when you get out of jail they're at you again. With that kind of shit going on, what do they expect you to do?

johnny gannon

A WORLD VIEW BEYOND MCKEON STREET

When we were younger we didn't realise how crazy everything was in Maroubra. You had Hinesy running around going mad, and Locko was a complete nutcase. It wasn't until I started travelling around Australia a bit that I started to realise how crazy it was. There were other guys as well who were complete mental cases; throw those two into the mix and it's a complete madhouse. It was way more full-on than it is now. Because of all the police surveillance, the cops are down there every five minutes these days, but it used to be like a lawless Wild West town. There was hardly a police presence and they didn't know the faces like they do now.

I think Maroubra's changed a lot. There's a lot of harder drugs around these days. We didn't know what hard drugs were when we were young. We knew what heroin was and to stay away from it, but there was no ice, no ecstasy. There's a lot more temptation and pressure on the kids today.

I hope crew aren't just coming to town because of the name the place has, trying to prove themselves in a thug way more than in a surf way. That's the thing I worry about for the future generations of Maroubra – that they're gonna take it the wrong way and think they have to be a thug to make a name for themself. If you wanna be a builder go out and be the best builder you can, you wanna be a surfer go out and surf the biggest waves you can, but don't come down here thinking you're going to get respect by trying to beat people up, because it's not going to happen. There are so many people to look up to down at the beach, guys who've made careers. You've got Reni, John Sutton, Koby, Mark, Richie, Ev; guys in MMA fights. I'd much rather the kids aspire to follow these guys and make careers for themselves.

I just don't wanna see one of the Maroubra kids do five years for some stupid assault when they were drunk. I'd much rather see 'em busting their arse working then going to Bali or overseas rather than going to juvey, then when they're old enough going straight into lock-up. Go travel, see the world. It's not all about Maroubra Beach, and Maroubra Beach isn't all about the Bra Boys; it's about the whole community. That community is pretty solid, and it's always been like that. You want to walk around the beach with your head held high, not with your hoodie on and your baseball cap over your eyes like you're not part of society. A lot of the guys these days have got kids and families; you want Maroubra to be a place you can bring your kids up, not a dark place where there's violence on the street and people walking past being abused. You want your mum to be able to walk down the street at night. That's the reason the Bra Boys bonded together in the first place – to make the place safe for our families and friends.

SUNNY

FROM THE SUN CLUB TO THE MCKEON STREET ELITE, THE MAROUBRA TRIBE EVOLVES

For the first time in six years I'm just sitting back, breathing, relaxed. For those six years it was just one thing after another; we had to stay sharp the whole time to get through it. It feels like it's only now that I can sit down and reflect on it.

It feels unreal to be back in Maroubra. For the past three years I've been living out of a suitcase, lounge surfing around the world from city to city, country to country. When we lost the family properties I had to put all my stuff into storage. It's only now that I've got all that stuff out and into a place of my own.

I just needed to have a place I could call home again. I wanted to rent a really nice apartment overlooking the beach. I wanted to look out the window and feel like I was on holidays, which is what I got. I look out my window and I can see the surf in the Dunny Bowl, I can see the whole beach down to South End, and I can see out over Mahon Pool. Life is good again.

Within a week of moving in I had my ritual sorted. I'll wake up, make a cup of coffee and stick my head out the window to check the waves, grab my board and head down for a surf. After a few waves I'll go and have breakfast at Zeebra Café – a BLT usually – but we try and share the trade around between all the shops in McKeon Street, especially during the winter. Tower owns Lozza's Café, which is a little takeaway hamburger joint opposite the pub, another place the boys frequent a lot. He's Bosnian I think, and he's a bit of a legend. In summer if there's a queue of 20 people he'll spot you and give a nod; you don't even have to order. The feeling among the community is still a bit mixed towards us – a bit of love, a bit of hate – but we've always got along great with the shopkeepers, those guys who see us every day.

Then maybe on a Thursday or Friday arvo I'll have a beer down at the pub. The Maroubra Bay is still a bit rough at times, nowhere near as full-on as it once was, but it's a good mix of surfers and crew hanging out. I'm not much of a gambler but the boys are – they love a punt – so we'll hang in the bar next to the TAB. It's our local pub and we love it. Anyway, we're banned from the Coogee Bay these days if the story in the paper is anything to go by.

The other good thing about being home is having time to spend with Kiyahna. She stays at my place most weekends, and I spend time up the coast with her, which she digs, because she's in love with surfing at the moment. You can't describe how good surfing with your daughter is. Our other big bonding exercise at the moment is that we're getting braces together. Kiyahna needs braces, and like any kid her age she was pretty embarrassed about the whole thing and none too keen on it. Even though I've only been to the dentist once in my life, my teeth aren't too bad, but I've said to her, 'What about if we get them together?' Suddenly she was stoked on the whole idea. But I can just imagine the reaction I'm gonna get when the boys at the pub see my new choppers.

Dakota? I just want Dakota to be happy.

The Abberton name is both a blessing and a curse for Dakota; it just depends on who he's talking to. If he's talking to a 16-year-old hottie down the beach at Maroubra, it might be a blessing, but if he's talking to the constable at Maroubra Police Station I don't think it would be doing him much good.

Mate, I know what it feels like for me walking into a place and you can hear people murmuring, 'That's one of the Abberton brothers,' or, 'That's one of the Bra Boys.' Imagine what it feels like for a young kid. There's a real stigma attached to it in certain circles. I don't want him to face a constant battle. We didn't plan any of this; it's what was thrown at us and we had to deal with it. I don't want him to go through all the trouble with the police we've had. I worry about that stuff.

His name has already got him into trouble. A couple of times there's been a disturbance with 20 kids there, and the cops have arrived and just dragged him off. He's had an order placed on him by the cops banning him from the beach, which was just ridiculous. Banned him from the beach over nothing. His mate Jesse got banned from the beach for *swearing*. Dakota and Jesse are surfers, for Christ sake. They're trying to ban them from the beach so they then go and hang on the street corner up in Lexo? It doesn't make sense. Would you rather 'em hanging on the streets doing nothing but looking for trouble, or would you rather them in the water surfing? That whole mentality is backwards. They're not really trying to solve anything. They're just banning the kids from the beach, the only positive influence most of these kids have had in their whole lives.

This fear the police are spreading is creating tension; something is going to give. The community has to understand that it's dangerous to spread fear about youth and minority groups. You've only got to look at Cronulla for that. Laws get changed, more police are dispatched out on the streets, more people end up in jail. And it's taxpayers' money being spent just for everything to repeat itself over and over. This whole thing where the police have open-ended powers doesn't work. You're better off spending the money on preventing all this stuff in the first place. Like what we're trying to do – get these kids when they're eight, take 'em surfing and get 'em off the streets, instead of waiting till they're 16 then locking them up. If you lock these kids up they become more powerful, because the streets are controlled to a certain extent from the jails.

This generation now, Dakota's generation, they've seen more harassment than we ever did. The cops have come down harder on them than they ever did on us, so how do you think these kids are going to react? What do you think Maroubra is going to look like in five years? The signs are there already, and it's not good. Anyone in the community here will tell you that since the Bra Boys were officially recognised as a criminal gang and the police tried to dissolve us, the troubles have gotten far worse, not better. All the cops have really achieved is the splintering of the boardriders club, as many older members have simply had enough. Enough of the riot squad parked at the beach every weekend, enough of the drug squad raiding the pub sometimes twice a night, Thursdays through Sunday. It's become impossible to relax at the beach.

The police and the big institutions around here have never really accepted what we do. We've asked the council, the police, the surf lifesaving clubs, the Seals Club to help put these programs in place for the kids, spend some money, but they've done nothing. There's this whole Maroubra bureaucracy who are very vocal when it comes to complaining about the street kids, but the best solution they can come up with is to lock the kids up or ban them from the beach.

As young kids, we tried to join Maroubra Surf Lifesaving Club but were knocked back. We could never join because our mum couldn't come down the beach with us. I remember being knocked back for nippers at both Maroubra and South Maroubra because a kid's parents had to be on the beach with them on Sunday mornings. When I was about eight we were in a restaurant and a group of older guys were there that I recognised from the surf club across the road. I remember one of them saying to his son, 'Don't go near those kids.' The old guard really had that attitude to the houso kids in the area. The surf lifesaving club, this 'safety house' on the beach, claims to be egalitarian, but in Maroubra it's not always the case.

I've got a theory why it's like that. After the First World War the surf clubs were inundated with returning servicemen. That's where the surf clubs get their regimentation and rules – the march-pasts, the drills, the boats on the beaches. It's got its roots in the war; that's why surf clubs are still so institutionalised today. After the Second World War it became even more regimented. Surfboards, which had just been introduced to Australia, were even banned from the beach, because the guys who rode them were free spirits who didn't like the rules of the surf club and were doing their own thing. If you wanted to get out in the water, you had to do it the surf club's way. That's what made Frank Adler from Maroubra form the Australian Boardriders Association in 1946, Australia's first rebel boardriding club. It's been us and them ever since. And it's not just in Maroubra.

Australia is famous for its surfing culture but, hard as it is to believe, it's been targeted with repressive laws and attitudes for generations. Think about it. When you go to a beach the first thing you might notice apart from the beautiful ocean is that it's full of signs: No skateboarding, No bikes, No dogs, No loitering, No drinking, No dumping, No alcohol, No ball games, No nude bathing. These signs are there to remind you that it's a place under control. Maroubra's not alone in this, but I don't think there's another beach in Australia where the local youth have been subjected to more laws. And look what it's led to. Now 10 kids standing together on the promenade checking the surf can be classed as a gang and forcibly removed with mace and batons. Is this Australia or North Korea?

Any time we try and do something positive for the beach we get shut down. In 2005 I was approached by a guy named Brad Farmer, a journalist and environmentalist who'd founded the Surfrider Foundation in Australia. He informed me that Maroubra had been voted as the second beach in Australia, behind world-famous Bells Beach, to be classed as a surfing reserve in recognition of its significance for Australian surfing culture. Guys like Nat Young, Midget Farrelly, Tom Carroll and Kelly Slater had been on the committee that voted for Maroubra. Brad explained that the reserve would help Maroubra and its boardriding community to gain some political recognition and help protect the beach itself. Randwick Council also planned to erect a bronze statue of one of Maroubra's surfing legends on the promenade. The council then discovered that the boardriders club had Bra Boys as members; two months later Brad tells me that the council would now only spend $5000 on the project. It was a slap in the face for local surfers, and Brad went back and told council as much. The next call he received was from the chief of detectives at Maroubra Police Station telling him that if he contacted the mayor or anyone from the council he would be charged with assault. The reserve went ahead without any representative from the local boardriding community and four measly plaques were buried in the ground to mark the occasion. But the really insulting thing was that the four plaques recognised three surfers from Manly and one guy from the surf club. Brad has since gone on to facilitate surfing reserves at Angourie, Cronulla and Lennox Head with the full support of each council. Randwick Council, meanwhile, has just spent $260,000 erecting signs prohibiting the flying of kites.

Before that night at the Coogee RSL club, the boardriders club was going really well. Today, Dakota isn't in boardriders and none of his mates are. In the two years after that the whole boardriders club fell to pieces. That whole ordeal sucked a lot of energy out of everyone, and all those kids who were 11 to 15 at the time, those vital years, well, you can fully see the effect that it had as clear as day. And today there are no institutions around they respect and can engage with; it's just rules, rules, rules. It's never what they *should* be doing, it's always what they *shouldn't*, and all the signs are there that it's heading back to a divided beach again.

I think the boardriders club is the key. That day on the beach once a month gives the older guys a chance to interact with the kids. You get a finger on the pulse of what's happening on the streets and on the beaches and in their lives. It's also where a young grommet is taught a bit of respect for the beach and for the older generation. You can't demand it off them; you have to earn it by looking after them and being there for them, even if that means pushing them into a 10-foot shoredump.

I'm even trying to get the young guys to form a rebel boardriders club, trying to get Dakota and Jesse Pollock and their mates to re-form North End Boardriders. That's what the beach needs. Those kids are like us 20 years ago, they're from similar social backgrounds – in Dakota's case the same background – they all surf, they're all tight, and they all like to have fun. They're also potentially likely to get into trouble. They inherited the fight like we inherited it. I think they're just starting to realise themselves that the best way to keep themselves together is a boardriders club, and a rebel one at that.

We've realised for a long time that getting kids into surfing as early as possible is a great way to keep 'em out of trouble. Once Ma passed away we wanted to make it our mission to do for other kids what Ma had done for us. And like it was with Ma, it didn't matter where you were from. And we looked and no other group was really doing it. The council does bits and pieces, but there no long-term programs that could take a street kid, or a kid from a broken family, and change him into an athlete, or someone who knows how to set goals and feel good about himself, or someone who knows that reward comes through hard work. Give the kids something to believe in, something that will take them off the street and give them a future they can see in their heads.

It's always better to influence from the inside and not the outside, but we're kinda to the point now where we're going, maybe let's see what happens if the Bra Boys do nothing for a while. The cops are going to realise pretty soon what we've been doing to hold the place together. We don't want to be the ones telling these kids what to do; that's what the cops do. I even fight with some of the other Bra Boys about how we should be treating this next generation. They want to take a harder line with some of the kids.

If the police are going to contribute to the process of making Maroubra a better place, the first thing they've got to do is pull back. I realise it's not going to happen overnight because there's so much animosity between the two groups, but it's the only way they'll solve the youth issues here. At the moment, the police and the authorities are banning kids from the beaches. But the beach is the only way out for these kids. It's not just to become a pro surfer; the beach is the social fabric of the place. And if this generation haven't got the mechanisms to hold it together – if no one realises that we need to embrace the boardriding culture of Maroubra and its surfers as a key ingredient to solving a lot of the youth problems here – then things will only get worse. Maybe that's why the Bra Boys tattoos seem to get bigger with every generation. As the authorities continue to battle the boardriding culture and the harassment increases, so too does the kids' resistance to it. I wonder when they will wake up and recognise that for all the good, the bad and the ugly, Maroubra Beach is a unique cultural place, and what's happening here represents what's happening in other parts of wider society. They want full control, but we won't let them take away our freedoms just because they don't understand or agree with who we are.

Dakota and his generation are going to be crucial to Maroubra. There are a lot of young Koori kids in that generation coming from La Per as well, and this next generation will be a lot more linked to the surrounding suburbs than ours. It's a whole new tribe growing up at the beach. It's coming full circle. It's going to be interesting to see where this next generation try and take it. All the ingredients are there for it to be good. Some of the bonds and the relationships between the community and families are a lot closer than they once were.

The only thing that's going to stay the same in Maroubra is the ocean. The tribe names will change. They always have. Dakota's mates are now the McKeon Street Elite. We've got to accept they're going to be different to us, and we should be embracing the change and helping them. Doing the same things that helped us. Not us saying, 'you have to do this, you have to get this tattoo'. It's not that; it's more respecting the culture of the place, acknowledging that it's changing, remoulding itself and that there will be new generations coming through ... and that these new generations will be doing their own thing.

However, all we can hope is to give them what the older generation helped give us. They gave us belief in ourselves and showed us a way to have a lifestyle in the ocean, with all the joy, challenges, passion and friends that go with it.

DAKOTA

DAKOTA ABBERTON DISCUSSES BLESSING AND BURDEN

I was so young I don't even remember my first surf, but I know my first board was a hand-me-down from Jai. It was a little Impact board, a thruster with black rails shaped way back in 1984. I've still got it around somewhere.

All three of my brothers got me out there; they just threw me on the board and sent me straight out here at North End. I don't think I had a choice really, but I just loved it straightaway.

I was 14 when I had my first surf at Ours. Koby come and picked up me and my mate Jesse from school and drove me straight out on his ski. It was pretty big. Really big. Driving out on the ski through Port Botany I was shitting myself. But I got dragged into a couple and it was fine, I loved it.

Then he towed me into that big one. I don't know how big it was, but as I was coming down the face I've just grabbed a rail and the thing has just broken over me. I got pinned into the reef and smashed, hurt my back a bit. Then it spat me out the back and straight into the path of the sets after it. I got another couple on the head while I was just sitting there on the shelf. I got pretty flogged.

Koby come in and got me on the jet ski; he was freaking out. He thought he'd killed me. I was a bit rattled by it but didn't freak out too much.

I've had a couple of good falls out there, but it's built my confidence pretty quickly. I'm just psyching for it to be on again next time. Every time the boys are over there now I'm onto it, me and Jesse. We've teamed up and got our own little tow team out there, while Kobe usually tows with Evo or Mark or Richie. I tow with Koby occasionally, which can be pretty sketchy. He always wants to get you the biggest one he can get. It's good for us having those guys out there.

We know that. No one surfs the place as good as them, and we love watching 'em.

I think that fearlessness might run in the family. I just love to give it a go. Once you're there you might as well. You've just gotta go with it, keep the family tradition alive.

When Jai was in jail it brought the whole family heaps closer. Anything could have happened. Jai could still be in there now for the rest of his life. I was about 12 when it all started. It was a pretty hard time, but I didn't know too much about what was going on. I think everyone tried to shelter me from it a bit. We're all still here today and that's all that matters.

Sunny is the head of the family, for sure. If something's going wrong he's the first one to pull me into line. Jai and Koby don't worry so much about it. Sunny has looked after all of them so he's used to doing it. Kobe takes on that role with me a bit because I'm the youngest brother and the closest to him. He's really strict on me and pushes me around a bit. I think he's stoked on doing it. When Koby was trying to keep me at school I just kept saying to him, 'But, mate, you left in Year 8!' It's all right, I beat him. I got to Year 9. Not sure how far Sunny or Jai got. I'm always getting people coming up and saying, 'You look like Sunny.' Then the next day someone will come up and say, 'You look like Jai.' I reckon I'm a bit of a mix of all three of 'em, really.

I see my brothers every day when they're home; I see Jai the most now because he's not travelling much. Koby's away the most, he was away for almost a year, and Sunny was away doing the movie for a while too. It's good having him back here. Sunny only just got this place a couple of months ago, so I come up and crash here quite a bit. I sleep right there on the veranda. The sun wakes me up and I stick me head out the window to check the surf.

I've just turned 18. All me mates are 18 now. I had my first beer in the Maroubra pub the day I turned 18. We'd snuck in quite a bit before, but it's not that easy these days. The pub is right there in McKeon Street, so you can't escape it. It's good, though, because it means everyone is always together – the older guys, the younger guys. It brings us all together. We're really tight with the older guys and we've got a lot of respect for what they've done. The boys have looked after us, for sure. They've got something pretty special. I hope we have a tight crew of guys who look after each other and are mates for 20 years.

They take us away on surf trips whenever they can. It's good: you get to see more of the world than just Maroubra. Koby took us to Bali two years ago. Me and Jesse pretty much were going out every night, which wigged Kobe out. That's when I got me big tatt done, in Bali. We saw a tattooist and it was a quarter of the price it was at home, so me and Jess thought we might as well get a tatt, and they were so cheap we thought we might as well make 'em big. A hundred bucks for me whole arm. Koby rocked up at the tatt shop when Jesse was halfway through his. He made Jess ring his mum and tell her. My mum didn't mind too much. It wasn't the first time one of her sons had come home with a tatt.

We get in a bit of trouble, but it's all little things. I reckon back in the boys' day there were bigger dramas. It's just all funny shit down here, stupid shit: throwing eggs, getting drunk, mucking around. None of it hurts anyone. It's all fun and laughs. It's hard for people from outside to know what it's like. They read the paper and think Maroubra's full of these bad little kids stealing shit, but we're just having fun. There's a lot worse people out there than us, heaps worse people.

The McKeon Street Elite? That was just me mates all mucking around. There's another group in Fenton as well. When we were young we'd just have little wars in the street and bash each other. I went and got me Bra Boys tatt done last Saturday up the Cross, at SleeveMasters. There were about six or seven of us got 'em done. It was a thousand bucks for six of us. We made a day out of it.

After Jai went to jail things changed a little bit round here. There were a lot more coppers around the place and it got a heap stricter, but it's still all good. We all still love the place and have fun being here. It's no different to when the boys were growing up; there's just some more expensive houses around here these days.

I've been singled out because of my name, for sure. I've had coppers say the worst things to me ever. But I'm allowed back into Maroubra now, so it's all good. I can laugh about it now. I couldn't come down Maroubra for a while. Nothing even happened down here to 'cause it, but they still banned me from being in Maroubra. Jesse and a few of me other mates got the same thing. If you get in any kind of trouble here, no matter how minor it is, they'll ban you from Maroubra as part of the bail conditions. Ban you from the beach. Even if it happened at Bondi, four suburbs down, they'll still ban you from coming to Maroubra. Having the Abberton name is good and bad, 50-50. It's all right with the girls, not so good with the coppers.

I've been training a lot lately, a bit of boxing, a bit of jujitsu. Jai wanted to send me up to the fighting camps in Thailand with his mate Matthew, and I wanted to do it. My brothers push me into everything they love. It'd be a good experience. I've just got to get out of here, ya know. I just want to get out of here as soon as possible.

I want to head over with Sunny to Europe later this year. There's another premiere of the movie over there and I'm going to go along with him. Maybe also Japan and Hong Kong as well. You've got to get out of here every now and then, but it's also that good coming home. I just want to go over there and surf and hang out for a bit. Just relax. Try and tune some French chicks, do some surf trips.

My brothers have always encouraged me to try and make something of myself. The Abberton name is there; I'd be stoked to carry it on and get some waves and try and make a living while I'm at it. I'd love to travel and surf, me and Jesse. We'll see where it takes us. I might as well take off and see what happens.

I don't want to die wondering.

Boarding Pass (stub)

Flight QF 434
Date 24AUG

Name DAVIDSON/JILLIANSA

Seat 50A
Class ECONOMY

From MEL
To SYD

Seq Nbr 134
Carrier QANTAS

QANTAS

Carrier
QANTAS AIRWAYS

Name
DAVIDSON/JILLIANSA

From MELBOURNE
To SYDNEY

Flight QF 434
Date 24AUG
Seat 50A
Class ECONOMY
Boarding time 1240
Seq Nbr 134
Gate

Service Information

Comments
ETKT

Please be at the boarding gate
well ahead of departure time

oneworld

qantas.com